Understan
Human Geography

A practical approach

Michael Raw

Bell & Hyman

First published in 1986 by
BELL & HYMAN
An imprint of Unwin Hyman Limited
Denmark House
37-39 Queen Elizabeth Street
London SE1 2QB

Reprinted 1986, 1987

British Library Cataloguing in Publication Data

Raw, Michael
Understanding human geography: a practical approach
1. Anthropo-geography
I. Title
304.2 GF43

ISBN 0 7135 2499 5

Designed by Chris Frampton, The Drawing Room, Warwick

Phototypeset by Tradespools Limited, Frome, Somerset

Printed in Great Britain by
Scotprint, Musselburgh

Contents

(Colour Section appears between pages 170 and 171)

Acknowledgements

The author and publisher would like to thank the following for permission to use photographs and illustrations:

Aerofilms 2.2, 2.11, 3.36, 4.2A, 7.16
Aycliffe & Peterlee Development Corporation 4.10
Photograph by BP Oil Ltd 5.9B
Patrick Bailey 2.14, 3.8
BBC Hulton Picture Library 1.6, 3.6
British Airports Authority 6.49
British Rail 6.38, 6.39, 6.41
British Sugar 5.6
Canadian Department of Energy, Mines and Resources 7.40
Stephanie Colasanti 1.1
Corby Development Corporation 4.10
The Danish Tourist Board 4.12, 4.20
DAS 6.24
Earthscan 7.84B
FAO 7.84A
Farmer's Weekly 7.6, 7.13
The Port of Felixstowe 6.11, 6.12
Ford Motor Company 5.20
French National Railways (Patrick Olivain, SNCF. CAV.) 6.2
Glenrothes Development Corporation 5.24
The Guardian (Victoria Brittain) 7.78
Tom Hanley 4.29, 5.51, 7.52, 7.68
Robert Harding Associates (© Tony Ang) 3.37, 4.33 5.46A and B
Hong Kong Tourist Association 4.48A and B, 4.49
Central Lancashire Development Corporation 4.10
Milk Marketing Board of England and Wales 7.21
Information and Documentation Centre for the Geography of the Netherlands, KLM Aerocarto 2.20, 4.33, 7.34, 7.37
Municipality of Metropolitan Toronto 4.26
Nippon Steel Corporation, Japan 5.32
Norsk Luftfoto og Fjernmaling 2.13
Northampton Development Corporation 4.10
Novosti Press Agency 3.38
Ordnance Survey 2.6, 2.7, 2.10, 2.30, 6.8
Oxfam 1.1, 3.11, 4.39A,B,C 4.42, 4.43, 4.50, 5.48, 7.60, 7.74A and B (Nick Fogden), 7.81A (Michael Behr), B
The Photo Source 1.1, 1.21, 6.1, 6.26, 6.31, 7.98
Michael Raw 1.1, 1.21, 2.26, 2.35, 3.30, 4.1B,C, 4.34, 4.51
Saskatchewan Department of Agriculture 7.45, 7.46, 7.51
Science Photo Library 1.9
Shell UK 5.9A
South American Pictures 7.90, 7.93, 7.104
Tony Sowerbutts 1.21
Spectrum Colour Library 3.17, 3.18
Swiss National Tourist Office 2.12, 2.25
The Times 2.28A and B, 4.47
Tyne & Wear Passenger Transport Executive 6.45, 6.47
UNEP (Sarah Errington) 7.76
Venezuelan Embassy 3.35
Warrington Runcorn Development Corporation 4.10

We would also like to thank the Information and Documentation Centre for the Geography of the Netherlands for permission to redraw Figures 4.33 and 4.44, and for the information in the two case studies on Netherlands' agriculture in Chapter 7. Finally, we would like to acknowledge that a number of the figures have been adapted or redrawn from work published by the following authors and publishers:

Figure 2.22 Mining operations in the Pilbara region of West Australia. Reproduction from *The Geographical Magazine*, London, August 1981, Brother Anslem
Figure 3.31 Location of City-Nord within Hamburg conurbation. *Geography*, April 1980, Husain
Figure 4.41 Tondo foreshore scheme. Reproduction from *The Geographical Magazine*, London, March 1983, Phillips and Yeh
Figure 4.46 Urban developments in Hong Kong and the New Territories. *Geography*, January 1980, Mountjoy
Figure 5.21 High tech industries along the Western Corridor. Source: *The Times*
Figure 5.49 The Damodar Valley. *Geographical Review*, 1979, Kumar Saha
Figure 6.3 A map of Europe and the Americas based on the cost of air travel from London. Source – *The Economist*
Figure 6.44g Africa's expanding railways. Source: *The Times*
Figure 6.50 Heathrow airport: origin and destination of passenger traffic. An advertisement produced by the *British Airports Authority*
Figure 6.53 Heathrow airport: layout. *British Airports Authority*
Figures 7.80a, b, c, d Based on an article by Vermeer, *Geographical Review* 1981
Figures 7.98, 7.99, 7.100. Based on an article by Hiraoka and Yamamoto, *Geographical Review*, 1979.

Preface

Understanding Human Geography is the first systematic text which covers the core areas of human geography at 16+. The book has been written with reference to the aims and content of the new GCSE examination, although it will also be appropriate for existing GCE, CSE and joint GCE/CSE syllabuses and for Scottish Higher examinations in geography.

It is therefore intended to appeal to a broad range of ability. Its general aim is to promote interest in human geography as a stimulating, worthwhile and relevant subject within the school curriculum. More specifically it aims to develop *knowledge* and *understanding* of places, spatial patterns and processes; to develop a range of geographical *skills*, including the presentation and interpretation of data in graphical and cartographical form; and to develop an awareness of some of the issues which arise from people's use of resources and the *values* which underpin them.

In writing this text I have been conscious of the need to maintain a balance between theory and generalisation, and empirical content. I have tried to avoid unnecessary abstraction in the belief that geography should be rooted in the study of the *real* world. For this reason, **Understanding Human Geography** places a strong emphasis on actual places and people, with many detailed case studies. Prominence is given to the British Isles in all sections of the book, reflecting the importance attached to the home country in GCSE guidelines and syllabuses. Examples from the developed world have been chosen from Western Europe, North America and Japan: the contrast they provide with Third World examples not only highlights global inequality, but demonstrates the problems of formulating generalisations in human geography at this scale.

A feature of the book is the large number of exercises integrated with the text which are designed to arouse interest and further understanding by 'doing'. Many exercises are based on tables, graphs, maps and photographs, and have been structured in order to provide an incentive for pupils of different ability. Statistical data are frequently used, but I have deliberately avoided all but the most simple statistical techniques, believing that at this level they are more likely to obscure rather than enhance understanding.

I owe a great debt of gratitude to the many people and organisations who have provided information and assistance in the preparation of this book. In particular I would like to thank Vincent Tidswell of the Department of Education, Hull University, for his many constructive comments on the original draft and his encouragement during the period of writing; Caroline Paines of Bell & Hyman for her efficient guiding of the book through the production process; and many of my former pupils at Bradford Grammar School who have laboured through most of the exercises, and have contributed significantly (though unwittingly) to their final development. I owe my chief debt to my wife, Ingela, whose support made it possible to write this book, and who, in spite of the demands of a young family, rarely complained!

M.D.R
Bradford 1986

Population and development

Rich and poor

There are enormous differences between countries in terms of poverty, wealth, population and way of life. These differences enable us to recognise two groups of countries: the so-called *developed countries* (DCs) of Europe, North America, Australasia and Japan; and the *less developed countries* (LDCs) of the 'Third World', found in Africa, Central and South America, South/South East/East Asia, and the Middle East.

There is no single factor which distinguishes DCs from LDCs: the level of development in a country is related to many factors, some of which help development and some of which hinder it. However, a low level of development is usually associated with:

1 rapid population growth – usually at least 2% per annum eg Egypt 2.6%, Kenya 3.9%, Thailand 2.8%

2 unbalanced exploitation of resources, with many LDCs typically dependent on the export of just one or two foodstuffs or minerals eg Cuba – sugar, Ivory Coast – cocoa, Nigeria – oil, Zambia – copper

3 lack of capital and sound government

4 ancient and conservative traditions and attitudes, which are often found among peasant farmers who may be reluctant to accept change

5 poor and limited industrial development, with the bulk of the population working in low productivity agriculture

6 poorly developed transport networks with few modern roads and rail links

7 low income and energy consumption per head of the population, and low standards of living.

Exercise

1 Look at the photographs (Figure 1.1) which give images of life in two DCs and two LDCs. Which photographs represent DCs and which ones LDCs? Describe briefly what each photograph tells you about the way of life (ie standard of living, type of employment, level of technology) in the two groups of countries.

Figure 1.1 Images of developed and less developed worlds

2 Study Figure 1.2 which is a type of graph known as a scatter diagram. It shows for a sample of countries the association between wealth (ie the *gross domestic product* – GDP – per head of the population, which is a measure of a country's total production of goods and services divided by its population), and dependence on agriculture (ie % of gross domestic product derived from agriculture). Describe in a short paragraph the association between the two factors shown on the graph.

3 Figure 1.2 relates one factor (% GDP from agriculture) to the level of development, and shows rather strikingly just how much more wealthy countries such as the USA and Sweden are, compared with Tanzania or Bangladesh or India. From the graph, make a list of those countries which you think are DCs, and those which are LDCs. What difficulty did you have in placing some of these countries into the two groups? Why?

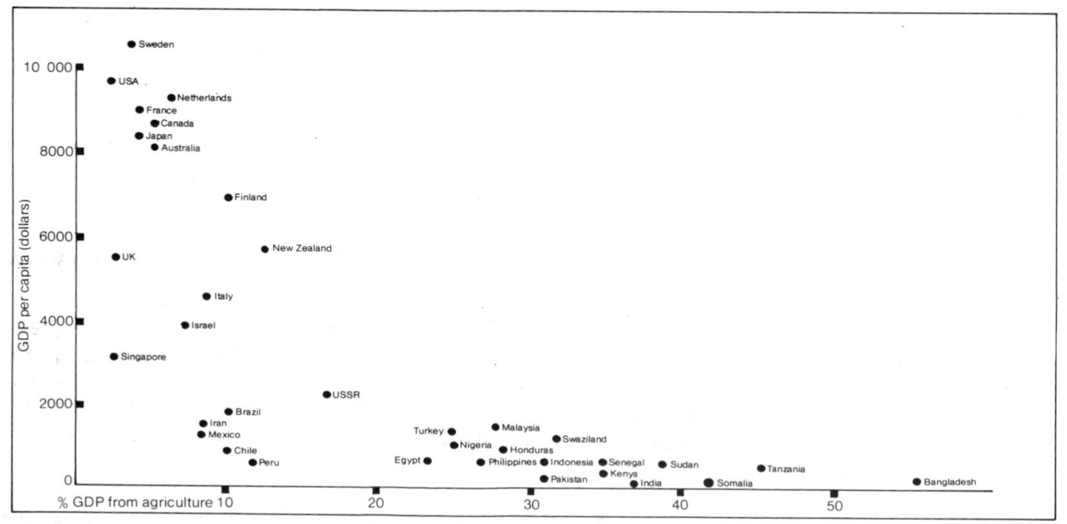

Figure 1.2 Economic development and dependence on agriculture

You now know that distinguishing DCs from LDCs is no simple matter. However, if several different factors are used, the problem of defining levels of development might be easier and more accurate. Figure 1.3 has the same sample of countries as Figure 1.2, but each country has *three* factors which in some measure are associated with development. For each factor the countries have been ranked in a sort of league table from 1st to 35th, according to their values. The league tables have then been divided into two equal parts, each with 17 countries, by taking the 18th value in each list. This middle value is known as the *median* and has been calculated for the three factors: % natural increase of the population per year, % urban dwellers and % of the population that is literate.

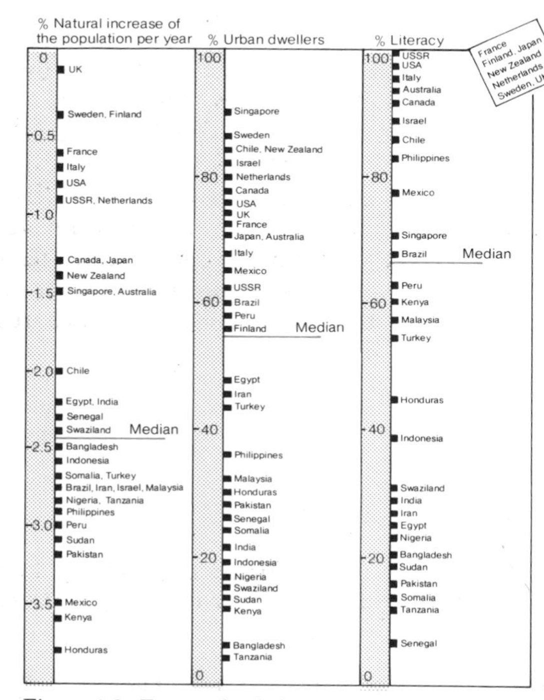

Figure 1.3 Factors for defining development

Exercise

1 Using the information in Table 1.1 plot a fourth league table for the % of the population aged 15 years and under. Calculate the median, and mark its position on your distribution. We have now ranked all 35 countries according to four different factors. It would seem reasonable to assume that those countries which always appear in the top half of each league table are 'developed', while those always appearing in the bottom half are 'less developed'. Make a copy of Table 1.2, and write in the name of each country in the appropriate category as shown.

2 Which of the five groups in Table 1.2 are likely to be most accurate and reliable as a measure of development?

3 Can you think of any reasons why this method could be inaccurate eg choice of countries, choice of factors? Comment on these and any other weaknesses you can think of.

4 How easy do you think it is to separate DCs from LDCs? How useful are these two labels for the countries which appear in the middle group in Table 1.2?

Table 1.1 % of the population aged 15 years and under

Australia	29.0	Israel	33.0	Senegal	42.5
Bangladesh	46.1	Italy	24.4	Singapore	38.8
Brazil	41.7	Japan	24.0	Somalia	37.2
Canada	29.6	Kenya	48.4	Sudan	47.3
Chile	39.0	Malaysia	43.8	Swaziland	47.8
Egypt	42.8	Mexico	46.2	Sweden	20.6
Finland	24.3	Netherlands	27.2	Tanzania	43.9
France	24.8	New Zealand	31.6	Turkey	41.5
Honduras	46.8	Nigeria	43.0	UK	24.3
India	41.6	Pakistan	42.4	USA	27.8
Indonesia	44.1	Peru	45.0	USSR	27.6
Iran	46.1	Philippines	47.0		

Table 1.2 Grouping of countries using four factors

4 values above median	3 values above, 1 below median	2 values above, 2 below median	1 value above, 3 below median	4 values below median
Canada	Brazil	India	Egypt	Iran

Although we shall make frequent use of the terms 'developed' and 'less developed' countries in this book, we should remember that it is not easy to decide to which of the two groups countries belong. Figures 1.2 and 1.3 suggest that there is no clear boundary neatly separating DCs from LDCs: the distribution of countries on these graphs shows a *continuous* trend, and only at the ends of the distribution is it possible to distinguish DCs and LDCs with any certainty. Furthermore, it may have struck you that within the two groups of countries there is great diversity. The USA and USSR are both regarded as 'developed', and yet on several of the factors we have looked at they are a long way apart. Thus although a division of the world into DCs and LDCs is useful, we should not forget that it may be an oversimplification, and that sometimes it hides the fact that there are enormous differences *within*, as well as *between* the two groups.

Exercise

1 Look at Figure 1.3 and Table 1.1 and write down the main differences between the USA and USSR.

2 Do the same for either Bangladesh and Iran or Tanzania and Mexico.

Population – the world scale

The dramatic growth of the world's population in the twentieth century has been on a scale without parallel in human history. Most of this growth has occurred since 1950 and is known as the population 'explosion'. Between 1950 and 1980 the world population increased from 2.5 to over 4 billion, and by the end of the century this figure will have risen to at least 6 billion (Figure 1.4). Growth of this size cannot continue indefinitely (if it did, it has been estimated that by AD 2600 there would be one person for every square foot of the earth's land surface, and in 1200 years' time the human population would weigh more than the earth!). Recent forecasts suggest that the total population will level-out at between 10 and 15 billion in the mid twenty-first century. Already there are encouraging signs that the rate of increase in many LDCs is beginning to slow down.

Nearly 70% of the world's population is found in LDCs (Figure 1.5), and 90% of the world's population growth between now and the end of the century will be in these countries. Rates of growth in LDCs are very high: 2–3% per year (Table 1.3), which means a doubling of the population every 20 or 30 years!

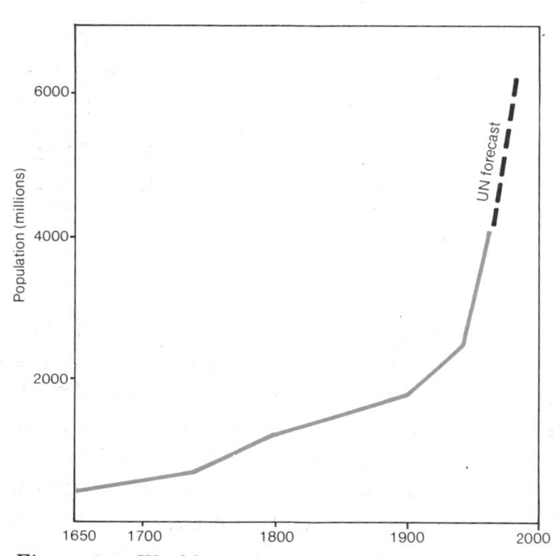

Figure 1.4 World population growth, 1650–2000

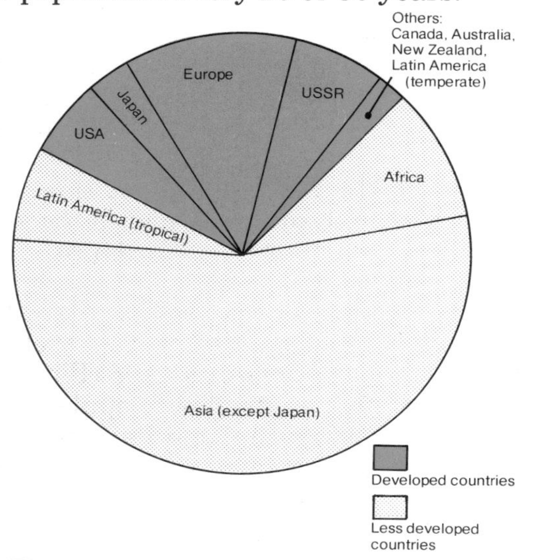

Figure 1.5 World distribution of population

Exercise

An increase in population is measured in terms of numbers per thousand. An increasing population doubles its size during an interval equal to 693 divided by the annual rate of increase. This means that a country with a growth rate of 30 per 1000 would double its population in 693/30 = 23.1 years.

1. Using the information on rates of population increase in Figure 1.3 calculate the doubling times for Sweden, Singapore, Chile, Bangladesh, Peru and Mexico.
2. Plot doubling times (*y* or vertical axis) against population increase (*x* or horizontal axis) as a scatter graph. Does the scatter of points follow a curved or a straight trend line? Describe in your own words how doubling times change with increases in population growth.

Causes of world population growth

Population increase (or decrease) is caused by the difference between the total number of births and deaths each year. If births outnumber deaths the population will increase; if deaths exceed births then the population will fall. Clearly, the world in the late twentieth century is passing through a period of rapid population growth, when births greatly exceed deaths.

The simplest way of measuring births and deaths is to relate the numbers each year to the total population. Births and deaths are usually expressed per 1000 of the population and are known as the *crude birth rate* (CBR) and *crude death rate* (CDR) respectively. The difference between these two *vital rates* is the *natural increase* rate. In DCs, CBRs usually range from 8 to 15 per 1000, and CDRs from 7 to 12 per 1000. In LDCs, CBRs are much higher, often between 30 and 50 per 1000, while CDRs average around 15 per 1000, and in many instances are little different from those of DCs (Table 1.3).

Exercise

Study the information in Table 1.3 and answer the following:

1 Which EEC countries are experiencing no population change?

2 Which EEC country is experiencing a natural decrease of its population?

3 Which country in a) the EEC b) South America has the fastest rate of population growth? What will be the doubling times for the populations of these two countries?

4 Can you think of any other factor which is likely to have an effect on the rate of population growth each year?

Table 1.3 Crude birth and death rates in the EEC and South America

EEC	CBR	CDR	South America	CBR	CDR
Belgium	13	11	Argentina	26	9
Denmark	12	11	Bolivia	47	18
France	14	10	Brazil	37	9
Greece	16	9	Chile	21	7
Ireland	21	10	Colombia	34	9
Italy	12	10	Ecuador	42	12
Luxembourg	11	11	Guyana	28	7
Netherlands	13	8	Paraguay	40	9
UK	12	12	Peru	41	14
West Germany	10	12	Venezuela	36	7

Ideas of population growth

The first idea or theory of population growth was presented by Thomas Malthus as long ago as 1798 (Figure 1.6). Malthus's idea was based on his observation of England's rapid population growth in the early part of the industrial revolution, and its consequences. He believed that the rate of population growth would always outstrip the growth of food supplies: population, he asserted, grew at a geometric rate (1,2,4,8,16,32...) while food supplies only increased arithmetically (1,2,3,4,5,6...). Thus, unless checked, population growth would eventually reach a resource limit, and further increase would produce a 'crash', with a massive number of deaths caused by famine, war and disease (Figure 1.7). The only way Malthus saw out of this dilemma was through the practice of birth control (or as he termed it, 'restraint'!).

Figure 1.6 Portrait of Thomas Malthus, 1766–1834

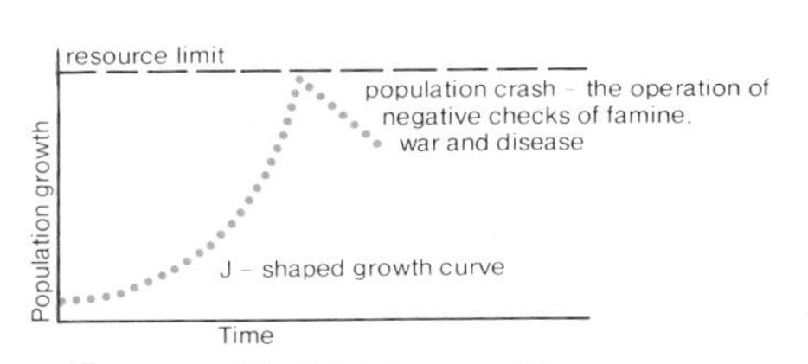

Figure 1.7 The Malthusian idea

Exercise

If Malthus's idea that population growth is geometric is correct, actual population growth curves should follow a J-shaped trend over time.

1 Do the population growth curves for the world's population (Figure 1.4) and Egypt (Figure 1.8) correspond to a J-shape?

2 Plot the data in Table 1.4 showing the growth of population in India, Pakistan and Bangladesh, as a line graph similar to Figures 1.4 and 1.8. On such a graph, time is always plotted along the horizontal (x) axis, and population on the vertical (y) axis. Does this graph confirm Malthus's view on the trend of population growth?

Table 1.4 Population growth 1750–1980: India, Pakistan, Bangladesh (millions)

1750	190	1911	303	1951	438
1800	195	1921	306	1961	532
1850	233	1931	338	1971	682
1901	285	1941	389	1980	818

3 If the growth of population were arithmetic, what form would the growth curve take?

The key idea in Malthus's theory – that population grows faster than food supplies – has aroused much discussion. The recent experience of Egypt lends support to Malthus's theory. Egypt is a country of some 42 million people, whose population is growing very rapidly (2.5% per year). However, although Egypt has an area four times greater than the UK, low rainfall confines farming almost entirely to the irrigated lands of the Nile Valley and Delta (Figure 1.9), and farmland comprises a mere one-fortieth of the country's total area. As population has grown, Egypt has extended its farm area, principally through the building of the Aswan High Dam (1960–70) which has added a further 550 000 ha of irrigated land since the 1950s. In spite of this achievement, Egypt faces a food problem, and is unable to feed its rapidly growing population (1.2 million extra mouths per year). Today, over half the country's food needs must be imported.

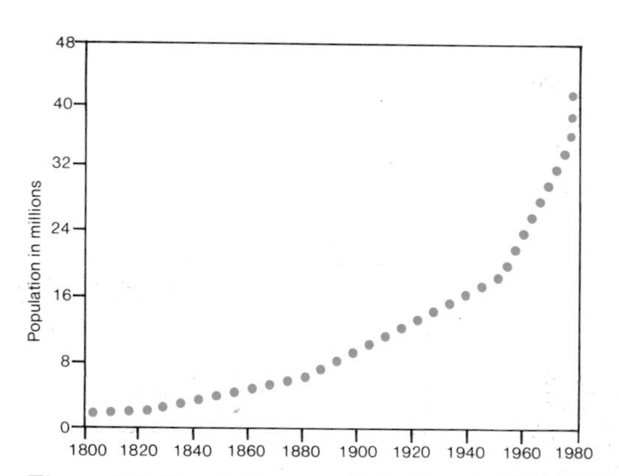

Figure 1.8 Population growth in Egypt, 1800–1980

Figure 1.9 The River Nile enters at the bottom of the photograph and fans out into the Rosetta Nile (left) and the Damietta Nile (right). Cairo is at the centre of the photograph. About 40 million people live in the 20 000 km^2 delta area.

While the recent experience of Egypt suggests that Malthus may have been correct, the population crash that he forecasted for nineteenth-century England never materialised. There are several reasons for this:

1 As population grew and pressure increased on home food supplies, it was possible to import foodstuffs (eg grain from North America, meat from Australia) in exchange for manufactured goods such as textiles, steel and machinery.

2 The growth of food supplies was not limited to an arithmetic rate: new farming methods such as rotations, the use of chemical fertilizers and machinery greatly boosted crop yields.

3 Effective, artificial birth control (contraception) was developed and adopted, thus reducing population growth to rates well below the potential maximum.

Exercise

In a number of LDCs (eg Mexico, the Philippines, India), scientific methods of farming based on new, high-yielding strains of cereals (particularly rice and wheat) and chemical fertilizers, have been introduced in the last 20 years, and have greatly improved output (see Chapter 7 page 221). Study Figure 1.10.

1 Describe the growth of population and cereal production in India 1970–80.

2 Has output of cereals kept pace with population growth? In the light of Figure 1.10 how accurate is Malthus's idea?

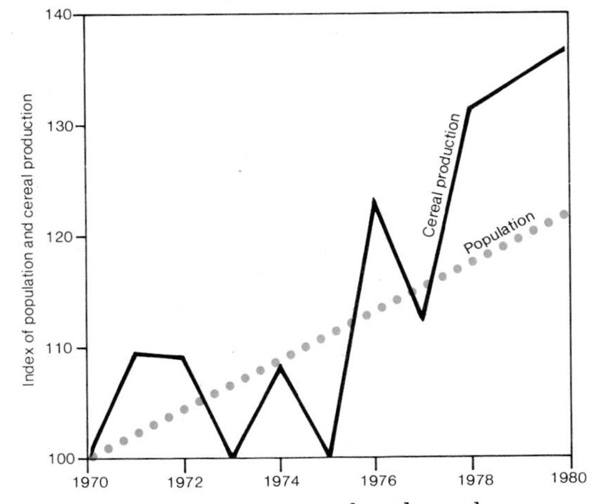

Figure 1.10 Population growth and cereal production in India, 1970–80 (1970 index = 100)

An alternative to the Malthus theory, is one which sees population following an S-shaped curve over time. Initially, growth is J-shaped and is similar to the geometric curve of Malthus, but as the population approaches the resource limit, growth slackens, and the curve flattens out, as the population accepts birth control. Eventually a balance is achieved between population and food supplies, and growth comes to a standstill (Figure 1.11).

Exercise

Plot the data in Table 1.5 showing Sweden's population growth AD 1750–2000 as a line graph. Which of the two population growth curves (J-shaped or S-shaped) best describes Sweden's population growth during this period?

Table 1.5 Population growth: Sweden 1750–2000 (millions)

1750 1.78	1830 2.89	1910 5.52	1970 8.04
1770 1.98	1850 3.48	1930 6.14	1980 8.31
1790 2.19	1870 4.17	1950 7.04	1990 8.40 (forecasts)
1810 2.40	1890 4.78	1960 7.50	2000 8.39 (forecasts)

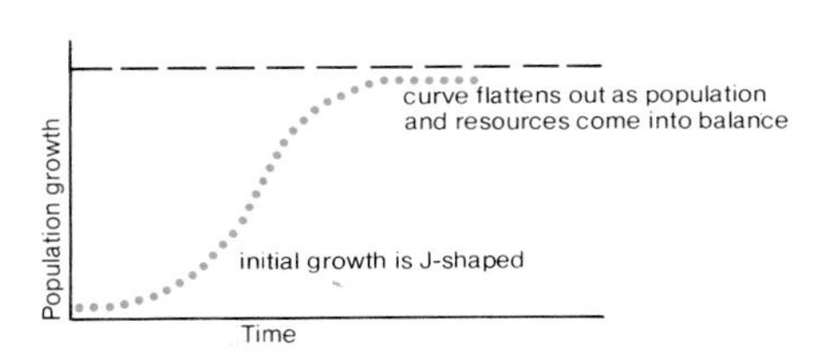

Figure 1.11 Population growth

As we have seen, few countries face a more urgent population problem than Egypt. The government, aware of the problems of rapid population growth and limited resources, have been committed to a policy of family planning and birth control since the mid 1950s. After a slow start, the number of family planning clinics increased from 18 in 1957, to 3703 at the end of 1979 (Figure 1.12). However, despite these efforts, of the six million women in the child-bearing years, less than one in five benefits from family planning services. Acceptance of birth control is particularly low in the rural areas of Upper Egypt, where often women will only accept contraception *after* having enough children. In contrast, family planning has been successful in the larger cities, especially in Cairo and Alexandria. The main hope for the future lies in a 'grass roots' approach, which is a village-based system of family planning where female volunteers, each responsible for around 250 women, give advice on birth control through house calls, and distribute contraceptives. This approach, which has operated since 1977, is already proving more successful than the setting up of family planning clinics.

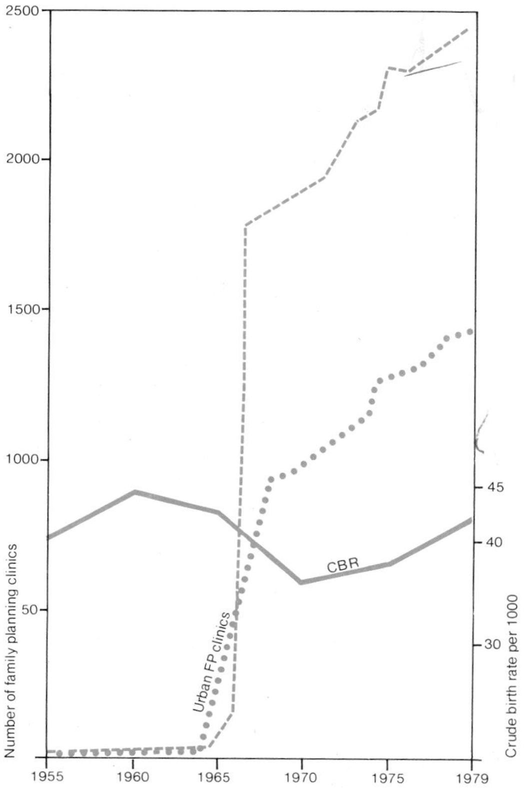

Figure 1.12 Growth of family planning clinics and changes in crude birth rate: Egypt, 1955–79 (after Hellen)

Exercise

What does Figure 1.12 tell you about the success of birth control through the setting up of family planning clinics in Egypt?

The third idea or theory of population change is sometimes known as the *population cycle* (Figure 1.13) and it links together population change and economic development. As a country undergoes economic development it experiences a sequence of changes in its birth, death and natural increase rates. At the outset the population is static because both birth and death rates are high; at the end of the cycle the population is again static, but now these vital rates are low. Thus there has been a transition from high to low *vital rates* – a process which takes many years – but in between, rapid population growth has taken place as the level of deaths has failed to match the very high level of births. This sequence of events has been observed in DCs over the last 200 years; it is, however, questionable whether the same events are occurring in LDCs today.

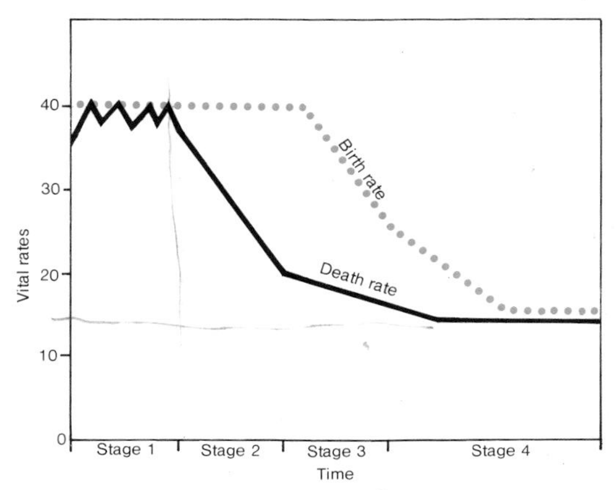

Figure 1.13 The population cycle

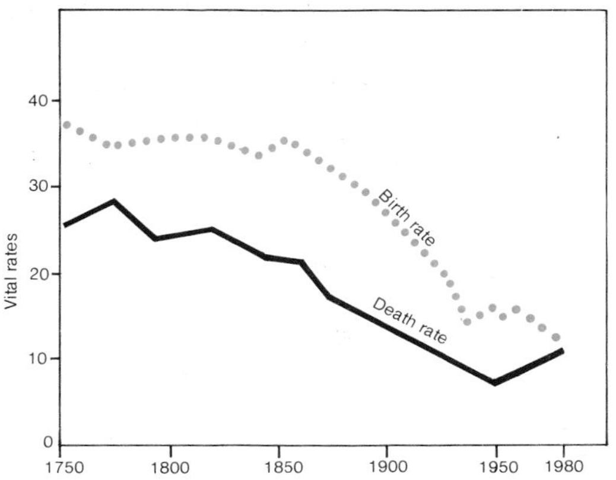

Figure 1.14 The population cycle in Sweden, 1750–1980

Table 1.6 The population cycle

Stage 1
High birth and death rates cancel each other out and the population is static. This stage is only found today among small tribal groups in areas such as Amazonia and New Guinea. These groups have a simple technology and depend on primitive agriculture and/or hunting and gathering.

Stage 2
There is a sudden fall in the death rate with the introduction of better medicine and better nutrition. The birth rate is not affected, and the result is rapid population growth. Many countries in the early stages of economic development, particularly in Africa (eg Ethiopia, Tanzania), are in this stage.

Stage 3
Population growth continues rapidly, but the birth rate slowly starts to fall as economic development progresses and voluntary birth control is accepted. This stage is typical of the more developed countries of the Third World eg Brazil, Venezuela.

Stage 4
Low vital rates, each cancelling the other out, means a return to a static population. This stage is typical of the high technology, industrial nations of Western Europe and North America.

Exercise

1 Look at Figure 1.14 showing the population cycle in Sweden. How many stages can you recognise on the graph? Which dates mark the approximate divisions between the stages?

2 Make a copy of Figure 1.13. Allocate the countries in Table 1.7, to one of the four stages of the population cycle, and label them on your graph.

Table 1.7	CBR	CDR		CBR	CDR
Afghanistan	45	21	Malawi	51	27
Argentina	26	9	Norway	13	10
Austria	11	12	South Africa	38	12
Cameroon	42	21	Switzerland	12	9
Chile	21	7	Uruguay	20	10
Israel	25	7	USA	16	9

3 Does the growth of population of England and Wales 1721–1981 follow the population cycle? Plot the data in Table 1.8 as a graph, and write a paragraph on how accurately the cycle fits population trends in England and Wales.

Table 1.8 Population trends: vital rates in England and Wales 1721–1981

	1721	1741	1761	1781	1801	1821	1841	1861	1881	1901	1921	1941	1961	1971	1981
CBR	31	34	35	35	36	35	33	30	33	30	22	15	17	16	13
CDR	31	35	30	30	25	20	22	21	20	17	15	12	10	11	12

Age structure

The age structure of a population can be represented by a graph known as a *population pyramid* (Figures 1.15A and 1.15B). The vertical axis of the pyramid represents the different age groups (usually five year age groups) and the horizontal bars show the percentage of people in each age group by sex (males usually to the left of the vertical axis, and females to the right). The shape of a population pyramid is controlled by three factors – births, deaths and migrations – operating over three or four generations. The two principal types of pyramid are 'regressive' and 'progressive'. *Regressive* pyramids typically narrow towards the base, indicating a declining birth rate and an overall ageing of the population. *Progressive* pyramids in contrast, have a wide and broadening base and suggest an increase in births and a more youthful population.

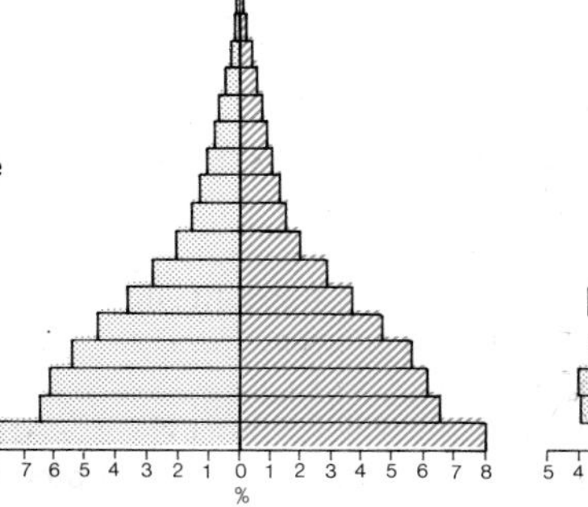

Figure 1.15A Age-sex pyramid for Brazil

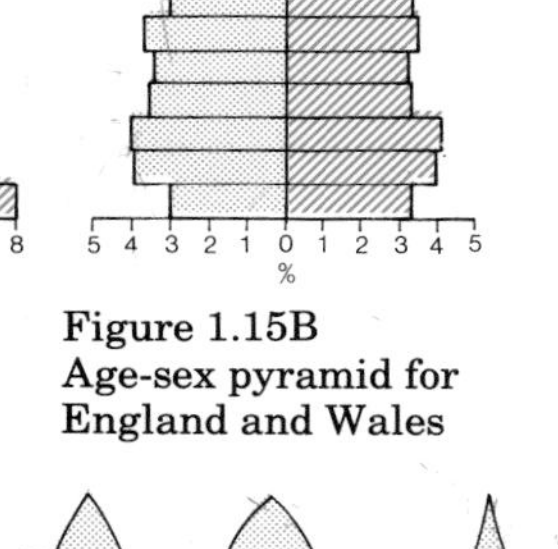

Figure 1.15B Age-sex pyramid for England and Wales

Exercise

1 Which of the generalised pyramids in Figure 1.16 best describes the age structure of a) England and Wales b) Brazil? (Figures 1.15A and 1.15B).

2 Copy the pyramids in Figure 1.16 and label each one from the following list:
- — high birth rate, falling death rate
- — low death rate and recent decline in birth rate
- — high birth and death rates
- — low birth and death rates
- — low birth and death rates with recent increase in birth rate.

3 Which pyramids would you consider to be a) regressive b) progressive c) stationary? Justify your choices.

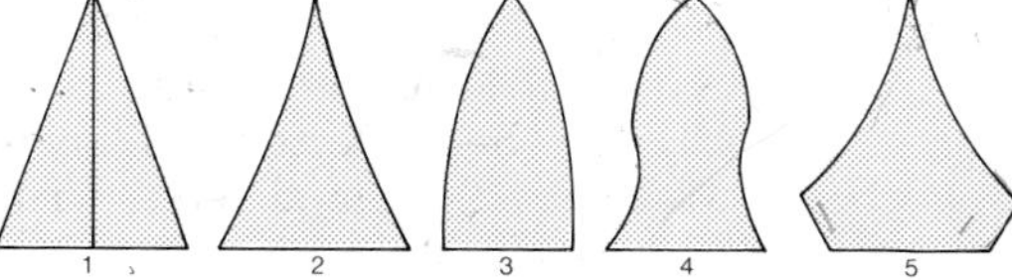

Figure 1.16 Types of age-sex pyramid

Important aspects of a population's age structure can be summarised using a number of simple measures or indices. Three indices which are particularly useful are:

1	dependency ratio:	children + aged/adults	children	= 0–14
2	old age index:	aged/adults	adults	= 15–64
3	juvenility index:	children/aged + adults.	aged	= 65 and over

Exercise

With reference to the bar charts of age structure shown in Figure 1.17, use the age indices to answer the following questions.

1 Which country has the highest level of dependency of young and old on its adult population?

2 Which country has the most youthful (juvenile) age structure?

3 Which country has the oldest age structure?

4 Both England and Wales and Honduras have high levels of dependency, but for different reasons. Study the bar graphs for these countries, and write a paragraph explaining how dependency differs between them.

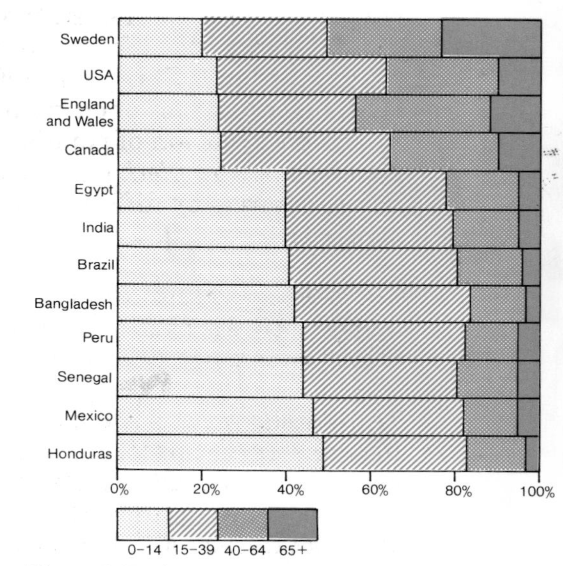

Figure 1.17 Age structure in DCs and LDCs

Figure 1.18 shows how Sweden's age structure has changed over the last 230 years. The graph tells us that there was little change between 1750 and 1850, but that since 1850 the trend has been towards a smaller proportion of children and an increasing proportion of older adults, and especially old people.

Exercise

1 Referring to Figure 1.18 and the population cycle, can you explain a) the declining proportion of children b) the increasing proportion of old people, in Sweden's population?

2 Draw two generalised population pyramids (similar to those in Figure 1.16) of Sweden's population in 1750 and 1981. Again, you will need to use your knowledge of the population cycle, as well as Figure 1.18, to complete this exercise.

3 What effects are the two trends evident in Figure 1.18 likely to have on the economic and social life of a country? Make a list of these, and then hold a class discussion on whether these effects are likely to be on the whole beneficial or adverse. Write up your conclusions.

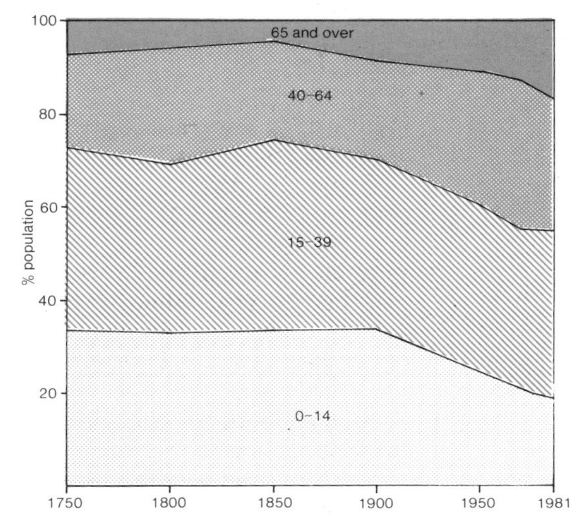

Figure 1.18 Changing age structure in Sweden, 1750–1981

Measuring and mapping population density and distribution

The density of population is the number of people per unit area eg per km^2, per mile^2, per hectare (ha), per acre. These measurements are known as *crude* densities because they are simply a ratio of population to area. In a city, a more useful measurement might be residential density ie the number of people for each km^2 or hectare of housing. In a country like Egypt, where the distribution of population is so uneven that 99% of Egyptians live on just 4% of the land area, a better idea of the pressure of population is given by density per unit of cultivated land. Thus, while Egypt's crude density is only 42 persons per km^2, its density per km^2 of cultivated land is over 1000!

The distribution of population is most effectively shown by mapping densities. *Choropleth* (or proportional shading) maps show how densities vary between areas by differences in colouring or shading, and are fairly simple to construct.

1 The density values for areas (eg counties, regions) are divided into several classes. All the classes should contain a least one value, and it is best if the set of values is more or less evenly divided between the classes.

2 The density values are marked (in pencil) on a base map, which shows the boundaries of counties or regions to which the values refer. Each area is then shaded or coloured: for black and white maps, tones should grade from light (lowest values) to dark (highest values). If colours are used, softer colours from the middle part of the spectrum (green, yellow) represent the lower values, and more striking colours (red, purple) the higher values.

Exercise

1 Complete the density calculations in Table 1.9.

2 Make a copy of Figure 1.19. Plot the densities of the provinces in Table 1.9 as a choropleth map, using the following classes: 0–200; 201–400; 401–800; 801–1600. Choose your own scheme of shading or colouring, and remember to draw a key.

3 Describe briefly the overall pattern of population distribution in the Netherlands ie where the areas of highest and lowest density are concentrated in the country.

Table 1.9 Density and distribution of population by province: The Netherlands 1983

	Area km²	Population	Density km²
1 Groningen	2338	560 700	240
2 Friesland	3353	595 200	178
3 Drente	2654	424 700	160
4 Overijssel	3813	1 038 400	272
5 Gelderland	5010	1 727 500	345
6 S.Lake Ijssel Polders	954	101 300	107
7 Utrecht	1332	923 200	693
8 North Holland	2670	2 308 000	?
9 South Holland	2901	3 129 900	?
10 Zeeland	1785	354 900	?
11 North Brabant	4958	2 094 000	?
12 Limburg	2171	1 080 500	?

Figure 1.19 The provinces of the Netherlands

World population distribution

Exercise

The main feature of population distribution at the world scale is its unevenness (Figure 1.20). By referring to Figure 1.20 and using an atlas:

1 Make a list of a) the most densely populated b) the most sparsely populated regions in the world.

2 Is it true to say that the 'developed' areas of the world are more densely populated than the 'less developed' areas, and that the tropics are less densely populated than the middle latitudes?

Explaining the distribution of population at the world scale is complex, but undoubedly a major factor is the irregular distribution and exploitation of

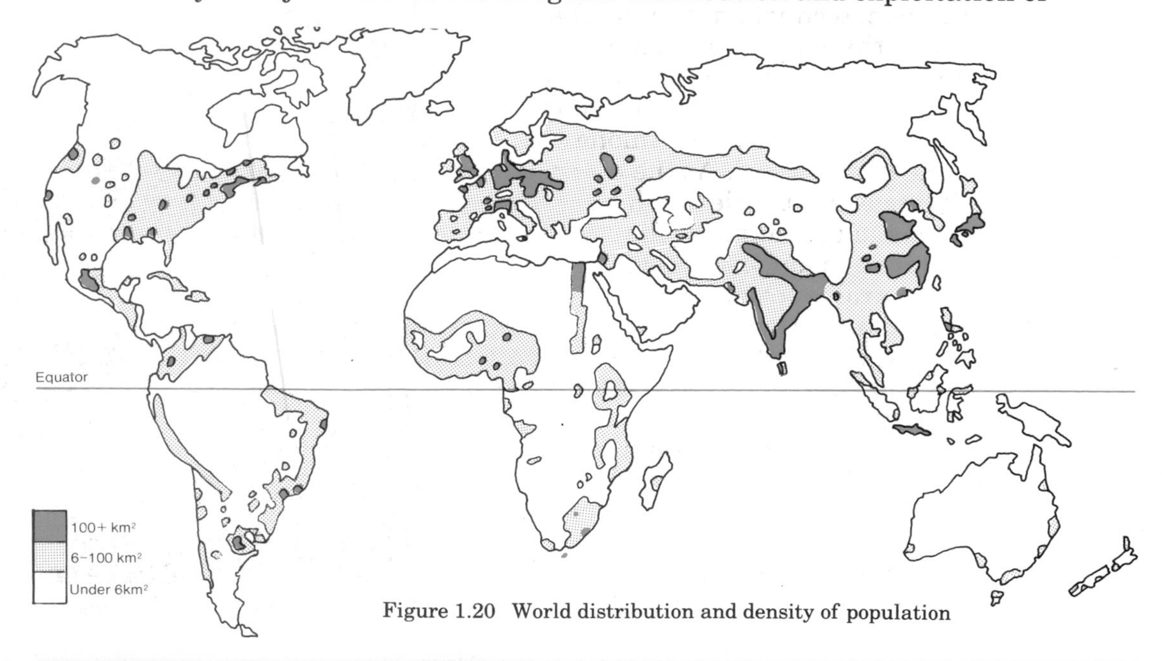

Figure 1.20 World distribution and density of population

natural resources, both today and in the past. A *natural resource* is any substance or physical property of a place (eg climate) that can in some way be used to satisfy a human need. Resources such as favourable soils and climate for farming (eg California, Paris Basin), mineral deposits and energy for manufacturing industry (eg the Ruhr coalfield in West Germany), and water supplies (eg the Nile Valley), often attract population and settlement. On the other hand, their absence frequently deters settlement.

Exercise

Look at the four photographs (Figure 1.21) of different parts of the world.

1 Which photographs show areas which are likely to support moderate to high densities of population, and which ones show areas with few resources and low densities of population?

2 For each photograph, describe what you think are likely to be the factors affecting population density.

The occurrence of natural resources alone does not automatically lead to settlement: countries such as Brazil and Zaire possess enormous mineral wealth, and yet owing to the operation of economic, technological and other factors, these minerals remain largely unexploited. Consequently, population densities in Amazonia and the Zaire Basin are among the lowest in the world. At the other extreme are countries such as Switzerland, Denmark, the Netherlands and Japan, with very few natural resources, but high population densities. In these countries the high level of economic development, technology, skills and education of the population are the key factors which explain high densities. Indeed it is arguable that these factors are more important than natural resources in determining the broad pattern of population distribution in the world today.

Figure 1.21 Resources and population density

Population distribution – the examples of India, Britain and Sweden

India

The average density of population in India (a country 13 times larger in area than the UK) is high – 198 persons per km^2 – though there are marked differences between regions. Areas of high density are either very favourable for farming or else highly urbanised. High densities are particularly associated with irrigation (compare Figures 1.22 and 7.67) and industrial development.

In spite of the rapid growth of towns and cities in the last 50 years, India's population is still overwhelmingly rural: four out of every five people live in the countryside and make their living from agriculture. High densities in the countryside are often found in areas with alluvial soils and a moist climate, with or without supplementary irrigation. This explains the high densities in a belt extending from eastern Uttar Pradesh, through Bihar, West Bengal, the Assam Valley and the Kerala coast. The upper Gangetic Plain in western Uttar Pradesh has similar high densities, based partly on rich irrigated agriculture and partly on an above average proportion of urban dwellers. The remainder of the peninsular coastlands, including the whole of Tamil Nadu, have lower rainfall amounts, but intensive irrigation in places, and a large urban population, has resulted in high average densities through Andhra Pradesh, Tamil Nadu and the coastal belt from Bombay north into Gujarat (Figures 1.23 and 1.24).

Figure 1.22 India: population distribution and density

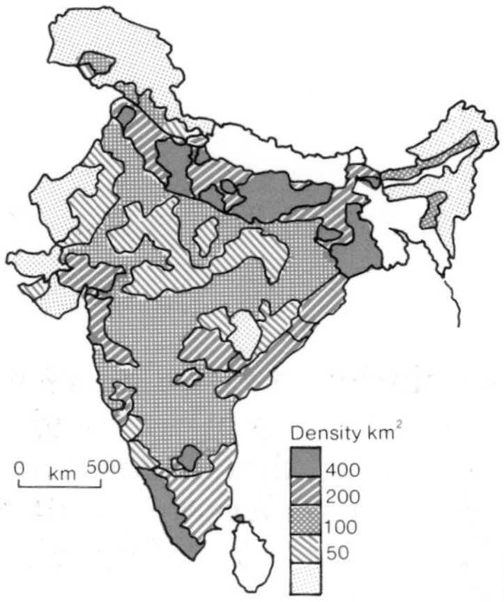

Figure 1.24 India: principal cities and places mentioned in the text

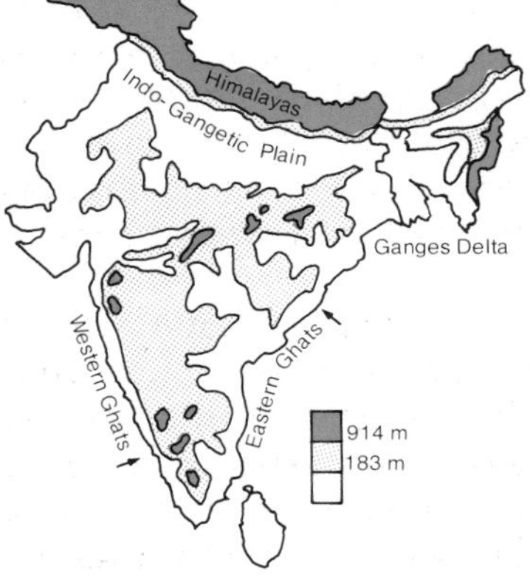

Figure 1.23 India: relief

Low average densities correspond with small proportions of urban dwellers in the hilly and remote areas of the Himalayas, the North East Hills, the Bastar Plateau and the hills of Orissa. Here resources favour neither agriculture nor urban growth. In central India, into Rajasthan and the swampy Kutch, low densities often coincide with poor soils, and rocky ranges or deserts, none of which favours productive agriculture. Agriculture here is partly nomadic and pastoral, with some seasonal, rain-fed cultivation.

The distribution of urban population is less influenced by natural resources. Calcutta, Bombay and Madras are all *millionaire* (contain more than one million people) and port cities, and Delhi, with a population approaching four million, is the historic capital of India. In Gujarat, the large urban population corresponds with a low overall density, and is explained by the many princely states which existed before independence, each with its own capital and administration. Once established, service centres of this kind tend to retain their importance.

Exercise

1 Draw an outline map of India and shade in the areas of high population density (over 200 per km^2) from Figure 1.22. Draw a second outline to the same scale on tracing paper, and using Figure 7.67 shade in those areas where more than 20% of the farmland is irrigated. Fix this second map as an overlay on your map of population density.

2 Describe briefly the similarities between the two distributions. How closely do they correspond?

3 Compare the map of relief (Figure 1.23) with that of irrigation. Would you say that relief influences the distribution of irrigated land? If so, can you suggest why?

Britain

In 1981 England and Wales had a total population of just over 49 million and an average density of 325 per km^2. With the inclusion of Scotland and Northern Ireland the total population was nearly 56 million, though the average density was reduced to 228 per km^2. (Can you explain this?) Even so, Britain is one of the most densely populated countries in Europe: only the Netherlands, Belgium and West Germany have higher average densities.

The high average density conceals many variations from one region to another. The inner suburbs of large industrial cities in northern Britain, such as Glasgow, Liverpool and Manchester achieve peak densities of more than 10 000 per km^2, while in remote upland regions such as the Scottish Highlands, central Wales and the northern Pennines there are extensive areas without any population at all.

The great concentrations of population are in the major urban areas or *conurbations*. Conurbations are made up of several towns and cities, which since the early nineteenth century have expanded and merged together to form huge, continuous built-up areas of housing, industry, offices, shops and transport networks. There are six major conurbations in England (See Table 1.10) and one – Clydeside – in Scotland. In addition there are a number of smaller conurbations and large, free-standing cities.

Table 1.10 Principal urban areas with population in millions: England and Wales 1981

Conurbations		Free-standing cities			
Greater London	6.696 m	Sheffield	0.477	Stoke-on-Trent	0.252
Southeast Lancashire	2.245	Bristol	0.388	Plymouth	0.244
West Midlands	2.244	Coventry	0.314	Derby	0.216
West Yorkshire	1.676	Leicester	0.280	Southampton	0.214
Merseyside	1.127	Cardiff	0.274	Portsmouth	0.179
Tyneside	0.805	Nottingham	0.271	Swansea	0.168
		Hull	0.268	Blackpool	0.148

Exercise

1 Using an atlas and Table 1.10, sort the following towns and cities into their appropriate conurbations:

Walsall	Croydon
Huddersfield	Bolton
Gateshead	Uxbridge
Bradford	Liverpool
Manchester	Oldham
Sunderland	Birkenhead
Solihull	Watford
South Shields	Leeds
Wolverhampton	Stockport
Dudley	Wakefield

2 In 1981, 76.2% of the population of England and Wales lived in urban areas, and 23.8% in rural areas, yet only 3% of the workforce was employed in agriculture. Can you explain this?

3 Construct a table (like the one below) and allocate the towns and cities in Table 1.10 to one of three groups: coalfield locations, coastal locations, coalfield and coastal locations. (Use the map showing Britain's coalfields – Figure 5.34 – and an atlas to identify the locations.)

Coalfield	Coastal	Coalfield/Coastal
Sheffield	Hull	Cardiff

4 Which of the towns and cities do you think were probably most attractive for industry in the nineteenth century? Explain your choice.

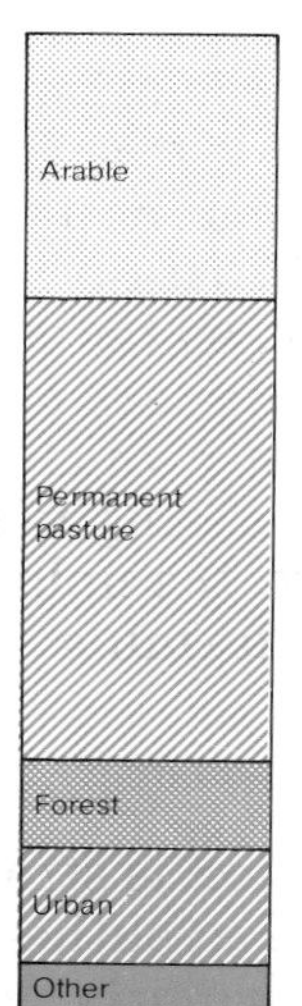

Figure 1.26 Land use in Britain

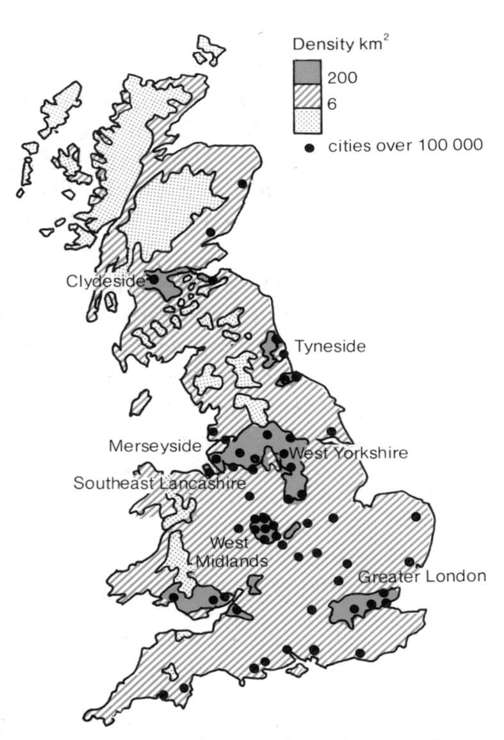

Figure 1.25 Distribution of population and major cities in Britain

A comparison of Figures 1.25 and 5.34 shows that the coalfields remain important centres of population, even though coal no longer has much importance for the location of manufacturing industry. We can say that the *initial advantage* of the coalfields has disappeared, but that in its place, other advantages have emerged which continue to make them attractive to industry. These advantages include pools of skilled labour (eg pottery at Stoke, steel at Sheffield), large markets for manufactured goods and services (particularly London), links between firms supplying/buying materials and components (eg the motor vehicle industry of the West Midlands) and good transport facilities. These advantages of large concentrations of population and industry are known as *external* or *agglomeration economies*. They explain a good deal about the distribution of population, not only in Britain, but throughout the developed world.

However, some concentrations of population and industry are located where they are because historically that is where the industry first started. Movement to a more profitable location would be too costly, and it is thus through *inertia* that population and industry remain where they are.

Nearly 90% of Britain's land surface is rural, supporting activities such as farming, forestry, water supply and recreation (Figure 1.26). In rural areas population densities are moderate to low, depending on the resources available to farming. Regions which have favourable combinations of climate, soil and relief, such as East Anglia and the Fens, may support densities of 50 per km^2 or more. In contrast, the upland regions of northern and western Britain offer limited scope for farming, and densities of just 2–3 per km^2 are widespread.

Sweden

Sweden's population is strongly concentrated in the southern part of the country, particularly in the central lake area between Stockholm and Göteborg, and in the far south (Skåne). The three 'län' or counties containing Sweden's three largest cities (Stockholm, Göteborg, Malmö) account for 36% of the total population. Population densities decrease northwards (Figure 1.28B) with the two most northerly län – Norrbotten and Västerbotten – supporting very low densities of just 2.7 and 4.4 per km^2 respectively. The most striking comment on the unevenness of Sweden's population distribution is the fact that the four most northerly län, occupying 55% of the total land area, contain only 11% of the country's total population.

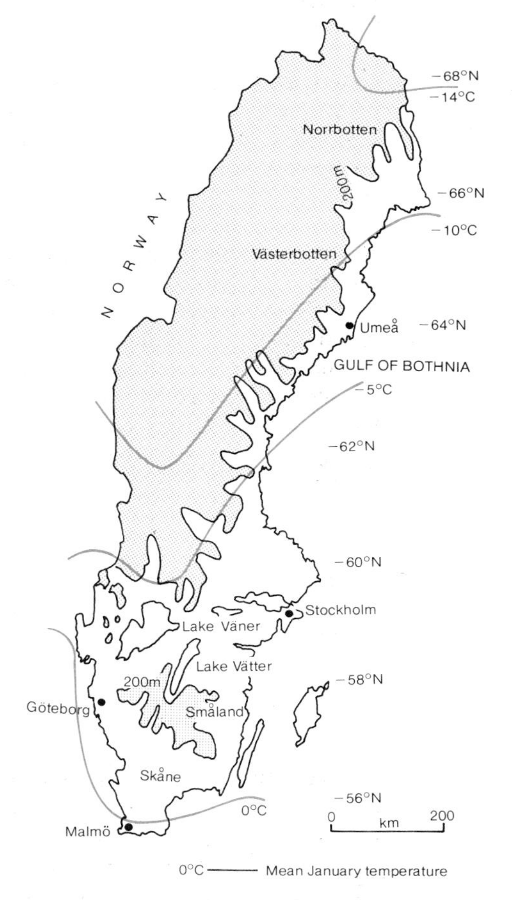

Figure 1.27 Sweden: latitude, altitude and temperature

Exercise

With reference to Figures 1.27 and 1.28B answer the following questions.

1 The three län with the highest population density lie to the south of which line of latitude?

2 These three län share a common feature in their location. What is it? How might this feature have affected population density?

3 How do you account for the lower population density of the two län which comprise Småland?

4 Where do you think that population is likely to be concentrated north of latitude 62°N? Briefly explain your answer.

Climate and *accessibility* are probably the two most important factors explaining the population distribution. The south has the warmest summers, the mildest winters and the longest growing season for farming. In addition, with the exception of the upland of Småland, soils derived from either glacial or lake deposits generally favour farming. The gentle relief and extensive plains in Skåne and around the central lakes also encourage farming. By comparison, the north suffers from a harsh climate and remoteness. (The distance from Stockholm to the far north of Sweden is equal to that from London to northern Italy!) In Norrbotten, along the shores of the Gulf of Bothnia, the growing season only lasts for $3\frac{1}{2}$ months, and in northern Sweden as a whole, farmland occupies just 3% of the total land area. Much of the land in the north is mountain and bog and soils are usually thin, waterlogged in summer and of little value. However, in other respects the north is well endowed with natural resources: HEP, timber, and iron ore are abundant. Even so, these resources have attracted little industrial development, and average population densities have remained low.

Figure 1.28 shows that Sweden's population distribution has not changed greatly since 1850. The towns and cities in the south have grown most rapidly, attracting migrants from surrounding rural areas, and giving the distribution a more concentrated appearance. This trend continues today: Stockholm's *net migration gain* (ie the difference between in-migrants and out-migrants) was greater than any other län in 1981. Meanwhile, modest population growth has occurred in the north during the twentieth century. Since 1963 the Swedish government has invested in the area in an effort to reduce unemployment and stem the steady outward flow of migrants. Investments by the state steel and state timber industries, by Saab in the manufacture of car components, as well as improvements in communications and the opening of a new university at Umeå, have helped to reduce, but not stop, out-migration. Indeed in 1981, Norrbotten's net migration loss was only exceeded by one other län in the whole of Sweden.

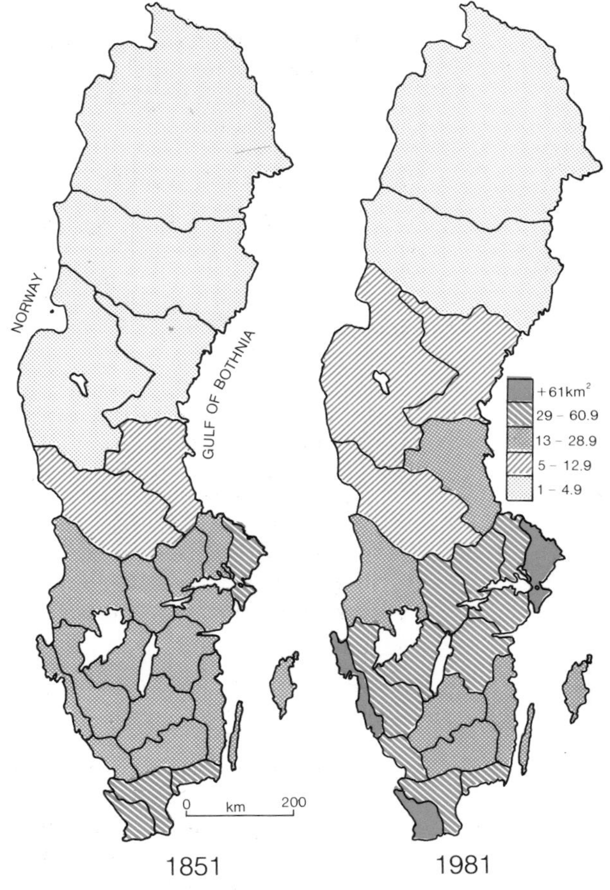

Figure 1.28 Population density in Sweden

Summary

In this chapter we have seen that the world is divided between developed and less developed nations. Although the definition of levels of development is difficult and often inconclusive, the division between DCs and LDCs explains many of the contrasts in population growth, structure, density and distribution at the world scale.

The world's population (or more specifically, the Third World's) continues to grow rapidly. There is no prospect of this growth ending until well into the twenty-first century. This growth has already caused problems for many Third World countries, several of which we shall study in the chapters which follow. However, we should not assume that these problems will only be confined to LDCs; many could spill over and affect DCs, and already problems such as poverty, food supply, ill-health and inequality are becoming world, rather than simply national issues.

Further exercises

1 Figure 1.29 shows the population cycle in India.
  a What stage has the cycle reached today? Explain your choice.
  b Make a copy of the graph and on it extend the trends of births and deaths into the future. Where the curves of the CBR and CDR meet, population growth should finally end. When might this happen in India? Do you think that your forecast is likely to be accurate?

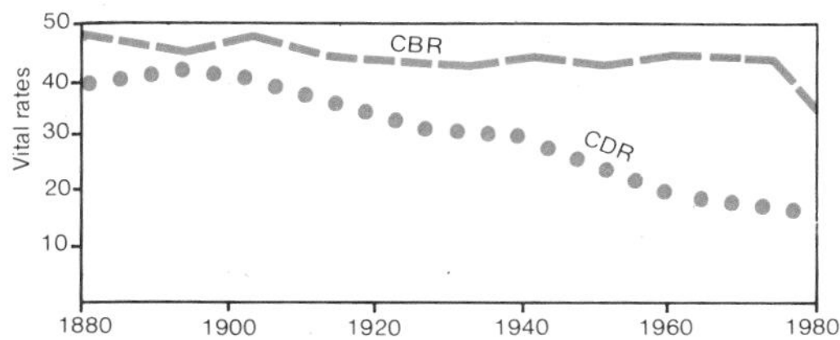

Figure 1.29 The population cycle in India

Table 1.11 Vital rates in an LDC

	CBR/ per year	CDR/ per year	Natural increase/ per year	% Natural increase/ per year
1945–50	48	23	?	?
1965–70	40	10	?	?

2 Table 1.11 shows vital rates in an LDC.
  a Calculate average natural increase and % natural increase rates for each period.
  b Draw a graph to show how changes in the pattern of natural increase shown above would affect the population structure of a country. Label the diagram to show the most significant developments.

3 'The distribution of population in the world is closely related to the influence of physical factors, particularly those of relief and climate.'
  a Explain with reference to population distributions in specific countries.
  b To what extent have the distributions in your examples been affected by developments in industry and agriculture?

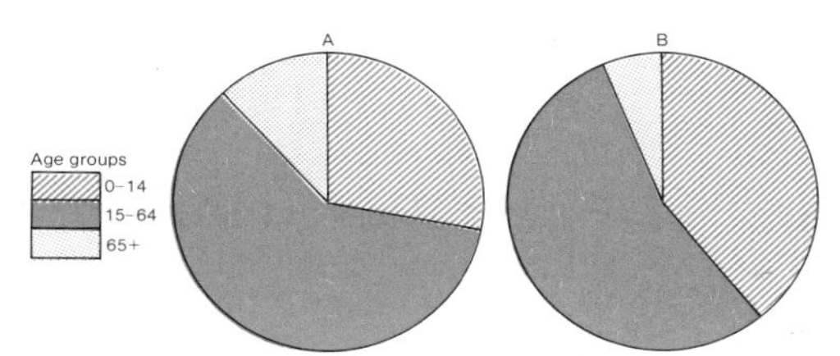

Figure 1.30 Percentage age distribution for two continents

4 The two diagrams, A and B, in Figure 1.30 show the age structure of the populations of two continents, one of which is in the developed world and the other in the less developed world.
  a Which diagram do you think refers to the less developed world?
  b Describe the main differences in age structure between A and B and suggest possible reasons for these differences.
  c For the diagram of the continent in the less developed world:
    — explain the importance of the size of the 0–14 age group in relation to the other two groups;
    — in what way is the percentage of the over 65 age group likely to have altered by the year 2090?

5 Define the following terms: crude population density; crude birth rate; age structure; choropleth map; industrial inertia; agglomeration/external economies.

CHECKLIST OF WHAT YOU SHOULD KNOW ABOUT POPULATION AND DEVELOPMENT

Key ideas	Examples
The world is divided into rich (developed) and poor (less developed) countries.	■ Defining DCs and LDCs is difficult. Differences are based on a combination of factors relating to population, income, occupation, trade etc. ■ Only at the extremes of the scale of development can countries be confidently labelled as 'developed' (eg USA, Sweden) and 'less developed' (eg Bangladesh, Tanzania).
The world's population is growing rapidly.	■ Current world population growth is almost entirely accounted for by LDCs. ■ Growth will continue until well into the twenty-first century. ■ Growth is caused by a surplus of births over deaths – the result of effective death control measures in most LDCs. ■ Births and deaths are measured per 1000 of the population, and are known as crude birth and death rates (or vital rates). ■ Within countries, migration can have a major influence on population growth eg population growth in southern Britain and southern Sweden.
There is an upper limit to world population growth	■ The ideas of Malthus ie natural checks such as famine and disease, to growth/The conflicting evidence from Britain, Egypt and India. ■ The population cycle, and the idea of voluntary control on births/The example of DCs, and the doubtful relevance of this idea to LDCs.
Populations can be grouped according to several criteria.	■ Differences between countries are evident in their age–sex structures, which are represented graphically as age–sex pyramids/The contrast between the young populations of LDCs and the ageing populations of DCs/The implications of these differences. ■ The distinction between rural and urban populations. ■ The division of the population according to occupation eg % working in agriculture or manufacturing industry.
The distribution of population is measured by density per unit area.	There are several measures of density: ■ The simplest measure is number of persons per hectare or square kilometre. ■ Other measures may give a better idea of the pressure of numbers on resources eg persons per hectare of farmland, persons per hectare of residential land.
The world distribution of population is very uneven.	■ The uneven distribution is related to the irregular distribution of resources eg favourable climate for farming, fertile soils, gentle relief, energy and mineral supplies. ■ Concentrations of population show great inertia, and remain long after the initial advantages have disappeared eg the coalfields of Western Europe. Factors such as external and agglomeration economies help to explain the survival of industry and population in these areas.

Settlement

The location of settlements

The location of settlements has two aspects:

1 the location of *individual* settlements and their characteristics

2 the distribution or pattern formed by *groups* of settlement within an area.

Individual settlements

Four characteristics of individual settlements interest geographers. These are site, situation, shape and function.

Site

The *site* is the area occupied by a settlement. There are usually good reasons for choosing a particular site, and these are often apparent from 1:50 000 and 1:25 000 maps. Most settlements are:

1 sited on level land which makes building cheaper and easier

2 found on well drained sites, free from the risk of flooding

3 sited close to a reliable water supply (eg a stream or a well).

Some larger settlements of historic importance occupy sites which could be easily defended in the past. Durham, Ludlow and Shrewsbury, for example, were built on natural defensive sites, surrounded by steep slopes and rivers. Durham City, sited on the core of an incised meander of the River Wear, occupies a classic *defensive* site: the ancient centre of the city is surrounded on three sides by a horseshoe loop of the river and the steep slopes of a deep gorge (Figures 2.1 and 2.2).

Figure 2.1 Durham City

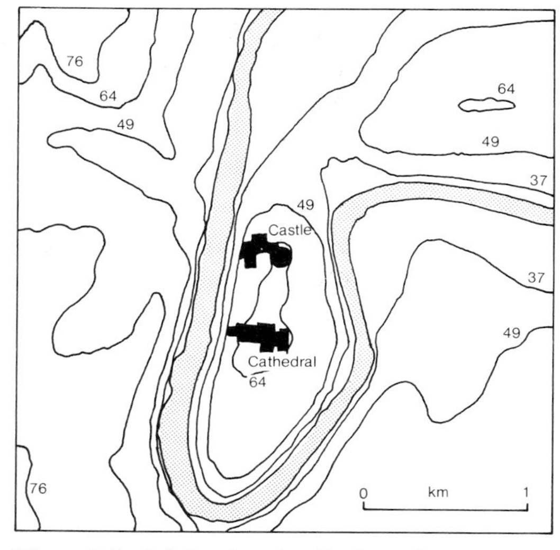

Figure 2.2 A defensive site: Durham City

Exercise

1 Make a sketch of the site of Durham (Figure 2.2). Label the following: steep slopes, incised meander, gorge, meander core, castle, cathedral.

2 Using the map and the photograph, where do you think is the main point of defensive weakness in Durham's site? How was this vulnerable area strengthened in the Middle Ages?

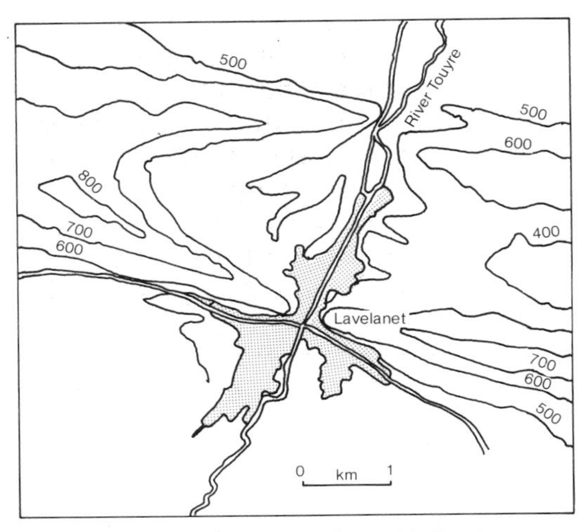

Figure 2.3 A gap town: Lavelanet (Ariège)

Situation

The *situation* of a settlement is its location relative to other settlements and surrounding areas. The link between a settlement and its neighbours, and to nearby areas, is through routeways. The situation of most larger settlements such as towns and cities, often gives them a high degree of accessibility or *nodality*, with roads and railways converging on them from several directions. Nodality frequently results from a situation where there is:

1 a convergence of valleys which are followed by routeways

2 a gap in a ridge or range of hills (Figure 2.3)

3 a bridging point, particularly the lowest bridging point on a river (Figure 2.4)

4 a central location in a flat area, giving access to other settlements and thereby encouraging trade.

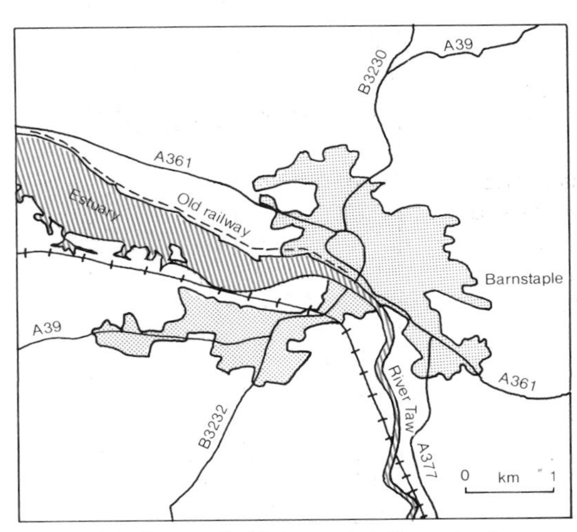

Figure 2.4 Lowest bridging point: Barnstaple

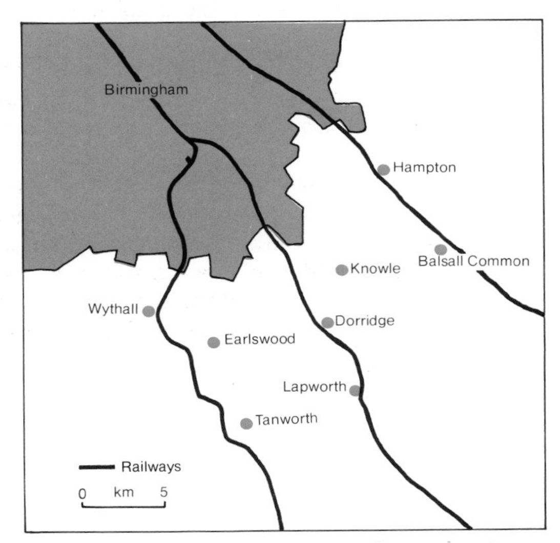

Figure 2.5 Expanded commuter villages: north Warwickshire

In many instances, it is the situation of larger settlements which has been responsible for their growth into towns and cities, and centres of commerce and trade. The city of Calcutta in north east India shows how, in some circumstances, the importance of situation can override the disadvantages of site. Calcutta was originally a small trading post, established in the Ganges Delta, occupying a low-lying and poorly-drained site. However, the disadvantages of site were compensated by a superb situation, as the natural trading outlet for the huge Gangetic Plain of northern India. Usually the situation of smaller settlements offers few advantages for growth. Exceptions are villages which have expanded due to their situation close to large centres of population and industry (Figure 2.5), and those in scenic areas which have benefited from the growth of the tourist industry in the twentieth century.

Exercise

1 Describe the site and situation of Corfe Castle (Figure 2.6). (See colour section.)

2 Give two reasons why the site of Ludlow would have been easy to defend in the Middle Ages (Figure 2.7). (See colour section.)

3 What is the main feature of Barnstaple's situation (Figure 2.4)? What evidence is there to suggest that Barnstaple is an important nodal centre?

Shape

Settlements vary enormously in *shape*, from thin, ribbon-like forms, to those that are almost circular. Shape is influenced by both physical and human factors. Steep slopes often hinder expansion while gentle slopes enable growth to take place. An exception to the latter are valley floors, where the problem of flooding often restricts building. Major roads attract development owing to the better access they provide: their effect is often to give settlements a ribbon or *linear* form. Less obvious are the effects of planning controls in conservation areas such as green belts, which in Britain often cause the boundaries of large towns and cities to end abruptly.

Exercise

1 a What are the factors which have most influenced the shape of Corfe Castle (Figure 2.6)?
  b Which of the following terms best describes the shape of Corfe Castle: circular, square, rectangular or linear?

2 Figures 2.8 and 2.9 show the location and extent of two towns 150 years ago. Assuming that the area of each settlement has increased fivefold, sketch what you think would be the likely shape of the towns today. Briefly explain the factors which have influenced shape.

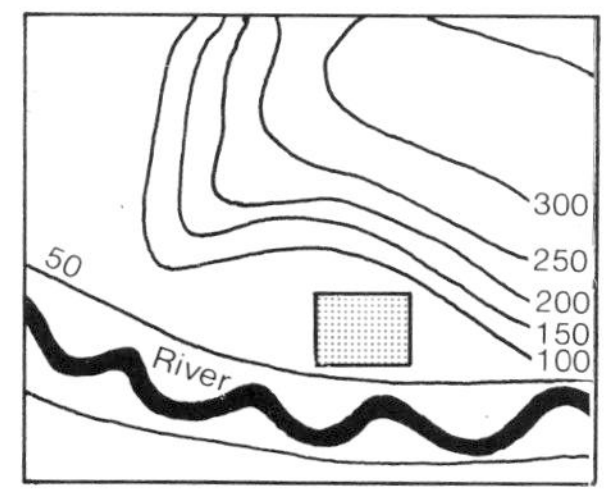

Figure 2.8

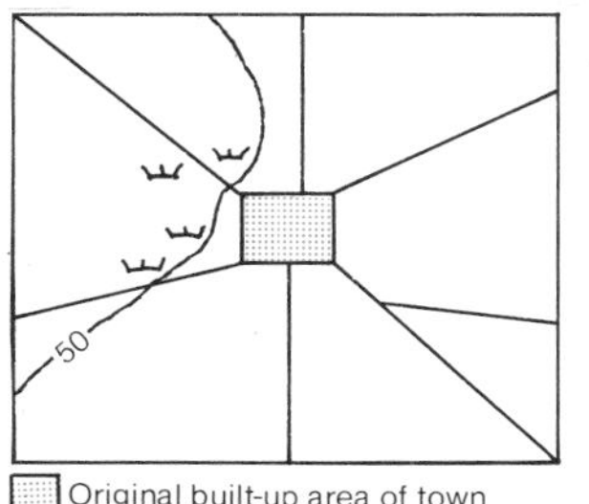

Figure 2.9

Much can be learned from large-scale maps of the internal layout of towns and cities. The central area, dominated by shops and offices, is known as the *central business district* (CBD) and is the focal point of routeways. Major functions found in the city centre, such as railway stations, bus stations, cathedrals and town halls, are shown on 1:50 000 and 1:25 000 OS maps. Around the CBD of most British cities is a zone of nineteenth-century terrace housing; evidence of this type of housing is a rigid grid pattern of streets, with rectangular blocks of closely packed houses. Beyond this zone, mid twentieth-century housing is identified by a more varied street pattern, with crescents, cul-de-sacs, circular and radial forms. These houses are larger and more widely spaced, with gardens.

Exercise

Look at Figures 2.10 (colour section) and 2.11 which show the town of Preston, in Lancashire, and answer the following questions.

1 a What is the approximate 6 figure grid reference of the point from which the photograph was taken?
  b In which direction was the camera pointing?
  c At what time of year was the photograph taken? Give two reasons for your answer.

2 Which two grid squares on the map cover the CBD? Explain your choice using both the map and the photograph.

3 Describe the street pattern in 5330. What type of housing is found in this area? Comment briefly on its probable age, density and its situation in relation to industry.

4 What evidence is there in the photograph of a) the type of housing you described in question 3 being demolished b) new housing being built to replace it?

5 How do the street patterns in 5231 differ from those in 5330? Use the photograph to describe the difference in housing between these areas.

Figure 2.11 Preston, Lancashire

Function

The *function* of a settlement refers to the main activities – commercial, industrial, administrative, residential – found there. Most towns and cities have several functions, some of which (eg ports, heavy industry) can be identified from large-scale maps. Others, such as administration and shopping, are not so obvious, but can usually be assumed from indirect evidence. *Central place functions*, which include shopping and other services, are found in all but the smallest settlements. In market towns they are the most important activities, as these settlements provide goods and services to the population over a wide area. However, it should be remembered that even in DCs the main function of most settlements is still agriculture, while in LDCs, such as India and China, villages are overwhelmingly agricultural.

Exercise

1. Make a list of the functions – commercial, administrative, industrial – in Preston from Figure 2.10.
2. Make a similar list from the aerial photograph of Preston (Figure 2.11).
3. Compare the usefulness of the map with the photograph. How else could you add further information on the functions in the town?

Figure 2.12 Nucleated settlement: the village of Boltingen in the Simme valley, Switzerland.

Figure 2.13 Dispersed settlement around the Trondheim fjord (64°N) in central Norway.

Figure 2.14 Dispersed settlement patterns: isolated farms and small hamlets in Swaledale, North Yorkshire.

Settlement patterns

Describing settlement patterns

The distribution of settlements in a region forms the *settlement pattern*. Geographers are concerned with the description and explanation of these patterns. Why, for instance, are settlements concentrated in some areas and yet absent from others? Settlement patterns fall into two types: nucleated and dispersed. *Nucleated* patterns are dominated by settlements which form tight clusters of buildings, such as small towns, villages and hamlets (Figure 2.12). *Dispersed* patterns are those where isolated farms are most important (Figures 2.13 and 2.14). In reality, settlement patterns usually combine both nucleated and dispersed types, with a mix of villages, hamlets and isolated farms.

Exercise

Figures 2.15 and 2.16 show settlement patterns in two areas of Warwickshire. Both maps show a variety of settlement types. Which pattern would you describe as 'nucleated' and which as 'dispersed'? Explain your choice in a few sentences.

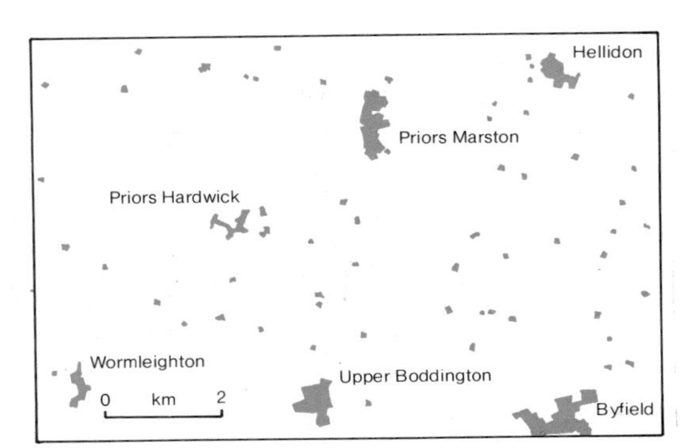

Figure 2.15 Rural settlement pattern: south Warwickshire

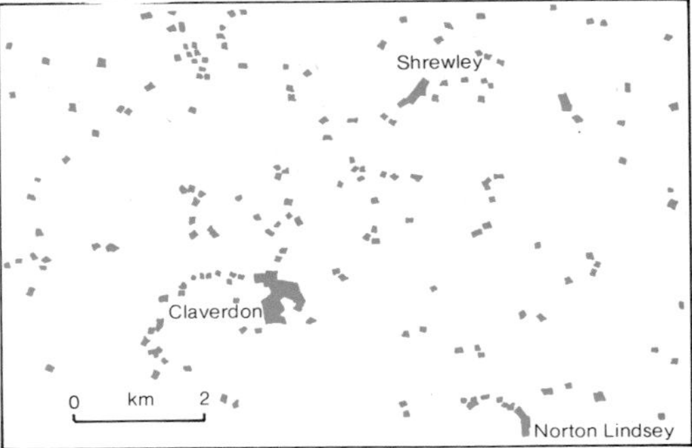

Figure 2.16 Rural settlement pattern: north Warwickshire

The *density* of settlement in an area often differs widely from place to place. Both settlement patterns for Warwickshire are, compared with most rural areas, fairly dense, and indicate a population density of perhaps 40–50 per km^2. This is because the resources for farming – climate, soils, slopes – are favourable, and farmers can earn a living from a comparatively small area of land. In contrast, Figure 2.17 shows an area around the Trondheim Fjord in western Norway where settlement is *sparse* and of lower density – probably less than 20 persons per km^2.

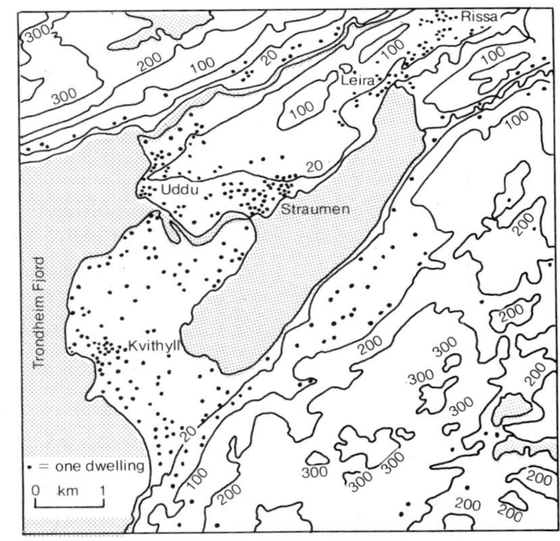

Figure 2.17 Settlement and altitude: western Norway

Exercise

Look at the photograph (Figure 2.13) of the Trondheim Fjord, and find this area in your atlas. What reasons could you give for the sparseness of settlement in this area?

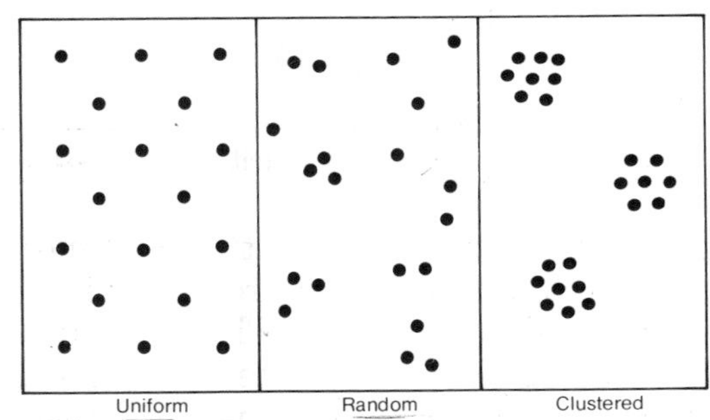

Figure 2.18 Settlement patterns

The distribution of settlement may be *uniform*, *random* or *clustered* (Figure 2.18). Uniform patterns, with settlements evenly spaced (See *Settlements as central places*, page 33) are rare, with just a few examples, such as the IJssel polders in the Netherlands, and the northern edge of the Negev Desert in Israel. In both cases, settlements have been carefully planned. In the Dutch polders, land newly reclaimed from the North Sea, has been laid out to achieve an efficient arrangement of farm holdings, and good access to the farms by roads. Apart from the farms, in each polder a number of villages and one or more larger places were planned to provide services such as shopping, education and administration.

Exercise

Figures 2.19 and 2.20 show part of the North East Polder in the Netherlands.

Figure 2.20 An aerial view of part of the North East Polder, taken in the early 1950s.

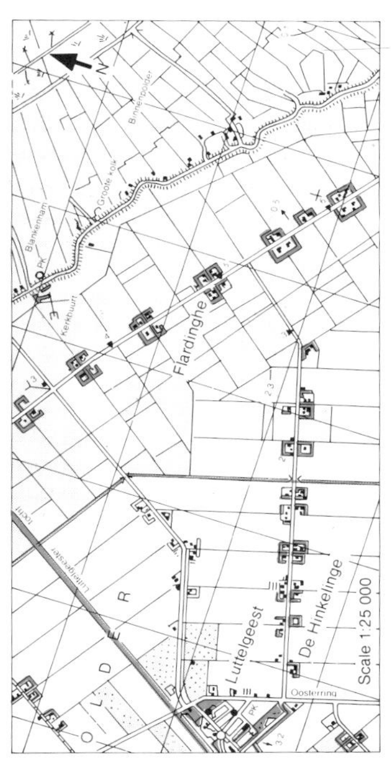

Figure 2.19 Settlement in the North East Polder, Netherlands

1 What is the name of the larger settlement shown in the foreground of the photograph? This settlement is a service centre for the farms in the surrounding area.

2 Make a sketch of a group of farms to show how they have been laid out in the polder.

3 90% of the land in the polder is first-class agricultural land. What other factor, evident from the map and photograph, has been important in permitting the planning of a regular settlement pattern in the area?

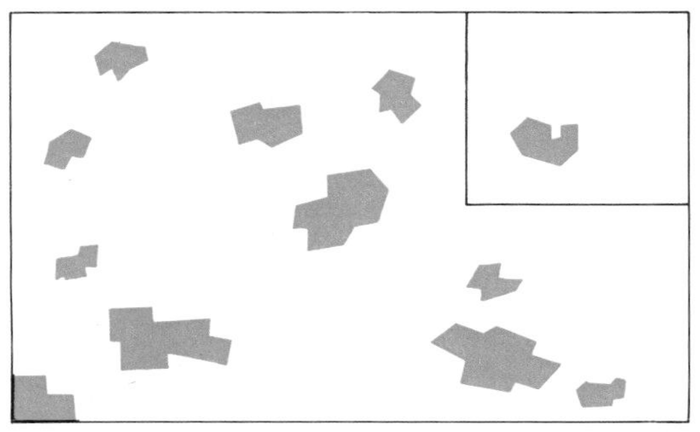

Figure 2.21 Distribution of good soils in a region

Uniform settlement patterns are exceptional: most settlement patterns are either random or clustered. It is the occurrence of resources which helps to concentrate settlement and determines their patterns. These resources, such as fertile soils, may show a random distribution when looked at on a regional scale, but when the viewpoint changes to a local scale, the same resources often appear to be concentrated in specific areas (Figure 2.21). In the large rectangle the distribution is random; in the small square, good soils are highly localised. If in this region the location of settlement is determined by the distribution of good soils, in the larger area the settlement pattern will be random, and in the smaller, clustered.

Factors affecting settlement patterns

The factors which affect settlement patterns can be grouped into two types: positive and negative. *Positive* factors attract settlement, while *negative* factors have the opposite effect. Among the most important influences are: mineral resources, water supply, altitude/slope, drainage and flooding.

Mineral resources

Not all settlements in rural areas are linked with agriculture. Mining villages in rural or semi-rural surroundings are common in the coalfield areas of Britain and Western Europe, and give rise to high population densities. Quarrying for rocks such as limestone, chalk and slate has a similar impact on settlement in some areas. Regions such as east Lancashire and the Cotswolds, which before the nineteenth century supported a prosperous, cottage-based, textile industry, are by comparison with other rural areas, densely settled, even though the resources for farming are relatively poor. In north west Australia in the Pilbara region (Figure 2.22) huge deposits of iron ore have been discovered in the last 25 years. Apart from its mineral wealth, the region has very little to attract settlement. Temperatures are above 32°C for several months, summer humidity is high and with a mean annual rainfall of 250–500 mm, vegetation is sparse and large areas are desert-like in appearance.

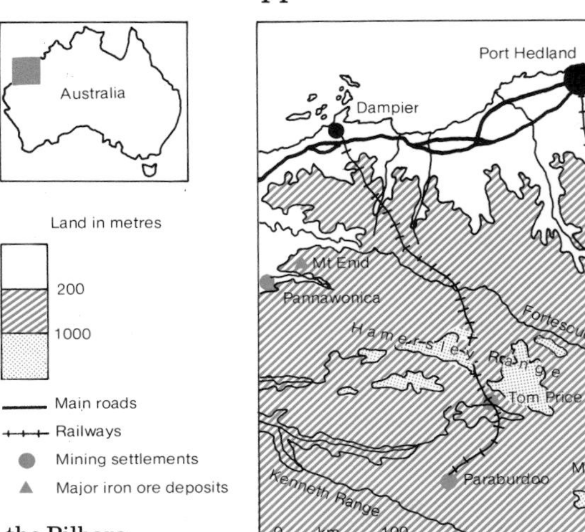

Figure 2.22 Mining operations in the Pilbara region of north west Australia

Water supply

Over most of the British Isles, *run-off*, in the form of streams and rivers, is abundant, and therefore has little influence on settlement patterns. However, in areas of *permeable* rock (such as the chalk of southern England or the limestone of the Peak District) surface water quickly disappears underground, and run-off is either absent or intermittent. Under these conditions settlement is often sparse, and confined to sites near springs or wells. Such settlements, attracted by permanent and reliable water supplies, are known as *wet-point* settlements. In areas of chalk, wet-point settlements are often located on a *spring-line*, at the foot of the scarp slope of an escarpment.

Exercise

Figure 2.23 shows a clustered pattern of settlement in southern England.

1 What evidence on the map tells you that chalk is permeable and clay impermeable?

2 Describe the density of settlement on the two different rock types. What type of site is occupied by settlement A?

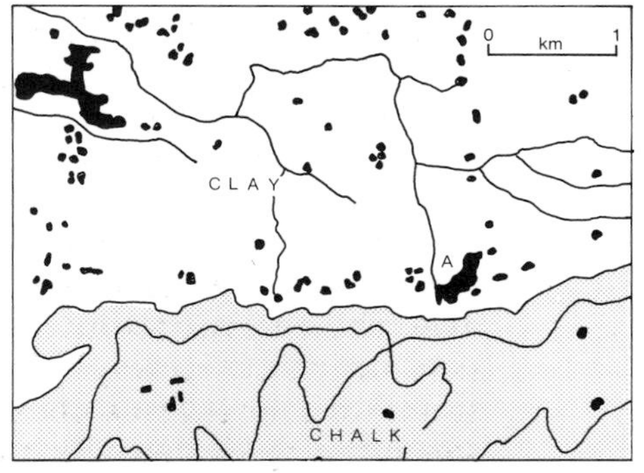

Figure 2.23 Settlement and water supply: South Downs

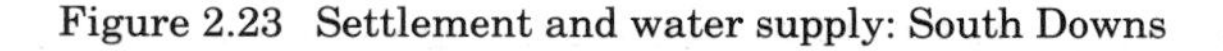

Altitude and slopes

The effect of altitude on settlement is indirect: altitude has a direct effect on soil and climate, and they in turn influence the types of crops which can be grown and their yields (Figure 2.24). When yields per hectare are low, farms are large and widely spaced, and the density of settlement is correspondingly low. Increasing altitude in Europe causes wetter and cooler conditions, which shortens the growing season for crops and reduces yields. These adverse conditions lead to the formation of infertile soils, which are poorly drained, acidic and contain few of the essential minerals needed for crop growth. For these reasons land above 300 m in north west Europe is usually sparsely settled.

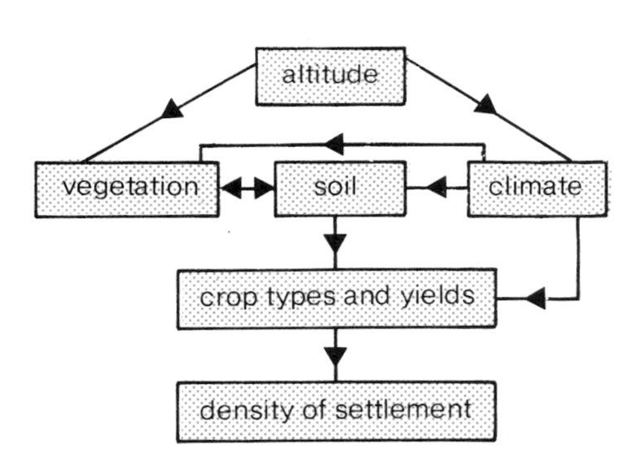

Figure 2.24 Altitude and rural settlement

Figure 2.25 The village of Saillon, in the Valais, Switzerland, overlooking the Rhône valley. Saillon occupies a site with a sunny, south-facing aspect (note the cultivation of vines in the foreground).

Regions of high altitude often have the further disadvantage of steep slopes. Slopes above 15° are difficult to cultivate with machinery, and if ploughed are likely to suffer from soil erosion caused by water moving downslope. Thus steep slopes often have little value for agriculture, and are usually left either wooded or under permanent pasture for rough grazing. However, in middle to high latitudes in the northern hemisphere in mountainous areas, settlements may be attracted to south-facing valley slopes. These slopes have a favourable *aspect* receiving more intense, and longer periods of sunlight than other slopes and even the valley bottom land. In the deep glacial valleys of the Alps, or in the mountains of Norway where the sun is low in the sky for much of the year, the shadowed northern slopes are avoided, and settlements cluster on the sunnier south-facing slopes which offer greater scope for farming (Figure 2.25).

Exercise

Figure 2.17 shows the pattern of settlement around the Trondheim Fjord in Norway. Test the statement that settlement has been influenced in its distribution by altitude, by completing the following table.

Table 2.1

Height of land (m)	% of land area in each height class	Actual % of dwellings in each height class
under 20	27	65.6
20–100	21	
101–200	20	
201–300	28	
over 300	4	

If altitude has no effect on settlement in this region, we should expect the proportion of dwellings in each height class (column 3 of the table) to be equal to the proportion of the total land area covered by each height class (column 2 of the table). Thus 27% of dwellings should be found in the 'under 20 m' class, 21% in the 20–100 m class, and so on.

1 Count the number of dwellings (one dwelling is shown by one dot) in each height class. The 'under 20 m' class has already been completed: it contains 252 dwellings, which is 65.6% of the total.

2 Calculate the % of dwellings in the height classes and complete the table. (There is a total of 384 dwellings on the map.)

3 Using the information in your table, together with the map, comment briefly on the effect of altitude on the settlement pattern of the region.

4 Apart from better resources for farming at a lower altitude, what other factor might explain why two-thirds of the settlements in the region are found in the 'under 20 m' zone?

Figure 2.26 The village of Larv in central Sweden. Like many villages in this area it occupies an elevated site, on a small hill or kame, of glacial sand and gravel.

Drainage and the flood hazard

Poorly drained areas such as lowland fens, coastal marshes and moorland plateaux deter settlement. Not only are buildings difficult to construct in areas which lack solid foundations, but soils which are waterlogged for much of the year limit cultivation. In fen and marsh areas settlements seek *dry sites*, which are elevated and well drained compared with surrounding lowlands (Figure 2.26). In the Fens of eastern England, early settlement was sited on boulder clay 'islands' (eg Ely) above the general level of the surrounding wetlands.

Under natural conditions, river valleys in lowland areas are liable to flooding at regular intervals. Consequently, settlements usually avoid the valley floor or *flood plain* and choose dry sites on terraces or benches above the level of the highest floods. Figure 2.27 shows part of the Severn Valley in Gloucestershire, where settlements have largely avoided the flood plain. However, although this area is one of the most flood prone in Britain, some settlements are sited on the flood plain, despite the hazard. In regions of very dense population, such as the Brahmaputra–Ganges delta of India and Bangladesh, the shortage of farmland and the pressure of population forces millions of people to live in areas exposed to the constant danger of flooding, sometimes, as in 1970, with disastrous consequences for life and property (Figures 2.28A and 2.28B).

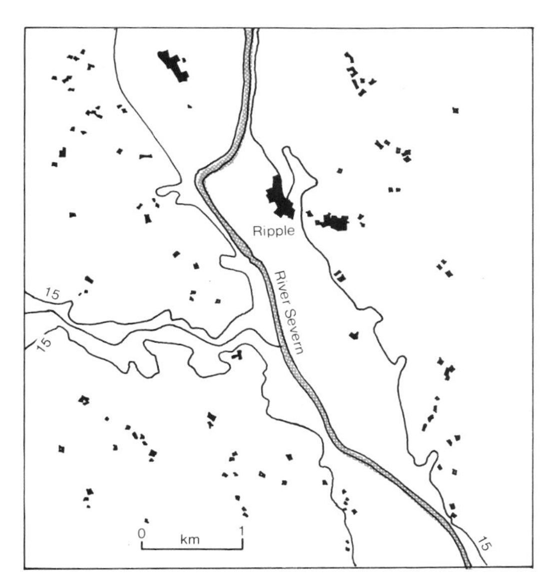

Figure 2.27 Settlement and the flood hazard: Severn Valley, Gloucestershire

Pakistan's flood disaster toll mounts to tens of thousands

By Our Foreign Staff

The possible number of deaths caused by the cyclone and tidal wave which hit the coast of East Pakistan on Thursday was put at 16,000 by Pakistan radio bulletins last night. The official figure has already reached 12,000.

Press reports, however, spoke of 25,000 dead and other unofficial estimates went as high as 100,000 or more.

About 10,000 people have died in the Noakhali district, which covers 2,440 square miles on the eastern edge of the Ganges river. As many as 5,000 are feared dead on the heavily-populated offshore island of Hatia, flooded by 10ft. of water.

More than one million people were made homeless when the cyclone swept a 20ft.-high tidal wave across 2,000 coastal islands. A pilot who flew over the devastation estimated that the affected area extended for 10,000 square miles.

Reports from Pakistan journalists say that some 5,000 people have been buried in mass graves on the southern tip of the Noakhali mainland, and it is said that stocks of cloth for religious burial shrouds had run out in the region by the time another 1,000 bodies were brought in.

President Yahya Khan, who returned on Saturday from a state visit to China, postponed his arrival in Rawalpindi and flew to the disaster area.

"Bodies which could not be buried have started decomposing. The air is filled with a bad smell, and the small number of survivors are without food. I saw about 800 bodies lying on both sides of the dam badly damaged by the tidal wave. I found one or two survivors in each house, mostly women and children."

Another report from the Ganges delta area said: "I saw at least 3,000 bodies littered along the road. Survivors wandered like mad people, crying out names of their dead ones. There were 5,000 bodies in graves, 100 to 150 in each grave."

Pakistan journalists reported that thousands of people had been swept away by waves. Bodies were found scattered over a large area, lying in paddy fields, tangled in the branches of trees and crushed under fallen buildings. One reporter said he had counted 300 bodies floating in a dam 60 miles south of Dacca.

The Indian Mercantile Marine Department said the 5,000-ton Indian cargo vessel Maha Jagmitra, with 49 crew members, was feared sunk in the Bay of Bengal.

Figure 2.28B Article from *The Times*, 16.11.1970

BENGAL'S DISASTER COAST

When natural disaster strikes some heavily populated corner of Asia the loss of life is almost unimaginable. The tragedy of Aberfan is immediate and crushing; the instantaneous flames in the dance hall at St. Laurent du Pont are far too close to common experience; but the dead bodies of East Pakistan—50,000? 60,000? possibly 100,000? There is no point of reference either in the number swept to their death nor in the manner of it. It seems that the tidal wave did most of the damage. How many of us can imagine such a wall of water advancing over land and flattening everything in its path? Even by the appalling record of disaster in this north-eastern corner of the Bay of Bengal this latest blow is phenomenal.

Most lives have been lost in the thickly populated islands on the seaward side of the vast Brahmaputra-Ganges delta area. It is not unusual for disaster in Asia thus to strike the most thickly populated areas. These islands offer the rich alluvial soil that will help the struggling peasant to pick up a living. In no less thickly populated parts of Java it is the volcanic zone that has the richest soil and that thereby catches the most people when a disastrous eruption comes upon them. On the face of it the mere record of disaster should keep people out of such areas—the last really serious cyclone accompanied by a tidal wave killed 6,000 in East Pakistan in 1960. But such are the conditions of life in this heavily over-populated province that any living to be had means the peasant must accept the risks.

A much wider area of East Pakistan is constantly subject to flooding, in great part due to the uncertain waters of the Brahmaputra River. Last year one message reported 300,000 homeless. This year six villages were washed away in July—and got as many lines in the newspapers—but by mid-August the numbers affected by flooding had reached two million. At that point President Yahya Khan decided that the general elections planned for October 5 would have to be postponed for two months as life would not have returned to normal in the affected areas before the date originally fixed. This postponement was challenged by the opposition parties. But even then the plea for a speedy return to civil government sounded rather specious. It would sound even more so now if a further postponement is decided upon. If, however, the loss of life in this latest and much greater disaster is particularly concentrated it might be argued that the elections can still be held early in December as planned.

President Yahya Khan was on a tour of China when this cyclone blew up. He has now returned home to face the task of rescue and rehabilitation. As yet not enough is known about the destruction to decide who and what can be saved or what kinds of succour are most urgent. Although cyclones are endemic along this coastline there are limits to what can be done both in advance warning and in the actual protection that can be offered. Much more within the scope of government action is the flood control that could save many hundreds of thousands from the suffering if not death that afflicts them every other year at least. International aid has before now been given for some of the projects that are in hand. The latest catastrophe should galvanize the government and at the same time wring the hearts of all those whose lives are lived far beyond the reach of such terrors. Here is an obvious priority for international aid.

Another immediate question is what might be the political effect of this blow falling on the febrile political atmosphere in East Pakistan. Not as much as the westerner might think is the probable answer. A catastrophe on this scale is not to be blamed on government, nor can a political party promise any balm for the sufferers. Their sorrow has long years of similar experience behind it; such resilience as they have in face of disaster does not turn to violence as a recompense. Fortunately the Pakistan Government has of late acknowledged the claims of East Pakistan to a greater share in economic development and welfare. Now a real effort must be made, backed by international aid and concern to limit the dangers to life.

Figure 2.28A Leader article from *The Times*, 16.11.1970

Exercise

Read the newspaper articles (Figures 2.28A and 2.28B) on the effects of the catastrophic floods which occurred in the delta area of Bangladesh (formerly East Pakistan) on 12–13th November 1970.

1 What was the cause of the severe flooding in this region?

2 What attracts people in such large numbers to the delta?

3 Which other part of the world is mentioned as attracting very high population densities, in spite of the constant danger of a natural hazard? What is the hazard in this case?

4 Why are peasants in the delta prepared to accept the risk of flooding?

5 What could the Bangladesh government realistically hope to do to lessen the effects of flooding in the future?

Exercise

1 Despite the flood hazard, flood plains often attract settlement. Can you think of any advantages that flood plains offer as locations for settlement?

2 Study Figure 2.29 which is a contoured sketch map of the relief and drainage of an area in central Somerset. The area is divided into six zones (A–F), each offering different opportunities for settlement. Zones A and C are part of the low-lying Somerset Levels; B is a low ridge of limestone; D is a gently sloping area at the foot of the Mendip Hills; E is the steeply sloping, west-facing side of the Mendips; F is the upland surface of the Mendips.

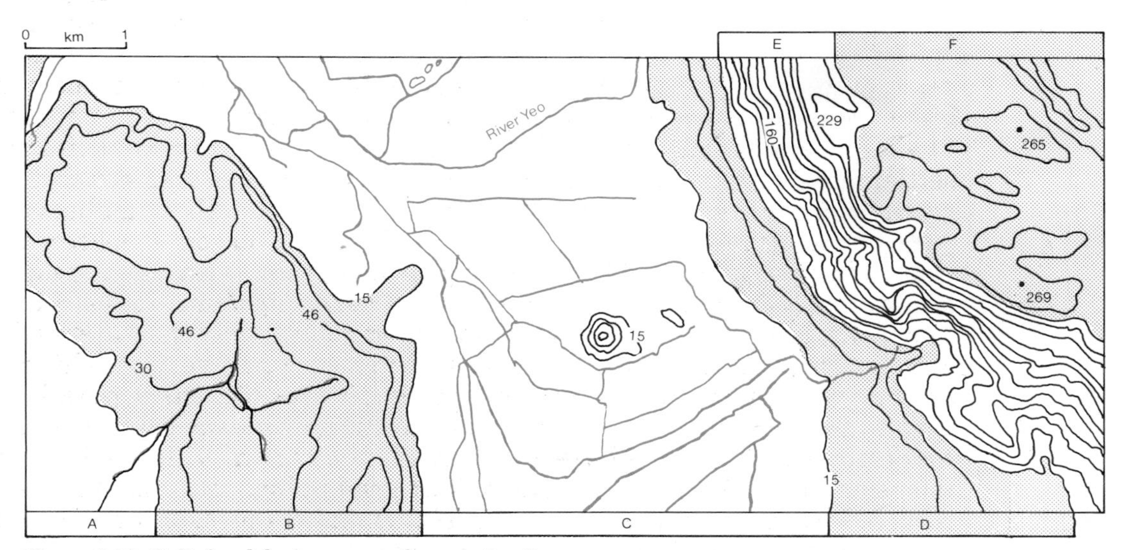

Figure 2.29 Relief and drainage map for question 2

a Assess the attractiveness of each zone for settlement using the five factors in Table 2.2. Make a copy of Table 2.2 and insert either a 1 or 0 against each factor. For example, in zone A there is a surface stream hence 'water available' is given 1, and 'lack of water supply' is given 0. Complete the scoring for all five factors in zones B–F.

b Add up the total positive and negative factor scores for each zone, and by subtracting the negative factor scores from the positive, calculate the final overall score of attractiveness for each zone. Zone A, for instance, has an overall score of 3 (4 positive and 1 negative factor).

c Compile a 'league table' of final scores for each zone.

d Compare your assessment of where you think settlement *should* locate, with the actual settlement pattern of the area (Figure 2.30 – colour section). What, if any, are the main differences between your expected pattern and the actual one?

Table 2.2

	Positive factors							Negative factors					
	A	B	C	D	E	F		A	B	C	D	E	F
Water available	1	1	1	1	0	0	Lack of water	0	0	0	0	1	1
Gentle slopes	1						Steep slopes	0					
Low altitude	1						High altitude	0					
Good natural drainage	1						Poor natural drainage	0					
No flood hazard	0						Flood hazard	1					
Totals	4						Totals	1					
Final total (positive minus negative factors)	3												

Settlements as central places

A *central place* is a settlement providing one or more services (such as shops, market, administration, entertainment) for both its own population, and people living in the surrounding area. All larger settlements are central places, though the importance of their service sector varies. For example, a market town such as Lincoln is *relatively* more important as a central place than an industrial town of similar size such as Scunthorpe. Not all settlements are central places: isolated farms, small hamlets and even some villages have no service functions, and depend on neighbouring, more important service centres.

Settlements vary in size and importance, but measuring these characteristics poses problems. Population totals are often used as the simplest measure, but other measures such as the number and range of services, or the number of jobs available, are equally valid. All three measurements are closely linked: settlements with large populations usually have a large number and wide range of shops and other services, and employ considerable numbers of people.

Settlements can be arranged into an order based on some measure of their size and importance. Such an ordering of settlement, with the largest and most important at the top, and the smallest and least important at the bottom, is known as a *hierarchy*. A feature of any hierarchy is that the *lower order groups* contain the largest number of items, and that as we move up the hierarchy the number of items in each group gets smaller, rather like the population pyramids we looked at in Chapter 1, page 10. This means that settlement hierarchies always have large numbers of hamlets and villages, but fewer towns and even fewer cities. The highest level in any settlement hierarchy is occupied by the *metropolis* – a single settlement of outstanding size and importance, such as London, Paris and New York.

Exercise

1 Figure 2.31 shows the populations and numbers of shops in settlements in Lower Wharfedale (North Yorkshire) plotted as a scatter graph. Copy the graph and mark on it the boundaries which separate first order (ie the most important settlement(s)) from second order, and second order from third order settlements or central places. The boundary separating third from fourth order (ie the least important settlements) has been drawn for you.

2 How many settlements are there in each of the groups you have defined? Do the settlements appear to form a hierarchy? Write a short paragraph of explanation.

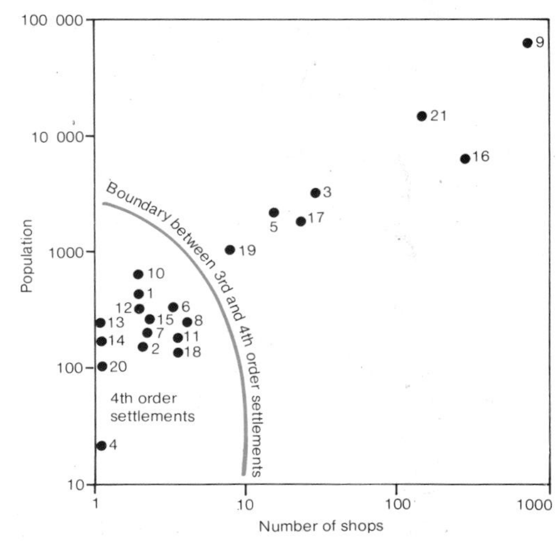

Figure 2.31 Population and number of shops: Lower Wharfedale, North Yorkshire

Central place theory

Central place theory explains the size and spacing of settlements. It tells us how settlements should be distributed when the aim is to supply the population with goods and services, as cheaply and efficiently as possible. This is done by ensuring that people travel the shortest distance in order to buy the items they need. In order to assess the influence of distance on settlement patterns, the theory makes a number of simplifying assumptions.

1 All settlements are central places; their only function is to provide goods and services.

2 People always buy the goods and services they need from the nearest settlement which can satisfy their requirements.

3 The region in which the settlement pattern develops is a uniform plain, where soils, climate and relief are the same everywhere. The cost of transport is the same in all directions; the population is evenly spread across the area; and all places are equally accessible.

Figure 2.32 shows what a settlement pattern would look like, given the assumptions and rules of central place theory.

The number and range of services found in a settlement is controlled by the number of customers it can attract. A minimum number of customers is needed to support each service. This number is known as the *threshold* population.

Table 2.3 gives an indication of the range of services found in the settlements of Lower Wharfedale. Typical of the villages and larger hamlets are post offices, pubs and general stores. These settlements provide *convenience goods*, which have low thresholds because they are bought often. They can be supported by just two or three hundred people. However, if a settlement has functions with higher thresholds, it must command a larger trade area. Items with a high threshold are called *comparison goods*, and are usually fairly expensive durables (eg clothes, shoes, electrical goods, cars), in contrast to convenience goods, which mainly consist of food items. Comparison goods are bought less often than convenience goods. Thus, more important, higher order settlements should contain a larger proportion of comparison goods and services than lower order settlements, and should command a larger trade area.

Exercise

1 Study Figure 2.32 then write out the following paragraph, inserting the missing words.
According to central place theory, settlements should be distributed in a ________ pattern. Each settlement or ________ serves an ________-shaped trade area, and the more important the settlement, the ________ the area it serves. The ________ trade areas fit neatly into the larger ones, a feature known as ________, thus ensuring that the whole of the ________ is served with a full range of goods and services.
population, triangular, nesting, hexagonal, central place, smaller, larger.

2 Make a list of other functions performed by settlements, apart from the provision of goods and services.

3 How many settlements of first, second and third order (importance) are there in Figure 2.32? Using the graph of settlements in Lower Wharfedale that you plotted, count up the number of settlements of first, second and third (combined with fourth) orders. Present the information for the two patterns as a table and write a brief report comparing the actual and theoretical hierarchies.

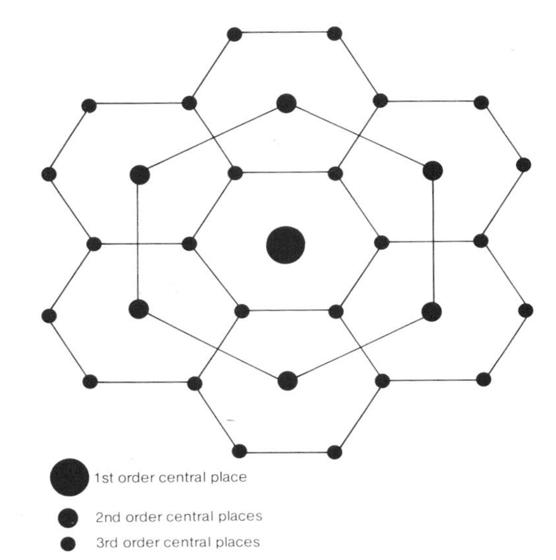

Figure 2.32 Pattern of settlements according to central place theory

Table 2.3 Central places and selected functions in Lower Wharfedale

	1	2	3	4	5	6	7	8	9	10	11	12
1 Arthington	x	x										
2 Askwith	x	x										
3 Burley	x	x	x	x	x	x						
4 Clapgates	x											
5 Collingham	x	x	x			x						
6 Follifoot	x	x	x									
7 Goldsborough	x	x										
8 Harewood	x	x										
9 Harrogate	x	x	x	x	x	x	x	x	x	x	x	x
10 Huby		x	x									
11 Kirby Overblow	x	x	x									
12 Kirk Deighton	x											
13 Leathley		x										
14 Little Ribston		x										
15 North Rigton	x	x										
16 Otley	x	x	x	x	x	x			x	x	x	
17 Pool	x	x	x									
18 Sicklinghall	x	x	x									
19 Spofforth	x	x	x									
20 Weeton		x										
21 Wetherby	x	x	x	x	x	x			x		x	

Key
1 Pub
2 Post office
3 Grocer/general store
4 Chemist
5 Independent shoes
6 Independent clothes
7 Multiple shoes
8 Multiple clothes
9 Boots
10 Woolworths
11 Gas or Electricity showroom
12 Marks & Spencer

Exercise

1 Which of the services in Table 2.3 are convenience type?

2 Why are only convenience type goods and services found in smaller settlements?

3 By referring to Figure 2.33 where, according to central place theory, should people living in the following settlements, travel to buy shoes: Follifoot, Sicklinghall, Leathley?

4 Which settlement should command the largest trade area? Explain why.

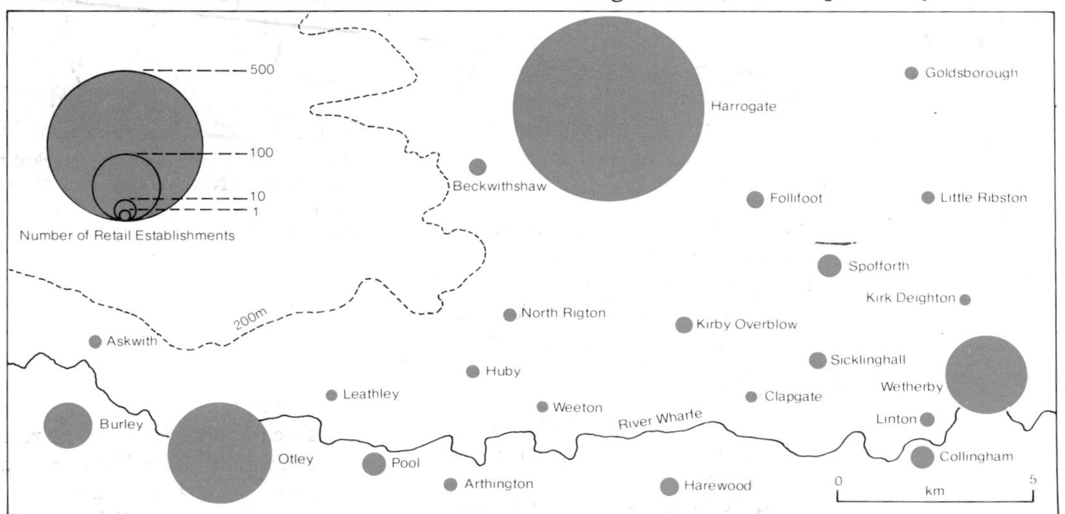

Figure 2.33 Central places in Lower Wharfedale

The distance that shoppers are prepared to travel to buy a good or service is known as the *range* of the good or service. Normally, shoppers travel short distances to obtain convenience goods (especially food) which are bought frequently and are relatively cheap, but longer distances to buy comparison goods. This is another reason why the trade areas of settlements which contain only low order services are smaller than those with higher order services.

Differences in the size of areas served by settlements should affect their spacing: hamlets and villages should be more closely spaced than market towns, while major cities should be the most widely dispersed type of settlement.

Exercise

1 a Test the idea that lower order settlements are more closely spaced than higher order settlements, by referring to Figure 2.33 and measuring the distance between each settlement and its nearest neighbour of the same size. Enter the distances in a table like the one below, and calculate the average distance for the two sizes of settlement.

Settlement size (number of shops)	Distance to centre of nearest settlement of same size	Average distance
over 100		
10 or less		

b Do your results support the idea that larger settlements are more widely spaced than smaller ones?

2 Richmond is a small market town in North Yorkshire (Figures 2.34 and 2.35) and an important central place for smaller settlements within a radius of 10–15 km. Using the information in Table 2.4 complete questions a–f.

Table 2.4 Shopping preferences for shoppers living in Richmond (percentages)

Place for shopping	Bread	Meat	Shoes	Furniture/ carpets
Richmond	95	92	53	16
Darlington	3	6	41	69
Teesside	2	2	4	7
Newcastle-upon-Tyne	0	0	2	8

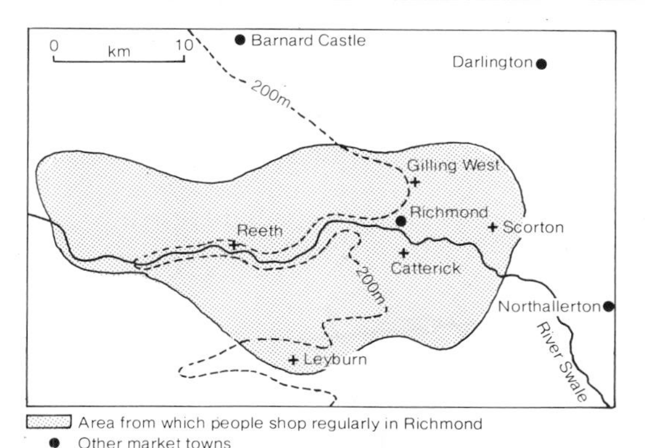

Figure 2.34 Richmond

Figure 2.35 Richmond: the market town for Swaledale in North Yorkshire. Note the size of the market square, indicating the importance of the town as a central place.

a Draw either two pie charts or two divided bar charts (one convenience and one comparison goods) to show the location of shopping for two of the items in Table 2.4.

b Why do you think that the vast majority of people living in Richmond buy their bread and meat in the town?

c What evidence in Table 2.4 suggests that furniture and carpets are a higher order good than shoes?

d In which town's trade area does Richmond lie for furniture and carpets?

e Given that the approximate distances travelled by shoppers to Richmond, Darlington, Teesside and Newcastle-upon-Tyne are 1 km, 18 km, 35 km and 65 km respectively, calculate the average range of the four goods in Table 2.4.

Example

To calculate the average range of shoes:

Richmond	53×1 km	=	53
Darlington	41×18 km	=	738
Teesside	4×35 km	=	140
Newcastle	2×65 km	=	130
			1061

range (ie average distance travelled) = 1061/100 = 10.61 km

f Are the four values for the ranges what you expected? Briefly explain your results.

The patterns of settlement based on central place theory (Figure 2.32) are idealised ones, which in reality are distorted by many other factors. Two such factors are present in the settlement pattern of Lower Wharfedale.

1 The high moorland areas in the western part of the region are unattractive and only sparsely settled.

2 The Wharfe Valley, followed by several important routeways, has attracted quite dense settlement.

A further difference between the theory and reality is that shoppers do not always aim to reduce their travelling costs to a minimum, by shopping at the nearest centre. For example, a particular centre might be chosen not because it is the nearest, but because it offers greater choice or is simply a more pleasant place in which to shop.

Exercise

1 Ask members of your family why they choose to shop in particular centres for comparison goods like clothes, shoes and furniture. Make a list of the factors they mention.

2 Compare your list with others in your class, and using information from the class as a whole, construct a bar graph to show the importance of these various factors.

Summary

Most settlements have a long history, and their survival suggests that their locations have been carefully chosen. Sites with good drainage, access to fertile soils, minerals and water supply, have been preferred, as have situations which promoted commerce and trade. At a larger scale, the distribution and density of settlement can be viewed as the result of forces which on the one hand attract, and on the other, deter, settlement.

Larger settlements are usually central places, providing goods and services for their own populations and those of surrounding areas. On the basis of the number and range of services they provide, settlements can be grouped into classes which form a hierarchy, from small hamlets at the bottom of the scale, to the metropolis at the top. The role of settlements as central places, supplying services supported by a threshold population, offers an explanation of their size, importance, and spacing in the landscape.

Further exercises

1 Explain in your own words the difference between the site and situation of a settlement.

2 What is a 'nucleated' settlement pattern? How does it differ from a 'dispersed' pattern?

3 Why is the CBD often regarded as the most accessible part of a city?

4 Define the following terms: nodality, spring-line settlement, gap town, convenience good, comparison good, central place, threshold, range, hierarchy.

5 Figure 2.36A shows the distribution of population by kilometre grid squares in an area measuring 10 × 10 km in north Lancashire. Figure 2.36B shows altitude in the same area, which varies from 15 m to over 500 m above sea level. You have already seen that population (and settlement) can be strongly influenced by altitude and slopes (relief) on page 29.

a Examine the effect of altitude on population density and settlement in this area.

76	168	152	283	351	400	381	427	433	427
107	215	183	198	290	381	429	459	426	457
91	152	198	183	290	411	427	411	381	520
46	137	198	198	273	305	229	213	503	510
46	122	137	183	213	198	168	198	244	432
30	76	167	183	183	152	152	152	274	426
15	46	107	122	122	137	229	229	168	198
15	30	76	107	107	152	266	259	198	168
22	30	61	76	107	137	152	168	168	152
15	30	46	76	91	107	123	122	122	137

Figure 2.36A Altitude by km grid square, north Lancashire

107	8	5	0	4	0	0	0	0	0
219	2	10	5	0	0	0	0	0	0
27	6	4	32	15	0	0	6	0	0
27	23	11	15	11	18	15	9	0	0
24	24	49	301	6	9	11	15	19	0
59	21	36	15	5	4	7	18	8	7
52	13	22	6	27	19	9	21	18	17
172	26	34	31	15	16	22	5	16	14
35	55	36	8	21	85	11	20	26	38
75	272	15	31	68	17	17	42	31	18

Figure 2.36B Population density by km grid square, north Lancashire

Either
by drawing two grid square maps to show population density and altitude. Use the following classes:
population: 0, 1–20, 21–40, over 40
altitude: 0–61, 62–152, 153–305, over 305
Shade or colour the maps (higher values should have the darker tones or more striking colours) and compare them.
Or
by drawing 4 divided bar charts, one for each altitudinal class. The bar charts should be divided up according to the proportion of grid squares with 0, 1–20, 21–40 and more than 40 people in them. Comment briefly on the effect of altitude on population density.

b Using either the maps or the graphs you have drawn, and the information on page 29, suggest reasons why population density should change with altitude.

6 Figure 2.37 shows the central place hierarchy of the largest cities in England and Wales.
  a Compare the distribution of these places with those in Figure 2.32 by:
  — counting the number of first, second and third order centres for each
  — presenting them as bar charts arranged in pyramid form
  — commenting in a short paragraph on the similarity/dissimilarity between the actual and idealised hierarchy.
  b Measure the average distance between second and third order centres and their nearest neighbours for the two distributions. (Measure in millimetres – actual distances are not important.) Again, comment briefly on any similarity/dissimilarity between the actual and idealised patterns.

Figure 2.37 Hierarchy of largest cities in England and Wales

The actual distribution of large towns and cities in England and Wales is clearly different from the regular, geometric pattern of central place theory. Given the many simplifying assumptions of the theory, this difference is to be expected. In reality, resources such as minerals and fertile soils are not evenly distributed, and this accounts for the clustering of major centres on the coalfields of the North and Midlands. Many of the largest cities, such as Birmingham, Manchester and Leeds, grew as industrial centres in the nineteenth century, and not as central places. The uneven spread of cities also reflects the limited scope for settlement in upland areas such as Wales, the Pennines, the Lake District and the South West Peninsula.

Key ideas	Examples
The original growth of a settlement is often related to its *site* characteristics.	■ Sites which attract settlements include those with a reliable water supply, good drainage, freedom from flooding and good defensive qualities eg surrounded by steep slopes or a river.
An important factor in the later growth of a settlement is access to the surrounding area.	■ A settlement's position in relation to access to the surrounding area is its *situation*. A favourable situation may be promoted by nearness to other places eg commuter villages around large cities, or villages close to tourist areas. Access is usually given by efficient transport networks, and settlements well connected to the surrounding region by transport routes are known as *nodal* centres. Physical factors often promote the convergence of routes on settlements eg valleys running through uplands, a gap in a range of hills, the lowest bridging point across an estuary.
The *shape* of settlements is influenced by physical and human factors.	■ The expansion of larger settlements may be hindered by physical factors eg flood plains, marshes, steep slopes. Planning laws (eg green belts in the UK) may restrict growth. Level, well-drained land, and roads which give easy access to a town or city centre, often encourage growth.
Large settlements have several *functions*, and distinctive patterns of land use.	■ Settlements may be centres of industry, services, tourism and trade eg ports. Distinctive types of land use – commercial, industrial, residential – are evident from large-scale maps and often show a preference for particular locations in towns and cities.
The distribution of settlements in rural areas shows various *patterns*.	■ Patterns may be uniform, clustered or random. The elements of settlement which form the pattern may be largely villages (*nucleated*) or isolated farms and small hamlets (*dispersed*). Settlement patterns are influenced by water supply, relief drainage, mineral resources, planning, etc.
Most larger settlements are *central places* and are ordered into a *hierarchy* by size and function.	■ Larger settlements provide services for their own populations and for those living in the surrounding area. The number and range of services provided is a measure of the importance of a settlement, and the basis of the settlement hierarchy, from tiny hamlets to regional capitals and the metropolis.
The higher the status of a central place, the more people it serves, and the larger its trade area.	■ Large towns and cities have many services such as theatres, art galleries and specialist bookshops, which need large numbers of people for their support (ie they have a high *threshold*). People will travel long distances for these services (ie they have a large *range*) – hence towns and cities command extensive trade areas. Hamlets and villages have only a few services eg church, pub, post office, which serve the local community. People will not travel far for these services. Thus these settlements have only small trade areas. ■ As a consequence of this towns and cities are fewer in number, and more widely spaced, than smaller settlements.

Urbanisation and urban growth

The growth of towns and cities

Today a large part of the world's population growth is occurring in *urban areas*, that is towns and cities (Figure 3.1). Indeed the population growth in urban areas is faster than that in the countryside, and it is forecast that by the end of the century an equal number of people will be living in urban and rural areas (Table 3.1).

Table 3.1 Growth of the world's rural and urban population (millions)

	1800	1850	1900	1950	2000
Rural	900	1000	1300	1700	3200
Urban	50	100	200	700	3200

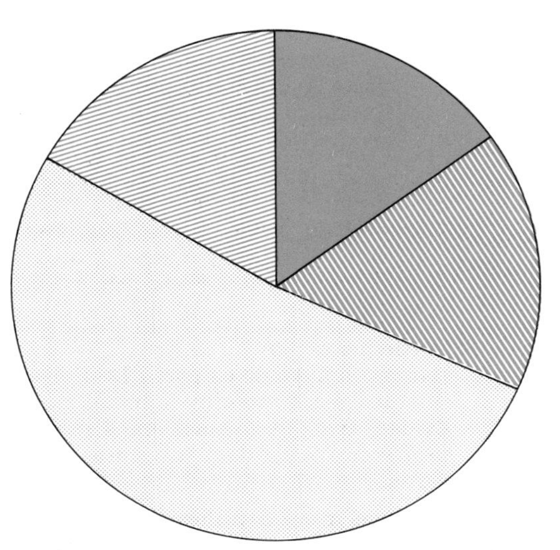

Figure 3.1 World's rural and urban population, 1980

Today, one person in two of the world's urban population lives in a town or city in the Third World. Urban growth appears to be coming to an end in DCs and the massive increases in the world's urban population expected in the near future will take place almost entirely in the cities of the Third World. This will mean that by the end of the century two in every three urban dwellers will live in Third World cities.

So far we have only referred to the increases which are expected in the total *number* of people living in towns and cities in the world. The term *urban growth* is used to describe this increase. *Urbanisation* on the other hand, means an increase in the *proportion* of urban dwellers, either in a region, a country, a continent or in the world (see Table 3.2).

Table 3.2 Urban growth and urbanisation

	Country A		Country B	
	1950	1985	1950	1985
Urban population	250 000 (25%)	500 000 (25%)	250 000 (25%)	1 000 000 (50%)
Rural population	750 000 (75%)	1 500 000 (75%)	750 000 (75%)	1 000 000 (50%)
Total population	1 000 000 (100%)	2 000 000 (100%)	1 000 000 (100%)	2 000 000 (100%)

Table 3.2 gives an imaginary example of urban growth and urbanisation. In country A the number of people living in urban areas doubled between 1950 and 1985; but because the numbers in rural areas also doubled, the proportion of urban and rural dwellers remained the same. We would say therefore that country A experienced urban growth, but *not* urbanisation. The total population

of country B also doubled in the same period, but the table shows that the urban population grew much faster than the rural population. The result is an increase in the proportion of urban dwellers: this means that urbanisation *as well as* urban growth took place.

Exercise

1 Plot the data in Table 3.1 as a series of bar charts (one for each date) showing the total population and the proportion which is rural and urban.

2 Which of the following statements is true?
— The world's population has undergone urban growth but not urbanisation since 1800.
— The world's population has undergone urbanisation but not urban growth since 1800.
— The world's population has undergone both urban growth and urbanisation since 1800.
Explain why you think that the answer you chose is the correct one.

3 Study Table 3.3 and answer the following questions.

a Assuming there is no movement of people from rural to urban, or urban to rural areas, in which countries is urban growth occurring?
b Again, assuming there is no migration, in which countries is urbanisation taking place?
c Explain the reasoning behind your answers to a and b.

Table 3.3 Rural and urban vital rates (per 1000)

	Urban		Rural	
	CBR	CDR	CBR	CDR
Equador	34	9	41	11
Honduras	52	12	39	8
Liberia	53	12	50	18
Panama	34	5	40	9
Sierra Leone	42	17	30	18

One indication of the speed of urban growth in the last 30 years is the large increase which has taken place in the number of cities with populations in excess of one million. In 1950 there were 70 *millionaire cities* in the world: today there are 154, almost evenly split between DCs and LDCs (Figure 3.2). It seems certain that the number of millionaire cities will continue to grow in the near future, to around 270 by the end of the century. Most of these new millionaire cities will be in the Third World, and their populations will be very poor (Figure 3.3).

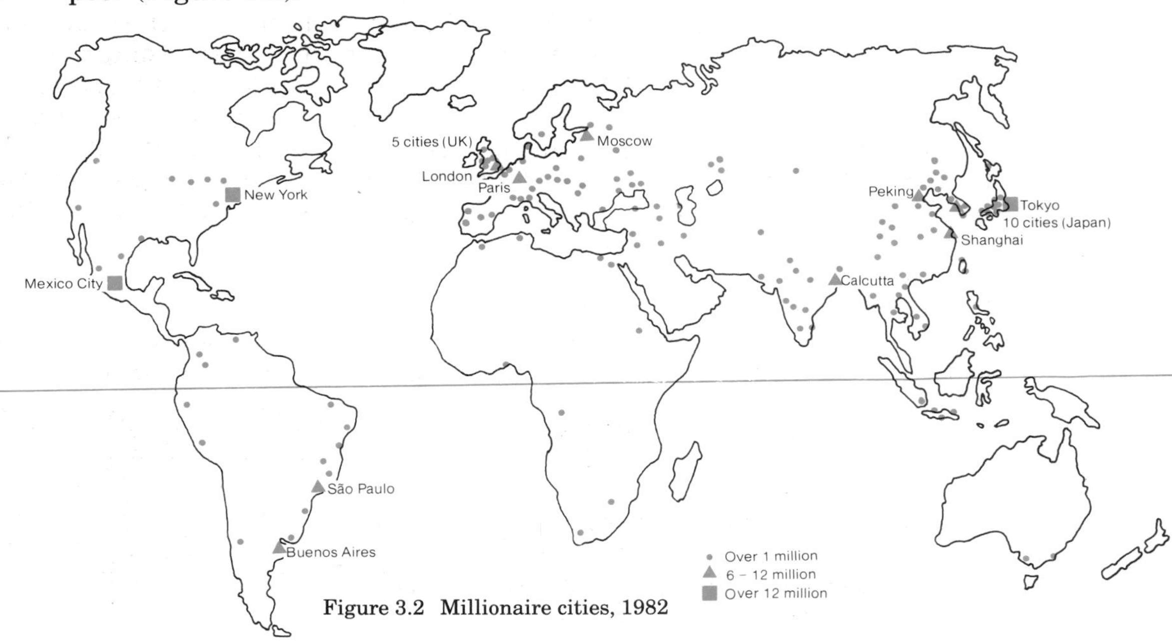

Figure 3.2 Millionaire cities, 1982

However, the most rapidly growing cities of all will be the so-called '*super-cities*', whose populations exceed 12 million. At the moment only New York, Tokyo and Mexico City are in this class, but by the end of the century they could be joined by a further 22 cities, 17 of them in LDCs!

Exercise

With reference to Figure 3.2:

1 Compile a table to show the number of millionaire cities in each continent. (The USSR to the west of the Ural Mountains is to be included in Europe.) From your table, illustrate the data by drawing a pie chart.

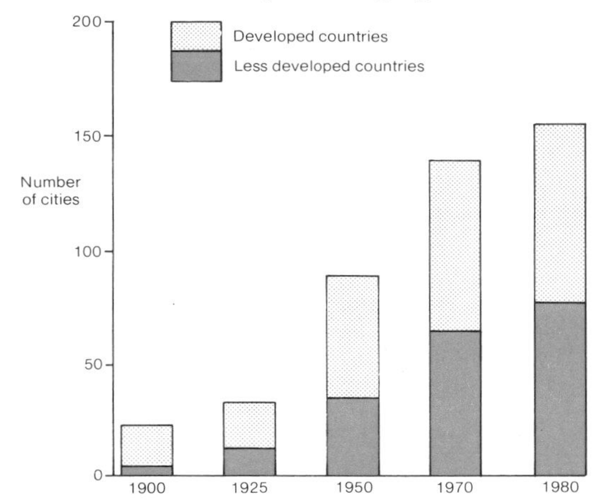

Figure 3.3 Growth of millionaire cities

2 Which country has the largest number of millionaire cities?

3 The USA, the USSR, China and India each have many millionaire cities. Can you think of any other feature they have in common which might help explain their relatively large number of millionaire cities?

4 The following cities will belong to the 'super-city' class by AD 2000: Bangkok, Bogota, Bombay, Buenos Aires, Cairo, Calcutta, Delhi, Jakarta, Karachi, Lima, London, Los Angeles, Manila, Mexico City, Moscow, New York, Paris, Peking, Rhine-Ruhr, Rio de Janeiro, São Paulo, Seoul, Shanghai, Tehran, Tokyo.
   a Use an atlas to locate each city, and plot them on an outline map of the world.
   b Seven of the cities in the list are in DCs. Which ones?
   c How many of the 18 super-cities in LDCs are port cities? Make a list of these port cities.

The rate at which cities in the Third World are growing today is similar to that at which cities in Europe grew during the nineteenth century, though no city in nineteenth century Europe could match Rangoon's current growth rate of 23% per year, nor Mexico City's 2.5 million population increase between 1970 and 1978! Although the total increases in population were by comparison modest, between 1821 and 1831 Manchester, Leeds, Glasgow, Liverpool, Birmingham and Bradford each grew at a rate of 4.5–6.5% per year, while London's population increased from one million in 1801, to nearly 2.5 million in 1851. Rapid urban growth occurred later on the continent, but was nonetheless spectacular: the population of Paris, for example, grew from 935 000 in 1841 to 2.66 million by the turn of the century.

As towns and cities have grown, so too has the proportion of people living in urban areas. This is the process of urbanisation, which first occurred on a large scale in Britain during the nineteenth century; by 1851, half of Britain's population were urban dwellers. Germany was the only other country to have a majority of its population living in towns and cities before the twentieth century. In contrast to the Third

Table 3.4 Population growth: nineteenth-century Leeds and twentieth-century Cairo

Leeds 1801–61 (% pa)		Cairo 1927–80 (% pa)	
1801–11	1.6	1927–37	1.2
1811–21	3.6	1937–47	3.7
1821–31	4.7	1947–60	3.0
1831–41	2.2	1960–66	4.3
1841–51	1.5	1966–76	1.6
1851–61	1.7	1976–80	3.2

World, urbanisation in DCs is virtually at an end, and in Britain the proportion of urban dwellers is beginning to fall slightly (Figure 3.4).

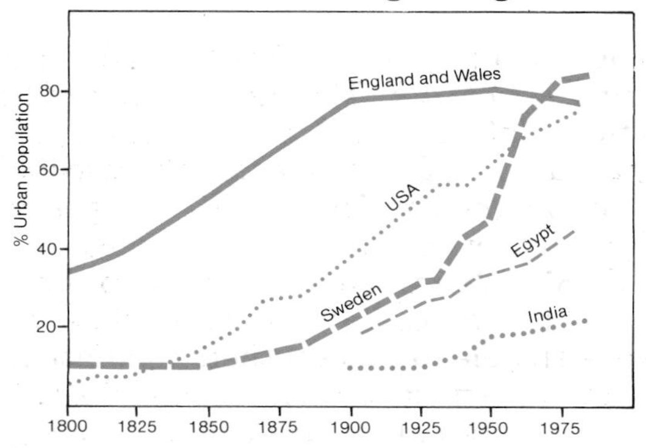

Figure 3.4 The progress of urbanisation: England and Wales, the USA, Sweden, Egypt and India

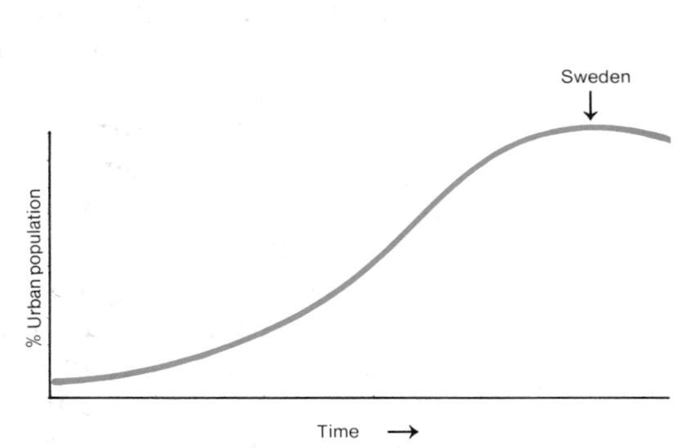

Figure 3.5 The progress of urbanisation

In many DCs, the progress of urbanisation has followed an S-shaped curve (Figure 3.5). Urbanisation is now at an end, with the % of urban dwellers either remaining constant at around 80% of the total population, or slowlybeginning to fall. The progress of urbanisation has followed three stages in DCs:

1 very slow growth, with most people employed in agriculture

2 rapid urbanisation associated with economic development

3 urbanisation ends, and the vast majority of people live in towns and cities and are employed in industry and services. A decline in the % urban population may take place as more people choose to live in the country and commute to the city.

Exercise

1 Make a copy of Figure 3.5 and mark on it the three phases of the cycle of urbanisation.

2 Figure 3.4 shows the progress of urbanisation in several countries. On your copy of Figure 3.5 show the progress of urbanisation in England and Wales, the USA, Egypt and India using the information given to you in Figure 3.4. (Sweden's progress has already been marked for you on Figure 3.5.)

3 In which of the countries has urbanisation developed
a) furthest b) least?

4 What is likely to happen to Sweden's urban population level in the future?

5 Is India's level of urbanisation likely to
a) fall b) stay the same c) grow rapidly in the future? Explain your choice of answer.

6 When did England and Wales enter stage 3 of the cycle?

7 Compare the dates at which the USA and Sweden entered stage 2 of the cycle.

The causes of urbanisation and urban growth

Britain 1800–50

We have already seen that a population can grow either through natural increase or migration or a combination of both. The rapid growth of the world's urban population since 1800 is the result of both factors. However, in Britain in the first half of the nineteenth century one factor was largely responsible for the growth of new towns and cities: migration. *Migration* is the permanent (or semi-permanent) movement of people from one place of residence to another, and in Britain between 1800 and 1850, this movement was from the countryside to the expanding towns and cities. Without this *rural–urban migration*, cities would not have been able to sustain their population growth. The new towns and cities which mushroomed between 1800 and 1850 were essentially industrial. Moreover, they were unplanned, overcrowded, insanitary death traps, where epidemics of cholera, smallpox and other diseases occurred frequently. Major cholera epidemics (the result of polluted drinking water) swept Britain in 1831, 1848 and 1866. Writers of the time painted a vivid picture of the squalid living conditions found in these new industrial cities. In 1832, 'Little Ireland', an area close to the River Medlock in Manchester, was described as:

> '... an unhealthy district which lies so low that the chimneys of its houses, some of them three storeys high, are little above the level of the ground ... surrounded on every side by the largest factories of the town, whose chimneys vaunt forth dense clouds of smoke, which hang heavily over this insalubrious region.'

In Wolverhampton in 1840, the worst housing, consisting of close courts and alleys, was described thus:

> '... a dense population is congregated in these places (and) in the formation of the buildings everything has been sacrificed to secure a large (financial) return.'
>
> '(they) are often of the worst construction, and in immediate contact with extensive receptacles of manure and rubbish ... and many have only one privy for several families ... Should any epidemic occur, its victims can scarcely be otherwise than numerous ... Even in the new buildings in the town, regard for the health of the public does not appear to exist, particularly as respects drainage and the facility of removing refuse ... and fever is constantly present.'

Exercise

Use these two short extracts of living conditions in parts of Manchester and Wolverhampton, and Figure 3.6 to answer the following questions.

1 In your own words, summarise the main problems of living conditions in Britain's new industrial towns of the nineteenth century.

2 Say what the main causes of these problems were.

Figure 3.6 (*right*) A Glasgow slum in the 1860s

It is not surprising that life expectancy in Britain's industrial towns and cities before 1850 was so low. In 1841, the average age at death in London was 36 years, and in Manchester a mere 26 years. Deaths among infants were especially high: 259 out of every 1000 children born in Liverpool in 1840–41 died in their first year, compared with a national average of 148. It is therefore apparent that Britain's towns and cities before 1850 were extremely unhealthy places, and that their enormous population growth in the first half of the century was only possible through a continuous inflow of migrants, who more than made up for those who died as a result of appalling living conditions.

After 1850 the introduction of public health controls and effective medical treatment helped to bring about an improvement in living conditions, and cities began to grow as a result of a natural increase of the population, as well as migration. From mid-century a number of acts of Parliament provided the necessary basis for improvement (Table 3.5).

Table 3.5 Acts of Parliament to improve living conditions in British cities 1848–75

Year	Act
1848	Public Health Act – set up a Central Board of Health and allowed it to establish Local Boards.
1866	Sanitary Act – helped to control the more obvious sanitary problems, though it was not adequately enforced.
1868	Local authorities were empowered to compel owners of insanitary dwellings either to demolish or repair them at their own expense.
1870+	Adoption of by-laws for the construction of new housing: minimum standards were laid down, which resulted in the familiar by-law housing built between 1870 and 1914 (Figures 3.7 and 3.8). Streets were a minimum width (to ensure sufficient sunlight); there were separate external WCs with back alley access to empty them. However, these houses had neither internal WCs nor baths.
1875	Artisans' Dwelling Act – allowed the compulsory purchase of insanitary areas either for demolition or improvement.
1875	Public Health Act – the country was divided into urban and rural sanitary districts, supervised by central government.

Exercise

Figure 3.9 shows the plan of four typical terrace houses built in Britain's industrial cities around 1850. Look carefully at the plans and answer the following questions.

1 Explain why these houses are known as 'back-to-back'.

2 How many rooms are there (excluding the cellar) in a) the two end houses b) the other houses?

3 How do you account for the difference in size between the houses?

4 How is access gained from one side of the block to the other? Why is access necessary?

5 Calculate the total floorspace for an end house (excluding cellar) and compare it with your own home. Assuming that the houses in Figure 3.9 had an average of 6 persons living in them in 1850, compare the amount of floorspace per person with that in your home.

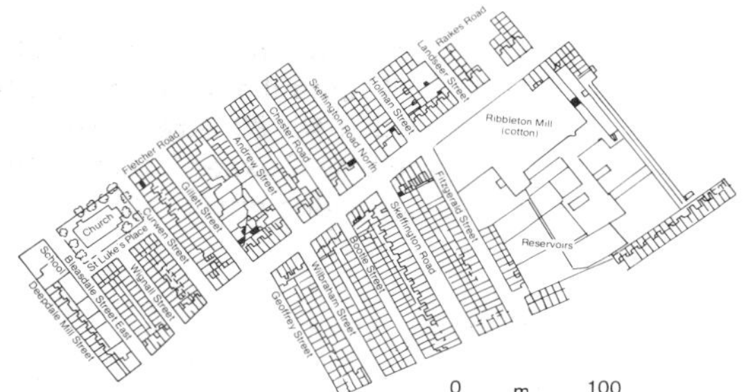

Figure 3.7 Nineteenth-century housing in Preston, 1893

Figure 3.8 Back-to-back terrace houses built in the 1880s, at Morley, near Leeds

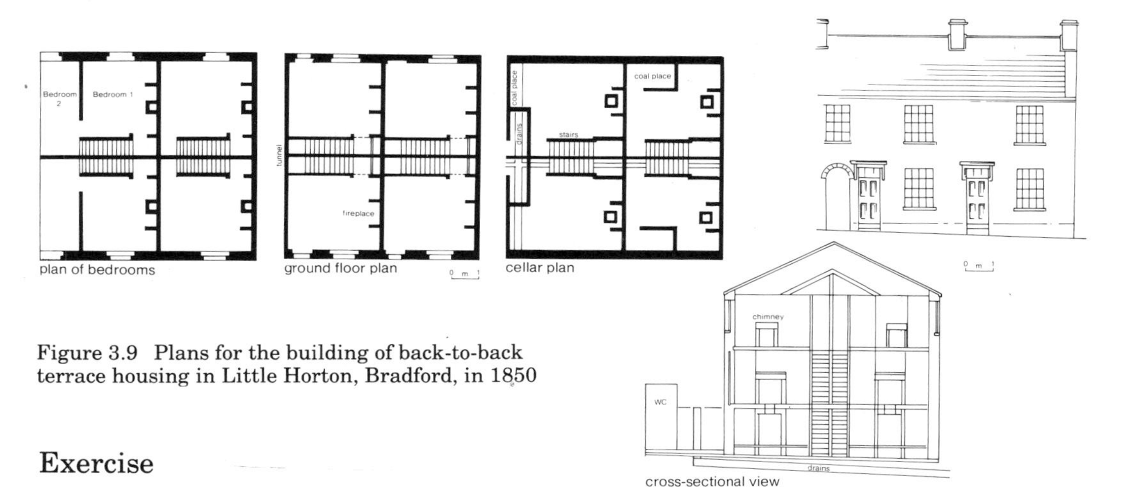

Figure 3.9 Plans for the building of back-to-back terrace housing in Little Horton, Bradford, in 1850

Exercise

Figure 3.10 shows changes in the crude death rate in England and Wales between 1845 and 1890.

1 Make a copy of Figure 3.10, and on the graph plot the following figures for the crude death rate in the industrial city of Bradford for the same period.

1845	27.2	1870	26.0
1850	28.0	1875	26.4
1855	27.8	1880	23.6
1860	25.0	1885	21.0
1865	26.8	1890	21.8

2 Describe the main differences in CDRs between England and Wales and Bradford in the period 1845–90. Are these differences what you would expect? Do the differences narrow or widen during the period?

3 On your graph, mark the dates of the main improvements in public health control and name them. Can you detect any relationship between the introduction of these controls and changes in the CDR?

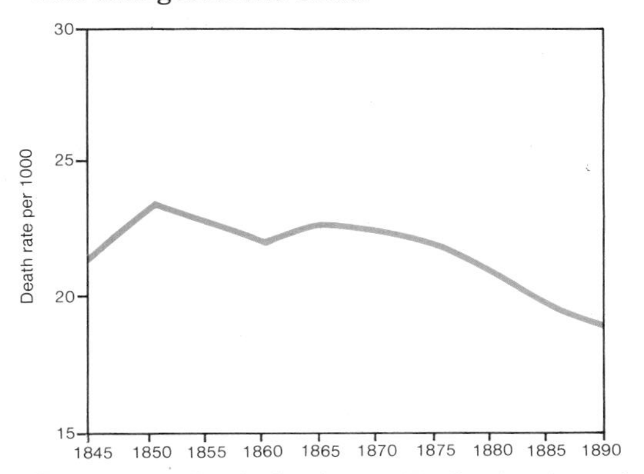

Figure 3.10 Crude death rate: England and Wales, 1845–90

South Asia

Between 1901 and 1981 India's population grew from 238 to 683 million. In this period the proportion classed as urban also increased, from 11% to 22%. Though this is a fairly slow rate of urbanisation, it hides an enormous absolute growth of urban population: from 23 million in 1901 to 148 million in 1981. Indeed there are nearly as many urban dwellers in India as in the whole of the EEC.

Urban growth has been mainly caused by migration: Bombay in the late 1950s had nearly 2 million migrants. At the same time, natural increase has played its part as Third World cities today are not the death traps that European cities were in the nineteenth century. Health care is better in the cities than in the countryside, and in some instances may be as good as DCs. This produces low death rates, and with youthful populations and high birth rates, natural increase is rapid.

Yet rural–urban migration continues apace, and living conditions in the cities, though poor by the standards of DCs, are often better than those in the countryside (Figure 3.11). Thus, whereas rural–urban migration in Britain in the nineteenth century was mainly caused by the attraction of jobs in new industries in the cities, in India, and throughout much of the Third World, it is

Figure 3.11 (*right*) Gurndaspur, Bangladesh. Most migrants to the large towns and cities come from small villages like Gurndaspur

lack of development in the countryside which is driving people into the cities. In other words, whereas in Britain it was the *pull* of the cities which caused migration, in India it is more often the *push* of poverty and unemployment in the countryside (Table 3.6).

Table 3.6 Factors affecting rural–urban migration

'PULL' FACTORS	'PUSH' FACTORS
Prospects of better material welfare and higher standard of living	Growing pressure of population on the land
Higher wages in urban occupations	Small holdings of land due to divided inheritance
Better job opportunities in the cities	Unemployment and underemployment
Less interest on loans compared with rural moneylenders	Crippling debts in rural areas
Information media, newspapers, radio, TV in cities	Information media seldom found in villages
More chance of social advancement	Static social structure
To join families already migrated to the city	No proper family planning in villages
Better medical facilities	Poor medical facilities
Better educational opportunities	Lack of educational opportunities
Proper housing, electricity, water supply and sewage disposal in cities	Lack of proper housing, electricity, water and sewerage
Transport and communication facilities	Insufficient transport and communications facilities
Impact of natural hazards less severe in cities	Hazards of flooding, drought, cyclones, etc.

In Bangladesh 40% of urban growth between 1961 and 1974 was due to migration, mainly to the three largest cities of Dacca, Chittagong and Khulna. Here too, push factors were dominant. The laws of inheritance in the country permit the division of property among all the children of the deceased, and this has the effect of producing tiny and fragmented farms. 38% of farms are little more than $\frac{1}{2}$ hectare in size, and 83% are less than 2 hectares. As an average family requires at least 2 hectares of good quality farmland to support itself, acute shortage of land is a major factor causing migration. The shortage of land also has another effect: farmers are often forced to occupy areas which are at risk from flooding, either by rivers or by the sea, sometimes with disastrous consequences, as we saw in Chapter 2 page 31. In addition, settlements in low-lying areas may be surrounded by stagnant water for several months during the rainy season, and in these areas malaria is a common disease. Disposal of sewage is also a problem and water supplies often become contaminated. A survey of migrants in Dacca found that 81% owned no land in the countryside, 64% were in debt to rural moneylenders, and that their average income as farmers was only £30 a year.

Undoubtedly, Bangladesh is unfortunate in the number of natural hazards to which it is susceptible, and in recent years these natural disasters have helped to swell the stream of migrants from the countryside. Floods in the Ganges Delta, cyclones, storms, droughts, landslides and river erosion are all a depressingly familiar aspect of rural life. The country lies in the path of tropical cyclones from the Bay of Bengal, and when storms coincide with high tides in the delta, storm surges pose a great threat to life and property. Nine cyclones between 1960 and 1970 resulted in the loss of 400 000 lives, 300 000 in 1970 alone. Such disasters are made worse by the destruction of crops and livestock, and the inevitable famine and disease which follow.

The factors listed in Table 3.6 amount to a powerful case for leaving the countryside for the city in LDCs. As we shall see in Chapter 4, conditions in the cities might be bad, but for most migrants they are even worse in the countryside. Of course, some migrants do return to their villages, disillusioned with the city, but the overwhelming majority stay; most would have little to return to, and though in a sense they have simply exchanged rural poverty for urban poverty, life seems to offer more hope in the city.

The migration game

Imagine that you are a newly married farmer living in a small village in north east India. You own a small farm of 2 hectares, and have savings of £100. Your farm gives you an income in 'normal' years of £100 (ie £50 per hectare). However, your income varies according to the weather and other factors (see Table 3.8) in any particular year. Each member of your family needs £25 a year to survive (ie for subsistence).

Your only source of income is your farm, though if you are able to save sufficient money you can make improvements such as sinking a tube well to provide irrigation water, or buying seeds of disease resistant varieties of rice (Table 3.7B – see Figure 3.12). If you are very successful you have the option of buying land and increasing the size of your farm. On the other hand, if you run into debt you must either use your savings to restore your balance to credit, or more drastically, sell your land and farm it on a sharecropping basis, giving half your crop each year to the landlord as rent.

Like everyone in your village you do not accept birth control: you believe that God decides the number of children you will have, and will provide.

The game ends when having sold all your land, and used all your savings, you are still in debt; then your only option is to migrate to the nearest town, and join the massive stream of people leaving the countryside in South Asia.

Table 3.8 Annual income and random events if land owner*

Area of farm (hectares)	Normal income (£50/ha/year)	Random events					
		1	2	3[1]	4[2]	5	6
2	100	80	40	60	60	160	120
3	150	120	60	90	90	240	180
4	200	160	80	120	120	320	240
5	250	200	100	150	150	400	300
6	300	240	120	180	180	480	360
7	350	280	140	210	210	560	420
8	400	320	160	240	240	640	480

[1] if a tube well has been drilled, income is normal
[2] if dwarf rice is grown, income is normal
* if the farmer is a sharecropper, income is exactly half that shown in table

Table 3.9 Balance sheet

Year	Farm area (ha); owner sharecropper	Family size	Yearly income			Yearly costs			Year balance	Total balance
			A	B	C	D	E	F	C – F	
0	2	2		—						100
1	2	3	80	—	80	75		75	5	105
2	2	3	120	—	120	75	100	175	–55	50
3										
4										
5										

A Income taking account of random events (see Table 3.8)
B Income from the sale of farm (£200 per hectare)
C Total income (A + B)
D Cost of subsistence for family (£25 per person per year)
E Cost of improvements (ie tube well or dwarf rice – £100 each)
F Total costs (D + E)

Example

The balance sheet (Table 3.9) shows that at the start of the game you own 2 hectares, have savings of £100, and no children. At the start of year one we select a number at random from the random number tables (Table 3.10). The first number (shown in bold in Table 3.10) is 1, and this refers to family size. Table 3.7A tells us that any number from 0–4 means that a child is born, and so the family increases to three. We then select random numbers consecutively, reading down the column. The second number, which is also 1, refers to random events (Table 3.7C) and tells us that yields are down by £10 per hectare, owing to an outbreak of malaria. Table 3.8 shows us that our income for this year will be only £80. Moreover, with an extra mouth to feed, the cost of living will rise to £75, leaving a surplus of just £5. In year 2, we read off the next two consecutive random numbers – 6 and 6. The first tells us that there has been no addition to the family this year, and the second that yields are up by £10 per hectare owing to a donation of chemical fertilizer from the EEC. As this is a good year, we decide to spend £100 on a tube well, which will help us overcome the effects of drought years in future. At the end of year 2 we are left with a total balance of £50.

Exercise

1 Make a copy of the balance sheet (Table 3.9), and run the game for either 20 years or until you are forced to migrate. Before you play the game, try and work out a plan which will enable you to survive for as long as possible.

2 Write an account of your experience. What was your plan? How did it work out? If you had to migrate, what factor finally forced you off the land? If you played the game again, would you alter your strategy?

3 Hold a class discussion to compare experiences. Was there any single factor which was mainly responsible for migration? Did those who survived longest have any features in common? (luck, small families, good decision making)

4 If you were eventually forced to sell your farm and become a sharecropper, did this prove disastrous? How do you think that the government might help farmers who fall into debt after one or two years of poor harvests?

Table 3.10 Random numbers

8030236467962133369003916933901334430219
61298961320812622260842003173313030613411
2333610102211181513236102374503190117352
942**1**3292935072672320745930304366775322797
8761926901602879747686063929738503275057

3756191803428603857444818645711613523556
6486663155048840103084380613588362046352
2269226958454923098198840504759927707279
2322142264891026742353912773781992436810
4238596472964657896722819456698418310639

1718013410983748938688596953788637268548
3945695394895897293329195094805731993891
4318114256194844450284290178657776848885
5944064568551665661338009576506767651883
0150343238003757478266591950871435597947

7914603547959071310385373870341664556649
0156636880261497238859228239708348344648
2576187129251551929601012818033511102784
2352108345064985354584088113525721236702
9164086254257416109731102748890642812910

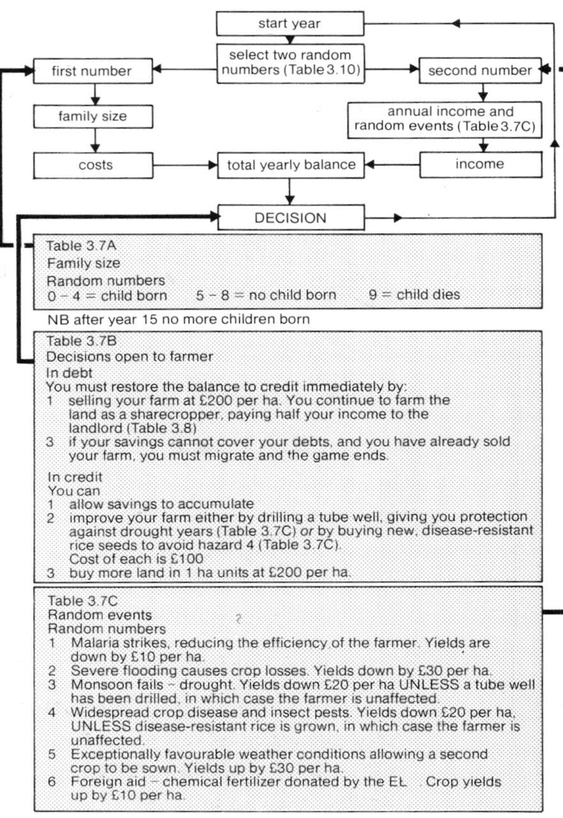

Figure 3.12 The Migration Game: rules

The USA 1970–80

In the last decade the growth of cities in the USA has been very uneven: among the 100 largest cities, Las Vegas grew most rapidly, recording a population increase of 69%; New York recorded the biggest decrease – a loss of 8.6%. However, the general trend was one of urban growth, and only 17 of the top 100 cities suffered an actual loss of population. This situation contrasts with the LDCs, where virtually every large city is growing rapidly. A further contrast is evident in Figure 3.13, for whereas in the LDCs it is the largest cities which are growing fastest, in the USA the trend is the complete reverse.

Exercise

1 Figure 3.14 shows the distribution of the USA's 50 largest cities, and the division of the country into three regions. Using this information and that in Figure 3.15, group the cities by urban growth % 1970–80, and complete a table like the one below.

	Number of cities losing population	Number of cities gaining population
North		
South		
West		

2 Write a paragraph describing clearly the main patterns of urban growth in the USA 1970–80.

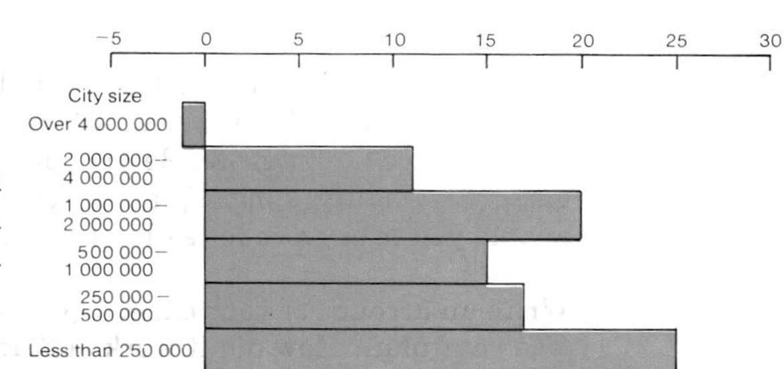

Figure 3.13 Percentage population change in US cities, 1970–80

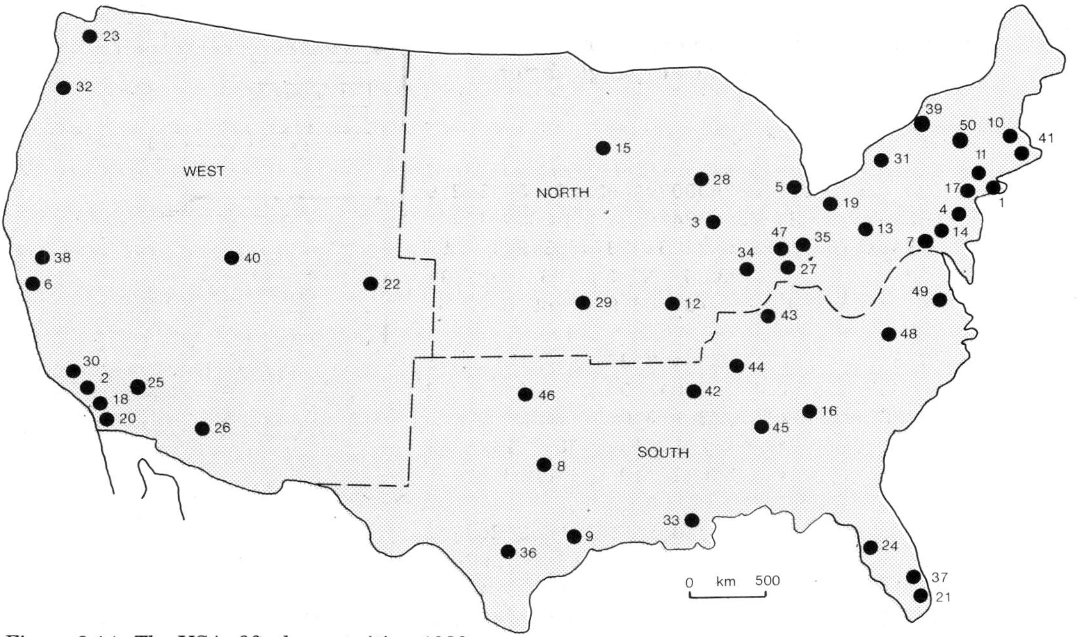

Figure 3.14 The USA: fifty largest cities, 1980

The geography of urban growth in the USA in the last decade is one of rapid population increase in most cities in the south and west, and low growth and often population decline in the north. The two regions in the north where urban decline has been most severe are: the great urban agglomeration in the north eastern states, known as Bosnywash, extending from Boston, through New

York to Washington; and the Lower Great Lakes region, including major cities such as Detroit, Pittsburgh and Cleveland (Figure 3.16). Urban stagnation and decline in these regions has been more than compensated by the very rapid growth of cities in Florida (Miami, Tampa, Fort Lauderdale), the Gulf States (Houston, Galveston, Dallas), California (Los Angeles, San Diego, San Francisco) and the Pacific north west (Seattle, Portland) (Figures 3.17 and 3.18). This pattern of urban growth is not new: the north has been losing population to the south and west for 30 years or more, but whereas in the past the northern cities continued to grow (albeit slowly), today, for the first time, many are suffering an absolute population decline. Migration is the cause of these changes, but unlike urban growth in LDCs, it is mainly a migration *between* urban areas, rather than the rural–urban migration which is so typical of the Third World. In explaining these movements of population, we shall, as in the previous section, consider both 'push' and 'pull' factors.

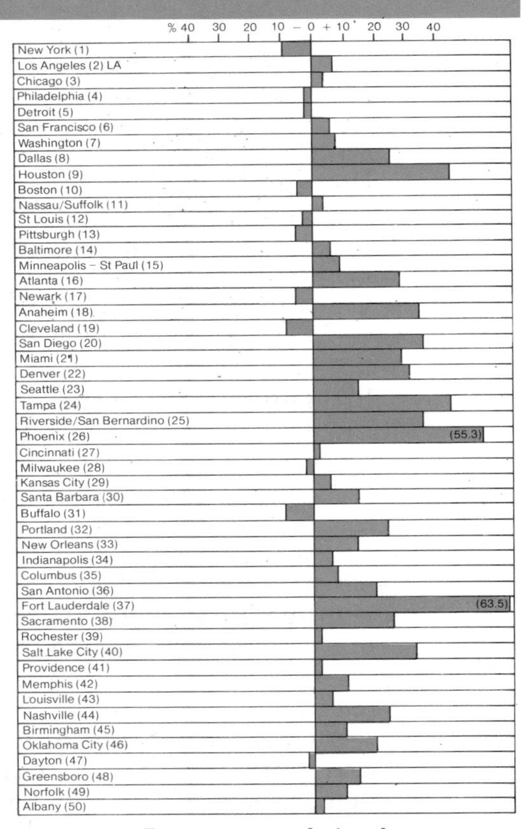

Figure 3.15 Percentage population change, 1970–80: USA's fifty largest cities (in order of rank size)

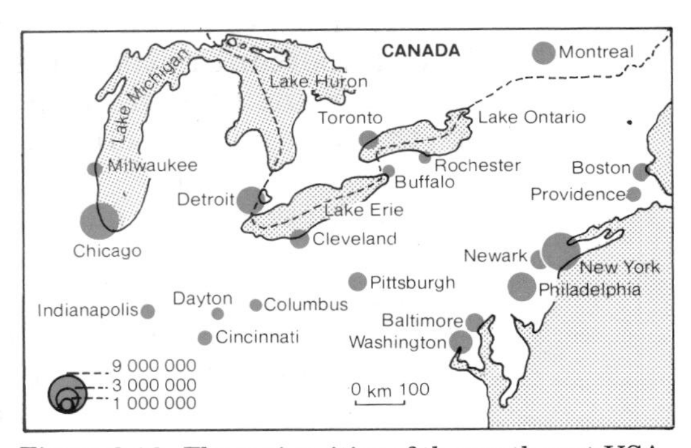

Figure 3.16 The major cities of the north east USA

Figure 3.17 (*below right*) Denver, Colorado, at the foot of the Rocky Mountains, is one of the fastest growing cities in the USA. Its favourable climate and beautiful surroundings have made it a major attraction for many new, high-technology industries

Figure 3.18 (*below*) Philadelphia, the fourth largest city in the USA, is one of several old industrial centres in the Bosnywash conurbation. In the last twenty years it has suffered population decline, and has been beset with problems of unemployment, overcrowding, high rents and taxes

'Push' factors in the north

Between 1969 and 1977 the north east lost 1.7 million jobs – a number almost exactly equalled by the growth of new jobs in the south and west. Bosnywash and the Lower Great Lakes region are the two oldest industrial areas in the USA, with many cities heavily dependent on long-established, declining industries, such as steel in Cleveland, coal and steel in Pittsburgh and cars in Detroit. Manufacturing industry dominates both regions, and Figure 3.19 demonstrates that, in general, where there is greatest dependence on this activity (rather than services, which create, for example, office employment), rates of urban growth are lowest. The reliance on heavy, low-growth industries, means a lack of modern high technology industries, such as electronics, and little investment in the latest technologies. Moreover, major cities in the north like New York, Philadelphia and Cleveland, are beset with problems of poor housing, high rates of crime, overcrowding, high rents and high taxes. New industries (which are less tied to the major cities as a result of better transport, inter-state highways, air travel, etc. and telecommunications) are choosing to locate in smaller, newer cities in the south and west, and the same is true of office companies. The older cities, particularly New York and to a lesser degree Chicago, Pittsburgh, Detroit and Philadelphia, have lost considerable numbers of headquarter offices to the south and west in recent years.

'Pull' factors of the south and west

The south and west are less dependent on manufacturing industry, and have a bigger share of fast-growing industries based on advanced technology. In California, two of the leading industries are micro-electronics (Silicon Valley near San Francisco) and aerospace, while in the Gulf States the location of the Johnson Space Centre at Houston, and the huge investment in space technology by NASA have given an enormous boost to the region. In addition, some regions have important natural resources which generate prosperous industries: examples include oil in the Gulf States, timber for pulp and paper in the Pacific north west, and the climate of the Sacramento area of California which supports horticulture and citrus fruit growing.

It is not economic factors alone which explain the attraction of the south and west. The most rapidly growing part of the country is Florida, where the sub-tropical climate (the south and south west USA is known as the 'Sunbelt') attracts older people on retirement from the northern cities, and offers great opportunities for outdoor recreation. The combination of a warm climate and great natural beauty are equally attractive along the whole length of the Pacific coast, from Seattle to San Diego. This migration of retired people has been made possible in recent years by earlier retirement and generous pensions. At the same time in the USA (and in most DCs) there has been an increase in the demand for leisure activities by all age groups. With improvements in transport and communications, for many industries and office activities it is no longer a disadvantage to locate outside the major conurbations; hence considerations such as climate and recreational opportunities figure more importantly in location decisions than ever before. An extreme example is the case of a New York office company which decided to re-locate on the Pacific coast, in order to be close to the snowfields, which would provide the managing director with all-year-round ski-ing!

Exercise

1 Summarise in a sentence the relationship between urban growth and dependence on manufacturing. (Figure 3.19.)

2 Cities A, B, C on Figure 3.19 represent Miami, Detroit and Houston, though not necessarily in that order. Identify each city, and explain your choice in each case.

3 If cities with high rates of growth are not heavily dependent on manufacturing, to what do they owe their prosperity?

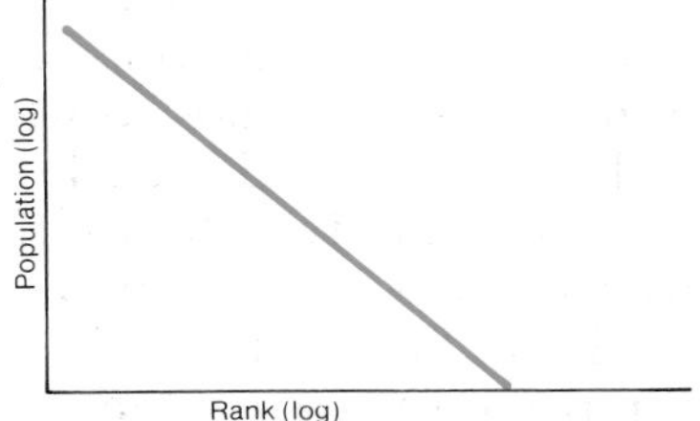

Figure 3.20 City size distribution following the rank-size rule

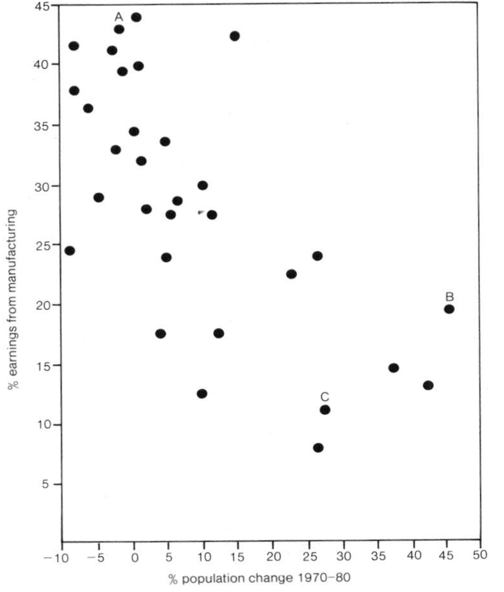

Figure 3.19 Percentage population growth, 1970–80, and dependence on manufacturing industry in the largest US cities

City-size distributions

Rank-size rule

We saw in Chapter 2 that urban places form a hierarchy with a few large, important places and many small places of less importance. One way of looking at urban hierarchies is to represent them as a graph (Figure 3.20) where the population of each city is plotted against its *rank* (ie its order of size within a country). For many countries (eg the USA, Australia, Switzerland) such a graph, when plotted on graph paper with a logarithmic scale, approximates a straight line. This means that the largest city is roughly twice the size of the second city, three times the size of the third, four times the fourth, and so on. This is the *rank-size rule*. It has been suggested that countries with this city-size distribution are often highly developed and highly urbanised.

Exercise

Figure 3.21 shows a rank-size graph of West Germany's 10 largest cities.

1 Copy the graph and draw in a second line to show the ideal distribution if it corresponded exactly to the rank-size rule.

2 Having drawn your rank-size curve, say how closely West Germany's city-size distribution corresponds to the rank-size rule.

3 Draw a rank-size distribution graph (similar to Figure 3.21) for Argentina. Use the data in Table 3.11, plotting the actual values on logarithmic graph paper, or if you are unable to obtain log graph paper, the log values in the Table on normal graph paper.

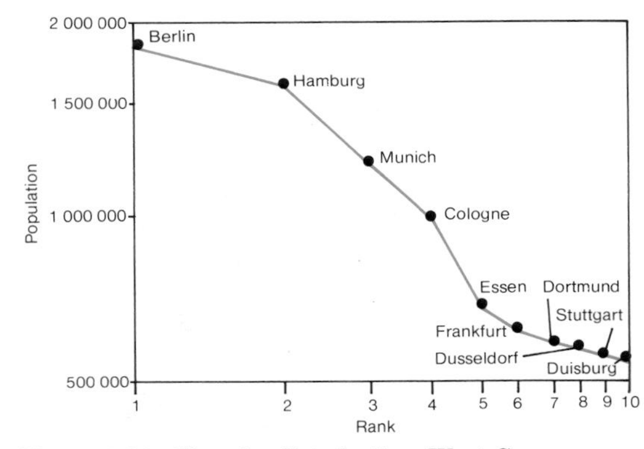

Figure 3.21 City-size distribution: West Germany

Table 3.11 Argentina – 10 largest cities

Rank	Log rank	City	Population	Log population
1	0	Buenos Aires	8.436 m	0.9261
2	0.301	Rosario	0.807	0.09069
3	0.4771	Cordoba	0.782	0.08932
4	0.6021	La Plata	0.479	0.06803
5	0.699	Mendoza	0.471	0.0673
6	0.7782	San Miguel de Tucuman	0.366	0.05635
7	0.8451	Mar del Plata	0.300	0.04771
8	0.9031	Sante Fe	0.245	0.03892
9	0.9542	San Juan	0.218	0.03385
10	1,0000	Bahia Blanca	0.182	0.02601

4 Draw in a second curve (as in question 1). How closely does Argentina approximate the rank-size rule? How does it compare with West Germany?

Primate distributions

If you have worked through the last exercise you will realise that Argentina does not correspond to the rank-size rule. In fact, Argentina is not exceptional: the majority of countries do not have a regular rank-size distribution of cities. Instead, these countries commonly have a largest city which is many times bigger than the second city – for example, Paris compared with Lyon, London with Birmingham, Copenhagen with Århus and Mexico City with Guadalajara. These large cities, which are disproportionate in size to the other cities in a country, are known as *primate cities*. Countries which have a primate city, also have a primate city-size distribution (Figure 3.22). For example, Lima, the largest city in Peru, had a population of 4.6 million in 1979, which is just more than one quarter of the total population in the country. Furthermore, Lima's position of primacy is increasing, and by 1990 it is estimated that it will contain nearly one third of Peru's population.

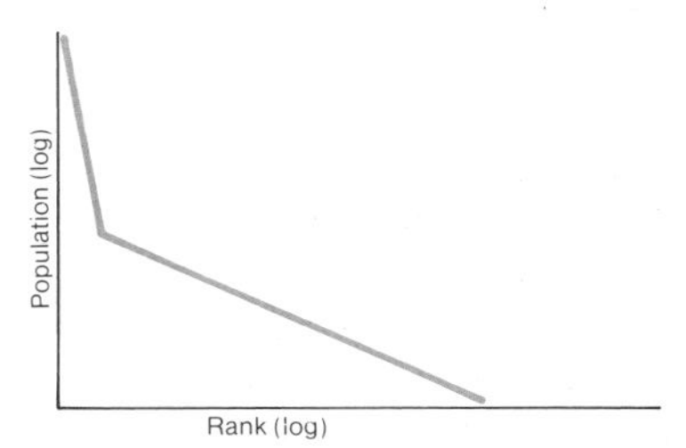

Figure 3.22 City-size distribution following a primate pattern

administrative centre of empire – rapid growth
transport routes
export of wealth limits growth of other settlements
manufactured goods and some investment
mineral/agricultural resources and wealth
HINTERLAND (minerals and agricultural resources)
Primate city
Gateway primate
Motherland
Colony
most settlements small trading centres shipping goods to gateway primate

Figure 3.23 Development of primate cities through the colonial system

Exercise

It is not easy to find an explanation for urban primacy, though it has been suggested that primacy is often a feature of countries which are less developed and poorly urbanised. Test these ideas for yourself by working through this exercise.

1 Calculate the remaining ratios in Table 3.12 for Senegal, Sudan, Sweden, Tanzania, the UK and the USSR.

Table 3.12 Ratio of population of largest to second-largest city

Country	Ratio	Country	Ratio	Country	Ratio
Australia	1.2	Honduras	1.8	Malaysia	1.7
Bangladesh	1.9	India	1.2	Mexico	6.0
Brazil	1.5	Iran	6.7	Netherlands	1.1
Canada	1.0	Israel	3.2	New Zealand	2.3
Chile	6.0	Italy	1.7	Nigeria	1.7
Egypt	2.2	Indonesia	2.9	Pakistan	1.6
Finland	3.0	Japan	3.0	Peru	10.9
France	8.6	Kenya	2.7	Philippines	1.5
				USA	2.4

Country	City	Population
Senegal:	Dakar	0.799
	Thies	0.117
Sudan:	Khartoum	0.334
	Omdurman	0.299
Sweden:	Stockholm	1.380
	Göteborg	0.694
Tanzania:	Dar-es-Salaam	0.757
	Mwanza	0.111
UK:	London	6.696
	Birmingham	0.920
USSR:	Moscow	8.011
	Leningrad	4.588

2 Compile a table of the countries in Table 3.12 arranging them into three groups: rank-size (less than 2.5); intermediate (2.5–3.5); primate (over 3.5). Compare this grouping with the one you compiled in Table 1.2 which gave an indication of level of development. Is it true to say that primacy is more a feature of LDCs than DCs?

3 Draw a scatter diagram of the % urban population (the x-axis can use the values in Figure 1.6), plotted against the ratios in Table 3.12. Does the scatter of points show any clear trend ie would we be justified in saying that the more urbanised a country is, the more closely it approaches the rank-size rule?

Many primate cities in LDCs are ports or *gateway* cities. When these countries were colonies, the port city had a vital function as a gateway, importing goods from the mother country, and funnelling mineral resources and agricultural products from the interior for export (Figure 3.23). Roads and railways converged on the gateway city, and it was here that most foreign investment in commerce and industry occurred. All this contributed to the growth of the gateway city at the expense of other settlements in the colony, until the gateway achieved a position of great dominance or primacy.

The effects of colonialism on city size were not confined to the colonies: the resources and wealth which came from the colonies permitted the growth of cities which were the administrative centres of great empires. It is unlikely that either London or Paris would have achieved such high levels of primacy without their nineteenth century connections with empire. Vienna is also an example of a primate city in Europe, whose size and importance can be explained by its role at the centre of the former Austro-Hungarian empire.

There are some countries, such as Australia and New Zealand, which at first glance appear to follow the rank-size rule (Figure 3.24). Closer study reveals that these countries in the nineteenth century were really a number of separate colonies, each served by a primate gateway. In New Zealand Auckland served the North Island, Christchurch the Canterbury Plains, Dunedin the more southerly parts of the South Island, and Wellington was the capital. Australia was originally five virtually independent colonies, each with its own primate gateway. However, when the state of Australia was created in 1901 the city-size distributions of the colonies were merged, and the original primate pattern became a rank-size one.

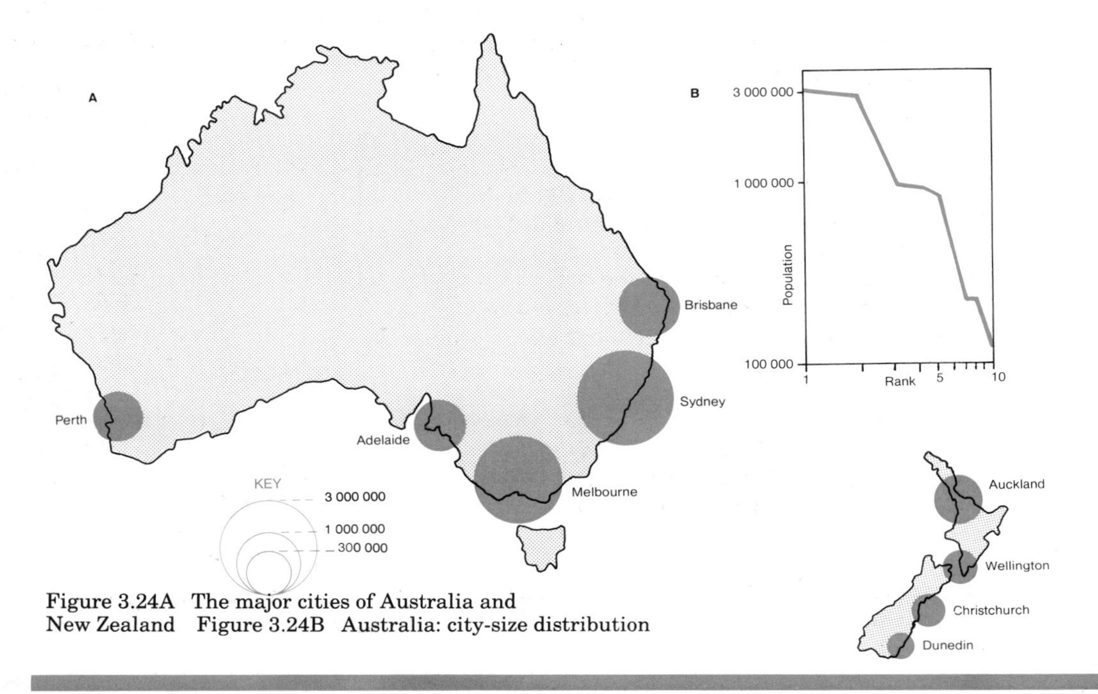

Figure 3.24A The major cities of Australia and New Zealand Figure 3.24B Australia: city-size distribution

Exercise

1 Using an atlas, pair the primate gateways and their territories in Australia.

City	Territory
Sydney	?
?	Victoria
Adelaide	?
?	Queensland
Perth	?

2 The Northern Territory of Australia never developed a primate gateway. By referring to your atlas, can you think of any reasons for this?

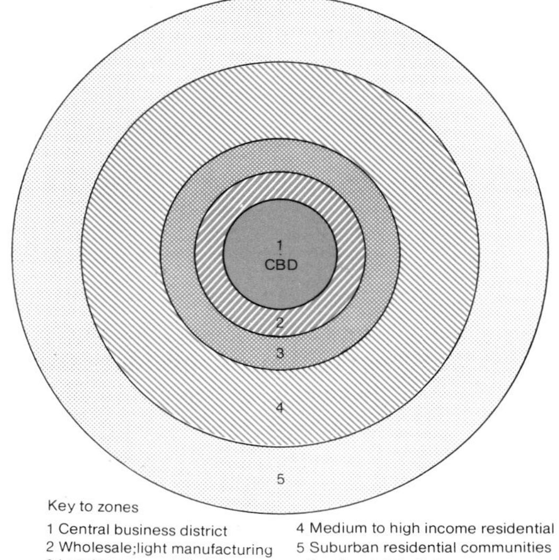

Figure 3.25 Urban land use zones

Land use in cities

The distribution of types of land use in cities often forms complicated patterns. To help us understand these patterns it has been suggested that land use frequently forms a series of *zones* or *sectors* or both.

Land use zones

Land use zones are a series of concentric rings of commercial, industrial or residential land arranged around the city centre or *central business district* (CBD) (Figure 3.25). These zones developed as the city expanded outwards from its centre in all directions, adding new areas of housing and industry along its edges each year, like the annular growth rings of a tree. The width of the zones varies: the inner zones are usually narrower than the outer ones because they were added at a time when urban transport was poorly developed, and people needed to be close to their place of work in and around the city centre. As transport improved with the development of the suburban railways, electric tramcars, and most recently private cars, the city grew outwards very rapidly, and each land use zone has become wider.

Exercise

In theory, the outward growth of the city and the developments in urban transport over the last 100 years should have had two consequences: as distance from the city centre increases, buildings should get newer; and as distance increases, the population density should fall.

1 Study the growth map of Birmingham (Figure 3.26). How does the age of the built-up area change with distance from the centre? Which period saw the most rapid increase of the city's built-up area?

2 Suggest reasons for the rapid growth of the city between 1905 and 1946.

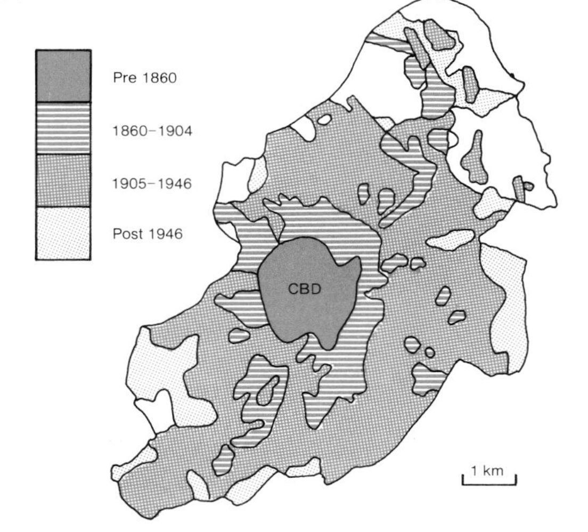

Figure 3.26 Birmingham: growth of the built-up area

Table 3.13 The CBD: characteristics

Land value	The highest land values and highest rents are found in this zone.
Land use	Dominated by commercial activities. Prestige office blocks close to the centre of the CBD in large cities; multiple or chain stores (with branches throughout the country), with large variety stores (eg Marks & Spencer, Boots, Woolworths, WH Smith) and department stores. There is an absence of housing and industry.
Traffic flow	Heavy flows of traffic with major routes converging on the CBD; congestion at rush hour times.
Pedestrian flow	Heaviest pedestrian flows found anywhere in the city. Shoppers and office workers.
Building height	Multi-storey buildings which signal the lack of space, high demand and the high cost of land at the centre.

3 Figure 3.27 shows the density of population in Leeds and Bradford in 1971. Describe how the density of population changes with distance from the CBDs of both cities. Where are the highest densities found, and why do you think that the CBD and adjacent areas have fairly moderate densities?

4 What type of housing would you expect to find in the squares of highest density? (Refer back to page 46 if you are unsure.) The highest density of any square kilometre in Leeds in 1971 was just over 10 000. This is a modest figure compared with some cities: in central Paris the *average* density is 24 000 km^2; in Manhattan (New York) the average is 29 000 km^2; and in Kowloon City (Hong Kong) densities in some parts rise to 150 000 people km^2! What type of housing do you think accommodates such high densities in Manhattan and Hong Kong?

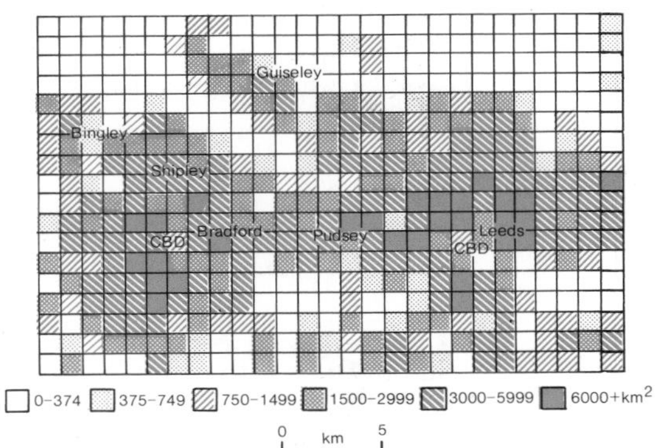

Figure 3.27 Leeds and Bradford: population density in 1971

5 Figure 3.28 shows the population density in Birmingham in 1971.

a Calculate the average population density in each of the five zones and complete the table below.

Distance from CBD	Average density (km^2
0–3 km	5455
3–6 km	
6–9 km	
9–12 km	
over 12 km	

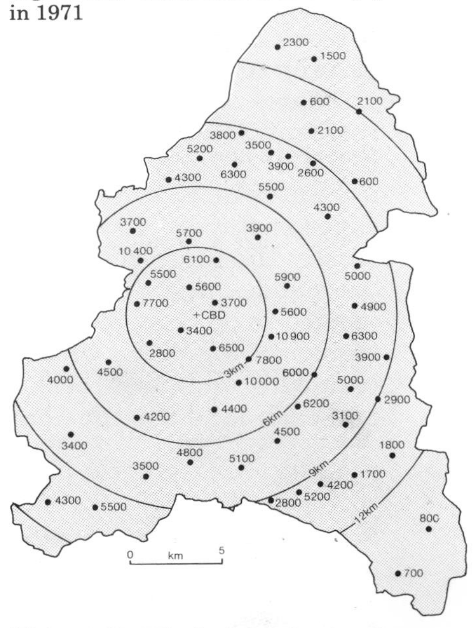

Figure 3.28 Birmingham: density of population (persons per km^2)

b Plot the densities in the table as a line graph, with distance on the horizontal (x) axis, and density on the vertical (y) axis.

c Write out the following paragraph, inserting the correct alternative answers. 'The density of population in Birmingham varies from *10900/10400* km^2 to *600/500* km^2. However, most densities are in the range *4000–6000* km^2/*6000–8000* km^2. In general densities *increase/decline* with distance from the centre. The exception is the *first/second* zone: this zone contains the CBD, and apart from housing has important areas of *industrial/commercial* land use. The highest densities are found in the *second/third* zone, which contains much *nineteenth/twentieth* century *semi-detached/terrace* housing. The outer zones are made up of housing built after 1945 at a relatively *high/low* density. *Terrace/semi-detached* houses dominate these zones, and sizeable garden plots help to reduce densities below *4000/2000* km^2.'

Zones of land use were first recognised in Chicago in the 1920s, where they resulted from successive waves of immigrants entering the city, causing it to expand outwards from the centre. Usually the immigrants first settled in the slum districts close to the CBD, displacing the original occupants who moved out into the next zone. This 'shunting' effect eventually spread throughout the city, and led to new zones of housing being added to the edges of the built-up area.

Many cities with zonal patterns of land use were not affected by immigration to any great extent. In these cases land use zones are explained by *competition* between different users. It is assumed that a plot of land is more attractive the closer it is to the city centre, which is considered the most accessible part of the city. Thus, commerce (shops and offices), industry and housing compete for land, and the user who bids the highest price or rent gains the use of the plot.

Exercise

1 Explain why the city centre is usually seen as the most accessible part of the city.

Look at Figure 3.29 which shows trends in land values with distance from the centre.

2 Which part of the city has the highest land values? Can you explain why?

3 Which type of land use is a) most affected b) least affected, by distance from the centre on its profits?

4 Suggest two reasons why it is so important that shops and offices locate in the city centre where accessibility is greatest.

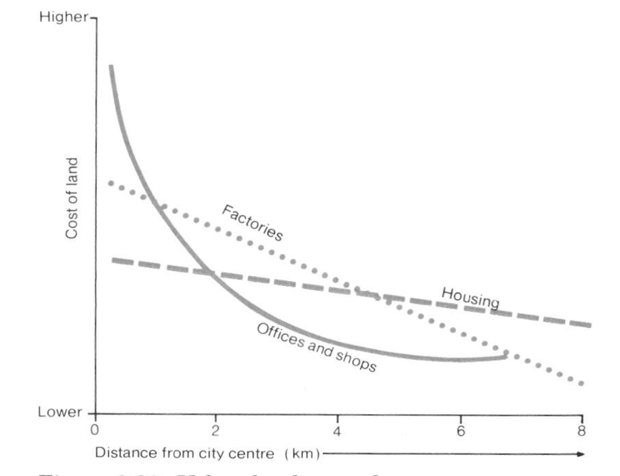

Figure 3.29 Urban land use values

5 From Figure 3.29 calculate the distance from the city centre where a) shops and offices give way to industry b) industry gives way to housing. Using this information draw a diagram to show the ideal pattern of land use, and shade and label each zone.

In many large cities in DCs *decentralisation* or the movement of commercial and industrial activities from the central area to the suburbs, has greatly modified land use patterns inside the city. Increasingly the CBD is no longer the most accessible zone: traffic congestion in and around the centre has been a serious problem for many years in major cities such as London, Paris, Tokyo and New York. Nor is congestion a problem confined only to cities in the developed world: cities such as Lagos, Calcutta, Bogota and Manila in the Third World face traffic problems as severe as those in DCs. While access to the centre has declined, the suburbs, thanks to the construction of motorways, ring roads, by-passes and airports, have become more accessible, and thus more attractive as locations for commerce and industry.

In the USA, France and West Germany huge 'out-of-town' shopping centres and hypermarkets have been built in the outer suburbs, to serve local, car-borne shoppers (Figure 3.30). In Britain progress has been slower and the country's first regional shopping centre in the suburbs, at Brent Cross in North London, was not completed until 1976.

Figure 3.30 A hypermarket, near Toulouse

In the USA, office jobs are also being decentralised at a rapid rate as offices choose to locate in specially built 'office parks' in the suburbs. These parks are often located close to motorway junctions and airports, and apart from offices, contain shopping and recreational facilities. This trend is also evident in London as offices locate in areas such as Croydon, or in towns such as Reading and Basingstoke outside the conurbation. One of the largest office park projects in Western Europe has just been completed in Hamburg: the City-Nord project covers 95 hectares on the inner ring road, 6 km north of the city centre, and has successfully diverted office expansion away from the overcrowded and congested CBD (Figure 3.31).

Industry has been established longer in the suburbs than office activities. Planned industrial estates such as Trafford Park in Manchester and Team Valley in Gateshead have proved increasingly attractive to manufacturing industry, compared to congested sites close to the city centre. However, it is not just easier access to customers and workforce that has prompted decentralisation of shopping, offices and industry: the suburbs offer other benefits such as lower rates and local taxes, cheaper land, more space for expansion and pleasanter surroundings.

Exercise

1 It is evident that decentralisation in Western cities has brought about several changes to the idealised pattern of zones described in Figure 3.25 and the diagram you drew in the last exercise. With these changes in mind, re-draw your land use diagram to show the effects of decentralisation.

2 Imagine that a large development company has decided to build a new, enclosed shopping centre with 60 shops, a sports centre and parking space for 500 cars, in a city of 500 000 people.
   a You represent the development company who want to locate the centre on a new site (at present used for farming) on the edge of the city. Write a letter to the Chief Planning Officer in the city, arguing the case for location in the suburbs rather than elsewhere.
   b Write a reply to this letter from the Chief Planning Officer, saying why you reject a location in the suburbs in favour of one in the city centre.

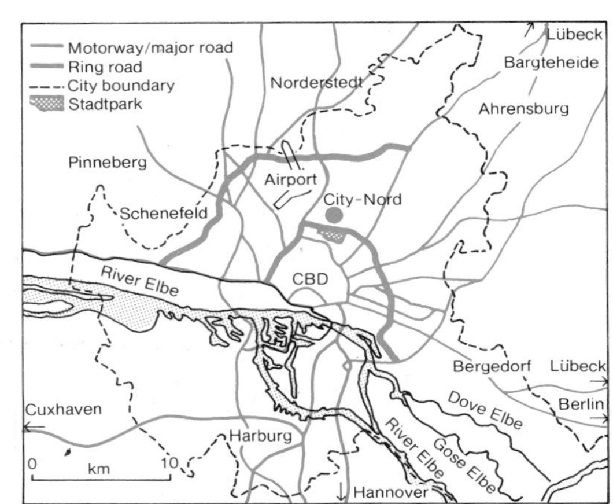

Figure 3.31 Location of City-Nord within the Hamburg conurbation

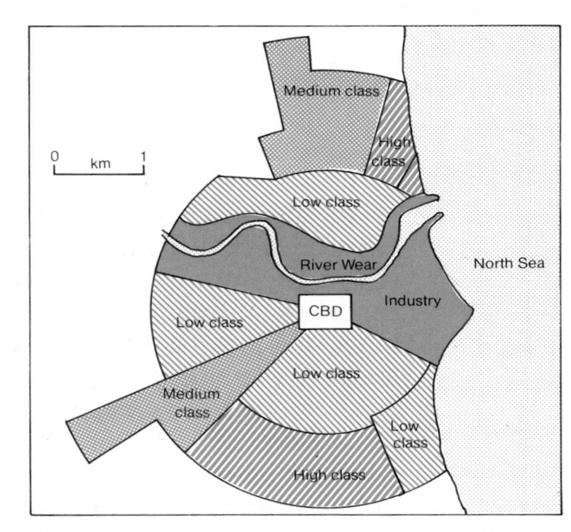

Figure 3.32 Sunderland: land use zones and sectors

Land use sectors

Sectors of land use are found in many cities, radiating from the centre towards the edge of the built-up area. These sectors often develop along important routeways, particularly major roads, and to a lesser degree along railways, canals and navigable rivers. Figure 3.32 shows that Sunderland has a well defined sector of industry along the Wear Valley, where shipbuilding and marine engineering are important activites. Once a certain type of land use has established itself in a sector, it tends to attract further development of the same type. For example, if a heavy industry first develops along a routeway, modern housing is likely to be deterred because of the unattractiveness of industry as a neighbour (eg noise, pollution, heavy traffic). In a similar way high class housing may form a distinctive sector, and by pushing up the price of land in the area exclude lower class housing.

Exercise

Figures 3.33 and 3.34 show the actual patterns of land use in Birmingham and Leeds respectively.

1 From the maps, construct two simplified diagrams of land use using zones and sectors.

2 Do you think that it is realistic to describe the patterns of land use in the two cities simply in terms of zones and sectors?

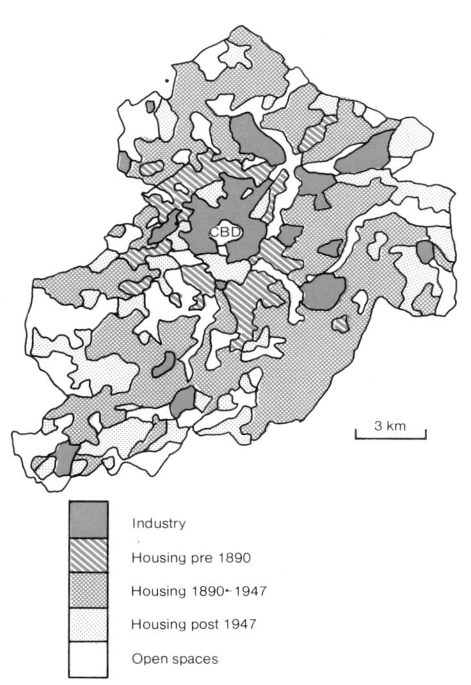

Figure 3.33 Birmingham: urban land use

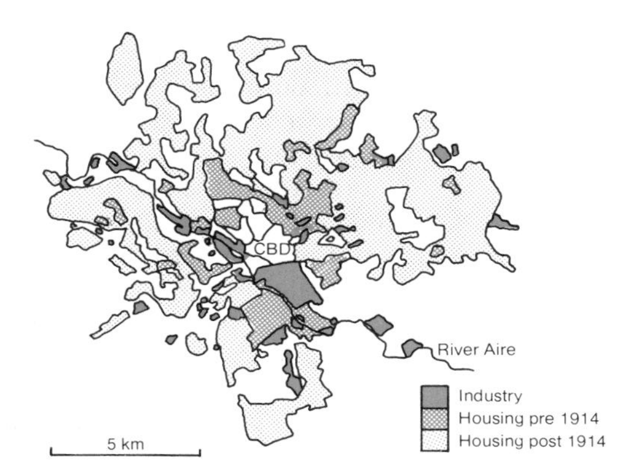

Figure 3.34 Leeds: urban land use

The idea of land use in cities consisting of a series of zones and sectors is clearly a simplification. In reality there are a number of factors which will distort these regular patterns. In British cities local authority planning is an important influence on land use: areas of slum housing in the inner suburbs close to the city centre have been demolished on a large scale in the post-war years, while council housing has been built on plots throughout the city which the local authority either owned or bought compulsorily. The physical geography of the site of any city will also distort simple zones and sector patterns. The coastal site of Sunderland limits the development of zones and sectors in an easterly direction, and in Leeds the flood plain of the River Aire forms a noticeable gap in the built-up area of the city towards the southeast.

Land use in non-Western cities

Most of the ideas about the land use and layout of cities which we have covered in this section are based on Western examples, from North America and Western Europe. However, most large cities in the world are not found in the West, but in the Soviet Eastern Bloc and in LDCs. Land use patterns in these cities are often very different from those with which we are most familiar in Britain or the USA – differences which stem from contrasting values, ways of life and government.

There are equally strong contrasts in patterns of land use between cities in LDCs and those in the West. In most Middle Eastern cities buildings are rarely more than two storeys high, and the city centre may be dominated more by mosques and other religious buildings than by commerce. As in many other parts of the Third World it is common to find shops, housing and small craft industries all occupying the same buildings. In India, the areas occupied by the former colonial administrators often form a distinctive enclave within the fabric of the city, while the older, unplanned parts of cities contrast with the modern high rise buildings and urban highways. The modernity of many Third World cities – for example a city like Caracas in Venezuela, which when seen from a distance gives every impression of being well planned and prosperous – can be misleading. While the rich may live in well appointed apartment blocks, the overwhelming majority of people occupy slums and shanty towns scattered in the foothills and narrow valleys around the edges of the city (Figure 3.35).

Figure 3.35 (*above left*) Caracas, capital and primate city of Venezuela. Does this view of Caracas correspond with your idea of a Third World city?
Figure 3.36 (*above*) Central London. The office towers on the right mark the financial quarter of 'The City'. Demand for office space in this area is so great that it produces the highest land prices and rents in the UK, and the tallest buildings to match.
Figure 3.37 (*left*) Traffic congestion in central London. For many commercial and industrial activities, the CBD is no longer the most accessible part of the city. In the last 30 years an increasing number of activities have moved out to the suburbs and to towns as much as 100 kilometres or more from the centre.

Table 3.14 Land use in western and Soviet cities

	Western cities	Soviet cities
Land values	There is competition for land by different uses. Land is usually occupied by the highest bidder.	All land is owned by the state, therefore there is no buying and selling of land. Land in the CBD should not be more valuable than elsewhere in the city.
Population density	Declines from the centre. It is often highest in the housing zone closest to the centre (apartments, terraces) and lowest in the outer suburbs.	Virtually the same throughout the city. The central area, in contrast to Western cities, often has much housing.
Building heights	The CBD is dominated by tall buildings owing to the high demand for land at the centre, and the small space available. Many older buildings in the centre have been replaced by more profitable multi-storey office blocks. Height declines with distance from the centre.	Buildings are of uniform height throughout the city. Many old buildings remain in the CBD, which compared with Western cities is low-rise.
Commerce	Concentrated in the CBD with high rise office blocks, department and variety stores.	Fewer shops and less employment in the CBD – in Moscow just four or five large department stores. Few shops of the same type. Shopping facilities in the suburbs serve local areas.
Industry	Close to the centre, industry is often found alongside housing. New industry is increasingly planned on industrial estates in the outer surburbs.	Industry is 'zoned' ie it is separated from housing, and confined to well-defined areas.
Housing	Wide variations in size and quality. Quality generally improves towards the outer suburbs. Large % of housing is owner-occupied.	Housing of uniform standard; mostly multi-storey apartment blocks. Most housing is state owned.
Transport	Private car ownership is important and creates traffic congestion in the centre.	Public transport only. Massive investment in rapid transit systems (eg Moscow metro) with cheap fares. Few people own cars and no congestion in the city centre.

Exercise

Study Table 3.14 and Figures 3.36, 3.37 and 3.38. Then answer the following questions.

1 Draw up a list of points in favour of
a) Western b) Soviet cities.

2 From the points you have listed in question 1 say which city you would prefer to live in and why.

3 You might feel that neither city is an ideal place in which to live. Combine what you think are their best features, and describe an ideal city, which is preferable to either London or Moscow.

Figure 3.38 Komsomol Square, central Moscow, Compare this view with that of central Toronto (Figure 4.26). What are the main differences?

Summary

In Chapter 1 we saw that the world's population was growing rapidly. If we study this growth in more detail we find that the world's urban population is increasing faster than the rural population, and furthermore, that urban growth and urbanisation are largely a feature of LDCs today. The causes of this growth are the transfer of people from the countryside to the city through migration, and the high rates of natural increase in most Third World cities. In contrast, in DCs the progress of urbanisation is virtually complete; the levels of urban growth recorded in the Third World today were paralleled by those of Europe and North America in the nineteenth and early twentieth centuries.

Soon urban dwellers in LDCs will outnumber those in DCs, and increasingly these people will live in the largest, millionaire cities. This trend has served to strengthen the primate position of many major cities in LDCs, a pattern of city size within a country which was often first established by the nature of colonial trade in the last century.

Urban growth has created distinctive patterns of land use within cities, which often take the form of zones and sectors. However, land use patterns vary widely inside the city, and there are great contrasts between Western cities and those in the LDCs and the Eastern Soviet Bloc.

Further exercises

1 Rural–urban migration does not affect a population equally: some groups are more likely to migrate than others. Most migrant groups consist of young people, particularly young adults under 25 years, while old people rarely migrate in significant numbers. Education is a factor which encourages migration, and it is usual to find the better educated people leaving rural areas for towns and cities in the Third World. Single people are more likely to migrate than those who are married, and on the whole, more men migrate than women. However, the latter does vary from one region to another: men predominate in migrations in South and South East Asia, but in South America, women frequently outnumber men. Thus, in relation to several factors, we can say that migration is *selective*. Figure 3.39 shows an age–sex pyramid for Calcutta (India).

a What does it tell you about the selectivity of migration in this part of India?

b Draw a similar pyramid to show the effects of rural–urban migration in a rural area sending migrants to Calcutta.

2 a Explain the meaning of the term *primate city*.

b Suggest reasons for the growth of primate cities.

3 Table 3.15 shows annual rates of population growth in four LDCs, and in one major city within each country.

a Suggest reasons why the two rates are different.

b What effect will this have on the distribution of population in these countries?

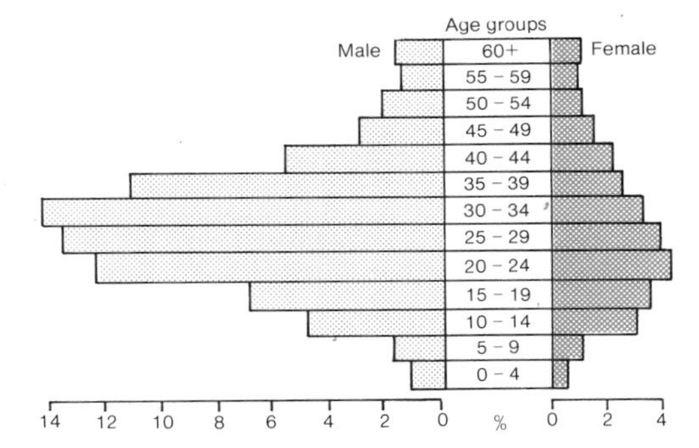

Figure 3.39 An age-sex pyramid for Calcutta

Table 3.15

Country	Total population (millions)	Annual growth %	City	Population (millions)	Annual growth %
Brazil	123	2.8	São Paulo	7.12	8.5
India	683	2.3	Madras	3.17	8.3
South Korea	38	1.8	Seoul	6.88	10.8
Zaire	28	2.8	Kinshasha	2.01	11.2

Table 3.16

	Population (millions)	% Urban	Population distribution by age (%) 0–14	15–29	30–44	45–59	60–74	75+
A	123.0	59.8	42	27	16	10	4	1
B	14.2	76.0	27	25	18	16	10	4
C	683.0	22.0	42	24	18	10	5	1
D	14.3	11.3	48	25	14	7	4	2
E	265.5	60.5	31	20	24	14	8	3

4 Table 3.16 gives information about five countries labelled A to E. These countries, not necessarily in the same order, are Kenya, the Netherlands, the USSR, Brazil and India.
- a Identify each country.
- b Say which countries are likely to be most developed and least developed, from the evidence in the table.
- c Is the % urban population related to age structure in this group of countries? If so, say how and explain why.

5 Figure 3.40 shows the cost of rents in the financial quarter or 'City' of London, which are among the highest in the world.
- a Draw a cross-section between point A (north bank) and point B (south bank). The base for your section will be the distance separating A and B on the map. **A vertical scale of 1 cm for every £5 of** rent will demonstrate how values peak in the centre of the 'City'.
- b On your cross-section, mark and name the approximate positions of the following: Bank of England, Stock Exchange, Royal Exchange, Liverpool Street and Cannon Street stations, and the River Thames.
- c Can you explain why rents are so high in this part of London? (For a general answer look back at page 59).
- d How could you explain the location of two British Rail stations in such a high priced zone?
- e To get some idea of just how expensive it is to rent floorspace in the 'City', measure the floor area of your bedroom (in square feet), and calculate how much it would cost to rent your bedroom for a year, if it were located next to the Bank of England! Would you expect there to be much demand for housing in the 'City' of London?

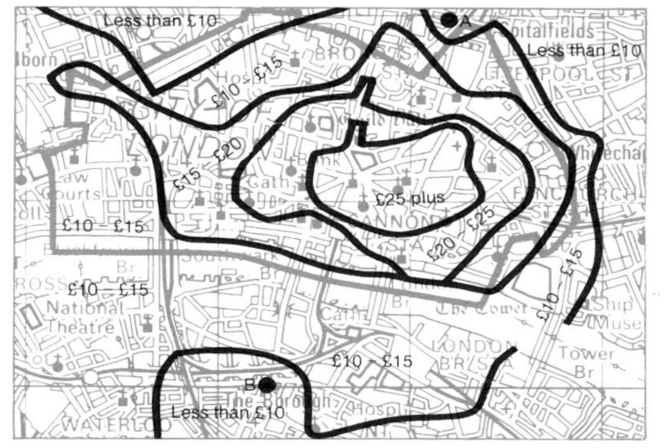

Figure 3.40 Office rents (square foot per year) in the City of London

CHECKLIST OF WHAT YOU SHOULD KNOW ABOUT URBANISATION AND URBAN GROWTH

Key ideas	Examples
The world's urban population is increasing rapidly.	■ Both the number and proportion of people living in towns and cities are increasing rapidly. There are important differences between DCs and LDCs: *Urban growth* – an increase in the number of urban dwellers – and *urbanisation* – an increase in the proportion of urban dwellers – are virtually at a standstill in DCs Urban growth is occurring with great rapidity in the Third World; urbanisation is also significant, but is taking place more slowly.

The causes of modern urban growth and urbanisation in LDCs differ from those of nineteenth-century Europe.	■ In nineteenth-century Europe urban growth and urbanisation resulted largely from rural–urban migration. Before 1850 European cities were extremely unhealthy places with high death rates. ■ Modern cities in LDCs, although very poor, are much healthier than those of nineteenth-century Europe. Urban growth therefore is the result not only of massive rural–urban migration, but also of natural increase in the towns and cities.
Rural–urban migration is caused by a combination of 'push' and 'pull' factors.	■ 'Push' factors are the poor living conditions found in the countryside, eg low incomes, high rents, few schools, limited health care, which encourage people to leave for the city. These factors are the main reason for rural–urban migration in the Third World today. ■ 'Pull' factors relate to the attractiveness of the towns and cities, and the opportunities they afford for employment, housing, education and a better standard of living. In nineteenth century Britain it was the lure of jobs in the new factories of the industrial revolution, that was mainly responsible for rural–urban migration.
Rates of population growth in cities are related to city size.	■ In LDCs the most rapidly growing cities are the largest 'millionaire' cities eg Cairo, Mexico City. ■ In DCs the largest cities and conurbations are declining in population eg London, New York. Smaller cities which offer a better quality of life are growing most rapidly eg Norwich (UK), Boulder (USA).
The hierarchy of settlement in many countries is dominated by one large city.	■ The dominance of a *primate* city is evident in many DCs and LDCs eg Paris, Vienna, Lima, Buenos Aires. Many primate cities are *gateways* and their development is related to colonialism. Where the distribution of city-size is more even, it is called a *rank-size* distribution eg USA, West Germany, India. Many rank-size distributions are in effect aggregations of former primate patterns eg Australia, Canada.
Towns and cities present patterns of land use recognised by their function.	■ The principal land uses are commercial (shops and offices), industry, housing and tended open spaces (parks and recreational areas). The various land uses show a preference for different locations in the city, and often form distinctive *zones* and *sectors*.
The central business district (CBD) is the focus of the city, and has the greatest concentration of shops and offices.	■ The CBD is the focus of public transport systems and is thus the most accessible location in the city. The high demand for land in the CBD results in high rents, which largely exclude industry and housing. To make the maximum use of limited space, multi-storey buildings dominate the CBD.
Land use patterns in cities in LDCs and the Eastern bloc are different from those in DCs.	■ Different values, societies, political beliefs and histories found outside of the West mean that Western cities are *not* typical of most world cities eg Soviet cities, Muslim cities.
Patterns of land use are undergoing change in Western cities.	■ Decentralisation is occurring widely in Western cities, as people, industry, offices and shops leave the central areas for the suburbs.

Cities and their problems

Part 1: Urban problems and planning in DCs

Cities in DCs face a number of urgent problems, some of which have occupied the attention of planners for nearly 50 years. They include the problems of housing shortages, substandard housing conditions, traffic congestion, urban sprawl and the decline of urban manufacturing industry. The case studies which follow describe the nature of these problems in the cities of Birmingham, Copenhagen, Toronto and Randstad, and the attempts of planners to solve them.

Birmingham

Birmingham, with a population of 920 000, is Britain's second largest city, and the centre of the West Midlands conurbation. It grew rapidly from the late eighteenth century as a major manufacturing centre, helped first by a national canal network which was focussed on the West Midlands, and later, by the development of the railways. The city's population grew from 70 000 in 1801, to 840 000 in 1911, as employment expanded in engineering and a variety of metal manufacturing trades, ranging from guns to jewellery. Today, Birmingham remains an industrial city, with 43% of its workforce employed in manufacturing, compared with a national average of 38%. Metals, motor vehicles and engineering are the leading industries. The city has also retained its importance as a communications centre, being at the hub of Britain's motorway network (Figure 6.25).

Birmingham's most urgent planning problem during the last 40 years has been the task of replacing its large stock of nineteenth century slum housing and meeting the shortage of housing for the city's growing population. A further problem has been the need to control the expansion of the city into the surrounding countryside, and prevent the kind of *urban sprawl* which occurred in the inter-war (1918–39) period.

Figure 4.1A Newtown, Birmingham, one of the city's original CDAs. The multi-storey blocks of 1960s urban renewal contrast with the remaining 19th century terrace housing in the foreground

Figure 4.1B (*above*) Urban renewal, Small Heath, Birmingham
Figure 4.1C Nineteenth century terrace housing in Small Heath, Birmingham

Solving the housing problem

In 1945 nearly all the houses in the inner city dated from the period 1829–75, and a high proportion were either slums or lacked basic amenities. For instance, in 1945 there were 29 000 back-to-back houses and 25 000 houses without a separate toilet. In 1946, the city started on a major programme of *urban renewal*, involving the clearance of the worst slum areas (Figure 4.2). 400 hectares of land in five areas of the inner city were compulsorily purchased, and nearly 30 000 slums demolished. The old terrace housing was replaced by many multi-storey blocks which were at a much lower density owing to the generous provision of public open space (Figure 4.1). The planners separated housing areas from industry, provided services such as shops and health centres, and designed road layouts to remove through traffic from the housing areas.

Exercise

In Britain this kind of large-scale urban renewal is known as *comprehensive redevelopment* and was the solution adopted to housing problems in most cities during the 1950s and 60s. Although the policy had obvious benefits, it also had disadvantages.

Figure 4.2 Birmingham: the redevelopment areas

1 Figure 4.1A shows a comprehensive redevelopment area (CDA) in inner Birmingham. Describe the housing which has replaced the old Victorian slums. How suitable would you say this type of housing is for a) single people or young couples without children b) families with young children c) old people?

2 The Victorian slums, although lacking decent living conditions, formed tight-knit communities, where people knew each other, and there was a strong sense of neighbourliness (rather like 'Coronation Street'). What effect do you think comprehensive redevelopment had on these communities? Do you feel that it is important for people to have a sense of neighbourliness, and of belonging to a community? Hold a class discussion on the advantages and disadvantages of urban renewal.

Today urban renewal in the original five CDAs is complete. In 1957 a further 15 CDAs were defined, containing 30 000 houses. Demolition of these houses is almost finished, and redevelopment is taking place.

In spite of this massive urban renewal programme, Birmingham still has over 100 000 houses which were built before 1914. Most are situated in a belt between four and five kilometres from the city centre, and though the houses are basically sound, many are without modern amenities such as baths and inside toilets. Attention is now being concentrated on these houses to prevent them from becoming slums. However, the policy of slum clearance and comprehensive redevelopment has been abandoned, partly because housing conditions are nowhere near as bad as they were 40 years ago, and partly because of the enormous costs involved. Planners also recognise that it was a mistake to break up local communities, and most houses, being basically sound, should last another 30 to 40 years with relatively minor improvements (Figure 4.1C). Today's policies, therefore, concentrate on *improving* existing housing by installing modern amenities, providing community facilities such as sports centres, swimming pools and clinics, and brightening up the appearance of neighbourhoods by closing streets to traffic and planting trees. Special areas for housing improvement have been set up throughout the city, known as housing action areas and general improvement areas (Figure 4.3). Housing action areas contain the worst housing in the city; grants of up to 75% of the cost of improvement are available in these areas. However, improvements are not confined just to housing: the aim is to raise the overall quality of the neighbourhood by encouraging the growth of new industries to create jobs, and by providing new schools, open spaces and other leisure facilities. By comparison, the general improvement areas have the more limited purpose of simply improving the standard of housing. Improvement grants of up to 60% of the cost of improvements are available from the city council in these areas.

Exercise

Figure 4.3 shows the distribution of urban renewal areas in Birmingham. Describe the distribution of each of the three types of urban renewal area. What do these patterns tell you about the quality of housing in relation to distance from the city centre? Can you explain why housing quality varies with distance from the centre?

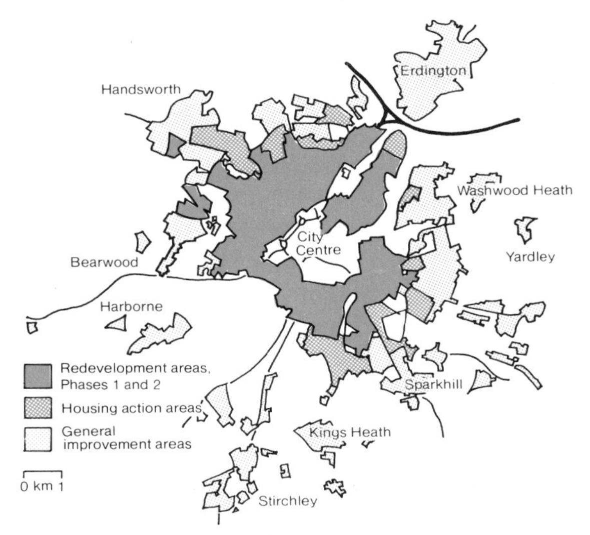

Figure 4.3 Birmingham: urban renewal areas

Overspill population and urban sprawl

As the slums of inner city areas such as Ladywood, Highgate and Nechells Green were cleared, they were replaced by housing of much lower density. This meant that not everyone who had lived in the inner city could be re-housed there. In the first five comprehensive redevelopment areas for example, the population fell from 103 000 before redevelopment to 37 000 on completion. At the same time the population of the conurbation continued to grow. It therefore became essential to develop new housing schemes to absorb this *overspill* population elsewhere. In the period before 1945 this problem of growth had been solved by allowing the city to expand outwards into the surrounding countryside of Warwickshire and Worcestershire. This expansion, known as urban sprawl, had, in the inter-war years, resulted in a massive loss of good farm land, denied residents living in the central part of the city easy access to the countryside, and threatened before long to see the built-up area of Birmingham merge with Coventry to the southeast (Figure 4.4). The planners' answer to this problem was the creation of a *green belt* – a zone of countryside which completely encircled the West Midlands conurbation, in which there were very strict controls to prevent housing and industrial development.

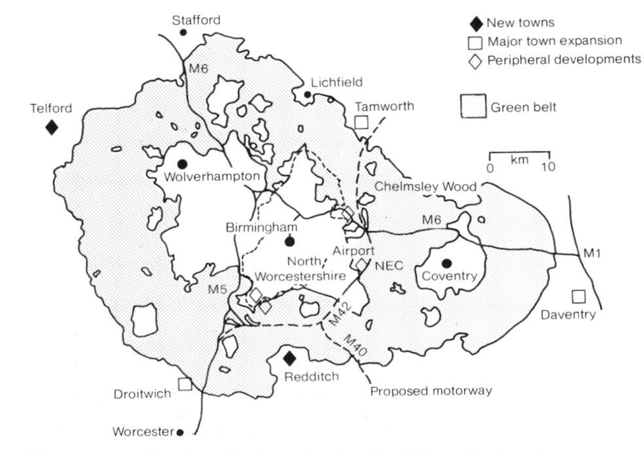

Figure 4.4 Regional planning in the West Midlands

Exercise

1 If the growth of a city was contained by a green belt, but its population continued to increase, people could be forced to move out to nearby towns beyond the green belt. If these people continued to work in the city, what problem could this create?

2 One of the purposes of green belts is to provide areas of countryside for recreation for city dwellers. Given your knowledge of where different groups of people live in the city (Chapter 3, pages 57–9) who is likely to have best access, and therefore benefit most from the green belt: high income groups; medium income groups; low income groups? Do you think that this is fair?

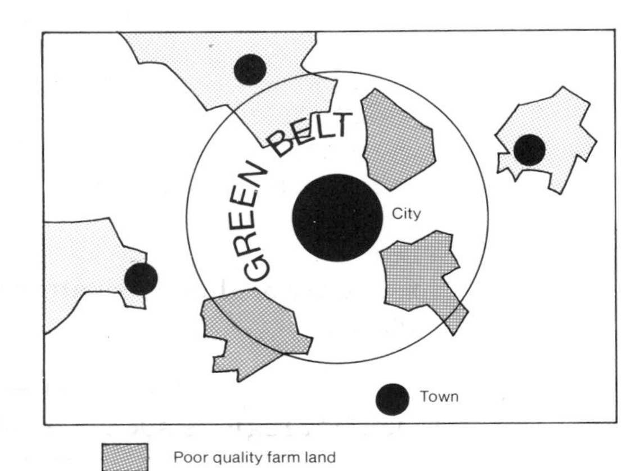

Figure 4.5 Green belts and the protection of farm land

Another disadvantage of the green belt idea is shown in Figure 4.5. If much of the green belt consists of poor quality farm land, this could be preserved while better quality land which lies outside the green belt could be zoned for building. However, despite these objections, the green belt has been the device favoured in Britain to limit urban sprawl around the conurbations and major cities (Figure 4.6).

Exercise

In Europe, the 'wedge and sector' idea (see pages 74–77 on Copenhagen) has been used instead of the green belt to tackle urban sprawl (Figure 4.7).

1 Explain how the 'wedge and sector' approach could help to solve the problem you considered in the last exercise.

2 Figure 4.5 shows how a green belt could protect poor farm land near the city at the expense of good land further away. Draw a similar diagram to demonstrate how a 'wedge and sector' approach could overcome this problem.

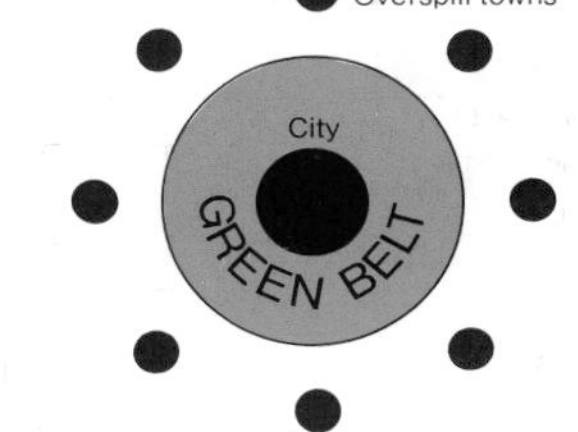

Figure 4.6 The green belt idea

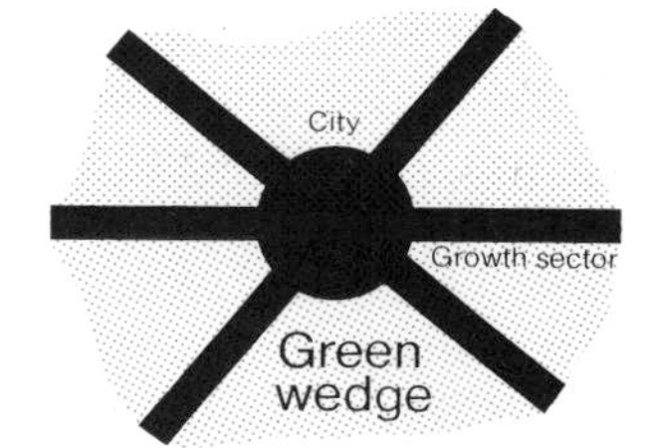

Figure 4.7 The 'wedge and sector' idea

It has proved impossible to solve Birmingham's housing problems entirely within the city's boundaries. Consequently, the housing shortage has resulted in the planned movement of households from the city, to nearby towns beyond the green belt. About 11 000 families have moved to towns with which Birmingham has an overspill agreement – principally Tamworth, Lichfield, Droitwich and Daventry (Figure 4.4). In addition, there are two *new towns* in the region – Redditch and Telford – which are designed to help solve the housing problems of Birmingham and the conurbation. Their combined population in 1981 was 166 000, but eventually they will house around 240 000 people. However, even these schemes could not provide sufficient new houses to meet the demand, and so the local authority extended Birmingham's boundaries and undertook two massive housing developments at Chelmsley Wood (13 000 houses), and in north Worcestershire (6000 houses) at Frankley, Kitwell, Hawkesley and Walkers Heath.

New towns in Britain

Since 1946 a total of 28 new towns have been built in Britain. As Figure 4.8 shows, the new towns vary considerably in size, and only one has reached its planned, target population. On the whole the new towns have been successful in fulfilling the two purposes for which they were designed:

1 to accommodate overspill population from the conurbations, resulting either from housing shortages after the war, or slum clearance programmes in the 1950s and 1960s.

2 to provide employment and more attractive living conditions in rundown industrial regions such as central Scotland, County Durham and South Wales.

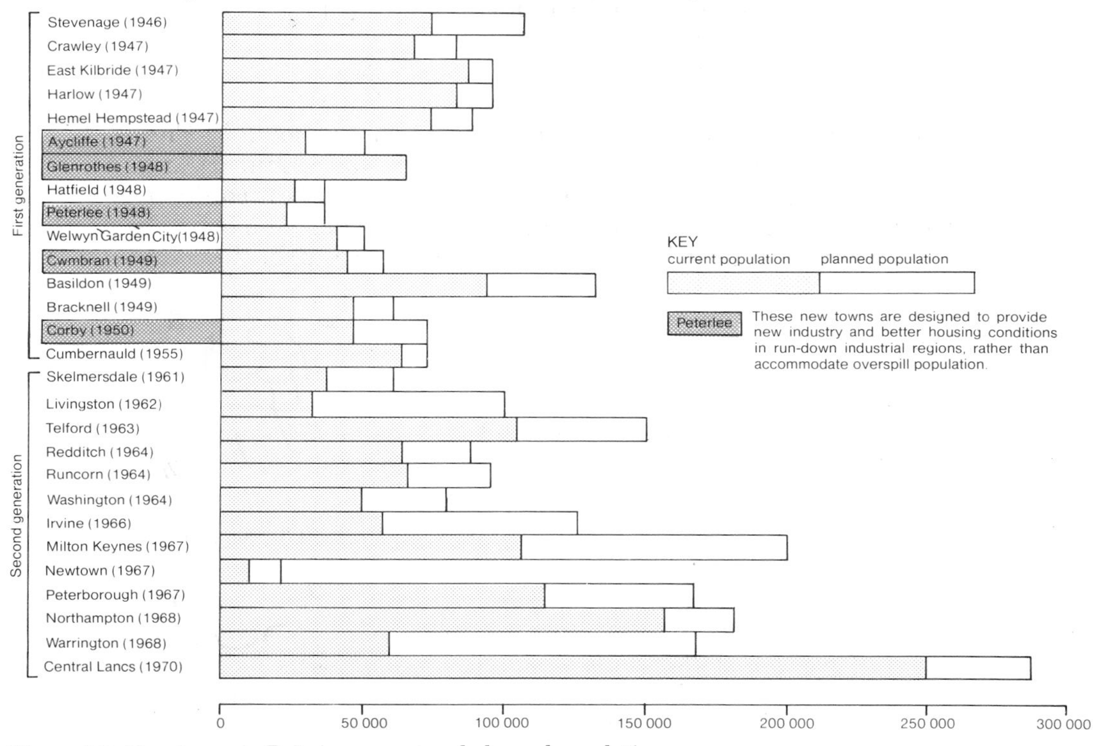

Figure 4.8 New towns in Britain: current and planned populations

The first new towns, built specifically to take overspill population, were in the South East, and were planned to serve London. Eight new towns were built outside the green belt, but within 50 km of central London. Stevenage (1946) was the first, and the last were Basildon and Bracknell in 1949. The towns were medium-sized, with target populations ranging from 29000 to 130000, and were near enough to London to permit daily commuting. To some extent therefore, though they helped to solve the capital's housing problem, they contributed to the problem of congestion in London. However, as they have grown, they have become less dependent on London for employment, and today many are important centres of employment in their own right, with modern light industries, and offices and services which have moved out from central London.

A second 'generation' of new towns was planned in the 1960s. They were larger than the first 'generation', and several were established towns, such as Northampton, Warrington and Preston-Chorley-Leyland (Central Lancashire), which were to be expanded. The three new towns designed to serve London –

Peterborough, Northampton and Milton Keynes – were situated much further from the capital than the first 'generation' new towns, well beyond the commuter zone. Apart from London (and the West Midlands), other conurbations acquired new towns to help solve their overspill problems in the 1960s: Merseyside was served by Runcorn and Skelmersdale; Manchester by Warrington and the Central Lancashire new town; Tyneside and Wearside by Washington; and Clydeside by Livingston and Irvine.

Exercise

1 Look at Figure 4.8 and answer the following:
 a Which is the smallest new town?
 b Which new town has expanded to its full planned population?
 c Which is the largest of the eight new towns designated to serve London, and built between 1946–49?
 d Which of the first 'generation' of new towns appears to have been least successful? Justify your choice.

2 By referring to the map of new towns (Figure 4.9), find out which of the seven major conurbations in Britain does not have any new towns.

3 The most recent new towns have been based on already established, and important settlements. What advantages do you think they can offer for their inhabitants and new industry, compared with new towns such as Peterlee or Skelmersdale, which started from 'scratch'?

Figure 4.9 New towns in Britain

Exercise

Figure 4.10 shows a number of newspaper advertisements published by new towns designed to attract investment by commerce and manufacturing industry.

1 Read the advertisements and complete your own table, like Table 4.1, to show the 'image' that each new town projects of itself. To give you an example, the advantages claimed for Aycliffe and Peterlee have been inserted in the table.

2 Look for similar advertisements in the national newspapers and extend the table. Can you find any other advantages claimed by new towns which are not included in the table?

3 Which factor in Table 4.1 is stressed most often by the new towns in their advertisements?

Table 4.1

Advantages claimed	Aycliffe and Peterlee	Central Lancs	Corby	Northampton	Warrington – Runcorn
Good labour force	*				
Government grants and other financial benefits	*				
Available sites and factory units	*				
Central location	*				
Good communications	*				
High tech industries famous company names	*				
Good housing/ schools shopping/ entertainment/ environment	*				

4 Explain what Northampton means with its slogan 'town keeps its promise'. (Refer back to the last section if necessary.)

5 You would probably expect the newer, second 'generation' of new towns to be most involved in advertising their attractions today. How many of the towns in Table 4.1 belong to this group? Given that Corby suffered the closure of its steelworks in 1981 and needs to attract new jobs quickly, can you suggest which of the remaining towns in the table might be considered least successful? (Have a closer look at Figure 4.8.)

6 Which of the advertisements would you say is a) most b) least effective? Give your reasons, and then re-design what you thought was the least effective advertisement (different lay-out, sketch map, slogan, etc.) in a way which you think would be more attractive.

Figure 4.10 Advertisements for new towns

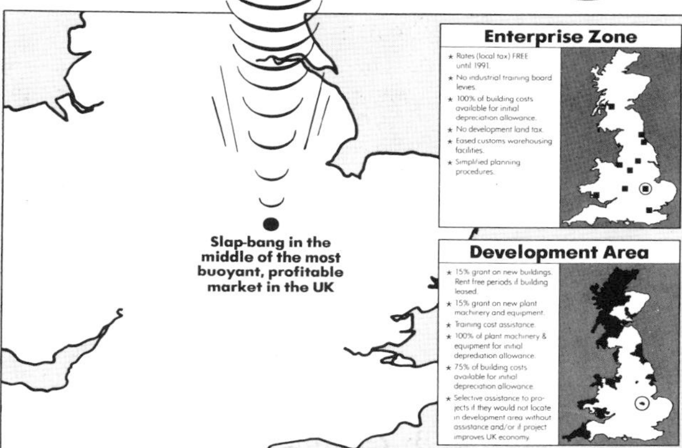

30 million people within a radius of 100 miles

The very last place you might expect to find both a development area and enterprise zone would be right in the centre of the UK market.

Yet here they are in Corby, and Corby is unique.

The combination of local and national government benefits can be incorporated into a tailor-made package for your particular company to reap the maximum advantages.

There are sites of up to 100 acres available now, as well as advance factories and a skilled industrial workforce on the doorstep committed to Corby's future. And because Corby is a steel-closure area, there are several added benefits for you, depending on your individual needs.

Take a closer look at Corby. You'll be impressed by the position, tempted by the incentives and understand the relevance of the slogan, Corby Works.

See us on Prestel Key ∗200 79 ♯

To: FRED McCLENAGHAN, Director of Industry, Corby Industrial Development Centre, Douglas House, Queen's Square, Corby, Northants.
Telephone: Corby (05363) 62571. Telex: 341543.
Please send me Corby's new brochure, THE WORKS.
Name
Position
Company
Address

CORBY WORKS

Warrington-Runcorn. The right move for...

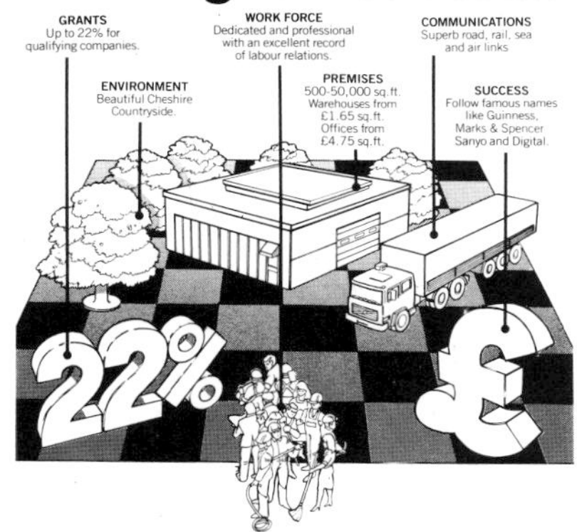

Could it be companies move to the North East because successful ones are already there?

It was in response to industrial demands that the network of roads, docks, and airports are now so well integrated in the North East. The same can be said for the rail services, thanks to George Stephenson who also had an affinity to this part of the country.

With two international airports, Teesside and Newcastle, and three major container and ro/ro seaports, the North East is the ideal location for regional, national and European distribution.

These are among the many reasons why companies considering expansion look seriously at the North East.

Two places in particular are generating considerable interest among industrialists.

Aycliffe & Peterlee – new towns that are attracting a significant list of prestigious names.

Companies which enjoy the full range of financial incentives – grants, tax allowances, rent-free periods for modern factory units.

At Aycliffe and Peterlee they draw upon the resources of skilled, adaptable and dedicated labour. Technicians and graduates trained and aware of modern work patterns and manufacturing methods.

To find out how Aycliffe and Peterlee can help you, contact our Business Team. A professional, practical and free service without obligation.

Providing guidance on the availability of labour, their skills and costs. The availability of factory space and sites, housing, education and leisure activities. Everything you require to know.

It could be successful companies like Flymo, Fisher Price, STC, Dewhirst, Ferranti, DJB, Tudor Foods, and NSK move to the North East because the open countryside is pretty exhilarating as well.

AYCLIFFE ✣ PETERLEE
Development Corporations
at the heart of the North East.

You know how it goes. Promises, promises. Growth tomorrow. Success sometime. Bear with us. All you need is faith.

Well, in Northampton the promise has been kept.

Eleven days isn't long. Less than a fortnight. But since 1970 Northampton has added one new firm, 45 jobs, 48 new homes, 65 people, 6250 sq ft of shops and offices, and 22000 sq ft of brand new factories – *every eleven days!*

And more good news. Nearly 70 overseas firms from 15 countries have moved to Northampton, bringing new investment and making this one of the UK's fastest growth points.

And no wonder. Distribution is no problem when your operating base is on the key stretch of the national motorway system. Right on the M1, midway between London and Birmingham. 50% of Britain's industry and 57% of its population is within 100 mile radius.

And the future? Better still. Continued growth, bigger markets, improved productivity.

So forget the good intention. Forget the brave new world tomorrow. Take success you can see. Take what you need right now in Northampton. The town that keeps its promise!

Factories from 3400 sq ft to 29000 sq ft. Rent free periods negotiable.

Send for your free information pack.

expanding
NORTHAMPTON
FREEFONE 4633 Lyndsey Clabburn
Northampton Development Corporation, 2-3 Market Square, Northampton NN1 2EN

Place names don't tell you the full story. If you're looking for Silicon Valley you won't find it on the M6. What you will find is Central Lancashire, with a remarkably high concentration of high technology companies.

Far from being the land of bobbins and brass foundries, it's where Dainichi-Sykes develop and programme their robots.

Where Plessey are now pioneering the latest in telecommunications systems.

It's also the home of British Aerospace's Tornado, the advanced multi-role combat aircraft.

And where companies like Rockwell, GEC and Thorn-EMI, to name but a few, are working towards tomorrow's world.

The way things are going Central Lancashire could soon be as well known for products featuring silicon chips as it is already for the kind which come with fish.

So if your business depends on high technology skills, don't ring international.

Ring Bill McNab FRICS, Commercial Director, on Preston (0772) 38211.

Central Lancashire
A BETTER PLACE TO BE

Copenhagen

Copenhagen is the capital and primate city of Denmark. Its present population is 500 000, but in the Greater Copenhagen region there are 1 750 000 people. This represents 35% of Denmark's population on just 7% of the country's land area. Copenhagen is an historic city, fortified in the Middle Ages (the fortifications were not dismantled until the mid-nineteenth century). It occupies a nodal situation, controlling the route from Germany to Sweden across the Øresund, and the sea route from the Baltic to the North Sea through the Kattegat (Figures 4.11 and 4.12).

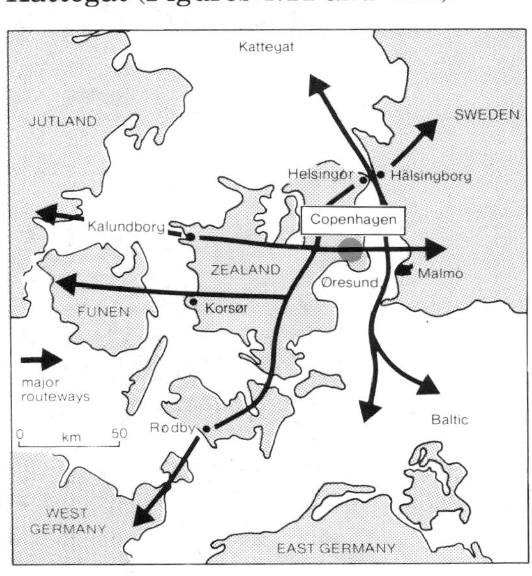

Figure 4.11 The situation of Copenhagen

Figure 4.12 Copenhagen: capital of Denmark and Scandinavia's largest city. This view of the central area of the city includes the cathedral in the foreground, and the tower of the town hall to the left

The city grew rapidly in the late nineteenth and early twentieth centuries when the development of industry attracted large numbers of migrants from the countryside. As the population grew, the city expanded outwards from its ancient core around the harbour. The inner suburbs around the CBD (Brokvartererne) were added between 1850 and 1920, and the outer suburbs (Yderdistrikterne) largely in the 1930s and 1940s (Figure 4.13). By 1950 the city had reached a peak population of 750 000. Housing in the older, inner suburbs was mainly cheap apartments at high density (Figure 4.14A), and there was an unhealthy mixture of industry and housing in areas such as Norrebro and Vesterbro. Much of this housing was built to low standards and was poorly planned: its replacement is one of the city's major planning problems today, a fact which may surprise you, given the modern, hygenic image of Denmark and the rest of Scandinavia.

Since 1950 the population of the city has declined rapidly (Figure 4.15) as large numbers of people have left for the wider Greater Copenhagen region. This trend is likely to continue, and planners forecast a population of only 418 000 by 1993. Those moving out are typically young families with higher incomes: those moving in are most often single people with lower incomes. (What effect is this likely to have on the city's age structure?) Indeed half of all households in the city are of one person, and only one in seven has children.

While the city's population has fallen, growth in the Greater Copenhagen region has been rapid: from 850 000 in 1930, to 1 750 000 in 1980. Although in the 1970s this growth slowed down, further expansion to 2 100 000 is expected by the end of the century.

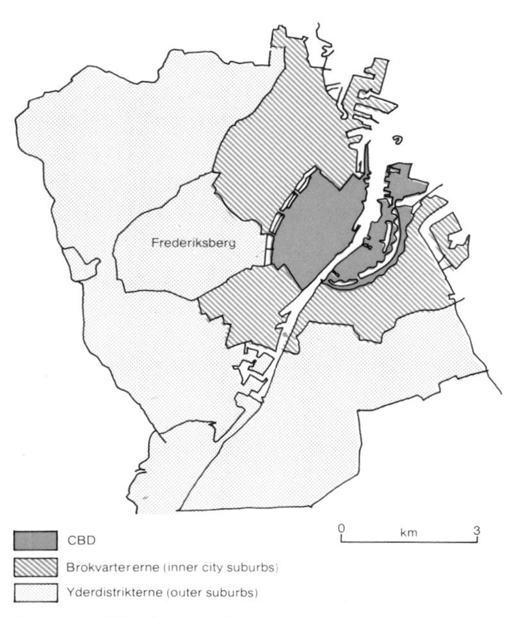

Figure 4.13 City of Copenhagen

Exercise

Figure 4.14 shows two residential districts in Copenhagen.

1 Describe the probable type of housing and comment on the density of development in each district. Is there any evidence of urban renewal in either district?

2 Suggest a possible location (ie inner or outer suburbs) for the two districts.

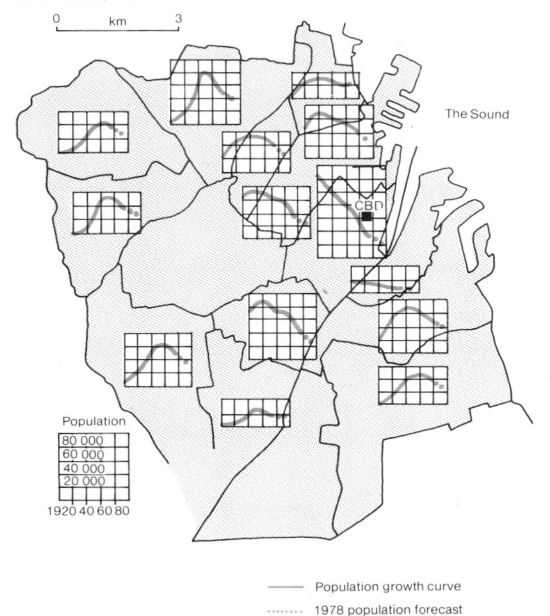

Figure 4.15 Population changes in Copenhagen

Figure 4.14 Housing districts in Copenhagen

Figure 4.15 shows patterns of population change in Copenhagen since 1900. Study the map and answer the following questions.

1 Is population declining in all parts of the city today? Where is decline most rapid?

2 How is the population likely to change up to 1990 in a) the central core b) the inner suburbs c) the outer suburbs?

3 In which part of the city did population decline first begin? Can you suggest reasons for this?

4 In the outer suburbs population growth continued until – 1940, 1960 or 1970?

5 Briefly summarise the major changes in population in different parts of the city.

Urban problems and planning

The major problem which has faced Copenhagen for the past 40 years has been how to control the growth of the city, and prevent urban sprawl into the countryside of eastern Zealand. Other problems include the replacement of old housing in the inner suburbs, and traffic congestion in and around the city centre. Since 1947 three separate plans have been devised to solve these problems. All three have encouraged the *decentralisation* of population and employment from Copenhagen into the wider Greater Copenhagen region.

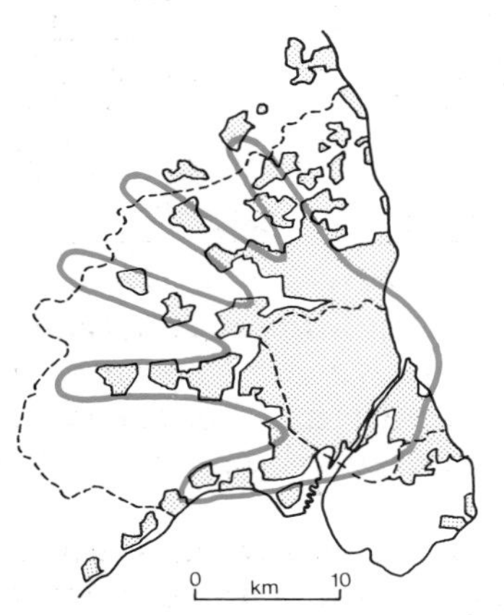

Figure 4.16 The Finger Plan, 1947

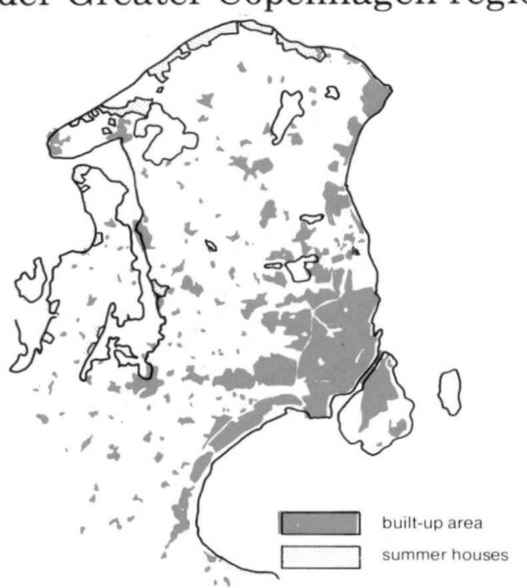

Figure 4.17 Greater Copenhagen region

In 1947 the first plan – the Finger Plan – was accepted. At the time the population of Copenhagen was growing rapidly, and could not be accommodated within the city. The Finger Plan (Figure 4.16) confined new development to five sectors which radiated from the city centre, like fingers on the palm of a hand (the palm, in this case, being the existing built-up area of the city). Between the fingers, wedges of open space were to be preserved for recreation. Each finger was to be served by a suburban railway, giving fast access to the city centre, which was important to shoppers and commuters. The plan therefore put people in close contact with the countryside, and at the same time gave them good access by public transport to employment and services in the city centre.

The 1947 plan was only partly successful: population growth during the 1950s was more rapid than expected, and the fingers could not contain all of the expansion, while the building of transverse roads linking the fingers together, meant that the planned finger development did not materalise fully.

The second plan in 1960 enlarged the two fingers pointing west and southwest, towards Roskilde and Køge Bay respectively. Stricter controls were placed on developments outside the fingers, especially in the scenically attractive area of North Zealand, which suffered badly from urban sprawl during the 1950s. By 1970 much of the new growth of Copenhagen had been successfully directed into the two preferred fingers, though urban sprawl had not been contained in all areas.

Exercise

Figure 4.17 shows the built-up area of Greater Copenhagen today.

1 Trace the outline of the built-up area, and draw in the fingers and palm of the famous 1947 plan. Shade the green wedges between the fingers.

2 How easy was it to identify the fingers? Would you say that the Finger Plan is evident in the built-up area of the region today? Comment briefly.

Although the population of Greater Copenhagen has remained static since 1970, the built-up area has continued to expand. This has been due to a trend towards smaller families (many more single person households and childless families) and to a demand for more living space, and a better standard of housing. The present aim of planners is to achieve a standard of housing which provides one room per family member, plus one extra room. The stock of older housing in the inner suburbs is cramped, lacking in basic amenities and of a high density. Many apartments suffer high noise levels from traffic, lack safe play areas for children, and are in need of replacement.

Table 4.2 Housing conditions in Copenhagen 1977

Amenities		Number of rooms per dwelling	
Flats without their own toilet	9%	1 room	41000
		2 rooms	118000
Flats without their own bath	42%	3 rooms	72000
		4 rooms	39000
Flats without central heating	33%	5+ rooms	18000

The third plan, introduced in 1973, continues the policy of dispersing population and employment from the city. The plan aims to construct 250000 new dwellings and create 150000 new jobs in the Greater Copenhagen region, outside the city's boundaries. As jobs follow population out of the city, it is hoped that the problems of traffic congestion, and lengthy journeys-to-work, will be eased.

The 1973 plan retains the original idea of fingers and wedges, but unlike previous plans, each finger now contains a major service and employment centre of its own (Figure 4.18). Each centre will be large enough to serve a population of 250000 people (ie larger than the second city of Denmark – Århus), which should relieve dependence and pressure on Copenhagen. Already, the southernmost centre of Tastrup is well on the way to completion. The new centres are located at places where the radial roads which converge on central Copenhagen cross the regional network of 'transport corridors' (Figure 4.19). Apart from roads, the corridors are also reserved for railways and pipelines for gas, oil and water. No housing is permitted along the corridors,

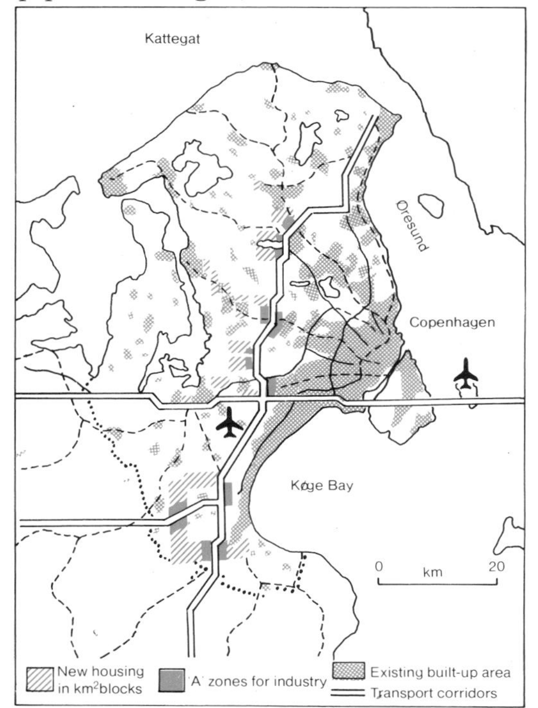

Figure 4.19 The 1973 plan for Copenhagen

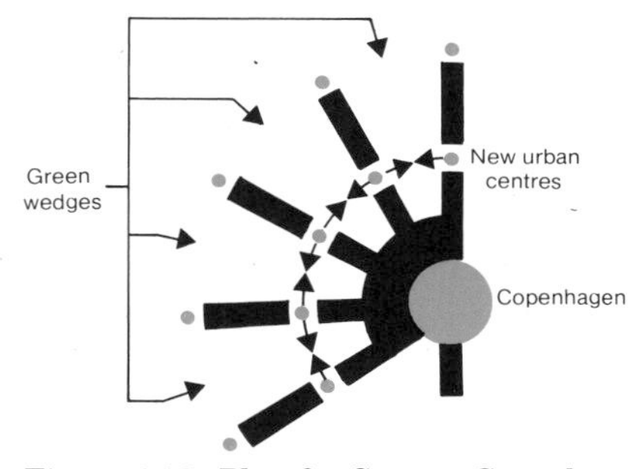

Figure 4.18 Plan for Greater Copenhagen, 1973

Figure 4.20 A group of modern flats in Høje Gladsaxe, Copenhagen. These flats were built in the 1960s and are located towards the end of the third 'finger', pointing NW, in the famous Finger Plan.

and industry is confined to reserved sites or 'A' zones. Housing is laid out in blocks of one kilometre square (each with 1000 dwellings) (Figure 4.19). The maximum width of development is two blocks, so that open countryside is never more than one kilometre from any dwelling. Further improvements to the transport system are planned which will eventually result in five new motorways to the city centre (one along each finger), three transverse motorways linking the regional centres, and two new suburban railway lines, one in the southernmost finger for the first time to Tastrup.

Exercise

Figures 4.21, 4.22, 4.23 and 4.24 illustrate the effects of decentralisation on employment and journeys-to-work in the city of Copenhagen.

1 Refer to Figure 4.21 and calculate by how much employment in Copenhagen has fallen during 1970–9. Which employment sector has been most affected by decentralisation?

2 Estimate the total employment in Copenhagen in 1979 (Figure 4.21), and using the information in the flow map of commuters (Figure 4.22) estimate the % of the city's workforce which commutes from outside the city. Does this figure suggest that decentralisation has been successful?

3 What effect has decentralisation had on the length (in km) of journeys-to-work to the city (Figure 4.23)?

4 What does Figure 4.24 suggest to you about a) the provision of public transport b) the provision of roads for use by private motorists in Copenhagen? What effect are these different journey times likely to have on the use of public transport?

5 Construct a *flow map* similar to Figure 4.22 to show the decentralisation of manufacturing firms from Copenhagen 1965–74. Use a scale for the flow lines of 1 mm for 50 firms.

Destination of firms	
Copenhagen (west)	400
Copenhagen (north)	100
Frederiksborg	90
Roskilde	40
Elsewhere	120

6 How far from the city of Copenhagen did most firms move? Suggest some reasons for the typical distance moved by the majority of firms.

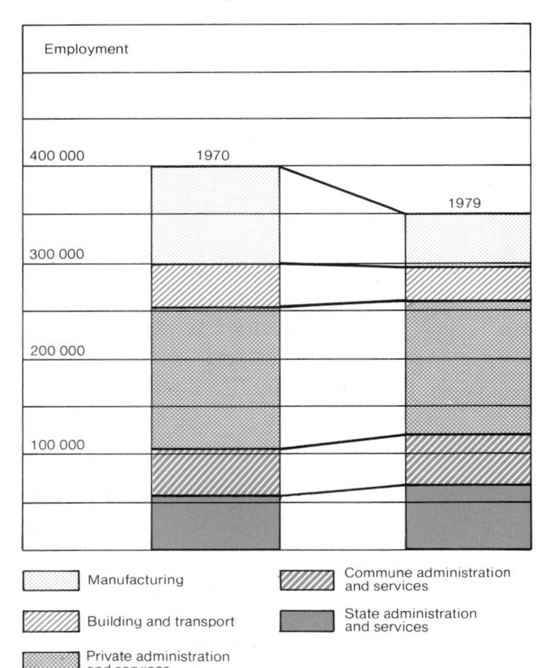

Figure 4.21 Employment changes: city of Copenhagen, 1970–79

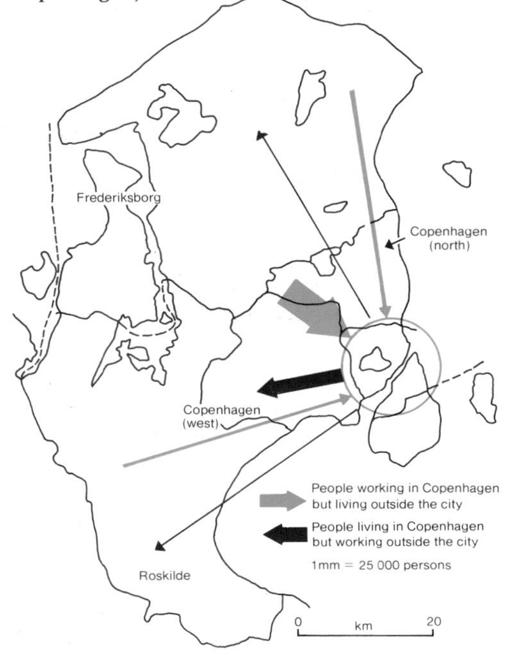

Figure 4.22 Journeys-to-work: city of Copenhagen

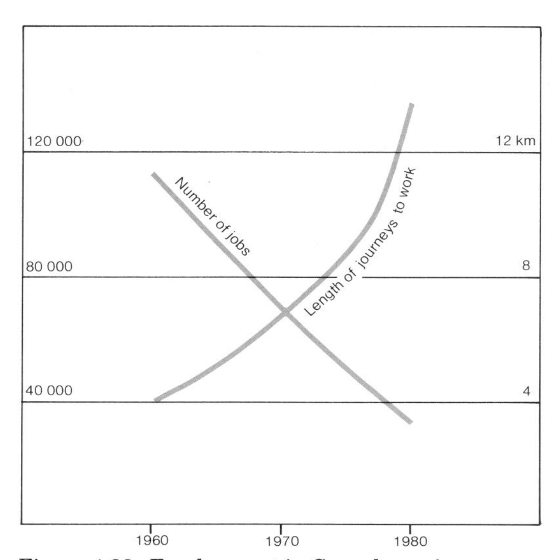

Figure 4.23 Employment in Copenhagen's commune and length of journeys-to-work, 1960–80

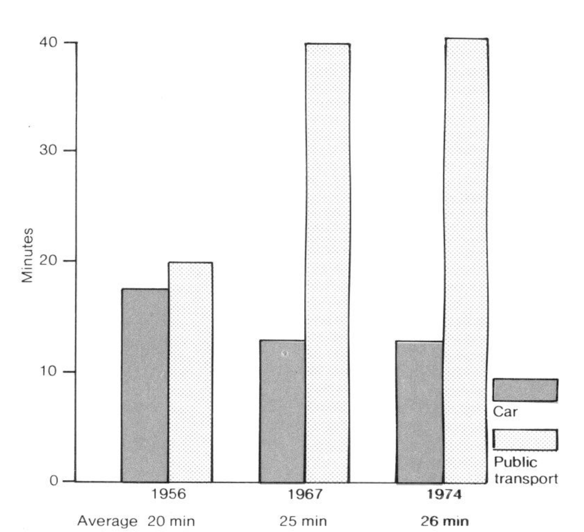

Figure 4.24 Length of journeys-to-work. Copenhagen 1956–74

Toronto

Toronto, located on the northern shore of Lake Ontario (Figures 4.25 and 4.26), is Canada's largest city. The city itself has a population of 600 000, but the wider built-up area of the Toronto region has a total population of 3 400 000. Several important functions are found in the city: as the capital of Ontario state, the city is a major administrative centre; it is the second largest port on the Lower Great Lakes, handling 1.3 million tonnes of freight in 1979, and connected to the Atlantic by the St Lawrence Seaway; its international airport is Canada's busiest, and served 14 million passengers in 1981; and it is a leading centre of manufacturing industry, with a diverse range of industries, including clothing, printing and publishing, food processing, metal fabricating and electrical engineering. However, the largest sector of employment is offices and services: 45% of jobs are in this sector, and most are concentrated in the city's CBD. Toronto is the financial capital of Canada, with its own stock exchange, the headquarter offices of the country's seven largest banks, and the headquarters of 43 of the 53 foreign banks in Canada.

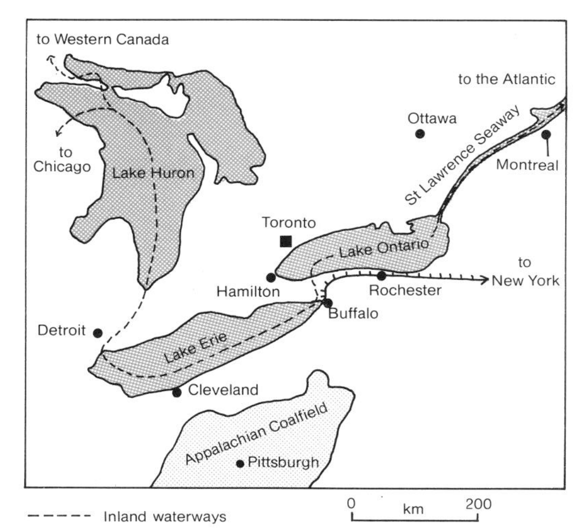

Figure 4.25 Situation of Toronto

Figure 4.26 View of Toronto's CBD from above the islands in Lake Ontario

Exercise

1 Plot the information in Table 4.3 as a bar graph (similar to Figure 4.21 for Copenhagen) and shade in the areas on the graph which represent the different employment sectors.

2 Which sector is a) growing most rapidly b) declining most rapidly? How does this compare with Copenhagen?

3 Taking account of its location in the CBD, can you foresee any problems that might be caused by the rapid growth of office activities in Toronto?

Table 4.3 % Employment in metropolitan Toronto

	1970	1974	1976
Offices	38.1	42.7	45.2
Retailing	10.0	9.5	9.3
Manufacturing	25.0	22.2	21.1
Others	26.9	25.6	24.4

Urban problems

Toronto, like most other cities in the Western world, faces a number of major problems, in particular the overdevelopment of office activities and traffic congestion in the central area.

The growth of population in the Toronto region has been very uneven since 1951 (Figure 4.27). While the population as a whole has increased rapidly, most of the growth since 1970 has occurred in the outer metropolitan suburbs of Scarborough and North York, and outside the metropolitan area , in districts such as Brampton and Mississauga (Figure 4.28). Population losses have been greatest in the central parts of the metropolitan area: the city of Toronto (Figure 4.27) suffered a 5.4% decrease between 1976 and 1981, which was similar to the decline experienced by Canada's second and third cities – Montreal and Vancouver.

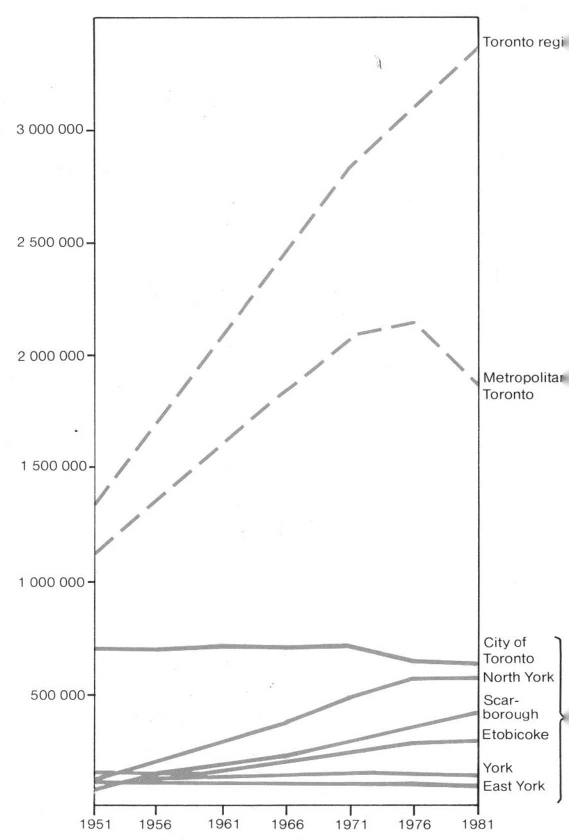

Figure 4.27 Population changes in the metropolitan Toronto and Toronto regions, 1951–81

Exercise

1 Using Figures 4.27 and 4.28 describe the pattern of population change with distance from the city centre.

2 Compare this pattern of population change with that in Copenhagen and Birmingham.

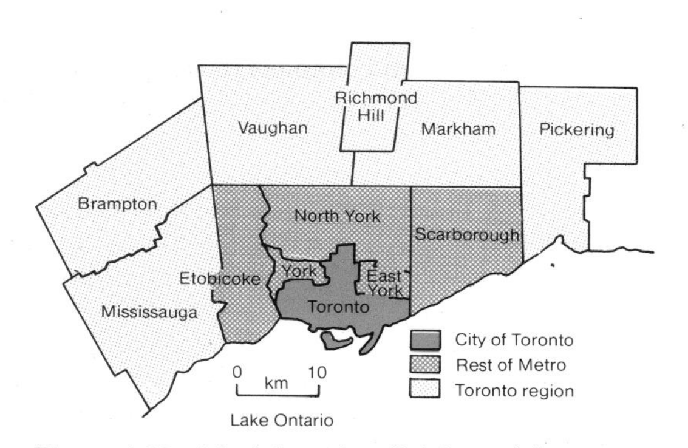

Figure 4.28 Administrative divisions of the Toronto region

The movement of people to the outer suburbs of the metropolitan area and the wider Toronto region has been caused by several factors:

1 a shortage of building land for new homes in the city and in older established suburbs such as York, East York and Etobicoke

2 cheaper family housing away from the centre

3 a decrease in the size of households in the central area of Toronto, from an average of 4.9 persons in 1951, to 2.1 in 1981. With one household per dwelling, this automatically means that fewer people can live in the central areas. The causes of this trend are the increasing proportion of old people in the city (many of whom live alone) and smaller families.

While the population of Toronto is gradually moving away from the older parts of the city, most employment in offices and retailing remains near the centre. This situation has forced commuters to travel longer distances than ever before. The central area of Toronto has a concentration of 500 000 jobs, and half of the people working there travel from outside the city each day. As journeys get longer, increasing strain is put on Toronto's transport systems, and traffic congestion around the CBD is severe at peak periods.

Other problems have appeared in central Toronto in recent years. They are summarised here by a planner:

> 'High office and bank towers emerged as the new landmarks dotting the skyline of Toronto. These developments transformed not only the skyline, but also the life of the streets of the city. They internalised retail areas within interconnected, underground malls, leaving behind windswept plazas and empty streets. Historic buildings were destroyed to make way for new construction and some of Toronto's most important landmarks were lost forever. Many old, low-rise residential neighbourhoods were also demolished to make way for high density tower developments, or simply for parking lots. Inner city residents began to have visions of Toronto turning into a typical American city, where life in the central city stops when commuters leave for the suburbs, and the city streets become lifeless after office hours.'

Exercise

1 State three effects that the development of high rise office buildings had on the life of the city centre.

2 Why did changes in the provision of shopping facilities leave behind 'windswept plazas and empty streets'?

3 What do you think is meant by an 'internalised retail area', compared with a traditional shopping street, lined with shop frontages? (See Figure 4.29.) Think of any modern, city centre shopping areas that you know, and make a list of their disadvantages compared with a more traditional shopping street (eg type and range of shops, shopper choice, access, etc.).

Figure 4.29 The Glasshouse Arcade: one of several internal shopping precints in Toronto's CBD

Solving the urban problems

Unlike Copenhagen or Randstad, the planners have not come up with any master plan to solve the problems of the Toronto region. Instead, the Official Plan covers only the city's central area, though its effects extend to the metropolitan area and the wider region. The Official Plan, approved in 1979, has several objectives. The three main ones are:

1 to disperse office jobs more widely throughout the Toronto region

2 to increase the number of houses in the central area, and so encourage people to live closer to their office and service jobs in the CBD, thus reducing journey-to-work lengths and times

3 to encourage the use of public transport at the expense of the private motorist, and thus relieve the problem of congestion near the city centre.

The key to the success of the plan is the dispersal of offices to the suburbs. This is essential because the city's transport system cannot cope with continued office expansion in the CBD. Planners have therefore put a limit on the amount of new office building in the CBD. Current office space is 5.8 million metres^2, and this will be allowed to rise to a maximum of 7 million metres^2 by 1991. All additional office development will take place in the suburbs, in specially designed *office parks*, and *office nodes* which are served by the subway and the suburban rail network (Figure 4.30).

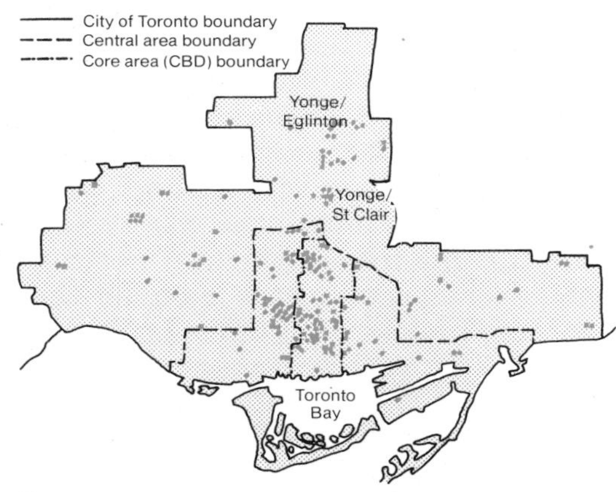

Figure 4.30 Distribution of office construction projects under way or completed in 1979

By 1981 the targets for restricting new offices in the CBD had been achieved, and many offices had been diverted to the suburbs (Table 4.4).

Table 4.4

% Distribution of office space	1976	1981
City of Toronto	72	64
Rest of metropolitan area	26	29
Rest of region	2	7

Exercise

As part of their plan to solve the congestion problem in the city centre, the Toronto planners have restricted the number of parking spaces available in the CBD to discourage commuting by car. Describe what you think might be the likely reactions of the following groups of people towards this policy:
— residents, living in the central area
— shoppers in the central area
— commuters
— businessmen with premises in the central area.

While the total amount of office space has increased in all parts of the region, the relative share of the city has fallen considerably, and this has allowed the public transport system to cope. Unlike most other North American cities, Toronto has continued to invest in its public transport system (subway, railways, buses, trams), despite competition from the private motorist. In the last few years there has been an increase in traffic on the subway and overground commuter trains, and only a slight rise in the use of private cars for journeys to the city centre. The rail services are particularly valuable because the network extends into the outlying districts beyond the metropolitan area, where population growth has been greatest in the last twenty years.

Apart from public transport, new housing has also been encouraged in the central area, with 10000 dwellings built between 1975 and 1981. This is one-third of the way towards the target of 30000 new dwellings by 1986. One result of this policy has been an increase in the population of the central area by 15000 between 1976 and 1981. This now means that half of the working population in this zone have jobs in the central area, and 35% are able to walk to work each day.

Future

The growth of population on the fringes of the Toronto region will continue, and as offices increasingly locate in these areas, commuting to the city centre should be reduced. However, this trend is beginning to pose a new problem: if offices are widely scattered in office parks throughout the region, they are very difficult and expensive to serve by public transport and commuters understandably take to their cars. To prevent this, planners are trying to concentrate new offices in centres served directly by the subway and overground railways (Figure 4.31). Already there are eight of these office nodes in the suburbs. They account for 11% of Toronto's total office floorspace, and as well as employment, provide shopping and recreational facilities. In addition, there are 13 smaller office parks in the metropolitan area, which although less well served by public transport, are growing rapidly like office nodes.

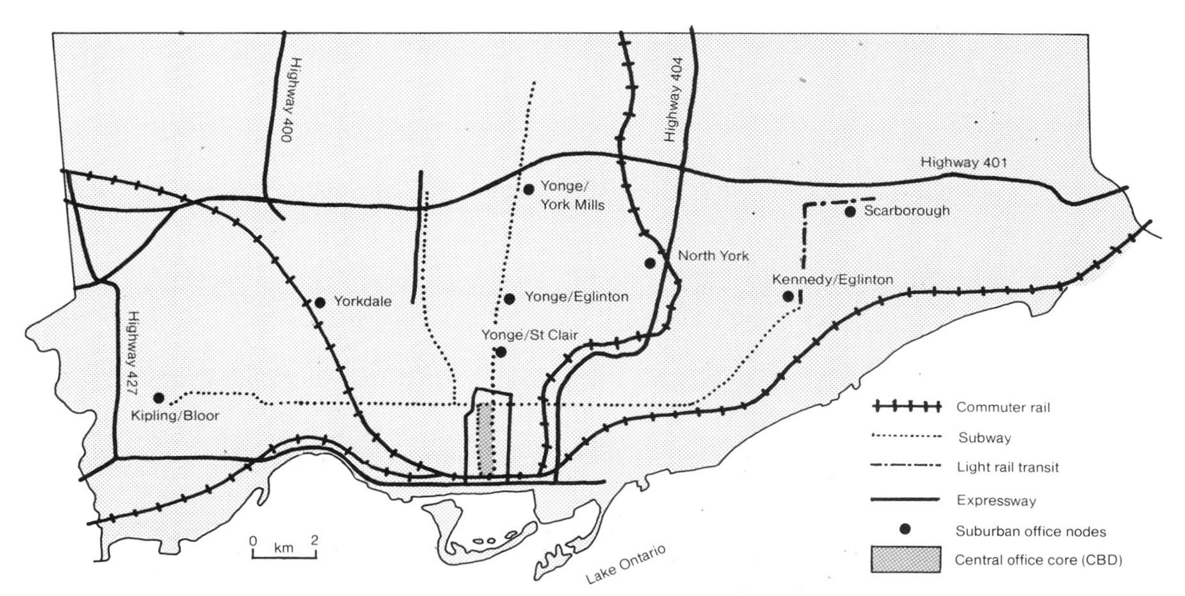

Figure 4.31 Toronto metropolitan region: urban transport network and principal office locations

Randstad, Holland

Randstad, or 'ring city', is the name given to a large concentration of towns and cities in the province of Holland in the western Netherlands. As Figure 4.32 shows, Randstad is not a completely ring shape, being open at its south eastern end. It is often described as a 'horseshoe', with a diameter of 50–60 km. At the centre of the horseshoe there is an open area, mainly devoted to agriculture, known as the 'green heart'. This rural core makes Randstad unique among the major cities of the world. Randstad, with a population of 5 900 000, is the fourth largest urban area in Western Europe, and with 42.6% of the Netherlands' population, it dominates the country.

Exercise

1 What term is used to describe a group of towns and cities which have expanded and merged into one vast urban area? (Refer back to Chapter 1, page 15 if you are unsure).

2 Look at Figure 4.32 and say whether you think this term applies to Randstad.

3 Which three urban areas in Western Europe are larger than Randstad? (They are listed in the exercise in Chapter 3, page 43.)

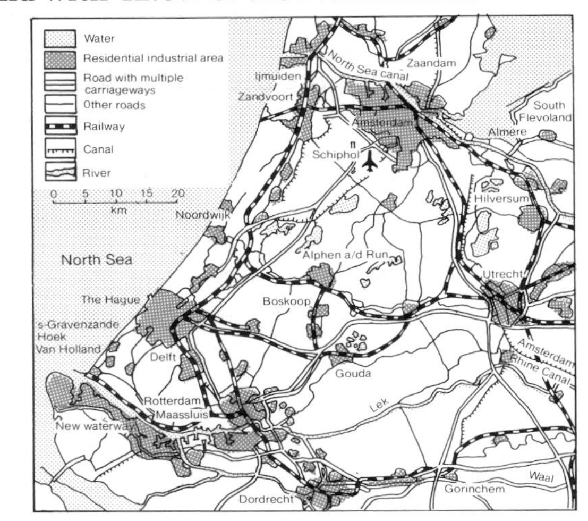

Figure 4.32 Randstad, Holland

Another unusual feature of Randstad is that, unlike Birmingham, Copenhagen and Toronto, it does not have a single city centre, but several, with each performing an important function for the city as a whole. The four largest centres are Amsterdam, Rotterdam, The Hague, and Utrecht (Figure 4.35). Amsterdam is the capital (but not the seat of government) and the main financial and cultural centre; Rotterdam is the largest port and the centre of heavy industry; The Hague is the seat of government; and Utrecht is an important conference and trade fair centre.

Exercise

Answer the following questions as a short essay, in three separate paragraphs.

1 Do you think that the shape of Randstad gives its inhabitants better access to the countryside, compared to a city like Birmingham, which has grown outwards from a single core?

2 Do you think that Randstad, with several centres, is likely to suffer more, or less, from traffic congestion, compared with Toronto or Copenhagen?

3 If the distinctive shape of Randstad means that access to the city from the surrounding countryside is fairly easy, can you foresee any problem to which this might give rise?

Figure 4.33 Amsterdam: the largest city in Randstad, and the financial, cultural and light-industrial capital of the Netherlands

Urban problems and planning

Randstad's urban problems and planning policies can be considered in two phases: 1950–70, and post-1970.

1950–70

During the 1950s and 1960s the population of Randstad grew more rapidly than any other area of the Netherlands. This growth was caused by high rates of natural increase and in-migration from other regions of the country. In 1960 planners, concerned about congestion in an already overcrowded Randstad, adopted a policy of dispersing population beyond the ring of the Randstad towns, and the further away the better. Such a policy is a very familiar one, and as we have seen, has been used to varying degrees in the cities we have studied in this chapter. In addition to dispersal, there was strict control over building in the 'green heart' to protect its rural character (Figure 4.34), and 'buffer zones' of agricultural land were established between the main towns, to prevent them from merging together.

Figure 4.34 The green heart of Randstad

Post-1970

By 1970 the nature of the urban problems had changed: some of the policies of the famous 1960 plan had failed, and a new approach was needed. Most striking was the trend of population: by 1970 the growth of population in Randstad had not only halted, but most of the cities were losing population (Figure 4.35). This prompted concern that there might be a similar decline in the provision of services such as schools and health care, and that the international status of Randstad might be threatened.

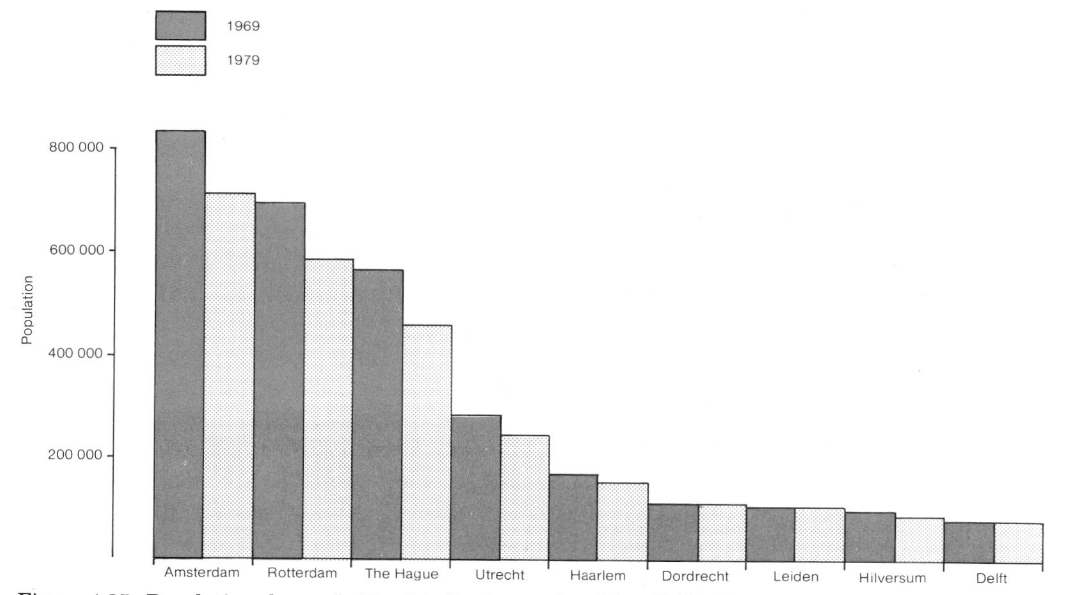

Figure 4.35 Population change in Randstad's nine major cities, 1969–79

Exercise

Figure 4.36 shows the rank order of size of the nine largest centres in Randstad, from Amsterdam (first) to Delft (ninth), and their rank order of % population decline 1969–79, from The Hague (largest) to Dordrecht (smallest). The diagram enables you to compare the size of a town with its rate of population loss. Study the diagram carefully and answer the following questions.

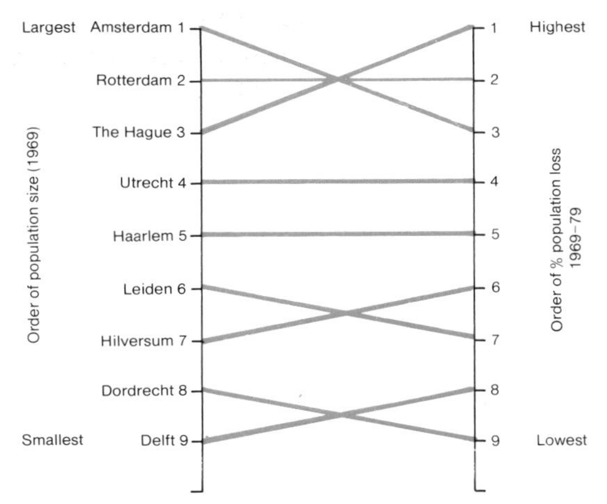

Figure 4.36 City size and rate of population decline in Randstad

1 Which towns suffered a greater % decline in their population than might be expected, given their size?

2 Which towns had a decline that was less than expected, given their size?

3 In which towns was the % decline in population in keeping with their size?

4 If all the lines in the diagram were horizontal, what would this tell you?

5 From the evidence of the diagram, would you say that there is a strong/moderate/weak relationship between size and rate of population decline?

6 Can you suggest any explanation for your answer to question 5?

The causes of declining population in Randstad are similar to those we have met in other cities. Many families left the city because living conditions in smaller towns and rural areas were more attractive (better housing, less congestion, less overcrowding, less pollution) and land and housing were cheaper. The growth of car ownership and incomes meant that it was possible to live outside Randstad and commute to the city, often over quite long distances. Also the trend towards smaller households, noticeable in Denmark and Canada, has had the effect of reducing the number of people that need to be accommodated in the city. Finally, during the 1950s and 1960s urban renewal in Randstad often meant that housing areas were replaced by office blocks, shops, parking lots and other non-residential forms of land use.

Although the 1960 plan aimed to encourage people to move out of Randstad to regions some distance away, in fact the majority settled close to the city, and urban sprawl took place into the 'green heart' and other areas of attractive countryside such as Gelderland and North Brabant. This movement increased the growth of long-distance commuting, and threatened congestion in the major urban centres of Randstad.

In the light of these problems, the policy of decentralisation was abandoned in 1976. The present aim is to encourage people to *remain* in Randstad, by reducing traffic congestion, building new houses and altogether making the city a more attractive place in which to live. The new approach emphasises urban renewal, and in particular replacing old houses with new ones (rather than with offices and industry as in the past), and wherever possible, filling empty spaces with housing developments. Nonetheless, some people will continue to leave Randstad, and to prevent unplanned sprawl they will be directed to a limited number of places, mostly near to Randstad. The largest of these places are *growth towns* (Figure 4.37) where at least 10 000 new houses will be built by 1990. The four growth towns are Breda, Groningen, Helmond and Zwolle.

Growth centres are smaller places where a minimum of 6000 new houses will be built by 1990. With the exception of Almere in the Flevoland polders, all of these growth places are existing settlements, with populations ranging from 8500 to 146 500.

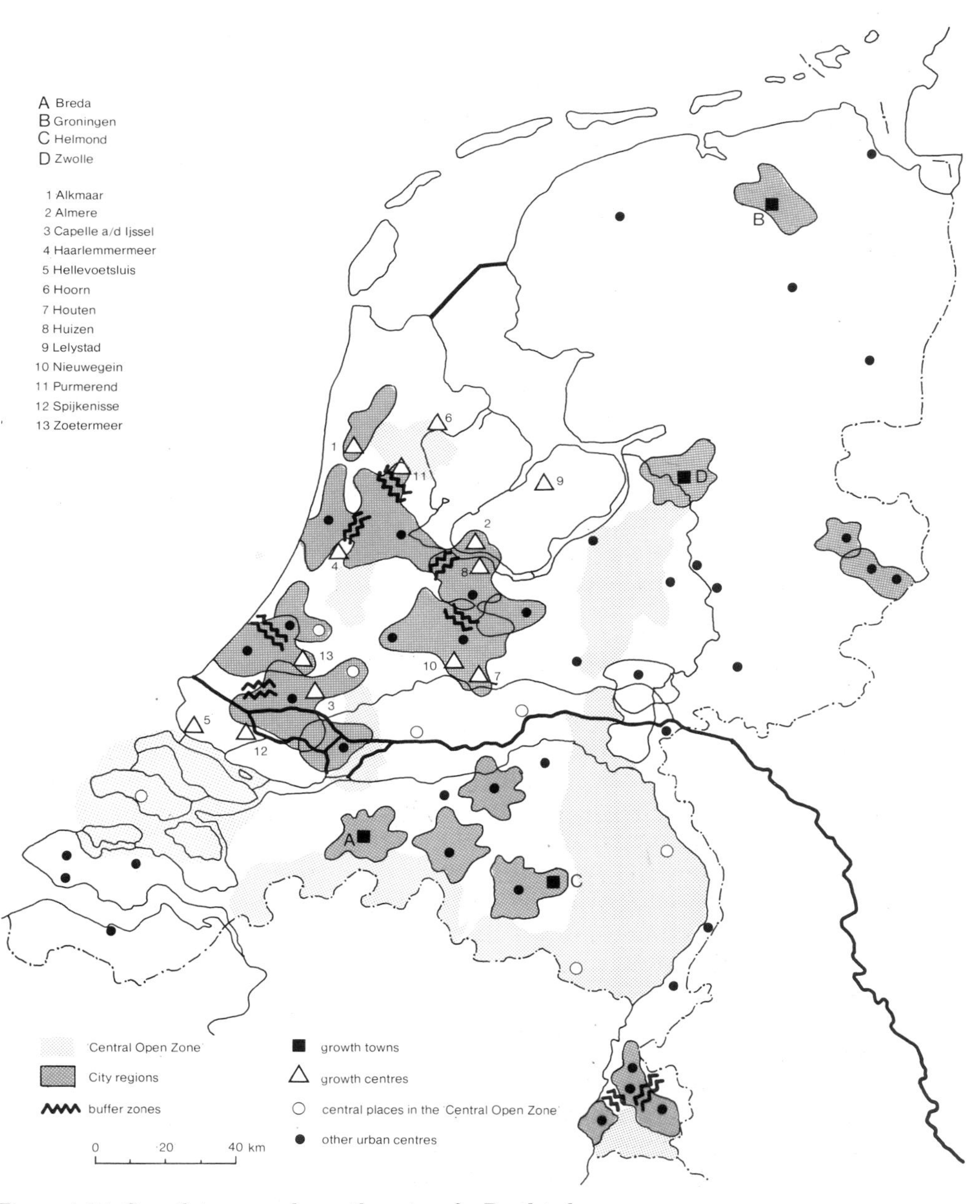

Figure 4.37 Growth towns and growth centres for Randstad

Thus in Randstad the former policy of dispersal has been largely reversed by an anti-dispersal one, where the aim is to achieve a larger share of the Dutch population for Randstad. However, the longstanding policy of preventing the towns and cities growing together, and keeping open the 'green heart', remains. Indeed the 'buffer zones', apart from stopping urban sprawl, will now be planned to serve as recreational areas for the inhabitants of the surrounding towns.

Exercise

Table 4.5 defines three zones in Randstad which are shown in Figure 4.38. The Randstad horseshoe is represented by the nine major cities; the fringe area is that immediately adjacent to the built-up area of Randstad; and the core area corresponds to the 'green heart'.

1. In which of these three zones has population change 1960–78 corresponded most closely with the 1960 plan?
2. Where did the 1960 plan suggest that population growth from the Randstad should be accommodated?
3. What does Table 4.5 tell you about the success of this dispersal policy?
4. Why do you think that the Dutch have been more concerned about the problem of urban sprawl than the Canadians, in the example of Toronto? (Clue – compare the size of the Netherlands with Canada.)

Table 4.5 Population change in Randstad: 1960–78

	1960	1978	% change
9 Randstad cities	2993000	2571000	−14.1
Fringe areas	365000	610000	+67.1
Core area	340000	523000	+53.8

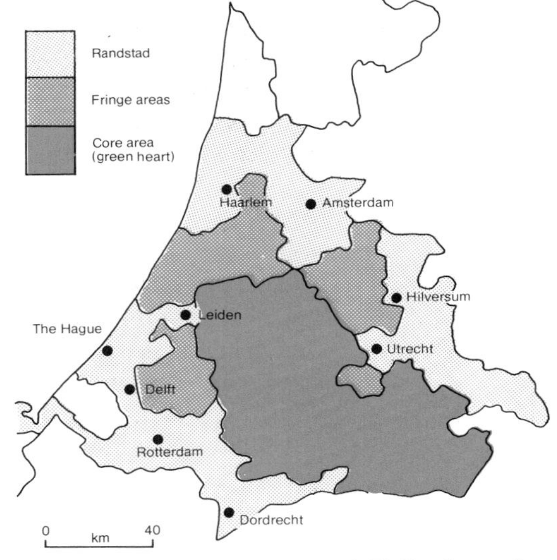

Figure 4.38 Regions of Randstad, Holland

Part 2: Urban problems and planning in LDCs

We saw in the first part of this chapter that cities in DCs today face a number of major problems. However, the problems which are typical of these cities, such as traffic congestion and urban sprawl, are insignificant compared with those found in the Third World: in Third World cities the problems are so serious, that they often concern the very survival of their inhabitants. The most obvious problem is the poverty of most urban dwellers, which expresses itself in a number of ways:

1. a shortage of housing
2. a lack of basic services necessary for urban life, such as sewage disposal and drinking water
3. a shortage of jobs.

The basic cause of these problems is the rapid growth of Third World cities in the last 30 years, which in turn is tied up with the lack of development in rural areas. People have moved from the countryside to the towns in such numbers, that the towns have been unable either to house or employ them. Most of the problems which are typical of cities in the Third World are to be found concentrated in the so-called *spontaneous*, or *squatter* settlements (Figure 4.39).

It has been estimated that two-fifths of the population of Third World cities lives in poverty. The most obvious sign of poverty is the low quality of much of the housing. For instance, in São Paulo, Brazil's largest city, 75% of all houses are self-built, squatter homes; in Nairobi (Kenya) and Lima (Peru) squatters represent 40% of the total population, and similar proportions are found throughout the Third World. The situation in Calcutta (India) is even worse: here, huge numbers are housed in squatter settlements; but below these are even more basic shelters, built in the streets from poles and sacking; and worst of all there are the 'pavement dwellers' – 200 000 people without any kind of shelter. Because the people are so poor, they are unable either to buy or rent accommodation, and in these circumstances have no option but to build their own houses. The result is unplanned squatter camps. Self-built houses can be made from anything – cardboard, tin, plastic, scrap wood, branches, cloth, concrete, brick, highway signs, roofing material and so on. Living conditions, though they generally improve with time, are often appalling, as the description of a squatter camp in Tijuana (Mexico) indicates:

> 'Many structures are little more than shacks and lack even basic amenities. Stairs and retaining walls are made from used tyres; discarded oil drums serve as water storage tanks, and outhouses take the place of sewers. Packs of dogs and flocks of chickens scurry among the numerous small children playing in the unpaved streets and in the mounds of trash on empty lots. Clouds of dust fill the air.'

The squatter camps often lack essential services such as a safe water supply, sewage disposal, electricity, schools, clinics and paved roads. The health of the inhabitants, particularly the children, is inevitably poor. A survey in the city of Medellin (Colombia) showed that 45% of its population were without electricity, 43% without sewage disposal, and 26% without a supply of safe drinking water. The problem of water supply is particularly acute for squatters in Lima because the city, sited at the foot of the Andes, has a dry, almost desert-like climate.

The location of many squatter settlements also causes problems. Squatters tend to settle on any vacant lots in the city, though they prefer ones which are close to areas of employment, like the CBD and industrial zones. However, many sites are hopelessly unsuitable for settlement. In Caracas (Venezuela) squatter housing has been built on steep hillsides and in narrow ravines on the edge of the city, where landslides and flooding are common. In Hong Kong, the squatter camps also cling to steep hillsides, where the provision of basic services is almost impossible. In Bogota (Colombia) several settlements are located in marshy areas and close to rubbish dumps, where there is the constant threat of disease; and as in most Third World cities, the squatter camps are concentrated in the outermost areas, where public transport to the city centre is often non-existent.

Finally, there is the problem of unemployment. The growth of employment has not kept pace with population increase (contrast this with what happened in the urbanisation of Britain in the nineteenth century – Chapter 3, pages 45–7) and there are not enough jobs available in manufacturing industry to satisfy demand. Once again, people have to rely on self-help, and find work in the 'informal' service sector, collecting rubbish, shoe-shining, running errands, street trading, cleaning cars and so on. Today, 67% of the working population of Calcutta is employed in service activities of this nature.

Exercise

Third World cities have been described as 'cities of the poor'. Read the extract on page 90 which describes the life of Kershar, aged 9 years, in the Indian city of Nagpur.

1. By any standards, Kershar's life is one of poverty. Make a list of factors described in the extract, which contribute to his poverty.
2. If an individual was described as 'poor' in Western Europe or North America, in what ways would his or her poverty differ from that of Kershar in India?

'I am looking through all this rubbish every day. It is my work. I am nine years old. I look for glass, paper, old iron things, plastic sandals. My brothers showed me how I sell to man who comes. I give money to my father and keep 2p for myself. I don't like this work. You work in sun all day. You get dirty.

I eat twice. Chapatis and potatoes in morning. Chapatis and cereal at night. My mother died two months ago. She was sick. She had TB. She had no doctor. No medicine at all. She died at home.

Now we stay in room which will be for night watchman when building is finished. My father works on building site. When work is finished we will move.

We make house where my father works. We make house from things we find around. We make many houses. Changing water make you sick. I would like to have proper house so we can always stay there. I do not like keep moving.'

(extract from *New Internationalist*)

Exercise

Study the photographs in Figure 4.39 which show squatter settlements in three LDCs.

1 Make a list of the building materials from which the squatter homes are made.

2 To what extent do the settlements appear to be 'spontaneous' or unplanned in their development?

3 Describe the sites of settlements B and C, and suggest:
 i the advantage of site B
 ii a possible reason for the choice of site C
 iii difficulties which might arise at site C in the provision of drinking water and sewage disposal.

4 What is likely to happen at site A after heavy rain? (Note the pools of water in the foreground.)

Figure 4.39B

Figure 4.39C

Figure 4.39A Squatter settlements in the Third World

Solving the desperate problems found in many Third World cities is a daunting task. However, much is being done, and in the next section we shall examine the progress which is being made in three cities, Kuala Lumpur, Manila and Hong Kong, particularly with regard to housing and the provision of basic amenities and services (Figure 4.40).

Kuala Lumpur (Malaysia)

Kuala Lumpur is the capital and largest city in Malaysia, and a centre of trade and communications. The city has grown rapidly since World War 2: in 1947 its population was 176000, compared with 820000 in the late 1970s. Much of this growth is due to in-migration from the countryside and from smaller towns, by people seeking jobs, higher incomes and better prospects for their children. Indeed, around 45% of all migrants were unemployed in their area of origin. However, poverty is also widespread in Kuala Lumpur, given unemployment, underemployment and low incomes. Squatters are the poorest group, and in the late 1970s comprised some 200000 people. Most of them find employment in labour intensive, traditional activities, such as petty trading; few jobs are available in modern, Western-style manufacturing and service industries.

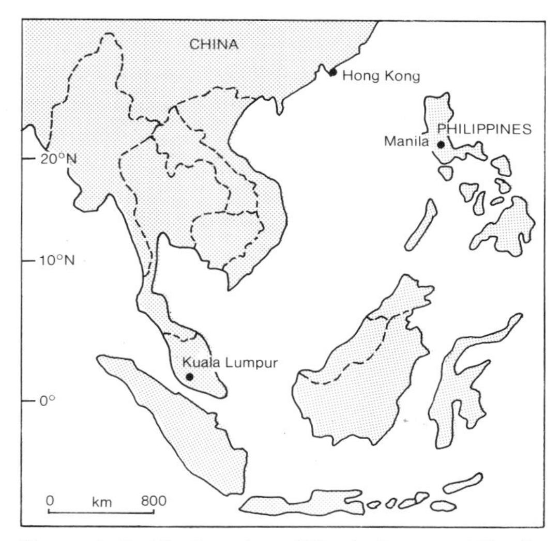

Figure 4.40 The location of Kuala Lumpur, Manila and Hong Kong

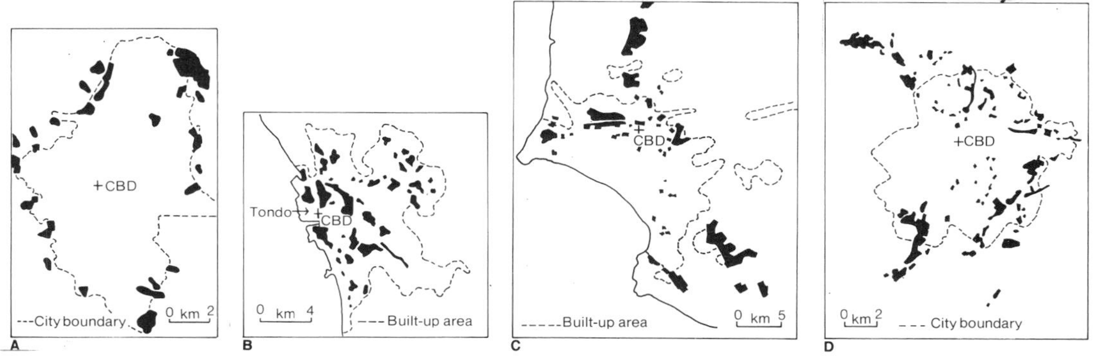

Figure 4.41A–D The location of squatter settlements A Medëllin (Colombia) B Manila (Philippines) C Lima (Peru) D Kuala Lumpur (Malaysia)

Squatter settlements

Squatter settlements are found throughout the city, though the largest ones are usually located in the outermost areas (Figure 4.41D). Squatter camps are found along roads, railways, river banks, waste land, undeveloped land and vacant lots – in fact anywhere where land is available, and preferably near to areas of employment. However, the squatter camps are themselves areas of employment, and often contain many tiny workshops engaged in motor vehicle repair, metal and woodworking, and the manufacture of concrete products.

Living conditions in many squatter camps are poor: in 1973 80% of squatters were without electricity, 75% had no piped water, and 35% lacked any sewerage facilities. Owing to the unhygienic conditions, squatters are subject to various diseases. A serious problem for children is the threat of fever, which is spread by a mosquito which breeds in household water containers, discarded cans, tyres, roof gutters and so on. Other potential breeding sites for mosquitoes include cesspools and polluted, stagnant water. Insanitary surroundings, together with overcrowded living conditions and inadequate diets, result in high death rates among infants and children in the camps.

Solving the squatter problem

In Malaysia, and in many other LDCs, the government does not regard squatter settlements favourably. Apart from being illegal, they are seen as centres of crime and disease, and tarnish the image of the capital city. Nonetheless, given the scale of the housing problem in Kuala Lumpur, the government has little option but to tolerate them. In the past, squatters were often evicted, but today the government has a more positive attitude, and seeks to solve the squatter problem in three ways:

1. by re-housing the squatters in conventional, low-cost housing schemes
2. by upgrading existing squatter settlements by providing them with services such as piped water, drainage and electricity
3. by developing 'sites and services' projects.

Relocation housing schemes

A number of low-cost housing schemes have been undertaken, notably in the Klang valley. Squatters are re-housed in multi-storey apartment buildings, where they are provided with essential services. So far, these low-cost schemes have not been very successful, and have not been able to meet the demand for minimum standard housing in Kuala Lumpur. Between 1976 and 1980, 73 million US dollars were allocated to the building of 13 000 new units, but by the end of the period the government had failed to build anything like this number. Furthermore, the schemes were disliked because they were often situated far from places of work, were poorly constructed and noisy. Even though rents were modest, the people had difficulty in meeting the charges for electricity and water. Thus, even if more low-cost housing were available, a sizeable proportion of the poor in the city could not afford to live in it!

Upgrading schemes

The problems associated with conventional low-cost housing suggest that there is a strong case for *improving* squatter settlements, rather than abolishing them. Squatters throughout the Third World have shown that they are capable of housing themselves in cheap and rent-free accommodation. However, what they cannot provide for themselves are the essential services such as water supply, sewage disposal and electricity. Therefore when money is scarce (as it is in all Third World cities) it is better spent on providing these essential services, than on housing. This is the aim of upgrading schemes, several of which have been introduced in Kuala Lumpur in areas such as Ampang, Kepong and Petaling Valley. These squatter areas on the edge of the city are supplied with services such as roads, water and electricity. Today there are stand-pipes, serving between 50 and 100 households, in approximately half of Kuala Lumpur's squatter settlements, and there are immediate plans to upgrade another nine. Although achievements have so far been limited, this policy of upgrading is cheap, and has great potential for improving some of the worst conditions in the squatter camps.

Sites and services schemes

The principle behind this scheme – which has been given financial support in many parts of the Third World by the World Bank – is self-help. Building lots are provided and laid out with water, drains, roads, lighting, and occasionally clinics and schools. Squatters are given modest loans for building materials, and are expected to build their own homes on the prepared sites (Figures 4.42

Figures 4.42/4.43 Low-cost housing schemes in the Third World

and 4.43). Another scheme provides squatters with a basic housing shell, or core, which can be improved and enlarged as circumstances permit. Such a core housing scheme in Salah South, in south west Kuala Lumpur, also provides drains, roads, shops and industrial sites.

The Malaysian government cannot hope to build conventional, low-cost homes for everyone, and has recognised that it must rely on the initiative of the people by either upgrading the settlements they have built, or providing basic services for sites, and encouraging self-help housing.

Manila (Philippines)

The 1960s and 1970s saw an enormous growth of slums and squatter areas in the Philippines, and particularly in the capital city, Manila. The main aim of planning in Manila has been to provide for 'basic needs' such as food, clothing, shelter and employment.

Tondo squatter settlement (Manila)
The Tondo foreshore area is part of the wider Tondo area in which 500 000 people live (Figure 4.44). The foreshore comprises 180 ha of reclaimed land on the north east shore of Manila Bay, and until recently was a notorious slum. The reclaimed land was originally to be used by expanding port activies around Manila harbour. The project did not materialise and, though vulnerable to occasional flooding, after four years 3000 families had settled on the land. In the 1960s the population grew rapidly, without the provision of any services, roads or sewers, and by the mid 1970s, 27 000 families were housed in just 17 000 shacks. The main attraction of the site was employment in the nearby North Harbour Docks, marshalling yards and a large public market. Moreover, the Tondo district is within 2 km of Manila's CBD.

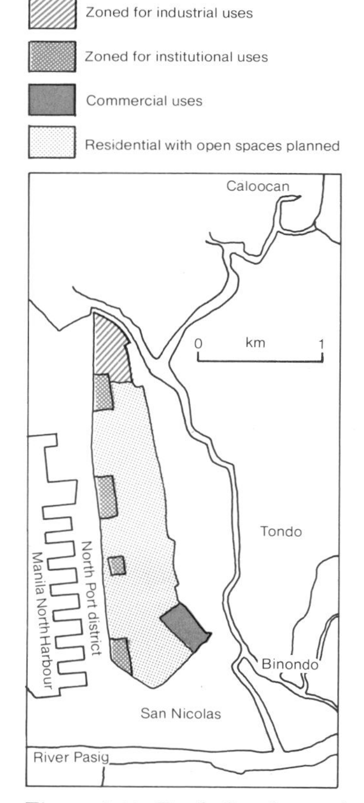

Figure 4.44 Tondo foreshore scheme: Manila

Recently, sites-and-services schemes have become an important means of tackling the housing problem, particularly in a poor country like the Philippines which cannot afford to build conventional, high-rise blocks, such as those in Hong Kong and Singapore. A new development in this area is the so-called BLISS project (Bagong Lipunan (New Society) Improvement of Sites and Services). The idea is to supply the basic needs of shelter and services, and at the same time encourage self-help among the squatters. Loans are provided by the government for each BLISS project providing there are good local prospects for employment. This is essential if the residents are to be able to afford to improve their houses and pay off their loans. Such a BLISS scheme has been successfully introduced into the foreshore area of Tondo. Land has been sold cheaply to residents, basic minimum services have been provided and most existing houses retained and improved. Initially, some core housing was provided, but today the emphasis is on self-built homes. The public services provided include water, sewers, electricity, the renovation of four schools and four health centres and the expansion of the local hospital. A major aim has been to improve job prospects, and with this in mind a technical training school has been established, and local employment created in industrial estates where some small firms have already set up successfully. In all 26 ha have been set aside for the development of industry.

The results of this scheme have been very encouraging: hundreds of squatter houses have been upgraded and people now have the security of owning their own land; 62% of homes have toilet facilities compared with 30% previously, and 80% have lighting compared with 50% before. In all, 27 000 families have benefited directly from this low-cost improvement scheme, based on a partnership between government and self-help on the part of the squatters.

Exercise

Figure 4.45 shows six vacant lots in a Third World city which are potential sites for squatter settlements. Study each location in terms of its site (slopes, liability to flooding), situation (nearness to areas of employment) and transport facilities.

1 Which locations are most likely to attract squatters? Give two reasons.

2 Which locations are likely to be least attractive? Again give two reasons.

3 Why is it that the least attractive locations (such as those you have listed in question 2) are often the location of squatter settlements in Third World cities?

4 Can you think of any particular problems that might be encountered if squatter settlements at locations 4 and 6 were to be upgraded?

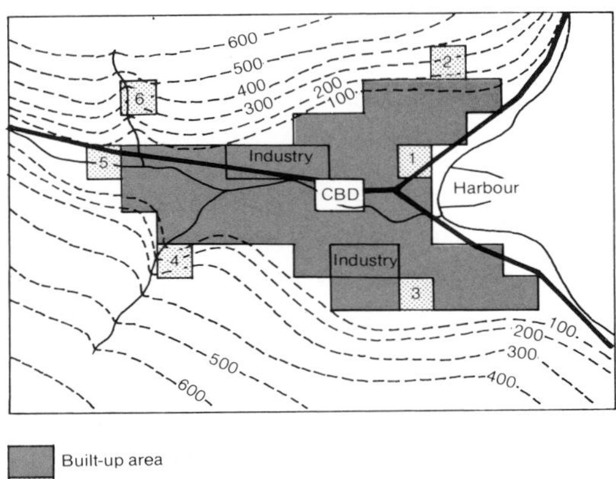

Major roads
Rivers
-400- Contours (metres)

Figure 4.45 Locating squatter settlements in Third World cities

Hong Kong

Hong Kong is one of the most densely populated areas in the world: in 1981 it had a population of 5 060 006 in an area about half the size of the county of Warwickshire. Its average density is over 4800 persons per km^2, though in parts of Hong Kong Island and the Kowloon peninsula densities reach 155 000 per km^2! (See Figure 4.46.)

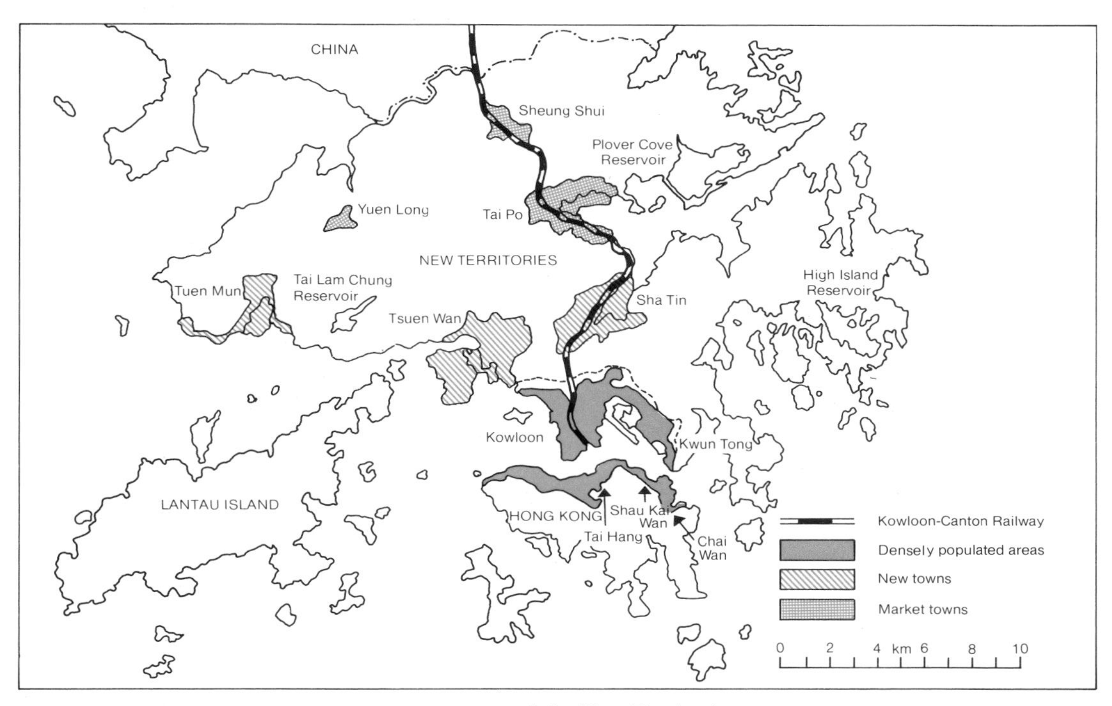

Figure 4.46 Urban developments in Hong Kong and the New Territories

Hong Kong's population has increased rapidly in the last 30 years, largely as a result of massive immigration from mainland China, and more recently from Vietnam. The scale and speed of this growth has caused a severe housing problem. The inability of the authorities to provide sufficient housing in the 1950s and 1960s inevitably led to the growth of squatter settlements. Vast areas of hillside squatter camps sprang up around the city, especially in northern Kowloon and at Tai Hang, Shau Kai Wan and Chai Wan on Hong Kong Island. Living conditions were primitive and insanitary: there was no sewage disposal, few water supply points, and the continual threat of fire, disease, landslide and typhoon damage. A further aspect of the housing problem was the enormous subdivision of existing housing: houses would first be split up into rooms for rent, and later, rooms would be subdivided into cubicles containing one or two bunk beds. In this way it was possible for up to 100 people to be crammed into a single house, giving the highest population densities found anywhere in the world.

Hong Kong's housing programme

In 1953 the housing problems in Hong Kong were brought into sharp focus by a disastrous fire, which swept through a squatter camp in Kowloon, and left over 50 000 people homeless.

FIRE IN KOWLOON SQUATTER AREA

OVER 50,000 HOMELESS

FROM OUR CORRESPONDENT

HONGKONG, DEC. 27

A conflagration in the squatter area of Kowloon on Christmas night made homeless more than 50,000 persons and imposed on the authorities unparalleled problems of emergency relief. Three perished in the fire.

Firemen, police, and social welfare officials were engaged all night in rescue and relief work, and both the Governor, Sir Alexander Grantham, and the Colonial Secretary, Mr. R. B. Black, visited the scene. The Government directed all resources towards meeting the emergency, which is one of the gravest of the post-war period. The armed services also gave valuable aid. Preparations for communal feeding, in which the welfare officials have had much experience in previous squatter fires, began at once, and 50,000 were fed yesterday, but the problem of sheltering such a number of victims is serious.

The magnitude of the task of resettlement is shown by the fact that the homeless exceed the total hitherto resettled since the resettlement scheme began, and the monthly average of persons resettled has lately fallen below 800.

GOVERNOR ON KOWLOON DISASTER

KINDNESS OUT OF TRAGEDY

FROM OUR CORRESPONDENT

HONGKONG, DEC. 30

The Governor, Sir Alexander Grantham, reflected widespread feeling in the colony when he told the Legislative Council this afternoon that, while the Kowloon squatters' fire had been a terrible disaster, "the help that has been given by all and sundry has been truly magnificent. Never before in Hongkong have I seen such a display of neighbourliness . . . in a disaster of this magnitude the first essential is to feed people and to care for the sick, and the second essential is to clothe the victims. All this has been done and is being done."

The third essential is housing the homeless, which is the most difficult task in view of the numbers involved and the absence of large buildings. Children, the aged, and the sick are now being accommodated, and the Government intends to rehouse the victims on the existing site as soon as possible. After roads and drains have been provided the Government will erect rows of two-storeyed fireproof houses.

The Governor added that much effort and money were needed for immediate plans, but he was sure that the council would provide the sum, probably £1m., required.

The Governor praised the way in which all the voluntary organizations, Army, Church bodies, and others came into action with speed and intelligence, adding: "Truly out of tragedy has come kindness."

Meanwhile contributions continue to flow in to the relief funds, of which the *South China Morning Post* fund already exceeds $300,000 within three days.

Figure 4.47 Extracts from *The Times* on the Kowloon squatter camp fire, December 1953

Exercise

Read through the extracts from *The Times* of the Kowloon squatter fire which occurred on Christmas Day 1953 (Figure 4.47).

1 What were the three immediate problems which faced the government after the fire? How did the government hope eventually to re-house the squatters?

2 The extract suggests that squatter fires were quite common in Hong Kong. Make a list of the factors which you think would make a squatter settlement a fire risk.

The Kowloon fire started a massive crash programme of re-housing in the colony, which in the 1970s included the development of three new towns and several expanded towns.

Since the mid 1950s over 2 million people have been re-housed in Hong Kong, largely in multi-storey tower blocks (Figure 4.48). Shortage of land has dictated this 'high-rise' solution, and though the provision of space for each family is not generous by European standards, it is low-cost, and most important it is housing that the people can afford. The first blocks were seven storeys high, but the continuing shortage of land and population growth have forced the construction of higher-rise towers of up to 32 storeys, often on land which would be considered too steep for building in the west. Recently, space allocation per family and facilities have improved, and many of the towers contain shops, restaurants and recreational areas.

We have seen that in Malaysia and the Philippines (and in most LDCs), governments have accepted the idea of 'self-help' in the provision of housing. Because squatters have effectively solved their housing problems for

Figure 4.48A Hong Kong – a view from Hong Kong Island to the Kowloon peninsula

Figure 4.48B High rise apartment blocks at the east end of Hong Kong Island. Note the density of housing and traffic in this street scene

themselves, many governments have granted them legal ownership of the land they occupy, and assistance to improve their houses and provide their neighbourhood with essential services. In Hong Kong, the land shortage and huge population growth makes this approach impossible: squatter settlements are too wasteful of land, and consequently when the land they occupy is needed for development, they are cleared, and the squatters are housed in temporary areas. Eventually, it is the aim that all squatter camps will be replaced by high-rise, low-cost housing schemes.

With virtually all suitable building land occupied in Hong Kong Island and the Kowloon peninsula, the government in the last 10 years has turned its attention towards the New Territories, bordering China. The New Territories, which comprise 90% of the area of Hong Kong, are on a 99 year lease from China, which will expire in 1997. Partly for this reason, and partly because the New Territories have been isolated from the rest of the colony by the Nine Dragon Hills, this area has always supported fairly low population densities. Most of the land which is not too steep has been used for rice cultivation, market gardening, and recreation for those living in the more crowded parts of the colony. However, the New Territories represent the only possible space where land for housing can be obtained. The problem of isolation has been largely overcome with the first road tunnel through the hills completed in 1967, and a dual tunnel opened in 1978. The new Hong Kong underground railway will eventually link the New Territories with the rest of the colony.

Housing developments in the New Territories have been based on the new town idea. By this means, new housing is concentrated in suitable areas, and as much of the rural landscape as possible is preserved as open space for recreation. Three new towns are being built: Tsuen Wan, Tuen Mun and Sha Tin (Figure 4.46). All three new towns are built around existing settlements, and a large part of Sha Tin is built on land reclaimed from the sea. The first new town plans were drawn up in 1975, and by 1985 the towns should contain almost 2 million people (Figure 4.49). Tsuen Wan is the largest, with a target population of 900 000, followed by Tuen Mun's 570 000 and Sha Tin's 450 000. In all three new towns 75% of housing units will be owned by the government. In addition to the new towns, three towns have been earmarked for major expansion: Tai Po, Yuen Long and Sheung Shui will undergo a fivefold growth and accommodate 500 000 people between them.

Exercise

1 Hong Kong's solution to its housing problem is very different from that adopted in most LDCs. Write a paragraph describing the differences between Hong Kong's programme and those of the Philippines and Malaysia.

2 Do you think that the Hong Kong approach would work in most other countries in the Third World? The figures below may help you decide.

	Average yearly income per person (dollars)	Population density (km^2)
Hong Kong	4205	4827
Malaysia	1194	51
Philippines	646	161
India	200	208

3 Do you think that Hong Kong's solution is more typical of DCs than most LDCs? Explain your answer.

Figure 4.49 Tsuen Wan new town, in the New Territories of Hong Kong

4 In the first seven storey tower blocks built in Hong Kong, an average of 2.2 m^2 was provided for each person. Since 1970, space allocation per person has increased to 3.2 m^2. How does this compare with the amount of floorspace per person in your home? (Note – if you attempted the exercise on page 46 you will already have information on the floorspace in your home.)

Although Hong Kong's efforts to solve its housing problems have been impressive and largely successful, illegal immigrants and refugees continue to pour into the colony at an alarming rate. In 1978, for example, 80% of Hong Kong's population growth was caused by immigration, and this shows no sign of abating. Unless some control over immigration can be enforced, no immediate end to the housing problem is in sight.

Summary

Today's cities are faced with considerable problems, most of which are caused by rapid growth. Many problems, such as inadequate housing, unemployment and poverty, are common both to Western and Third World cities. What distinguishes Third World cities is not so much their problems, but their size and seriousness. For instance, Birmingham's problems of re-housing are trivial compared with those of Manila or Kuala Lumpur, and Copenhagen's attempts to reduce overcrowding become insignificant when we learn that 200 000 people in Calcutta have no shelter at all. However serious problems such as traffic congestion and urban sprawl may seem to us, the problems which Third World cities face concern the very survival of the people.

One of the features of planning in DCs is that similar problems are approached in different ways. Compare the green belt idea with the wedge and sector solution; urban renewal with urban improvement; and decentralisation in Copenhagen, with centralisation in Randstad. In DCs planners can hope to solve many urban problems; in LDCs this is often not the case, and increasingly the people must rely on self-help. Throughout the Third World, urban dwellers have successfully proved that they can not only house themselves, but also create their own employment. Many governments are now encouraging this spirit of self-help by providing squatter settlements with basic services, supporting sites-and-services schemes, and removing legal obstacles to the squatters' ownership of land. It is this approach which offers the best hope for improving the quality of city life for the people of LDCs.

Further exercises

1 Table 4.6 lists the possible solutions to the problems of slum housing and poverty in Third World cities. Make a copy of the table and alongside each solution write what you think are its advantages and disadvantages. In completing the table you should pay particular attention to factors such as:
a) cost to the government or city authorities
b) the ability of squatters to pay for loans, rents and so on c) whether the solution is a realistic one, given the enormous scale of problems in the Third World.

2 Study Figures 4.50 and 4.51 which show the outer zones of two cities in different parts of the world.
  a Describe four differences between the characteristics of the two areas.
  b Suggest where the people who now live in the area shown in Figure 4.50 originally lived.
  c Why do you think that people moved to the area shown in Figure 4.50?
  d Suggest where the people who now live in the area shown in Figure 4.51 originally lived.
  e Why have the people moved to the area shown in Figure 4.51?

3 Look at the distribution of squatter settlements in four Third World cities (Figure 4.41).
  a Where in the city are the poor people mainly concentrated?
  b List the factors which are likely to have caused this pattern. Would you say that they are mainly 'push' or 'pull' factors? (Refer back to Table 3.6.)
  c Compare the distribution of poor people in Third World cities with the distribution of slum housing in Birmingham (Figure 4.3). Describe the differences, and briefly suggest reasons for them.

4 Compare Hong Kong's new town programme with that of Britain (pages 71–3) under the following headings:
— size of new towns
— speed of construction
— purpose of the new towns.

5 a Of the four 'primary' urban problems shown in Figure 4.52 only one is found to be important in Toronto. Can you say which one?
  b Why do you think that in Toronto and other North American cities, urban

Table 4.6 Solutions to the problems of slum housing and poverty

Solution	Advantages	Disadvantages
Upgrade squatter settlements		
Sites-and-services schemes		
Conventional low-cost housing schemes		
Eviction of squatters and clearance of squatter settlements		

Figure 4.50

Figure 4.51
Contrasting housing areas on the outskirts of two cities

sprawl is not regarded as such a serious problem as in Western Europe?

c Which of the four cities that you studied in the first part of this chapter has faced the most serious problem of replacing old and substandard housing? Can you explain why the housing situation was more severe in this city than the others?

d Which city has been most concerned that continuing decentralisation, resulting in loss of population and jobs, would affect its status or importance?

e By looking at Figure 4.52 and the work you have done in this chapter, fit the correct planning solutions to each of the four cities:

Toronto Copenhagen Birmingham Randstad	green wedges and urban corridors; green belts, new and expanded towns; reconcentration of people and employment in the city; dispersal of employment from the centre of the suburbs;

f While the populations of most Western cities have declined in recent years, the number of households has generally increased. Can you explain this? How has the increase in the number of households caused problems in the cities you have studied?

6 Figure 4.53 shows three simplified city plans: city A has a single centre and is located on the coast or lake shore; city B also has a single centre, but can be approached from any direction; city C comprises four separate settlements, each with its own centre, and linked together by routeways.

a Which plan best describes Copenhagen, Toronto, Randstad and Birmingham? Give your reasons.

b Which plan is most likely to lead to traffic congestion in the city centre? Do the cities with the worst congestion which you have studied in this chapter have this type of plan?

c Which plan is least likely to cause congestion? Explain your choice.

7 Figure 4.54 shows the pattern of population change in the Bradford Metropolitan District between 1971 and 1981.

a Describe the distribution of those areas which gained, and those which lost population during this period. Does this pattern of change follow the trends in

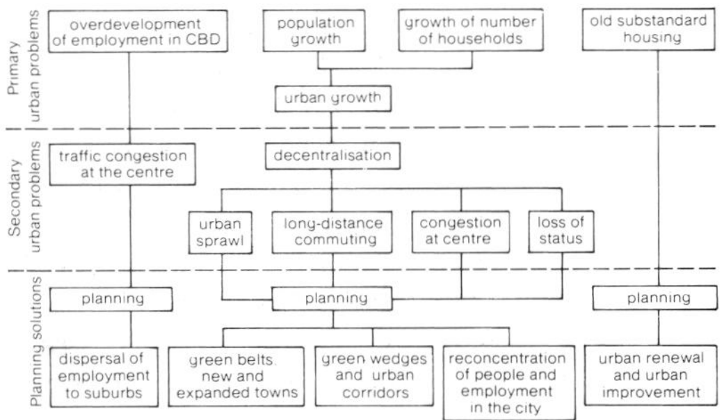

Figure 4.52 Urban growth and planning in Western cities

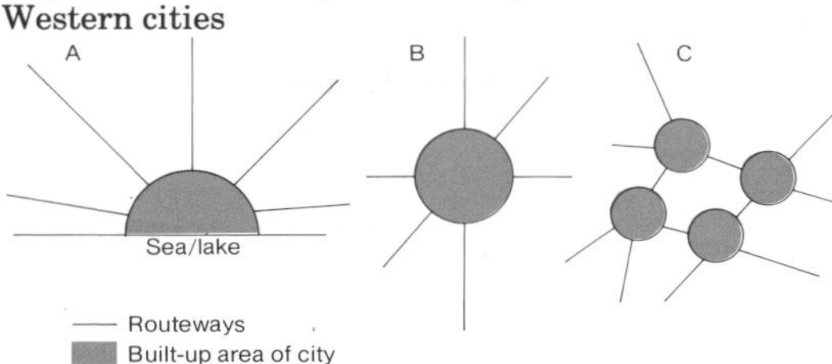

Figure 4.53 Generalised city plans

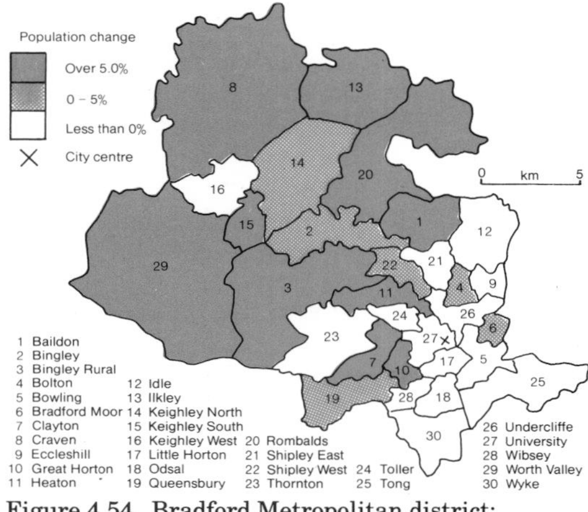

Figure 4.54 Bradford Metropolitan district: population change, 1971–81

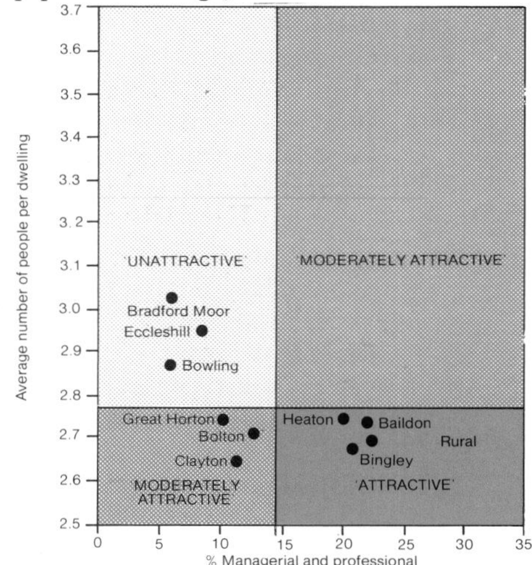

Figure 4.55 Grouping areas of Bradford Metropolitan district according to their attractiveness as places in which to live

other Western cities that you have studied in this chapter?

To explain these changes we could test the idea that the more attractive an area is (eg good housing, low unemployment, nearness to countryside) the more likely it is to increase its population. If we try to examine the truth of an idea like this, we refer to it as testing a *hypothesis*.

b Test this hypothesis by first dividing the 30 areas of the metropolitan district into three groups on the basis of their attractiveness. In this example we are going to measure attractiveness by using two factors: the average number of people per dwelling, and the percentage of the working population who have 'top' jobs (ie professional and managerial). Plot the information in Table 4.7 as a graph (Figure 4.55) and label each area as either 'attractive', 'moderately attractive' or 'unattractive'. The first 10 areas have already been plotted and grouped in Table 4.8.

c Having grouped all 30 areas, construct a map (using the outline in Figure 4.54) to show their distribution by shading the most attractive areas in the darkest tone, and the least attractive in the lightest.

d Compare your map with that of population change 1971–81 (Figure 4.54). How similar are the maps? Write a paragraph and comment on the accuracy of the hypothesis that the more attractive an area is, the greater is its population growth.

Table 4.7 Bradford Metropolitan district 1981

Districts	Average number of people per dwelling	% Professional/ managerial
Baildon	2.75	22
Bingley	2.59	21
Bingley Rural	2.70	22
Bolton	2.70	13
Bowling	2.83	6
Bradford Moor	3.03	6
Clayton	2.65	12
Craven	2.59	16
Eccleshill	2.93	8
Great Horton	2.73	10
Heaton	2.76	20
Idle	2.59	14
Ilkley	2.75	30
Keighley North	2.68	13
Keighley South	2.51	9
Keighley West	2.79	9
Little Horton	2.74	6
Odsal	2.79	12
Queensbury	2.73	11
Rombalds	2.59	35
Shipley East	2.59	9
Shipley West	2.86	22
Thornton	2.67	15
Toller	2.92	11
Tong	3.00	7
Undercliffe	2.90	10
University	3.69	9
Wibsey	2.80	14
Worth Valley	2.72	17
Wyke	2.75	11

Table 4.8 Grouping areas of Bradford according to their attractiveness

Attractive	Moderately attractive	Unattractive
Baildon	Bolton	Bradford Moor
Bingley	Clayton	Bowling
Bingley Rural	Great Horton	Eccleshill
Heaton		

CHECKLIST OF WHAT YOU SHOULD KNOW ABOUT CITIES AND THEIR PROBLEMS

Key ideas	Examples
Housing shortages and poor quality housing are a feature of cities in DCs and LDCs.	■ Shortages of housing are most acute in Third World cities where populations are growing rapidly and there is little money to house people. The result is self-help housing in the form of spontaneous settlements or shanty towns eg Calcutta, Bogota, Manila. ■ Housing shortages in DCs may occur because of smaller families, a larger number of old people, demolition of housing areas in the city and their replacement with offices or industry eg Randstad. ■ Housing in Third World cities often lacks essential amenities such as electricity, pure drinking water, sewage disposal, proper roads.

	■ Older housing in cities such as Birmingham or Copenhagen may lack facilities such as internal baths and WCs. Overcrowding is often a feature of older houses in the inner city.
Various solutions are used to tackle the housing problem.	■ In LDCs the most common solution is to allow the people to build their own housing in squatter settlements. This may be encouraged by supplying the people with building materials, or giving them legal ownership of the land. Government assisted housing includes low-cost schemes eg multi-storey apartments in Hong Kong and Singapore, and more basic 'core' housing. Conditions in shanty towns may be improved by installing essential services like water and electricity, or promoting sites-and-services projects eg Manila, Kuala Lumpur. ■ The problem of housing shortages in many DCs has been solved by decentralisation of the population – moving people to new towns, expanded towns or housing developments in the suburbs eg Randstad, Copenhagen, Birmingham. Substandard housing (slums) has been tackled through slum clearance programmes eg Birmingham, and more recently by improving older housing.
Many cities are unable to provide employment for a large proportion of their citizens.	■ In Third World cities few jobs are available in 'organised' service industries or modern manufacturing. People have to rely on self-help and create their own jobs. ■ In DCs unemployment in the city is often a problem in the inner suburbs where many firms have either closed down or moved out in the last 20 years.
Urban sprawl is a serious problem in cities in DCs.	■ The problem of urban sprawl is the loss of countryside both for agriculture and recreation. The problem is most urgent in small countries like Denmark, the UK and the Netherlands. ■ Solutions to the problem include green belts (UK), green wedges (Copenhagen) and buffer zones (Randstad).
Traffic congestion is a common problem in most large cities.	■ In DCs urban traffic problems may result from: — overdevelopment of office jobs in the CBD so that the transport system becomes overloaded eg Toronto — decentralisation of population faster than jobs, so that long-distance commuting becomes necessary eg Randstad. ■ Solutions take two forms: — move employment from the centre to the suburbs eg Toronto, Copenhagen — improve public transport eg rapid transit systems eg Toronto, Newcastle (see Chapter 6), motorways eg Copenhagen. ■ Note that in Randstad the policy is to encourage people back into the city and cut down long-distance commuting, and in Toronto new housing near the city centre means that many people can walk to work in the CBD.
Poorly developed transport systems are a problem in many Third World cities.	■ The lack of public transport is particularly a problem for the poorest people, living on the edge of the city in shanty towns. It is common for people to walk miles to their work in the city centre each day.

Manufacturing industry

Part 1: Employment and industry in DCs

For any country or region we can group occupations into three sectors. The *primary* sector covers occupations concerned with producing raw materials, such as farming, fishing, forestry, mining and quarrying. The *secondary* sector is mainly manufacturing industry, but also includes electricity generation and building. Finally the *tertiary* sector covers all service activities, such as employment in shops, offices, health care and education, as well as transport and communications.

Exercise

1 Look at the list of materials given in the exercise on page 105. How many different primary industries are represented in the list? Can you name them?

2 Countries differ in the extent to which they rely on each of the three employment sectors. In Chapter 1 we saw that LDCs depend much more heavily on the primary sector than DCs. Look at the information in Figure 5.1 and write a sentence stating a further difference in employment between DCs and LDCs.

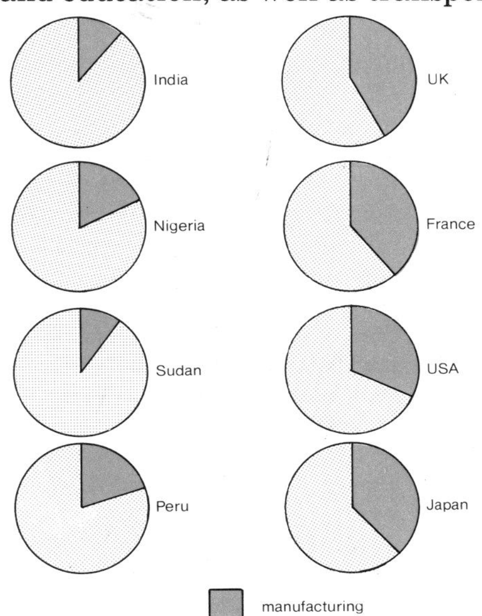

Figure 5.1 Proportion of workforce in manufacturing

It may surprise you to learn that the largest employment sector in most DCs today is not the secondary, but the tertiary sector. This is partly because machinery has steadily replaced labour in most manufacturing industries, and partly because rising living standards have created a demand for more and better services in health care, leisure and education. This points to the fact that the pattern of employment in any country tends to change through time. Take manufacturing in the UK: in 1951 it employed almost half of the workforce; 30 years later it accounted for just over one-third. Figure 5.2 shows in more detail how the employment structure in the UK has changed since the early nineteenth century. The trends are similar to those experienced by other DCs in this period. However, we should be careful not to assume that countries in the Third World today will automatically follow this same trend.

Exercise

1 In 1831 the UK's level of urbanisation was around 40%, which is roughly the same as that of Egypt today. However, although the proportion of urban dwellers was similar, the pattern of employment in the two countries was very different. Study the figures in Table 5.1 and say what the main differences are.

Table 5.1 Employment structure of the UK (1831) and Egypt (1983)

	% Primary	% Secondary	% Tertiary
UK	24.6	40.8	34.6
Egypt	42.5	17.5	40.0

2 When people migrated to the towns and cities in the UK in the nineteenth century, in which sector do you think that most of them found jobs? (Refer back to Chapter 3, page 45, if you are unsure.) How do you think that this compares with modern Egypt and other LDCs? (See Chapter 4, page 89.)

3 From your work in the last chapter, describe the kinds of jobs that people find in the tertiary sector of Third World cities.

4 Does the evidence in Figure 5.2 and Table 5.1 suggest that employment changes in LDCs might be taking a different path to those of DCs over the last 150 years? Justify your answer in a few sentences.

5 Refer to Figure 5.2 and then copy out the following paragraph, inserting the terms primary, secondary or tertiary in the appropriate spaces.
'At the start of the nineteenth century most of the UK's working population was engaged in the ________ sector, and the vast majority worked in agriculture. Yet by 1821 ________ activities had taken over as the leading sector, and the ________ sector continued its decline until the present day. Until 1861, most of the growth of the secondary sector was at the expense of the ________ sector, as massive numbers of people left agriculture to work in manufacturing industries in towns and cities. Between 1861 and 1891 the importance of the secondary sector remained more or less unchanged, but while ________ activities continued to decline, the ________ sector grew rapidly. Today this sector employs over 60% of the workforce, and this proportion seems certain to increase in future. Meanwhile there has been a steep downturn in the ________ sector in the last 20 years – a trend which is likely to continue as manufacturing industry becomes increasingly automated.'

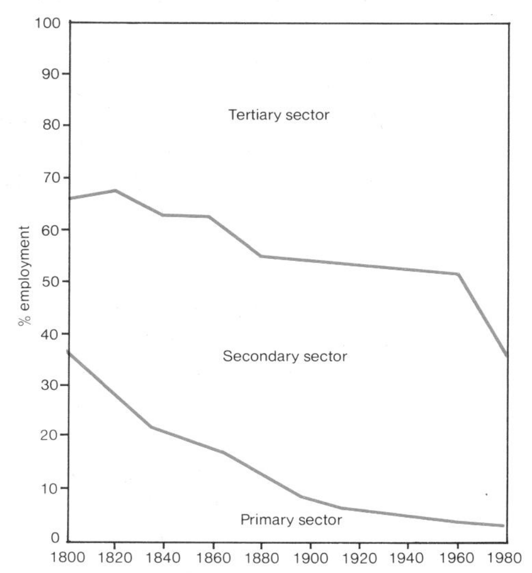

Figure 5.2 Changing UK occupational structure, 1800–1980

The location of manufacturing industry

Manufacturing industries are concerned with two activities:

1 *processing* raw materials to produce finished or semi-finished products eg the smelting of iron ore to produce iron and steel

2 *assembling* manufactured items to produce finished goods eg assembling electronic components to produce computers or video recorders.

Exercise

1 Group the following industries into processing and assembly types:
brick making, oil refining, motor vehicle manufacture, shipbuilding, wood pulp manufacture, cheese making, sugar beet refining, aircraft manufacture.

2 The manufacture of a finished product from raw materials often involves an intermediate stage, with the production of refined or semi-finished materials. Re-order the information in Table 5.2 to show the links between raw materials, semi-finished and finished products in the seven industries. An example – timber/woodpulp/paper – is given in the table.

Table 5.2

Raw material	Semi-finished product	Finished product
timber ⟶	wood pulp ⟶	paper
iron ore	molasses	cloth
sugar cane	ethylene	aluminium foil
limestone	alumina	steel sheet
crude oil	pig iron	concrete
cotton	cement	paint
bauxite	yarn	sugar

In choosing where to locate an industry, the decision-maker's main consideration is the need to make a profit. *Profit* is the difference between income and costs (Figure 5.3); as costs of materials, labour and energy often vary from place to place, they often influence location decisions.

Transport costs cover the cost of bringing materials to the factory, and of taking the finished products to market. These two elements of transport costs are known as *collection* and *distribution* costs respectively. If transport costs are very high for an industry, as for example in oil refining and brick making, a location may be chosen which will reduce the cost of transport to a minimum. The actual location chosen will depend on the level of collection and distribution costs: if collection costs are higher, it will make sense to locate at the source of materials, and such an industry is said to be *material-oriented*; on the other hand, where distribution costs are higher, a location at the market would give higher profits, and the industry would be *market-oriented* (Figure 5.4).

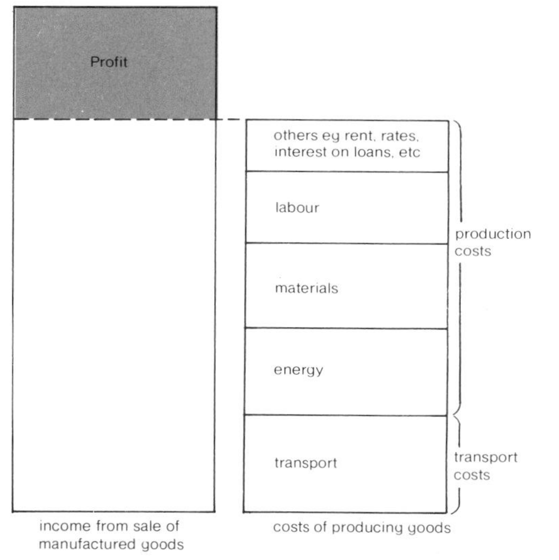

Figure 5.3 Income, costs and profit in manufacturing industry

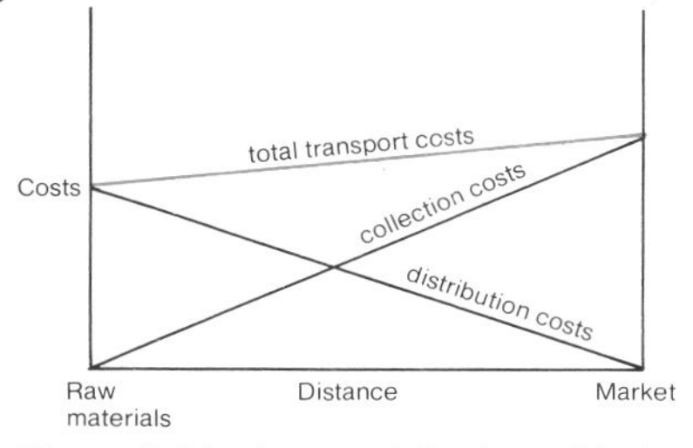

Figure 5.4A A material-oriented industry

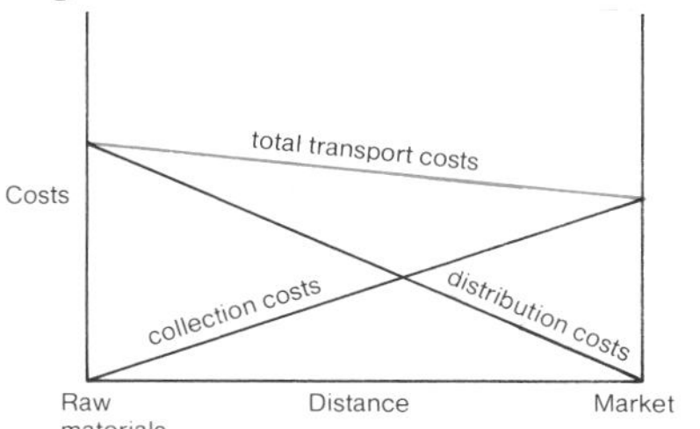

Figure 5.4B A market-oriented industry

The steel industry is a good example of a material-oriented industry. The iron ore smelted in blast furnaces rarely contains more than 65% of iron, and sometimes the proportion may be as low as 30%. This means that the raw material for steel making undergoes a considerable weight loss in the manufacturing process. If the iron ore is transported any distance then the steel industry will be paying for the transport of large quantities of waste material and its collection costs will be very high. In contrast, finished steel is 100% pure, and the cost of distributing it to the markets will be much lower. In this example, where collection costs exceed distribution costs, a location at the source of iron ore would be most logical.

There are a few manufacturing industries where the finished product has greater weight or bulk than the materials. In the brewing and soft drinks industry, and in the making of ready-mixed concrete, this occurs because water (which is available virtually everywhere) is added to the product. Clearly in this situation distribution costs will exceed collection costs, and the industries will be market-oriented.

Exercise

1 We have seen that an industry can increase its profits by reducing its costs. Can you suggest another way in which profits may be increased?

2 Table 5.3 shows collection and distribution costs for a manufacturing industry. Complete the calculations in the table and draw a graph like those in Figure 5.4. Where should this industry locate?

3 Bearing in mind the effect of collection and distribution costs on the location of industry, try to explain the following statements.
  a Industries processing raw materials are more likely to be material-oriented than those processing semi-finished materials.
  b Assembly industries such as electronics and motor vehicles may be little affected by either collection or distribution costs.

4 A simple measurement which tells us whether an industry is likely to be material- or market-oriented, is the *material index*. This compares the weight of a finished, manufactured item, with the weight of the materials needed to produce it.

$$\text{Material index} = \frac{\text{weight of materials*}}{\text{weight of finished product}}$$

(* Materials which are assumed to be available everywhere, like water or sand, are excluded from the calculation.)

If the index is more than 1, it tells us that the materials weigh more than the finished product. As they should therefore be more expensive to transport than the finished product, the industry should be material-oriented. An index of less than 1 means that the finished product is heavier than the materials, and that the industry should locate at the market.
Calculate the material index for the zinc smelting industry from the information given in Table 5.4. Would you expect the industry to be material- or market-oriented? Explain your conclusion.

Table 5.3 Collection and distribution costs for a manufacturing industry

Distance from raw materials to market km	Collection costs £ per tonne	Distribution costs £ per tonne	Total costs £ per tonne
0	0	50	50
10	10	45	55
20	20	40	60
30	30	35	65
40	40	30	?
50	50	25	?
60	60	20	?
70	70	15	?
80	80	10	?
90	90	5	?
100	100	0	?

Table 5.4 Weight of materials and finished product: zinc smelting industry

Materials	Weight (tonnes)
Zinc concentrate	1.00
Coal	1.45
Fireclay	0.10
TOTAL	2.55
Finished product Slab zinc	0.54

5 Sugar refining using sugar beet has a high material index (around 8), for the sugar beet undergoes considerable weight loss in the manufacturing process.
  a Where would you expect to find the sugar beet factories located?
  b Compare the distribution of sugar beet growing areas (Figure 5.5A) with the distribution of sugar refineries (Figure 5.5B). One method of doing this would be to copy Figure 5.5B onto tracing paper, draw circles with a 25 km radius around each refinery, and place your tracing as an overlay on Figure 5.5A. Is the distribution of refining what you would have expected from the material index?

Figure 5.5A Distribution of sugar beet growing areas in England and Wales

Figure 5.5B Distribution of sugar beet refineries in England and Wales

Figure 5.6 A sugar refinery near Peterborough, Cambridgeshire. This is one of the 13 refineries operated by British Sugar, all of which are located in the main beet growing areas of the UK

Manufacturing industries in the UK

Oil refining

Crude oil is a mixture of many different kinds of liquid. Oil refining involves the separation of crude oil into its different parts or *fractions*, by the process of distillation. In a refinery, crude oil is distilled in a tall steel tower known as a fractionating column (Figure 5.7); the fractions which rise highest in the column are light fractions and include gasoline and naphtha, and those that condense at lower levels are heavy fractions, such as fuel oil and bitumen. A further process carried out at the refinery is 'cracking', where some of the heavier fractions are broken up by applying great heat, and converted into lighter fractions, particularly gasoline, for which there is a greater demand.

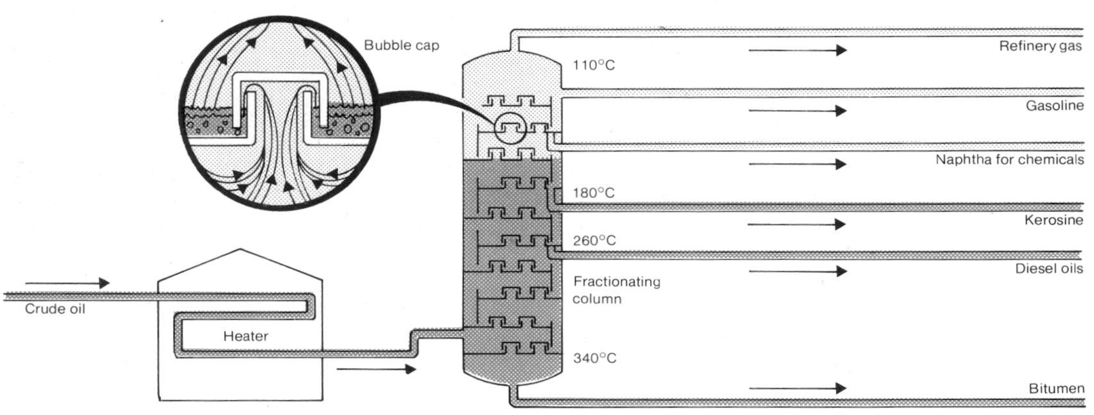

Figure 5.7 The oil refining process

Distribution of oil refining

Without exception, all of the UK's major oil refineries are located on or near the coast (Figure 5.8), where crude oil can be imported cheaply by tanker. However, although the raw material of refining has pulled the industry to the coast, access to markets is the most important influence, and most refineries are designed to serve particular regions. Thus Shell's Stanlow refinery serves north west England, Grangemouth (BP) serves most of Scotland, and Fawley (Esso) much of London and the South East.

Crude oil is transported by tanker and by pipeline, though the only refineries linked directly to oilfields by pipeline are at Grangemouth and Teesside. The oil tankers which transport crude oil to the refineries are huge vessels, up to 250 000 tonnes in the UK, and vessels of this size require special deepwater

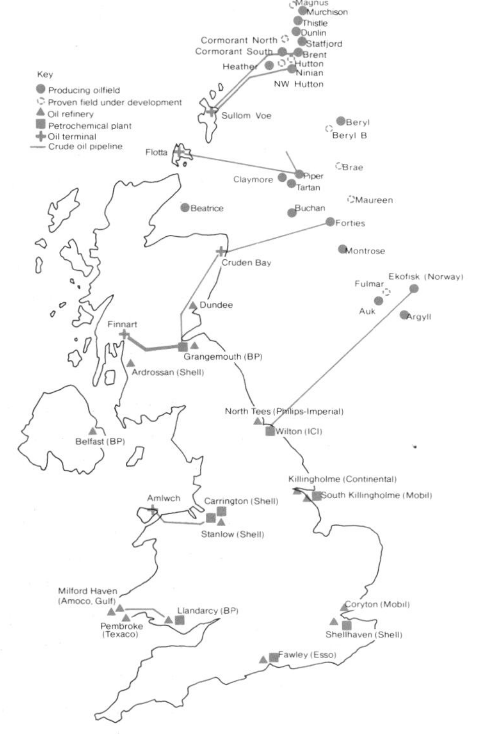

Figure 5.8 The distribution of the UK's oil and petrochemical industries

terminals to off-load their cargo. Modern refineries are sited therefore, either at deepwater locations (eg Milford Haven, Fawley) or are linked by pipeline to deepwater terminals (eg Stanlow, Figure 5.9).

Figure 5.9A Shell's oil refinery at Stanlow, Cheshire

Figure 5.9B BP's oil refinery at Grangemouth, Scotland. Grangemouth primarily serves the Scottish market. Can you name the estuary in the background and say what the advantages of the Grangemouth site are from the photograph?

Exercise

1 Figure 5.10 shows how oil tankers have increased massively in size in the last 90 years. This is because it is cheaper to transport each tonne of oil in larger ships. For example, a 100 000 tonne tanker burns only 40% more fuel than a 50 000 tonner. These savings are known as *economies of scale*. Make a list of other savings that make larger ships cheaper to operate than smaller ones.

2 Can you think of any disadvantages associated with the use of very large oil tankers?

3 Study Figure 5.8 and name the three refineries linked to deepwater terminals by overland pipeline. These refineries were first built when tankers were much smaller than today. Can you suggest any reasons why these refineries were not relocated at the deepwater terminals? (Refer back to Chapter 1, page 17 and the idea of industrial inertia.)

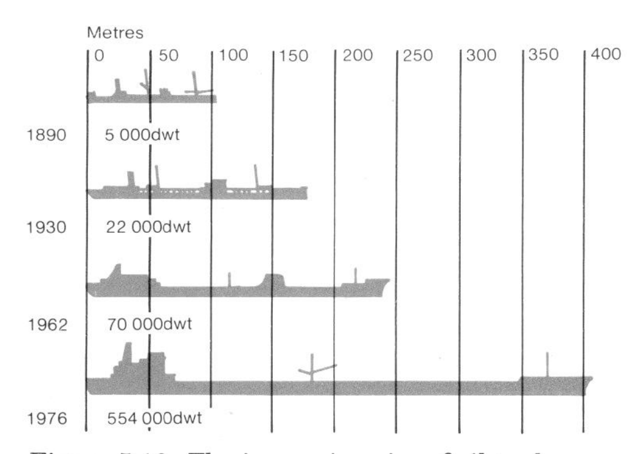

Figure 5.10 The increasing size of oil tankers

Although most refineries are located close to major markets, Milford Haven in west Wales is by any standards, rather isolated. In spite of this by the early 1980s it had four major refineries with a combined capacity greater than any other region except the South East. The attraction of Milford Haven is its superb deepwater anchorage, which means that it can handle tankers of 250 000 tonnes. It is also a shorter haul to Milford Haven from the Middle East oilfields, than to any other refinery complex in the UK, and Milford Haven has large areas of cheap flat land, which the industry needs for refinery plant and storage.

Table 5.5 UK oil refining and regional populations 1981

	Population (millions)		Refinery output (million tonnes)
South East	16.893	Fawley	14.0
		Kent†	10.4
		Coryton	9.5
		Shellhaven	8.5
North West	6.45	Stanlow	12.2
Scotland	5.167	Grangemouth	8.8
Yorks and Humberside	4.878	South Killingholme	9.4
		Killingholme	6.0
North	3.087	Teesport*	5.2
		North Tees	5.0
Wales	2.777	Pembroke	9.1
		Milford Haven (Esso)	8.5*
		Llandarcy	5.5
		Milford Haven (Gulf)	5.2
		Milford Haven (Amoco)	5.0
Northern Ireland	0.764	Belfast	1.5
		(† closed 1983 * closed 1985)	

Exercise

1 Use the information in Table 5.5 to draw a scatter graph to illustrate the statement that the oil refining industry is essentially market-oriented. Population should be on the horizontal (x) axis, and refinery output on the vertical (y) axis.

2 On your scatter graph, draw in what you think is the best-fit trend line giving an equal scatter of points on either side of the line. Which region shows the greatest divergence from the trend line? Can you suggest why this is so?

Fawley oil refinery

Fawley, located on Southampton Water, is the largest refinery in the UK, and the centre of Esso's refining operations. Although there was a small refinery on the site as early as 1921, the modern refinery dates from 1951. The location of Fawley has a number of advantages.

1 The site is extensive and flat, covering in all over 1300 hectares.

2 There is a deep and sheltered anchorage in Southampton Water which can accommodate tankers of up to 150 000 tonnes.

3 Its coastal location makes it easy to distribute refined products by tanker to other regions of the UK and to the continent.

4 Water can be taken from the estuary for cooling required in the refining process.

5 It is close to the major markets for oil products in the UK, in London and the South East.

Petrochemical manufacture at Fawley

Closely associated with the rapid growth of oil refining since 1945, has been the development of an entirely new manufacturing industry – petrochemicals. Refined oil products, known as *feedstocks*, provide the basic materials for the manufacture of a wide range of products, including plastics, paints, fertilizers, synthetic fibres and cosmetics.

In 1958 Esso built its first petrochemical plant at Fawley, adjacent to the refinery. Naphtha and gas oil from the refinery are vaporised at high temperatures and broken down or cracked to form ethylene, propylene, butylene and other chemicals essential for the petrochemical industry. The petrochemical industry is therefore *material-oriented*, and is found concentrated around the major oil refineries (Figure 5.8). At Fawley (as well as other locations such as Stanlow and Teesside) a large industrial complex has developed around the refinery. Apart from Esso's own petrochemical activities, the Esso refinery supplies a number of other chemical companies on nearby sites, such as Monsanto, Hythe Chemicals, Enoxy Chemical and the International Synthetic Rubber Company. Also tied to the complex are the power stations at Fawley and Marchwood which are oil-fired, while Air Products supplies industrial gases to the various industries, and Re-Chem International processes chemical waste from the petrochemical plants (Figure 5.11).

By clustering together, linked industries can reduce their costs: clearly transport costs will be lowered, contact between producer and consumer is made easier, and many other costs, such as energy, roads and water supply can be shared. This concentration of related or linked industries arises because of these advantages or *external economies*. (See also Figure 5.12.)

Exercise

1. Figure 5.9 shows the Stanlow oil refinery and petrochemical complex in north west England. From the photograph, briefly describe the main features of the site and explain their advantages to refining and petrochemical activities.

2. Use an atlas to find the name of the estuary shown on the photograph. In which large industrial city does the canal on the photograph terminate?

3. Name the location of the deepwater terminal which supplies the complex with crude oil (Figure 5.8).

4. Can you suggest why there are few housing areas located close to the complex?

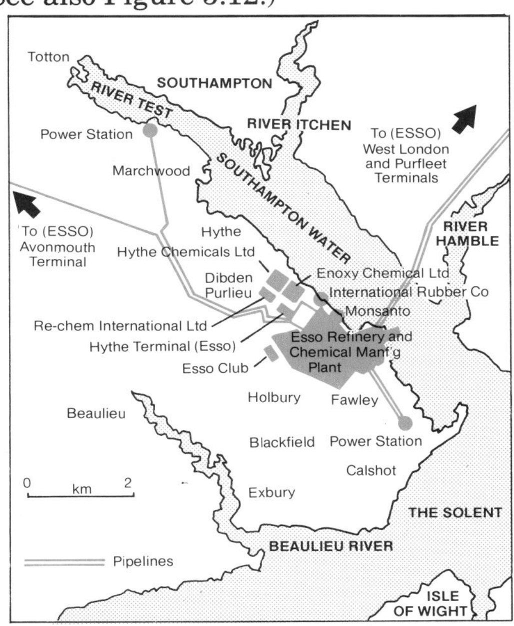

Figure 5.11 Location of the Fawley complex

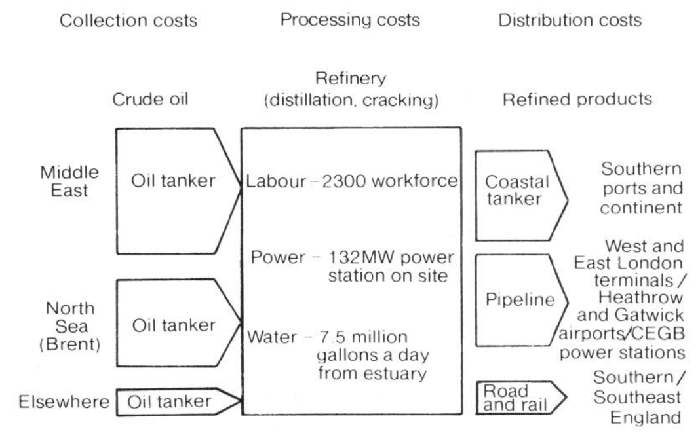

Figure 5.12A Fawley oil refinery: costs

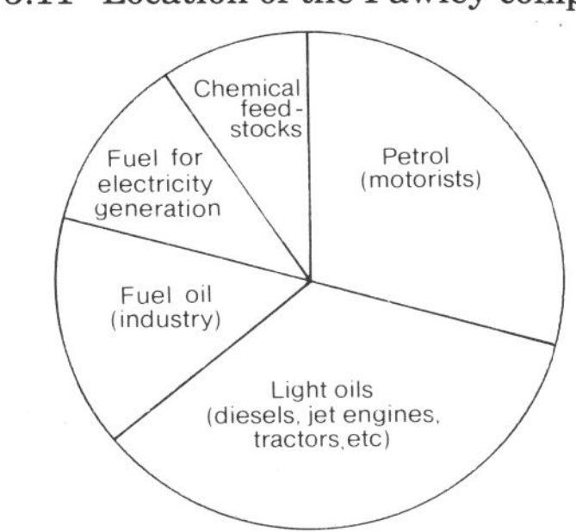

Figure 5.12B Markets for Fawley's refined oil products

Motor vehicles

This is one of the UK's leading manufacturing industries: it directly employs nearly 470 000 people, and provides indirect employment in the manufacture of components for more than twice this number. The industry is essentially an *assembly* industry, where hundreds of components supplied by different manufacturers are brought together for assembly at a plant such as Longbridge in Birmingham (BL) or Dagenham in Essex (Ford). The modern vehicle industry is highly automated, and the use of robots in the assembly stage is increasing rapidly. For instance, more than 500 robots are now used in European Ford plants, and by the end of 1985 this will have increased to 1200. This calls for massive investment – in 1980 Ford invested £205 million at Halewood (Merseyside) to produce the new Escort model. The use of robots gives the largest manufacturers, such as Nissan, Ford (Europe), Renault and Volkswagen, an advantage over smaller producers such as BL and Talbot.

The development of the motor industry in the UK

The UK motor industry developed in the late nineteenth and early twentieth century in small workshops concentrated in the West Midlands and South East. Many of the firms had originally specialised in the manufacture of related products, such as horse-drawn carriages and bicycles, where many of the skills were similar to those required in the motor industry. The West Midlands and South East had a number of advantages for the industry: both had a strong tradition of engineering, and both were well placed in relation to the main market for motor vehicles (in southern Britain). The West Midlands in particular had a great concentration of metal working and engineering industries: steel and non-ferrous metal producers, foundries, metal shaping and metal stamping workshops, and assembly industries swarmed together in the Black Country between Birmingham and Wolverhampton, and were able to provide the components and the skilled workforce for the new motor industry. This clustering of related industries reduced transport costs and the risk of delays and disruption on assembly lines, and brought important savings or external economies to the motor industry.

Exercise

By the early 1960s, the two traditional regions for motor vehicle manufacture dominated the industry, with major assembly plants at Birmingham, Coventry (2), Oxford, Luton and Dagenham. Look at the distribution in 1981 (Figure 5.13). Describe the pattern and identify any changes which have occurred in the last 20 years or so.

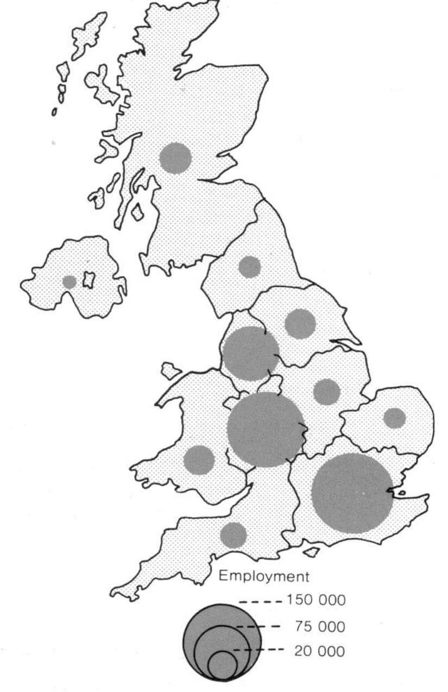

Figure 5.13 UK motor vehicle industry, 1981

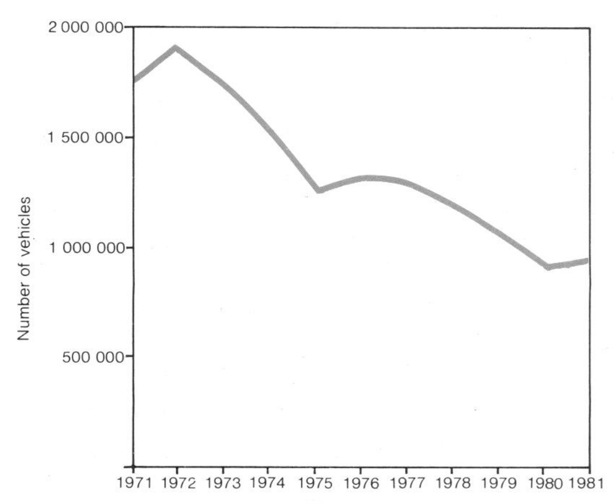

Figure 5.14 UK car production, 1971–81

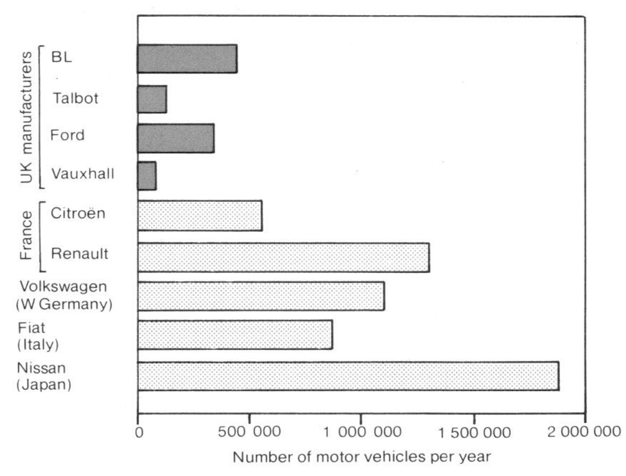

Figure 5.15 UK's leading manufacturers compared with some foreign manufacturers

The decline of the UK motor industry

Until the early 1970s the motor industry was the most prosperous manufacturing industry in the UK: today the industry is in decline. In 1972 the UK ranked as the fifth largest producer of motor vehicles in the world; by 1981 it had slipped to eighth place, but more significantly the output of vehicles had fallen by more than half in this period (Figure 5.14). Today the entire UK output of vehicles is less than one million a year. The main cause of decline has been competition from more efficient foreign manufacturers, particularly Japan, West Germany and France. For example, in 1981 a typical Japanese factory produced 30 cars per worker per year, compared with 15 in West Germany, and just 7 in the UK!

Exercise

1 Figure 5.15 suggests another reason for the decline of the UK motor industry and BL in particular. Can you say what it is? (You may want to refer back to the first paragraph in this section.)

2 Compare Figures 5.15 and 5.16 and name the car manufacturing companies which have a larger output of vehicles than the whole of the UK's.

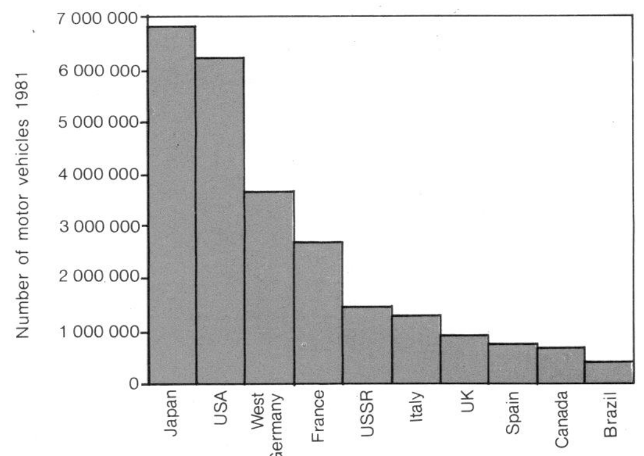

Figure 5.16 World's leading motor vehicle manufacturing nations

The importance of an industry in a region can be measured by comparing the % of the regional workforce employed in that industry, with the overall national %. This measure is the *location quotient* (LQ).

ie $$LQ = \frac{\text{regional \% in industry A}}{\text{national \% in industry A}}$$

Example

In Table 5.6 the location quotient for the motor vehicle industry in Scotland is 0.87%/1.8% = 0.48. As the location quotient is less than one, this tells us that the motor industry is less important in Scotland than it is in the UK as a whole.

Exercise

1 What does a location quotient of a) more than 1 and b) 1, tell you?

2 Calculate the location quotients for the regions in Table 5.6

3 Which regions have above average concentrations of the motor industry?

4 Which region has the greatest dependence on the motor industry? How great is its dependence compared with the average?

Table 5.6 Employment in the UK motor vehicle industry

	% Total workforce
UK	1.8
North	0.62
Yorkshire and Humberside	0.86
East Midlands	0.90
East Anglia	1.07
South East	1.68
South West	0.72
West Midlands	6.04
North West	2.38
Wales	1.90
Scotland	0.87
Northern Ireland	0.37

Specialisation by a region in a particular industry can prove to be a weakness if that industry declines. With few prospects of alternative jobs in other activities, high unemployment can result. The West Midlands is an example of a region which is overdependent on a single industry – motor vehicles and its associated metal and engineering trades. We have already described how the motor vehicle industry has declined in the last few years; with the fortunes of the West Midlands so heavily dependent on this industry, it is not surprising that this region today has one of the highest levels of unemployment in the UK (Figure 5.17).

Exercise

Using the information in Figure 5.17, which region has suffered the greatest decline in the unemployment league table 1970–82? How have the other regions where motor vehicles manufacturing is important fared?

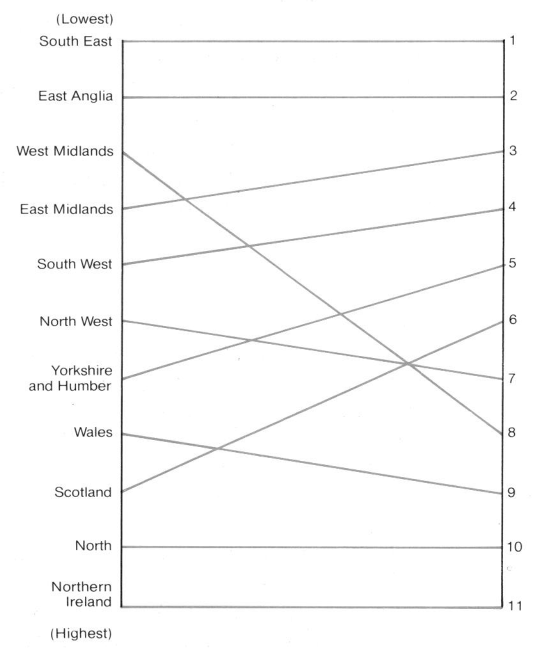

Figure 5.17 (*right*) Unemployment in the UK, by region, 1970–82

The Ford Motor Company

Ford is a large, US owned company, with factories in several European countries, including the UK. In Europe it employs 130 000 people, of whom 60 000 are in the UK, and produces around 1.4 million vehicles a year in plants in West Germany, Belgium, Spain and the UK (Figure 5.18).

The first Ford factory in the UK was a converted carriage works at Trafford Park in Manchester, which was opened in 1911. As demand grew, there was a need for a larger factory to serve the European market. In 1924 Dagenham in Essex was chosen as the location of the new factory. The site, on the north side

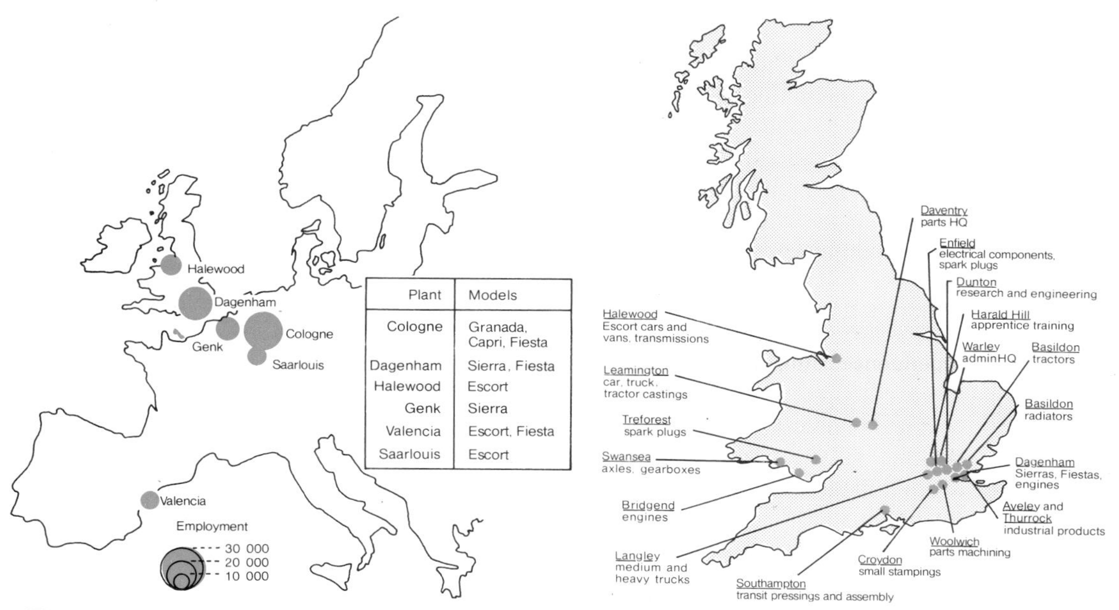

Plant	Models
Cologne	Granada, Capri, Fiesta
Dagenham	Sierra, Fiesta
Halewood	Escort
Genk	Sierra
Valencia	Escort, Fiesta
Saarlouis	Escort

Figure 5.18 Ford's car assembly plants in Europe

Figure 5.19 Ford's locations in the UK

of the Thames estuary, was flat and extensive, permitting the layout of long assembly lines and allowing plenty of room for future expansion. Its situation gave it excellent links to European ports for export, and finally there was a large supply of labour on a vast new housing estate nearby. The factory was completed in 1931, with is own blast furnace, foundry, wharf and power station. Today the plant covers nearly 4 km^2, employs 23 000 people, and has a capacity to produce 1000 cars a day. Although there are Ford plants at 18 other locations in the UK (Figure 5.19), Dagenham is by far the largest employer.

Exercise

1 Figure 5.19 shows the distribution of Ford's operations in the UK. Based on this information, write a paragraph which would explain why Ford was reluctant to locate on Merseyside. In terms of making the highest profit, where do you think Ford would have preferred to locate?

2 Using the air photograph (Figure 5.20) make a sketch map of the Dagenham site, and add the following labels: blast furnace, wharf ($\frac{1}{2}$ km long), River Thames, power station, assembly areas, local authority housing estates (for labour), flat site (essential for layout of a modern assembly plant).

Figure 5.20 Ford's Dagenham assembly plant, on the north bank of the Thames estuary

Ford's Halewood plant on Merseyside is its other major assembly plant in the UK. Halewood was opened in 1963 and, unlike Dagenham, is located outside the traditional regions of motor manufacture. In the early 1960s Ford was looking to expand its UK operations, preferably in the South East or West Midlands. However, government policy meant that the company had to locate its new plant in an *assisted area* (Figure 5.22) where unemployment was high, and where there had been a decline in traditional industries. Ford chose Merseyside where unemployment was nearly 30 000, and where employment in the docks and port industries had fallen appreciably. (Vauxhall and BL also built new plants on Merseyside at about the same time.) The Halewood site, like Dagenham, is extensive and flat, and adjacent to a large estuary. It is well served by road, rail, air and sea communications. The plant employs 13 000 people, making Ford the largest private employer on Merseyside, and like its sister plant in Saarlouis (West Germany) it has a capacity to produce 1000 Escorts a day.

High technology industries

Electrical engineering employs nearly 630 000 people in the UK; that amounts to more than twice the number employed in the mining and quarrying industry, motor vehicles and textiles, and six times the number employed in the iron and steel industry. Within this sector is the fast growing electronics industry, based on advanced technology, and the manufacture of computers, microchips, microprocessors, telecommunications equipment and so on. These are the so-called 'high tech' industries.

The initial centre of high tech industries was Silicon Valley in the USA, in the Palo Alto–Santa Clara–San Jose area, south of San Francisco Bay in California, where the first factory was set up in 1958. Silicon Valley remains the leading centre of high tech in the USA, although in the last 10 years it has been challenged by a new concentration in Colorado in the Boulder–Denver–Colorado Springs area. In the UK two centres of high tech industries stand out: the 'Western Corridor' following the route of the M4 between West London and Bristol, and the central lowlands of Scotland ('Silicon Glen'), with a particularly strong concentration in Glenrothes in Fife. Many cities have their own 'silicon cells' eg Birmingham at Five Ways. Can you think of one in a large city near you?

The high tech industries make items of low bulk and high cost, and thus transport costs are not important when choosing a location. Industries for which transport costs are of little significance are termed *footloose*. However, this does not mean, as we shall see later, that the high tech industries are free to locate anywhere.

The Western Corridor

The Western Corridor (Figure 5.21) has proved the most attractive area for high tech industries in the UK, and indeed the Thames Valley in Berkshire has been described as the UK's answer to Silicon Valley! The triangle formed by the towns of Reading, Bracknell and Wokingham is at the centre of this new industrial zone.

There are several reasons why high tech has become so important in this region.

1. The M4 gives good access to the UK's traditional electronics industry in the London–Slough area, and can draw skilled workers from a wide region. The M4 also gives easy access between firms, which is important in the assembly of complex equipment.

2. Closeness to Heathrow Airport: Heathrow is a major international airport and the high value products of high tech can easily be transported by air to markets throughout the world. Many American companies, such as Hewlett-Packard

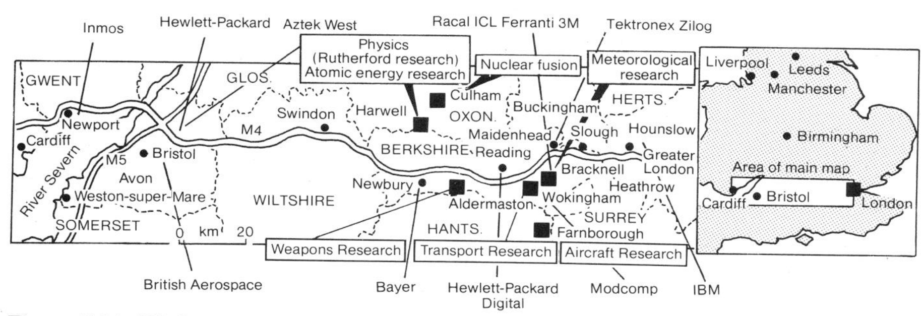

Figure 5.21 'High tech' industries along the Western Corridor

and Honeywell, established their European bases in the Western Corridor to be near Heathrow, which has constant flights to North America (Figure 6.50).

3 A pool of labour, skilled in electronics, had already been established in the region in the 1950s by British companies such as Ferranti and ICL. With the invention of microprocessors based on silicon chips in the early 1970s, the only people with the skills to develop them in the UK were electronics engineers in mini-computers, who were already concentrated along the M4.

4 Many big government labs in the area act as a magnet for high tech businesses. There is the Harwell nuclear research establishment, the Rutherford physics lab, the Culham fusion research centre, the nuclear weapons lab at Aldermaston, and several others. These labs have special skills, buy a great deal of scientific equipment, and most importantly create new ideas which can be developed commercially by the nearby high tech industries.

5 The area is attractive to its highly skilled workforce. There are good schools, pleasant countryside, pubs, restaurants and golf courses, and there is easy access to London's West End with its shops and entertainments.

The high tech industries are continuing to expand in the region, moving westwards along the line of the motorway: a new industrial estate has opened in Reading, and sites are being developed at Swindon, Bristol and as far west as Weston-super-Mare. A large technology park – Aztek West – has been built at the M4–M5 interchange outside Bristol: the skills of Bristol workers trained as aerospace engineers with British Aerospace and Rolls Royce, who can make high precison products, are an additional advantage at this western end of the M4.

Exercise

1 Heathrow airport is a major reason why the high tech business has developed in the Western Corridor. Figure 6.50 shows the origin and destination of regular airline flights from Heathrow. Study the diagram, and then answer the following questions.
   a To which US and Canadian cities are there direct flights from Heathrow?
   b Use an atlas to draw a sketch map showing the location of these cities, and calculate the percentage of foreign destinations which are in North America.
   c Does this information confirm the statement that Heathrow has good connections with North America? Make a list of the USA's 15 largest cities (Figure 3.15) and find out to which ones there are direct flights from Heathrow.

2 Some older industrial cities in the UK, such as Manchester, Liverpool and Newcastle, have not attracted many high tech industries. Can you think of any reasons why these cities have proved unattractive? (Refer back to Chapters 3 and 4.)

Glenrothes – 'the micro-chip capital of Britain'

You may be surprised to learn that today more people are employed in high tech industries in Scotland than in the traditional industries like shipbuilding and steel making. The success of central Scotland in attracting electronics industries since the 1960s has earned it the title of 'Silicon Glen'. Many of the firms which have established branches in the region are foreign owned, and there has been an especially large investment by American companies.

Exercise

1 Complete the calculations in Table 5.7, and compile a second table with the towns arranged in order of their dependence on the electronics industry (ie the smaller the population per firm, the greater the dependence).

2 What do the first four towns in your revised table have in common? (Look back at Figure 4.9 if you are unsure.)

Table 5.7 The electronics industry in Scotland 1983

	Number of firms	Population	Population per firm
Glasgow	24	762228	31760
Glenrothes	22	32700	?
Livingston	14	38594	?
Aberdeen	12	190200	15850
East Kilbride	12	70259	?
Edinburgh	10	419187	?
Dundee	7	174746	?
Cumbernauld	6	47702	7950
Irvine	2	32852	?

3 These towns have an advantage over some of the older, larger towns in Table 5.7 when it comes to attracting new industry. Study Figures 5.22 and 4.9, and describe in a sentence or two what this advantage is.

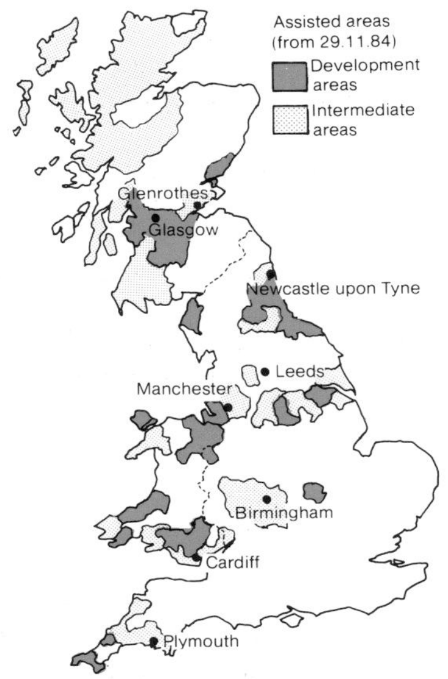

Figure 5.22 Assisted areas in Britain

Glenrothes is a new town in an assisted (intermediate) area. Grants are available for manufacturing and service industries from central Government. However, they are no longer obtainable automatically as they were before 1985. Glenrothes is also eligible for grants from the EEC's regional fund. Only the development areas now receive grants automatically.

Regional development grants

Buildings: manufacturing and some services can qualify for a grant of 15% of the cost of the new buildings.

Plant and machinery: a similar grant of up to 15% of the cost of new plant and machinery is available.

Loans: the Glenrothes Development Corporation gives loans on the cost of premises at preferential rates.

Rent free: rent free periods of up to two years can be offered in certain circumstances.

Glenrothes Development Corporation builds factories and workshops ahead of requirement. This practice ensures that there is normally a substantial amount of factory space available for incoming companies.

Premises from 93m² upwards and smaller workshops are available. The basic design of all units is sufficiently flexible to cater for a developer's specific needs, either as purchaser or tenant. Leases are negotiable for periods of up to 40 years with breaks for review of rent every five years.

Glenrothes has one of the best strike-free records in the UK – no stoppages have commanded national newspaper attention for fully 15 years – and has been commended in the British Parliament as an outstanding example of good industrial relations in Western Europe.

Many long-established companies in the town state that they have lost no production time due to disputes.

The high level of education within the town combined with good standards of housing, shopping, social services and leisure amenities give Glenrothes workers a quality of life they appreciate and are keen to sustain through steady employment.

Management recruitment: Glenrothes is situated within one hour's drive of five universities that yield a continuous flow of highly qualified personnel.

The Corporation or local Employment Service can provide information about the skills and availability of labour, as well as prevailing wage rates. Publicity for vacancies, practical assistance with recruitment and interviewing facilities are available free to incoming employers.

There is a good labour supply. A population approaching 250 000 lives within 30 minutes' drive-to-work distance and the work force within the new town is exceptional in that more than 70% are professionally qualified or skilled personnel.

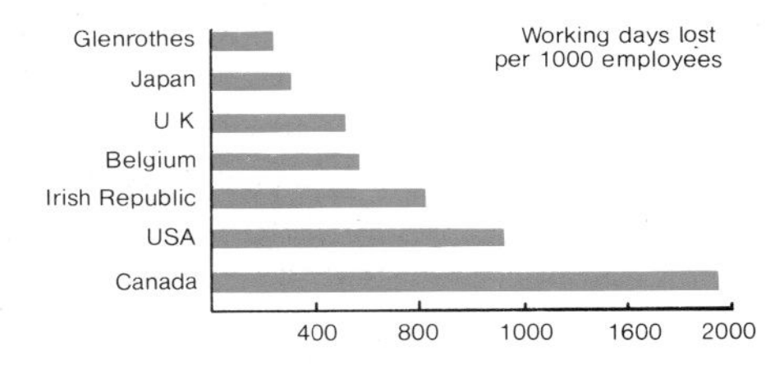

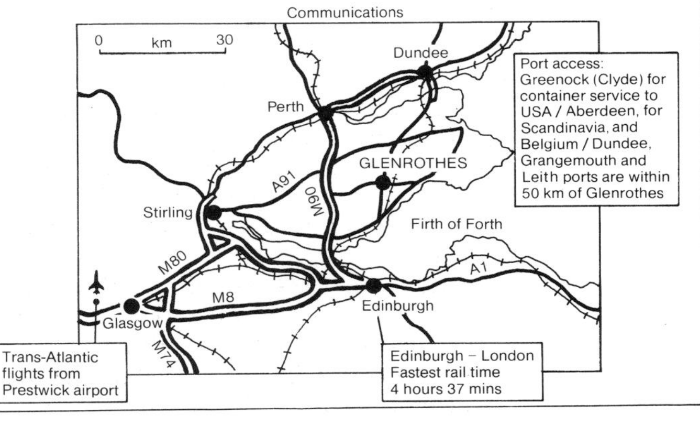

Figure 5.23 Glenrothes new town

The undisputed centre of Silicon Glen is Glenrothes new town in Fife (Figures 5.23 and 5.24). In 1983 the town had almost 20% of its workforce engaged in electrical engineering, the majority in high tech industries manufacturing such items as microcomputers, microprocessors, microcircuits, precison instruments and telecommunications equipment. Of the 22 electronics firms in the town, 8 have their headquarters in the USA and use Glenrothes as a base for their European operations.

Exercise

1 Using the information in Table 5.8 calculate the location quotient for electrical engineering in Glenrothes. Write a brief note on the importance of the industry to the town.

2 Today the electronics industry is booming and creating prosperity for the town. However, in the longer term could this specialisation create problems for Glenrothes? Write a brief paragraph of explanation.

3 Over one-third of the electronics companies (mainly the largest) are American owned, with their headquarters in the USA. In what way could it be a disadvantage for the town to rely heavily on foreign, rather than British, firms?

Table 5.8 Employment in electrical engineering 1983

Total	Glenrothes %	UK %	Location quotient
3018	19.6	3.2	?

Figure 5.24 Glenrothes new town, Fife. Note how industry is separated from housing, on spacious industrial estates

Glenrothes new town was designated in 1948 to support the development of the coal industry in the depressed mining area of Fife (similar to Peterlee in County Durham). However, by 1963 there was little future for coal mining in the area, and the role of the new town was changed to that of a centre for the development of eastern Scotland. Its target population was increased from 32000 to 55000 and it became an assisted area, with special financial help given by government to new firms locating there. From the mid-1960s, electronics firms began to locate in the town; GEC, manufacturing telecommunications equipment, was one of the first. The most recent, ACT, located there to build a new design of micro-computer. Today, Glenrothes remains an assisted area (Figure 5.22), but its success in attracting new industry has meant that its assisted status has been downgraded from *development* to *intermediate area* (see Figure 5.23).

Exercise

1 Imagine that you are a planning officer working for Glenrothes New Town Development Corporation, and that your job is to attract industry to the town. A large American electronics firm wants to set up a new branch plant somewhere in the UK and Glenrothes is one of several locations being considered.
  a Write a report based on the information in Figures 5.23 and 5.25 setting out clearly the advantages that Glenrothes has to offer under the following headings: grants and other financial assistance; factory buildings; communications; labour force; recreation. (Have a look at the situation of Glenrothes in an atlas in relation to the coast and the Scottish Highlands.)

2 Figure 5.26 shows the plan of Glenrothes.
  a Look carefully at the distribution of industry and comment on its distribution; is it near the centre or edge of the town?
  b Say what reasons there might be for separating industry from housing.
  c Estimate the distance people might have to travel on average from their homes to their places of work – would it be less than 2 km, 5 km or 10 km?

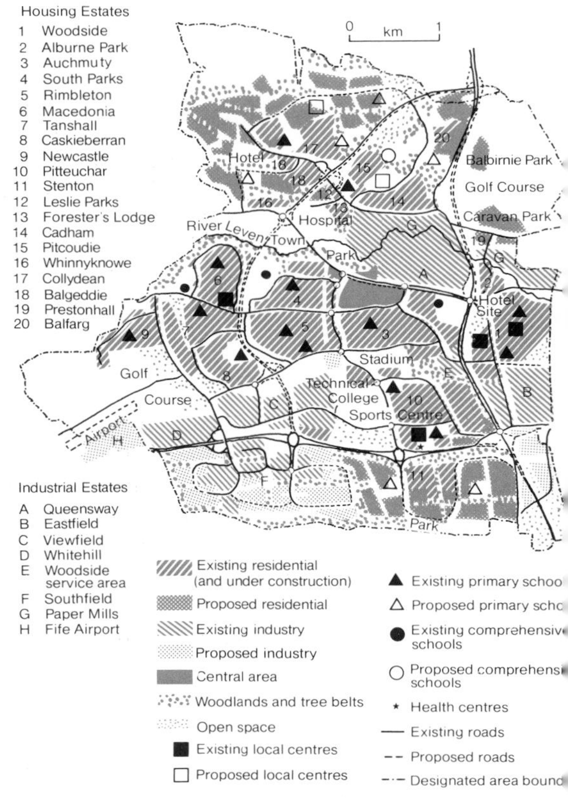

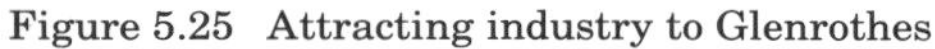

Figure 5.25 Attracting industry to Glenrothes

Figure 5.26 Progress plan for Glenrothes

It is interesting to know the reasons given by ACT for moving to Glenrothes. They were certainly influenced by the factors described in Figure 5.23, but in addition they attached great importance to the nearness of Scotland's eight universities which could supply highly skilled engineers and new ideas for the electronics business, and also to the beauty of Scotland's scenery.

The miracle of Japan

Japanese manufacturing industries, which employ 40% of the country's workforce, have grown rapidly in the last 25 years. Today Japan is the world's largest manufacturer of motor vehicles and merchant ships, as well as being one of the world's three largest producers of steel, electronic equipment, chemicals and refined oil products. Japan's industrial success has been remarkable because the country has few energy and mineral resources of its own: for example, Japan has virtually no oil or natural gas, and has to rely heavily on imports of minerals such as iron ore, copper and zinc. In all, 82% of the country's energy needs have to be imported: Japan's own energy resources are limited to a few small coalfields in northern Kyushu (output less than 20 million tonnes a year), some hydro-electric power, and deposits of uranium which can be used in the country's nuclear power stations.

No other major industrial country depends so much on imported materials as Japan. However, in recent years there have been signs that some of the heavier industries (such as steel, shipbuilding and chemicals), which depend most on imported materials, have begun to decline. At the same time, new industries such as electronics, which depend on knowledge, and not on expensive imports of energy and minerals, have shown the most rapid growth.

Exercise

1 Study Figure 5.27 which shows energy production and consumption in Japan and the UK. Write an account of the main differences between the countries, paying attention to the following: a) the amounts of energy produced and used b) the importance of the different types of energy.

2 Suggest two reasons why the UK's energy position could be said to be stronger than Japan's.

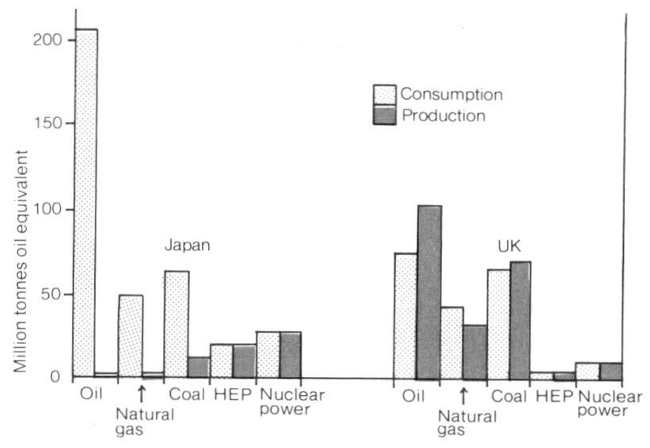

Figure 5.27 Energy production and consumption in Japan and the UK

Modern manufacturing industry started much later in Japan than in Europe and North America: it was not until the replacement of Japan's feudal rulers in 1868 that industrialisation got underway. The new government encouraged industry, and gave support to a number of very large industrial organisations known as *zaibatsu*. They were usually owned by one family, and had interests in several different sectors of industry. Current examples are Mitsubishi and Sumitomo, which manufacture items ranging from cars and steel, to ships and electronic equipment.

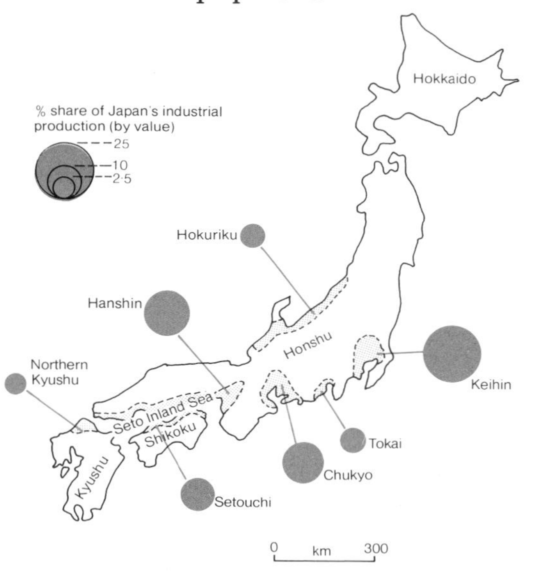

Figure 5.28 Japan: major industrial regions

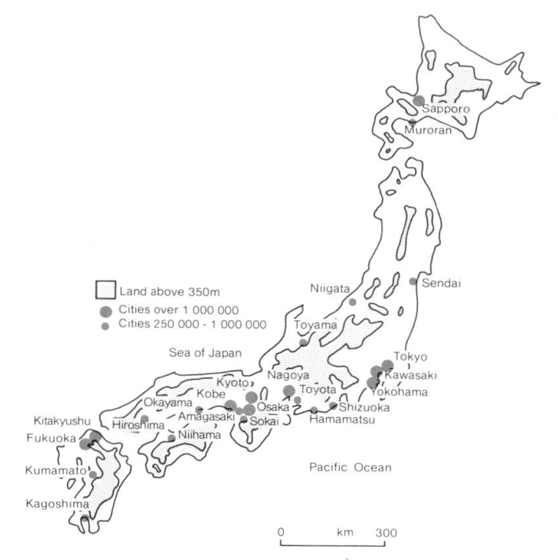

Figure 5.29 Japan: principal cities

The distribution of Japanese industry is mainly concentrated in a few large industrial regions on the coast (Figure 5.28). This results partly from the mountainous nature of Japan – only 20% of the land is habitable – and partly from the dependence on imported materials. The largest concentration of industry is along the Pacific coast, including the Seto Inland Sea. Three-quarters of Japan's manufacturing industry is found here, in a belt which stretches 1200 km from Tokyo Bay, westwards as far as northern Kyushu. The Pacific coast belt also contains Japan's four largest cities (Tokyo, Yokohama, Osaka and Nagoya) (Figure 5.29), and its three biggest industrial regions. Keihin, the principal industrial region, is located on the Kanto Plain, which is the largest area of lowland in the country; its focus is Tokyo, with a population of more than 11 million. Hanshin, centred on Osaka, is second in importance to

Keihin, and Chukyo, between Tokyo and Osaka, accounts for around 11% of Japan's industries. There are, in addition, a number of smaller industrial regions in the Pacific belt, especially Setouchi, Tokai and northern Kyushu. The only large industrial region outside this zone is Hokuriku, on the coast of the Sea of Japan.

Exercise

1 Japan consists of four large islands (Figure 5.28).
  a Which is the largest?
  b Which is the smallest?
  c Which is the most northerly?
  d What is the distance between southern Kyushu and northern Hokkaido? How does it compare with the distance from west Cornwall to northern Scotland in Britain?

2 By referring to Figures 5.28 and 5.29 allocate Japan's principal cities to their correct industrial regions. Copy and complete the table below.

Keihin	Hanshin	Chukyo	Setouchi	Northern Kyushu	Hokuriku	Tokai	Others
Tokyo	Osaka	Nagoya	?	?	?	?	?

Japan's steel industry

The Japanese steel industry is one of the largest, as well as the most efficient and advanced, in the world. With an output of 99 million tonnes in 1983, only the USSR and the USA have larger steel industries. One-third of Japan's steel production is exported, making Japan the world's leading steel exporter (Figure 5.30). The industry is dominated by five major producers: Nippon Steel (the world's largest steel company); Sumitomo (the world's biggest producer of pipes and tubes); Nippon Kokan; Kawasaki Steel; and Kobe Steel. Three-quarters of the total production is accounted for by the six largest steelworks, at Fukuyama, Mizushima, Yawata, Wakayama, Chiba and Kimitsu (Figure 5.31).

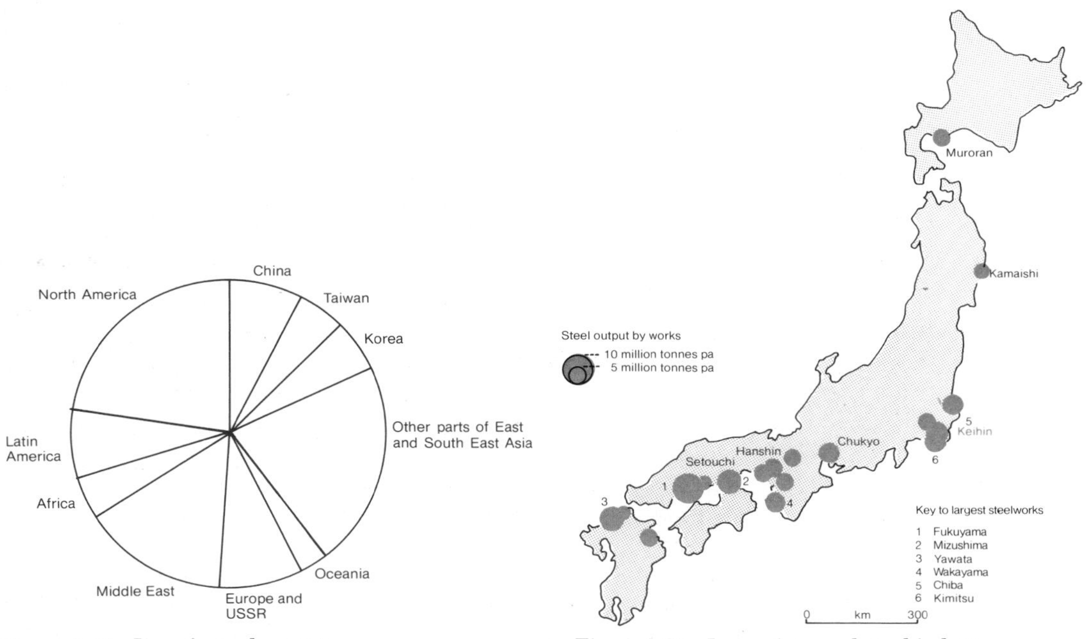

Figure 5.30 Japan's steel exports

Figure 5.31 Japan: iron and steel industry

The changing distribution of the steel industry

The iron and steel industry was first developed towards the end of the nineteenth century, largely through government investment. It was located at both ends of Japan, well away from the main centres of population, attracted by resources of coal (Kyushu, Hokkaido) and iron ore (Kaimaishi and Hokkaido). With increasing dependence on imported coal and ore, coastal sites within the main market centres dominated the location of the industry after 1950. Huge investment in new plants took place in these areas. Most of the plants were very large by European standards, and were fully *integrated*, with iron smelting, steel making and steel shaping (into items such as plates, tubes and beams), all taking place on the same site. Some were planned to serve a specific market: the Nagoya works for instance, was primarily built to supply the Toyota car assembly plant in nearby Toyota City. Most of the new steel plants were sited on land reclaimed from the sea in shallow coastal areas such as Tokyo Bay (Figure 5.32) (especially Chiba on the eastern side of the Bay), Osaka harbour, and in the case of the newest plant, Ogishima, on a reclaimed island! The massive costs of reclaiming land were largely paid for by the government, as was the building of new deepwater harbours. The reclaimed lands were then sold out at bargain prices to private industries.

Exercise

1 Apart from reducing the costs of imported raw materials, what other advantage does a coastal location have for Japan's steel industry?

2 Why do you think that the Japanese government has gone to such expense to reclaim land for industry from the sea.

3 Can you suggest two advantages of reclaimed land as a site for a modern steelworks?

4 Suggest what the likely advantages are of *integrated* steel works.

Figure 5.32 The Kimitsu steelworks occupies a 10 km^2 site, on reclaimed land on the eastern shore of Tokyo Bay. It produces nearly 6 million tonnes of steel a year. Iron ore is imported from Australia and Brazil, and coking coal from the USA, Canada and Australia, through its own deepwater terminal.

The modern Japanese steel industry brings coking coal and iron ore from distant sources such as Australia, USA and Latin America by cheap sea transport in the form of huge bulk carriers. Today, Japan's own resources provide only 10% of coking coal, and 1% of iron ore used by the industry. Steel is produced in large, modern plants which use the latest technology, and outputs of steel per worker are much higher than in Europe and North America. Many of the steel companies have interests in related industries such as shipbuilding and chemicals, and this has led to the development of huge complexes of heavy industry at tidewater, again often on reclaimed land as along Tokyo Bay and around the shores of the Seto Inland Sea.

Exercise

Re-read the section on Japan's steel industry, and find the missing words/figures for Table 5.9.

Table 5.9 Iron and steel in Japan and the UK

	Japan	UK
Production	In 1983 Japan produced ________ million tonnes of steel, over ________ being for export. There are eight works each with a capacity of over 5 million tonnes a year, the largest being ________ in western Honshu.	The UK industry produces around 15 million tonnes of steel a year. Only a small proportion is exported. There is only one works with a capacity of more than 5 million tonnes – Redcar-Lackenby on Teesside.
Raw materials	The Japanese industry relies almost entirely on imported materials. ________% of coking coal, and ________% of iron ore is imported.	The UK has abundant supplies of coking coal, but depends heavily on foreign iron ore. In 1981 14.6 million tonnes of ore were imported, while domestic production was less than 1 million tonnes.
Changing location factors	The first steelworks, built with government assistance, were located near to supplies of raw materials in ________, ________, and ________. Domestic supplies of coal and iron ore were small, and as the industry grew it came to rely more on imports. By 1950 the industry was already established on the coast, close to the major markets and sources of materials. After 1950 huge areas of land were reclaimed from the sea in districts such as ________ and Osaka Harbour. These areas were the site of other heavy industries too, such as ________ and ________.	The large-scale industry first developed on the coalfields. By 1850 areas such as Stoke-on-Trent and the West Midlands dominated the industry. The high cost of transporting coal at this time tied the steel industry to the coalfields. After 1878 it became possible to smelt the phosphoric ores of the East Midlands (the invention of the Thomas-Gilchrist process), and as less coal was needed for smelting by this time, new works were built on the orefields at Scunthorpe and Corby. After 1945 dependence on imported iron ore increased. New works were located at tidewater (Port Talbot, Redcar, Llanwern), and Scunthorpe and Ravenscraig were served by deepwater terminals. Sites with large areas of cheap, flat land were chosen to accommodate the much larger integrated works.
Modern distribution	Although most of the original steel making centres survive, the industry is strongly concentrated at tidewater, in the ________ coast belt. This reflects the importance of imported ________ and the pull of the main Japanese ________. All the major industrial regions have their own steelworks serving the local manufacturing industries.	The industry is concentrated almost entirely on or near the coast. Virtually all coalfield and orefield steelworks have closed. Sheffield is the only large coalfield centre which survives, producing special, alloy steels. The industry has remained in the traditional steel making regions and has not been pulled towards the main market in south east England.

Japan's shipbuilding industry

Although like all shipbuilding industries in DCs the Japanese shipbuilding industry has undergone considerable contraction since the mid 1970s, it easily remains the world leader, and is responsible for about half the tonnage launched each year. Like the steel industry, shipbuilding was started by the industrialisation policy of the government after 1868. Today it is dominated by seven companies, with the two largest – Mitsubishi and Ishikawajima-Harima (IHI) – having about half of Japan's capacity. Shipbuilding is closely linked with the steel industry (Nippon Kokan, Sumitomo and Kawasaki are major steel and shipbuilding companies) and heavy engineering, which supplies component parts.

Exercise

'The main centres of the steel industry are also the leading shipbuilding areas'. Comment on this statement by a) describing the distribution of shipbuilding in Japan (Figure 5.33) and the UK (Figure 5.35) b) saying to what extent steel making has a similar distribution (Figures 5.31 and 5.34).

Figure 5.33 Japan: major shipyards

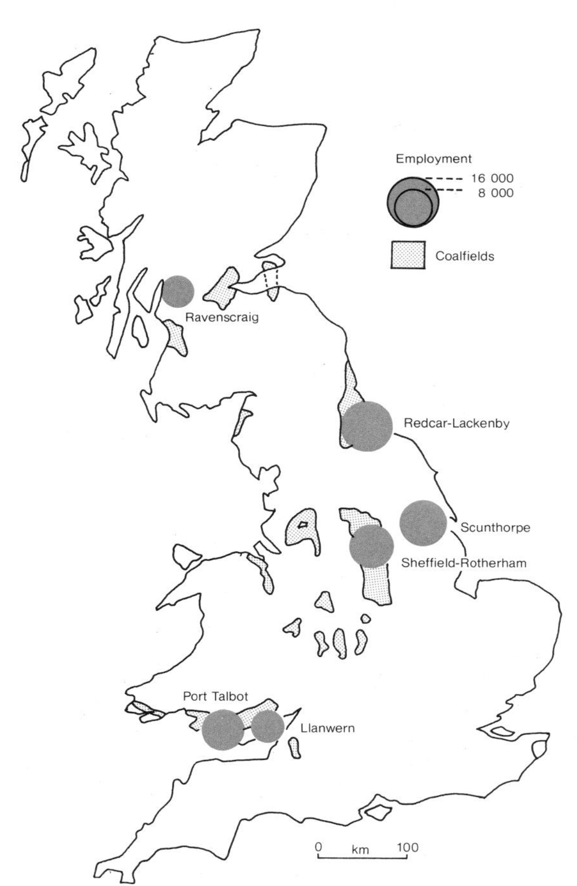

Figure 5.34 UK principal steel making centres and major coalfields

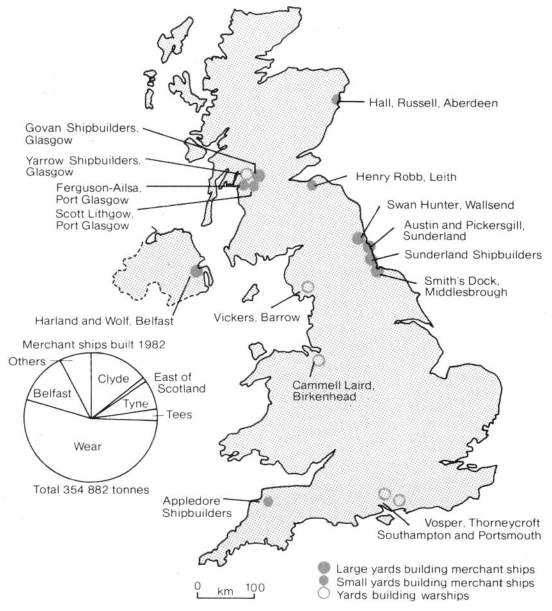

Figure 5.35 UK shipbuilding industry

You will have noticed from the last question that shipbuilding in Japan is mainly found in the largest industrial regions, notably in Keihin (Yokohama), Hanshin (Osaka), northern Kyushu (Nagasaki) and several medium-sized towns in Setouchi. This even distribution throughout the Pacific coast belt is the result of a deliberate policy by the shipbuilding companies to locate their shipyards nationwide. Each company has several yards which specialise in one particular type and size of vessel. IHI for example has two shipyards in each of Setouchi, Chukyo/Tokai and Hanshin. Its yards for super-large vessels over 200 000 tonnes are at Yokohama and Kure, while 100 000 tonners and specialised vessels are at Nagoya and Chita (Tokai).

Japan has been the world's leading shipbuilding country since 1956, when it overtook the UK. Its rapid post-war growth, which peaked in the early 1970s when production reached 19 million tonnes in one year, resulted from two factors. First there was a large increase in world trade, and particularly in the movement of crude oil, between the late 1950s and early 1970s. New tankers with larger capacity were needed, and Japan invested heavily in plant and equipment to meet the demand for very large ships. Second, Japan pioneered new shipbuilding methods, which speeded up delivery, reduced costs, and made it possible to build ships of more than 200 000 tonnes. Most important was the introduction of a new assembly line system called 'block building'. In contrast to the traditional 'layer' method, where the ship is built outdoors from the keel upwards, the shell is built in blocks, which are assembled indoors, and then lifted onto the stock by heavy cranes.

Four-fifths of ships built in Japan are for export, often for oil and mineral companies. However, there is a large surplus of oil tankers in the world today, and little demand for new vessels. Three-quarters of tonnage (around 9 million tonnes) are bulk carriers, built for traffic such as minerals, gas and grain. However, the industry is running at barely half its capacity, and further reductions are likely in the future. Some cities have been badly hit by the decline of shipbuilding (eg Harshima in Setouchi), but because Japanese workers are guaranteed a job for life, this has not caused unemployment. Instead it has often meant a transfer of shipyard workers to related industries, which are often controlled by the same parent company. Meanwhile, for the first time Japanese shipbuilders are facing severe competition themselves from Third World producers. South Korea, which has labour costs only one-third of those of Japan, is the biggest threat, and is beginning to have the sort of impact on Japanese shipbuilding, that Japan had on European yards throughout the 1960s and 1970s.

Japan's motor vehicle industry

In 1958 Japan produced less than 200 000 vehicles. Today Japan is the world's largest producer, and one in every three new motor vehicles is made in that country.

The Japanese motor industry, which includes assembly, body and parts factories, employs 650 000 workers. Production is, however, highly automated and efficient, reflecting the enormous investment which has taken place in the last 20 years. Although there are eight manufacturers in Japan, there are two which dominate the industry (Figure 5.36). Nissan (Datsun), which is concentrated in Keihin; and Toyota, based in the Chukyo region.

We saw in pages 112–16 earlier in this chapter, that motor vehicle manufacturing is essentially an assembly industry. Although in Japan the assembly works often produce some important parts (such as engines and gearboxes), as in the UK, they rely on large numbers of outside component manufacturers. Because of the close links between assembly plants and

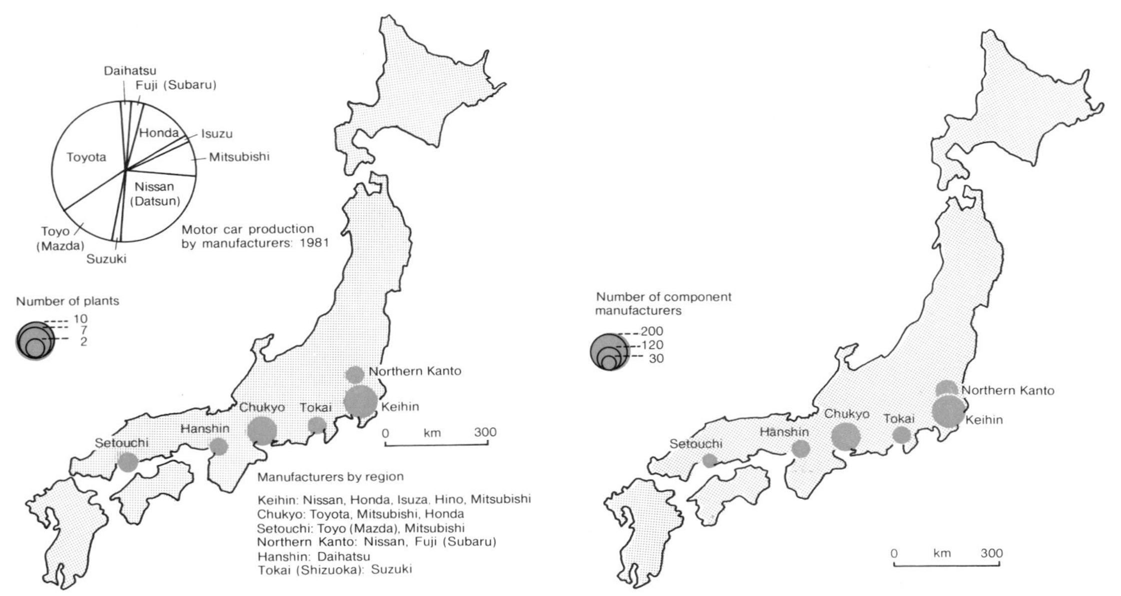

Figure 5.36 Japan: motor vehicle assembly plants

Figure 5.37 Motor vehicle component manufacturers

component suppliers, it is an advantage if they locate together (Figure 5.37). In this way transport costs are reduced, and the flow of parts and information between the different branches of the industry, are made easier. These benefits, called *external economies*, are apparent in Keihin: here the large assembly plants of Nissan and Honda are able to obtain virtually all their parts from the local region. Even within the smaller industrial region of Chukyo, Toyota and Mitsubishi can buy more than half the components they need locally. Keihin is the largest manufacturing centre, with the main concentration of assembly, body and parts factories stretching in a belt from south east Tokyo, through Kawasaki, to Yokohama (Figure 5.38). With the great expansion of the motor industry in the 1960s, Nissan, Honda, Isuzu and Hino all built new assembly plants on the outskirts of the conurbation, where there was more space and land was cheaper. There has also been some transfer of body and parts plants to this outer zone. Southern Tokyo, formerly the centre of the motor industry in Keihin, now has just two assembly plants, though the district retains its importance as the principal area for parts manufacture. Thus, in Keihin, there is a pattern of assembly works towards the edge of the conurbation, which are closely linked to the parts factories found mainly in the older districts of inner Tokyo. A similar pattern is found in the West Midlands of the UK, with the older areas of the conurbation between Birmingham and Wolverhampton containing large numbers of parts manufacturers, and the two big assembly plants – Longbridge and Solihull – located on the southern outskirts.

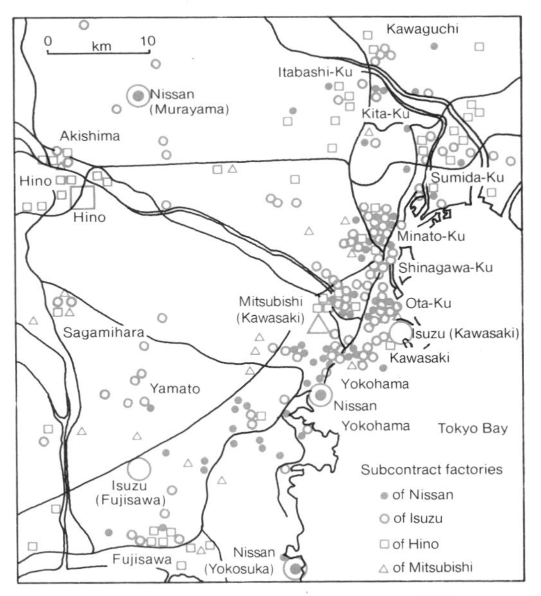

Figure 5.38 Distribution of the motor vehicle industry in Keihin

In the Chukyo region, factories are centred on Nagoya (Mitsubishi) and Toyota City (Toyota). Toyota City (282 000) is a one industry town. 90% of its workforce is employed by the Toyota company, and to underline this dependence its name was changed from Koromo to the company name!

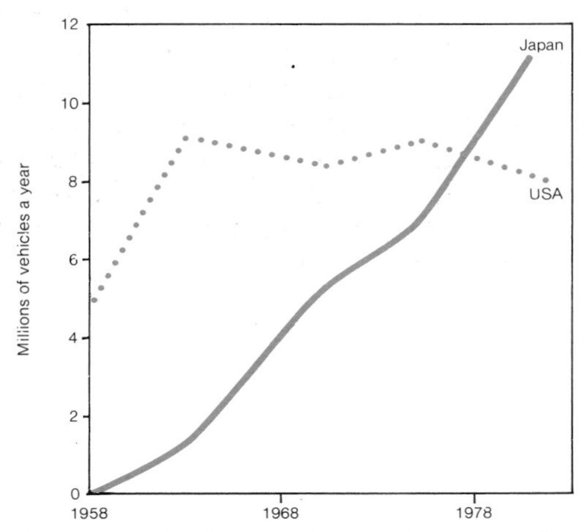

Figure 5.39 Production of cars and commercial vehicles: Japan and the USA, 1958–81

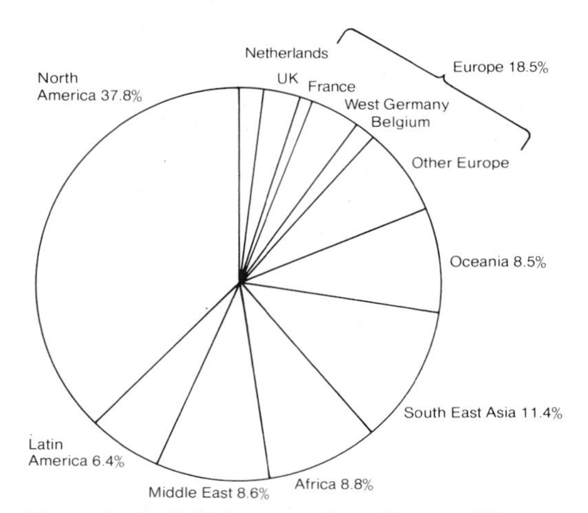

Figure 5.40 Vehicle export from Japan, 1981

The success of Japan's motor industry (Figures 5.39 and 5.40) has led to competing countries imposing limits or quotas on Japanese vehicle imports. Recently, this policy has slowed down the growth of exports. To overcome this, several Japanese companies have built factories in the USA and Europe. These are usually joint ventures with American or European companies. For example, Toyota and General Motors are planning to build a new factory for small cars in California; Nissan started building trucks in Tennessee (USA) in 1983; Honda will soon be producing small cars from a new factory in Ohio; Nissan has joint production with Alfa Romeo in Italy: and in 1986 Nissan will open its first assembly plant in the UK at Washington new town in north east England. Thus, Japanese manufacturers are beginning to develop production on a worldwide basis, and follow the example of *multinational* US motor manufacturers such as Ford and General Motors.

Exercise

1 Using the information in Table 5.10 calculate the number of vehicles produced per worker per year (ie productivity) in the Japanese and UK motor industries.

Table 5.10

	Workforce	Vehicles produced 1981	Vehicles per worker (ie productivity)
Japan	650 000	11 179 962	?
UK	470 000	1 184 205	?

2 Suggest reasons for the differences in productivity.

3 Virtually all Japan's major industries have grown rapidly since 1950. However, in the last few years, the 'big three' of steel, shipbuilding and motor vehicles, have faced a number of problems. For each industry, describe briefly the nature of these problems, and the effects they have had.

4 In 1973 world oil prices increased fourfold. Why do you think that the 'oil crisis' hit Japan particularly severely? (To remind yourself look back at page 120.)

5 Explain why you think it is in Japan's interest to move away from heavy industries like steel, shipbuilding and chemicals, and concentrate instead on items like machine tools, video machines and word processors.

Part 2: Manufacturing industry in LDCs

In LDCs manufacturing industry usually employs less than 20% of the workforce. Unlike DCs, the manufacturing sector in LDCs consists of two parts: the *modern*, and the *traditional*. The modern sector is similar to manufacturing in countries such as Japan and the UK: it relies on a highly skilled workforce, a large investment in plant and machinery, and efficient transport, and is often concentrated in the major cities. In contrast, the traditional sector is essentially a 'cottage' industry (rather like Britain before the industrial revolution), scattered in villages and small towns, and based on simple crafts such as weaving and pottery making. In many LDCs, the traditional sector provides the bulk of the jobs available in manufacturing industry.

Exercise

Many countries have encouraged the development of small-scale, traditional industries, particularly in rural areas. Give three reasons why traditional industries might be said to be more appropriate for LDCs than modern industries. (Think of cost, imported fuel and materials, type of labour, and technical knowledge.)

In the last 30 years many LDCs have attempted to modernise through *industrialisation*, hoping that this would transform the country to a high level of development, as it has in Europe, North America and Japan. Typical of the large-scale industries which have been introduced are those based on local raw materials, such as textiles using cotton or jute, or cement based on limestone. Industries like these depend on a fairly low level of technology and simple skills, and contrast with the advanced technology of industries such as electronics and motor vehicles in DCs.

Industrialisation in the Third World is usually just one part of a plan to develop a country's resources, which includes agriculture, transport, education and health care, as well as industry. In some countries, notably India, Nigeria and Egypt, industry has received most attention. Planning in these countries usually covers periods of five to ten years, and sets out targets for output, employment and growth. India is now into its sixth five-year plan; Nigeria's 1981–5 plan is its fourth. Egypt's Programme of National Action 1973–82 was a typical plan, which gave special emphasis to industry, and aimed to double the national income in the space of 10 years.

Exercise

Look at Figure 5.41 which shows differences in manufacturing in eight countries.

1 What are the main differences in manufacturing between DCs and LDCs as illustrated in Figure 5.41?

2 Try to explain the differences between DCs and LDCs with particular reference to food and agriculture-based industries, textiles, and machinery/transport equipment.

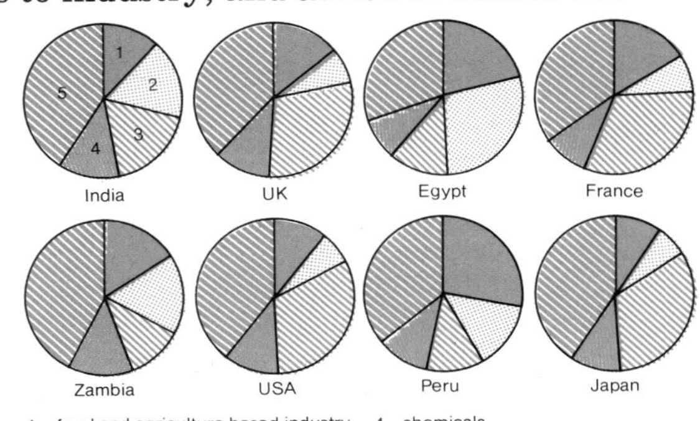

Figure 5.41 Importance of manufacturing sectors by value

Nigeria

Industrialisation

One in every three or four Africans is a Nigerian. Although no one knows for certain how many people live in Nigeria, reliable estimates put the population at around 80 million, making it easily the largest country in Africa. Since 1960, when Nigeria gained its independence, it has been the policy of the government to modernise the country through industrialisation. In 1950 manufacturing industry contributed less than 1% to Nigeria's income: today the proportion is around 10%. However, despite expansion, the manufacturing sector is small compared to DCs, and Nigeria remains heavily dependent on the export of raw materials such as crude oil and agricultural products. (See Figure 5.43.)

Exercise

1 Read carefully through the list of disadvantages to industrialisation in Nigeria in Table 5.11. Rank the disadvantages in order of difficulty (1 to 7) in a table. Compare your rankings with those of others in your class. Write a short paragraph to justify your choice of the most serious disadvantage.

2 Extreme dependence on the export of just one or two raw materials is a feature of the trade of many LDCs, including Nigeria (99%), Zambia (96%), Sudan (100%) and Peru (89%). With this in mind, study Figure 5.43 and answer the following questions.
   a Assuming that the total amount of exports was unchanged, what is the common feature of all the items exported by Nigeria?
   b Describe how Nigeria's trading position became weaker in the period 1960–78.
   c Try to explain the disadvantages of Nigeria's trading position in 1978 by referring to the range and the types of goods exported.

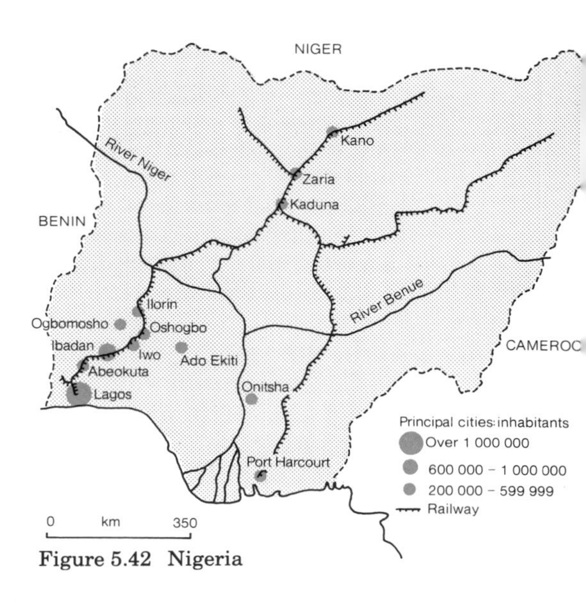

Figure 5.42 Nigeria

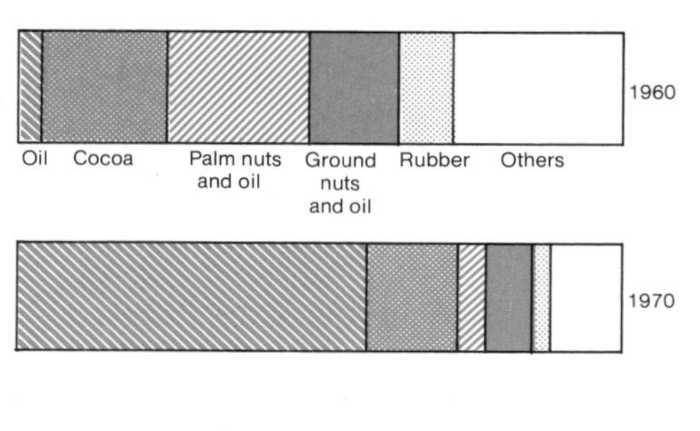

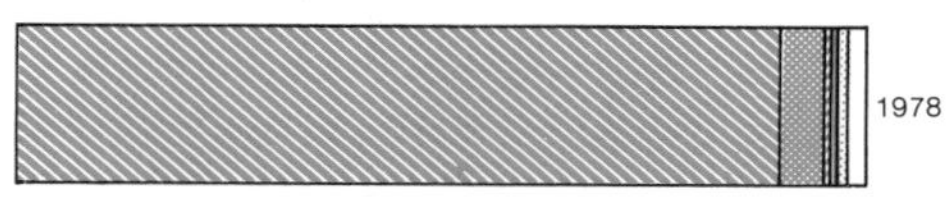

Figure 5.43 Nigerian exports by value, 1960–78

Table 5.11 Industrialisation in Nigeria

Factor	Advantages	Disadvantages
Natural resources	Nigeria has plentiful sources of energy, especially crude oil and natural gas. In 1982 crude oil production was 64 million tonnes, and Nigeria is one of the world's largest exporters. Natural gas, found along-side oil in the Niger delta, could become as important as oil in the next few years. Coal deposits are small, but supplies for the new steel industry are being developed at Lafia and Obi. HEP is generated at dams on the Niger at Kainji and Jebba. The Kainji Project provides power for the whole country, water for irrigation, and fishing in the artificial lake behind the dam. Other minerals include tin (2.6 million tonnes of ore a year), iron ore (new deposits at Itakpe and Agbaja) and limestone.	Nigeria is heavily dependent on the export of crude oil to finance industrial development. 90% of Nigeria's exports by value are crude oil. At current production rates, known reserves are only sufficient until the end of the century. Industrialisation was boosted after 1973 following the fourfold increase in oil prices. In the early 1980s prices fell, and Nigeria lost important income. Oil production peaked in 1974 when output reached 112 million tonnes.
Capital	None	There is a shortage of money for investment in industrial projects. Ambitious plans for the expansion of the rail network in the 1981–5 programme have been trimmed because of lack of funds. With an average annual income of only 700 US dollars per person, there is limited scope for savings by the population. Nigeria relies heavily on investment from DCs (West Germany, the USSR, the UK), from multinational companies (Shell, BP, VW, Nissan), and from organis-ations like the World Bank and the OECD.
Markets	There is a large potential domestic market of 80 million people, and an even larger market in West Africa.	The majority of Nigerians are too poor to afford many of the products of industry. It is difficult to compete in foreign markets with the manufacturing industries of DCs.
Labour	With a large and growing population there is no shortage of labour in ***quantity***.	The labour force is largely unskilled. There are acute shortages of scientists, technicians, craftsmen and managers. Although 62% of the population have received primary education, only 13% have had any secondary schooling.
Transport	There is already a transport network which by Third World standards is well established. There are 105 000 km of roads, 3524 km of railways, with a major improvement in the latter already underway. Port facilities at Lagos, Sapele, Port Harcourt, Warri and Calabar are good.	The rail network is sparse and narrow gauge. Several of the 19 state capitals are not served by rail. Most roads are unmetalled and many are impassable in the rainy season. Providing a comprehensive transport network is made difficult by the sheer size of the country.
Population change	None	With a high birth rate (50 per 100) and a falling death rate (20 per 1000) population is growing rapidly. Unless growth is controlled, there is the danger that gains made through industrial development will have little impact on people's standard of living.
Government	None	Five governments have been overthrown by force in the period 1960–83. Unless there is stable government, longterm planning and attracting investment is difficult. Many governments have mismanaged the country and corruption has been a major problem.

Distribution of industry

The early stages of industrialisation in LDCs often lead to the concentration of manufacturing industry in the largest city and its surrounding region. This *core* area grows rapidly, while the rest of the country, or *periphery*, remains starved of industry. It is suggested that at a later stage, industry will spread out from the core, and establish itself in the smaller towns and cities in the rest of the country. Figure 5.44 explains how the core region comes to dominate manufacturing industry in a LDC.

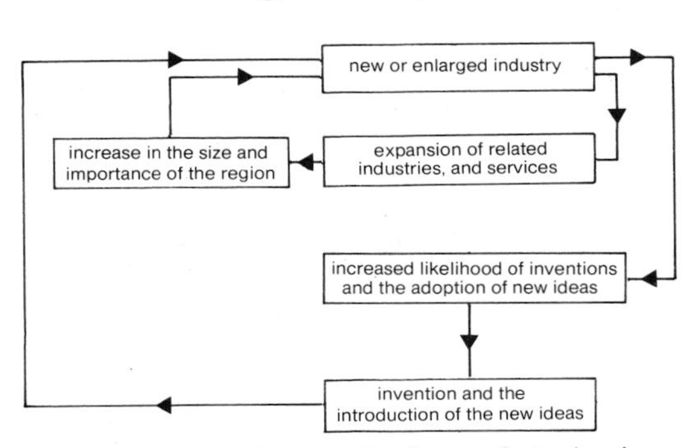

Figure 5.44 Nigeria: growth of manufacturing in the core region

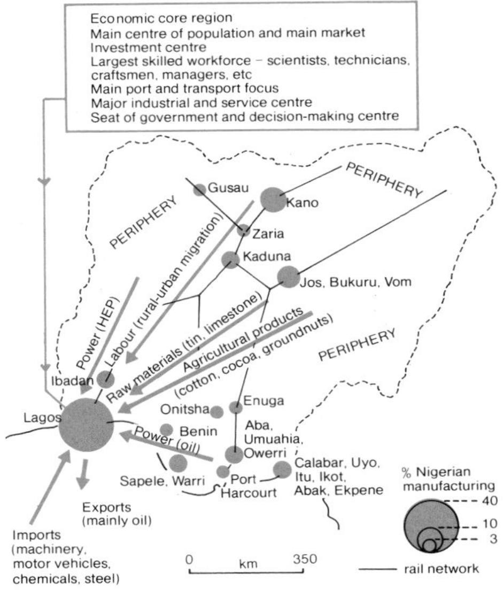

Figure 5.45 Nigeria's core and periphery

In Nigeria, Lagos, the capital and largest city, is at the centre of the core region (Figure 5.45). This region has 40% of the country's manufacturing industry, and the proportion is increasing. As Lagos is Nigeria's largest port, many industries are concerned with processing and assembling imported materials (Figure 5.46).

Figure 5.46A/B Old and new port facilities at Lagos, Nigeria's largest port and major centre of manufacturing industry

The Nigerian government would like to see a more even spread of industry throughout the country. There are two reasons for this:

1 most Nigerians do not live in the Lagos region and badly need employment

2 Lagos, like many cities in DCs, has a problem of congestion. The government has started to put into effect its ideas by developing the new steel industry (see

pages 133–4) well away from Lagos, and by building a new capital city at Abuja (Figure 5.47) in the centre of the country. Other steps taken by the government include giving financial assistance to firms to provide essential services like water and electricity, and directing new industries to locations close to raw materials, rather than close to the market.

Exercise

1 The following African countries have all their manufacturing industry concentrated in a single, core region: Gambia, Liberia, Rwanda, Central African Republic. Using your atlas, find the name of the largest city (core region) where all the industry is located.

2 Refer back to Chapter 3, pages 54–6 and find out if either of the following descriptions fits Lagos: gateway city; primate city.
You should note that Lagos has a population of 1.48 million, while Nigeria's second city, Ibadan, has a population of 0.85 million. Explain your answer in a short paragraph.

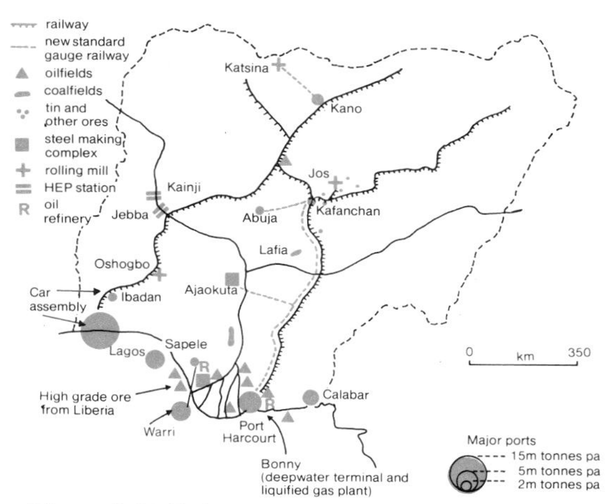

Figure 5.47 Industry in Nigeria

Nigeria's steel industry

The development of a new steel industry in Nigeria is one of the largest projects in black Africa, and of great importance to the country. Apart from saving on imports of steel (steel was Nigeria's third largest import in 1981), it should encourage the growth of steel-using industries, create employment, and generate essential skills.

The project involves the construction of two steel making complexes and three rolling mills (Figure 5.47). The two steel making plants are at Ajaokuta in Kwara state, and Warri (Delta Steel Company) in the Niger delta. The Ajaokuta works, completed in 1983, has a capacity of 1.5 million tonnes of steel a year, and is located near to local raw materials. Low grade (33%) iron ore deposits are being developed nearby at Itakpe Hill; coking coal, which at present is imported, will be replaced by deposits at Lafia and Obi. The plant has been built by the USSR and many Nigerian workers have been trained in the USSR.

The Warri plant started production in 1982, and will eventually employ 4000 workers, mainly Nigerians. The plant is on the coast and has access to the ports of Warri and Sapele, and unlike Ajaokuta depends on imported materials, including iron ore from neighbouring Liberia. However, in common with Ajaokuta, Warri has been built with foreign capital and expertise, in this instance provided by a group of West German companies. Together, the two plants should be able to meet about half of Nigeria's demand for steel.

The three rolling mills, with a combined capacity of nearly 1 million tonnes, are widely dispersed at Jos, Katsina and Oshogbo. Steel will be taken from Ajaokuta and Warri for shaping at the mills, though this will mean improvements in the rail network. Warri is not linked to the railway system: the current plan is to transport steel from the plant by road, but given the poor state of many Nigerian roads, steel might be shipped to Lagos by sea, and then by rail to the mills. A new rail line is being built between the Ajaokuta plant and Port Harcourt, and the Katsina mill will be linked to Kano by a new standard gauge line.

Exercise

1 In Japan and the UK steel making and steel shaping are usually found on the same site. Can you suggest any reasons why the two processes have been a) separated b) dispersed so widely, in Nigeria?

2 Compare the location of Nigeria's two steel works with those of Japan a) before 1900 b) after 1950.

Other modern industries

Vehicle assembly, using car and commercial vehicle kits imported from Japan and Europe, has become an important industry. Assembly of kits has the advantage of reducing the cost of vehicles, and providing jobs in Nigeria, rather than at Dagenham or Tokyo. Honda and Mitsubishi both started assembly in 1981 – Honda in Lagos, and Mitsubishi at Ibadan. Three other Japanese firms are planning to build commercial vehicle assembly plants. European manufacturers include Peugeot (60 000 cars a year), VW (29 000 cars, mainly 'beetles') and BL. In 1981, 121 000 vehicles were assembled, mainly in the Lagos region.

Although most of Nigeria's oil is exported as crude, there are two refineries near Port Harcourt and Warri which serve the domestic market. A new development at the Bonny deepwater terminal is the construction of a liquified natural gas plant.

Improving the transport system

Industrial development depends on an efficient transport system. In the 1970s Nigeria invested heavily in port facilities to relieve the problem of congestion, particularly at Lagos. The leading five ports are shown in Figure 5.47. (Note that oil traffic has been excluded from the figures.) Sapele in the delta region is a completely new port, opened in 1982. It is located 100 km upstream of the Benin River, and is designed to serve central Nigeria, from the delta to Kano, including the new federal capital at Abuja. There are six berths, including ro-ro and container facilities (see Chapter 6, pages 151–2). A new container terminal has been built at Apapa port (Lagos) and other berths have been modernised with new handling equipment. Excluding oil, Lagos handles two-thirds of Nigeria's trade. Nigeria's deepest port is the Bonny oil terminal near Port Harcourt, which can accommodate 60 000 tonne vessels. This is the main outlet for exported crude oil, and coking coal and iron ore will be landed here for the new steel industry.

Attention in the 1981–5 development plan was switched from the ports to the railways. A five phase programme of development has been accepted, which will cover the period until 2006, and will eventually link all 19 state capitals. A major aim is to replace the existing narrow gauge system (1.067 m) with standard gauge (1.435 m) track. The first phase is already well advanced and involves the building of a new line from Port Harcourt to the Ajaokuta steel works, and then as far as Kafanchan, with an extension to Abuja. The new line will, as far as possible, run parallel to the existing narrow gauge track. An essential rail link which will have to be completed as soon as possible, is that between the new Katsina rolling mill and Kano in the north. The plan to develop the railways, like the plan for steel, relies heavily on foreign capital and know-how. French, Brazilian, British, Swiss, Yugoslav and Chinese firms are all involved in the improvement of the rail system, and in supplying new locomotives and rolling stock which will be needed as the standard gauge network is extended.

India

Although one of the poorest countries in the world, and with only 11% of its working population employed in manufacturing industry, India is still the world's thirteenth largest industrial power. In the 'organised', modern sector its leading industries such as steel, textiles and chemicals are comparable to those found in DCs. However, at least half of India's manufacturing jobs are in the 'informal' sector, either in small-scale workshop industries, or in the countryside, scattered throughout half a million villages.

Village industry

Village industries may account for between 35 and 40% of manufacturing employment in India (Figure 5.48). They are based on traditional crafts such as weaving, wood carving, basket making and metal engraving, use little capital and rely almost entirely on muscle power. A measure of their importance is the fact that they exported goods worth £900 million in 1981, and their total output was valued at £2000 million. In addition they have an enormous value in providing essential goods for India's rural population. Textile production is the largest single village industry, employing about one in every four workers; indeed the textile village industry is nearly as large as that in the modern sector.

Figure 5.48 Village industries in India
A Handloom weaving
B Pottery
C Charcoal burning

The government has taken some steps to protect village industries from competition from large-scale, modern industry. For instance the cotton industry is provided with cheap, machine-made yarn, and the manufacture of saris, worn by virtually every woman in India, is reserved for the village industry. Even so, compared with the modern sector little money has been invested in village industries since India began to plan for development in 1955, and because the modern sector is usually given preference, shortages of materials are a common problem.

It is doubtful whether industrialisation can make any great impact on improving the lives of the majority of Indians. For all the huge sums of money spent on modern industries in the last 30 years, this sector has increased its workforce by a mere 12%. This situation contrasts with that of rural industry, which is largely ignored by the government, and yet because it is *labour intensive* is able to employ millions of people throughout the country. The development of rural industries offers a sensible and cheap alternative, and there is an urgent need to encourage employment in the countryside in non-agricultural activities. This could be done by expanding and improving existing handicrafts, and by diverting industries related to agriculture, such as cereal milling, fruit canning, cotton ginning and leather production, to rural areas.

Exercise

1 Many village industries tend to be seasonal in character. Can you say why?

2 Look back to Chapter 3, pages 47–9 on South Asia, and explain how the development of village industry might help to solve some of the major urban problems of LDCs like India.

3 Refer to Chapter 1, pages 14–15 and suggest why there is such an urgent need to encourage the growth of rural industry in India.

The Damodar Valley – case study of a heavy industrial region

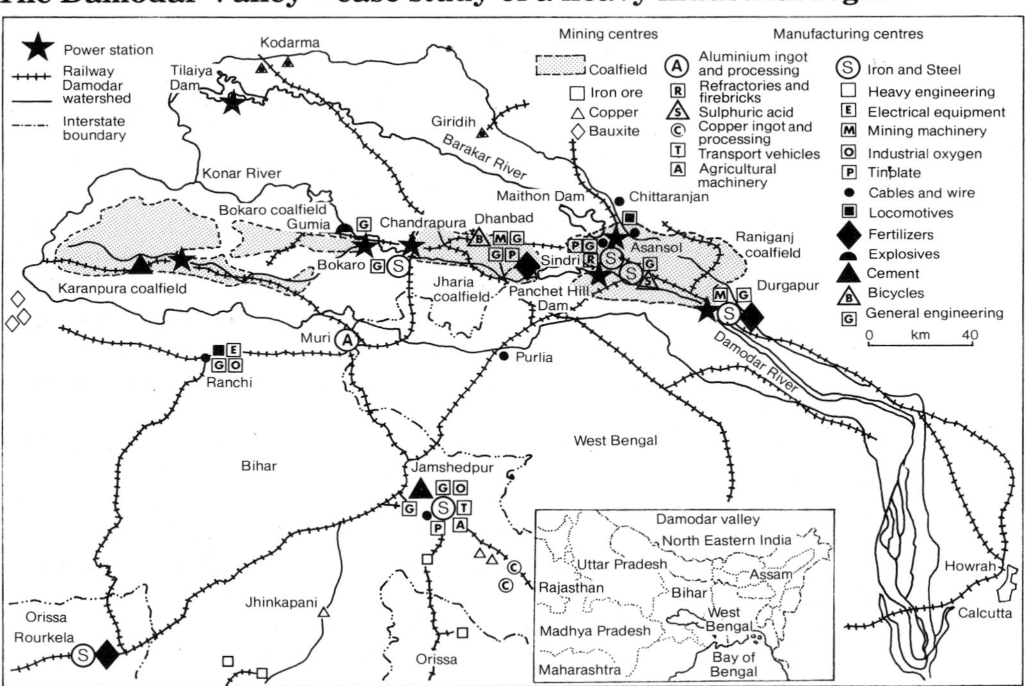

Figure 5.49 The Damodar Valley

The Damodar Valley in north east India (Figures 5.49 and 5.50), which extends across the states of Bihar and West Bengal, is a region of heavy industry based on local raw materials, especially coal. The region is the third largest concentration of industry in India, after Bombay, and Hooghlyside (Calcutta) which lies only 150 km to the east. This area provides between 6% and 7% of India's total employment in the modern sector, and with a population of 9 million, the Damodar Valley industrial region can be compared with major industrial regions in the developed world, such as the Ruhr coalfield in West Germany, the Pittsburgh region on the Appalachian coalfield of the USA, and the Yorks, Notts and Derby coalfield in the UK.

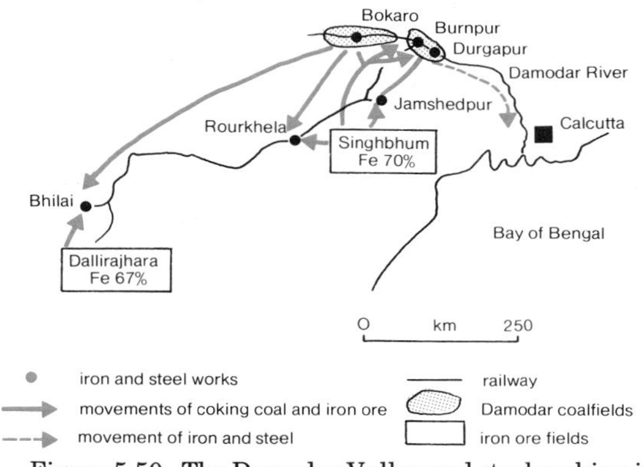

Figure 5.50 The Damodar Valley and steel making in north east India

Figure 5.51 Jamshedpur steelworks in Bihar. The works occupies a mid-point location between Damodar coking coal and Singhbum iron ore

The coal deposits of the Damodar Valley extend westwards from the Raniganj field in West Bengal, to the Jharia, Bokaro and Karanpura coalfields in Bihar, over a distance of nearly 300 km. These are India's largest coalfields, and account for two-thirds of the country's annual production of 124 million tonnes (1981). The coal deposits include valuable coking coals, which are the basis of iron and steel production in the whole of north east India.

North east India, and the Damodar Valley in particular, is the centre of India's iron and steel industry. Six of India's seven steel making plants, responsible for an output of nearly 10 million tonnes in 1981, are located in the north east, three in the Damodar Valley. The industry is attracted to the region not only because of the coking coals, but also because of the high grade iron ore deposits found in the Singhbhum region in Orissa, just south of Jamshedpur. Indeed Jamshedpur was the location of India's first iron and steel plant, built between 1907 and 1911 by the Tata Iron and Steel Company (Figure 5.51). The works occupies a favourable location, between the Damodar coking coal and Singhbhum iron ore, as well as being close to the huge market of Hooghlyside. Burnpur, located on the coalfield, is the only other works built before Indian independence in 1948.

Since 1948 the steel industry has grown rapidly with foreign assistance. The Durgapur works was built by Britain; Rourkhela by West Germany; and Bhilai by the USSR. Bhilai is the largest plant, and is most distant from Damodar (745 km). Even it depends on Damodar for coking coal, though it obtains iron ore from Dallirajhara, 100 km to the south. Bokaro (also built with Soviet assistance) has similar advantages to Durgapur; a major feature is its hot strip mill, and it has been planned eventually to achieve an output of 10 million tonnes of steel a year. All the steelworks in the region are fully integrated, making products which include steel sheet, rails, plates and beams. Figure 5.50 also shows the movements of coal and iron ore to the steelworks and to the main market, Hooghlyside, in north east India. All the shipments are by rail, some over very long distances. Several lines have been electrified and use power from the thermal and hydroelectric power stations in the Damodar Valley.

The coalfield and the steel industry have attracted many other related industries to the region (Figure 5.49). Refractory bricks for lining blast furnaces, are made from local clay; fertilizers are manufactured using naphtha, a by-product of the coke ovens of the steel industry; coal is burnt in several thermal power stations in Damodar; and heavy engineering industries such as the building of locomotives, rolling stock, mining machinery and heavy cables depend on steel produced in the region.

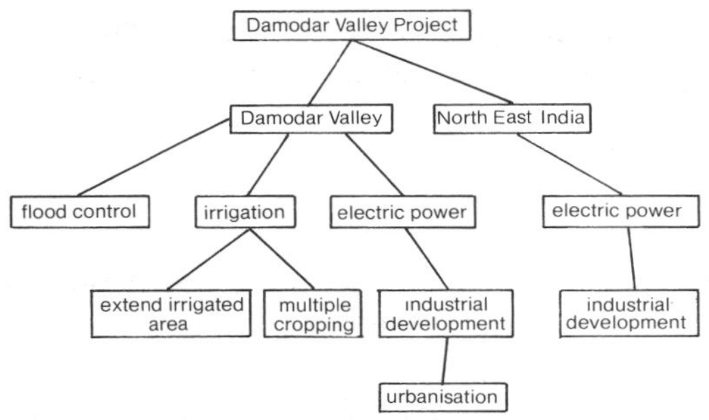

Figure 5.52 Benefits of the Damodar Valley Project

Planning in the Damodar Valley

In 1948 the Damodar Valley Corporation (DVC) was formed to plan the development of the region. The DVC has three aims:

1. to develop the power resources of the valley
2. to extend the area of irrigated farmland, especially in the lower valley
3. to protect the lower valley from flooding (Figure 5.52).

Before the Damodar River was controlled, its flow varied greatly from season to season. 80–95% of its flow was concentrated in the monsoon or rainy season, lasting from June to October. Flooding in the lower valley, below the confluence of the Damodar and the Barakar (Figure 5.49), where the channel was heavily silted, was common. At the same time, the low flow of the river during the dry season from November to May, made irrigation, and therefore cultivation, impossible for half the year.

The main feature of the DVC's plan, designed to tackle these problems, was the building of several dams on the Damodar and its largest tributaries, in order to even out the river's flow. The dams would store surplus water during the monsoon season, and release it gradually in the rest of the year. Apart from giving flood protection and water for irrigation, the dams would also generate HEP. Further electricity would be produced by the building of a number of thermal power stations along the river which would use local coal as fuel.

In all, four dams were built and they have proved very successful in protecting the lower valley from flooding. The area of irrigated land has been increased, and by 1977 320 000 ha in the lower valley were provided with water through the new irrigation canal system. However, the heavy demand for water by industry, and for domestic use, has not made it possible to grow a second or third crop a year on any scale. Three HEP stations, at Tilaiya, Maithon and Panchet Hill (Figure 5.49), and three coal-fired power stations at Bokaro, Chandrapura and Durgapur have been built by the DVC. They have a total capacity of 1242 MW, and today the Damodar Valley, with only 8% of the combined population of Bihar and West Bengal, generates 37% of all the power used in the two states.

Cheap power has led to the rapid growth of industry and towns in the valley. Urban growth has been particularly strong in the upper valley in the towns of Bokaro, Chandrapura, Maithon and Panchet Hill, all of which are close to power plants. In contrast, the older industrial areas on the Raniganj coalfield in the lower valley have shown little growth. Today the towns of the Jharia coalfield form a conurbation of nearly 1.25 million. Industries which have been attracted to the valley are those which require large amounts of cheap power, such as steel and aluminium smelting, and those linked to steel production, like heavy engineering. The effects of these developments are not confined to the

Damodar Valley: nearly two-thirds of the power generated in the valley is 'exported' to other areas, notably to Hooghlyside, India's second largest industrial region.

Exercise

1 Study the figures on employment changes 1961–71 in north east India in Table 5.12, and then copy out the paragraph below, putting in the correct words.
'In spite of huge investment in the *traditional/modern* sector the proportion of the population engaged in non-agricultural jobs has *increased/decreased* only slightly in the Damodar Valley, and *increased/decreased* in Bihar and West Bengal in the period 1961–71. In Bihar and West Bengal the population is becoming *more/less* dependent on agriculture. This is because the number of new jobs in manufacturing and service industries *is/is not* keeping pace with population growth, in a part of the world where most people are employed in *farming/manufacturing/services*.'

Table 5.12 Non-agricultural employment as % of total workforce

	1961	1971
Damodar Valley	37.6	43.2
Bihar State	23.2	19.6
West Bengal State	46.2	42.5

2 In view of the paragaph you have just written, what chance do you think that the development of modern industry, following the lines of the Damodar Valley Project, has in solving India's employment problems? What in your opinion is the alternative?

3 In what sense is urbanisation in the Damodar Valley similar to that which occurred in Britain in the nineteenth century? (Look back to Chapter 3.) How does it differ from urbanisation taking place today in cities like Manila and Kuala Lumpur? (Re-read Chapter 4, pages 88–94.)

Summary

Manufacturing industries are concerned with processing materials and assembling manufactured items to make finished products. In DCs manufacturing employs a large, but declining proportion of the workforce. This trend is likely to continue as industry relies more on automation and advanced technology.

Industry is usually located in areas where it can make a profit. Locations which are chosen may have several advantages, including skilled or cheap labour, linkages with other industries, markets, materials, low transport costs and so on. However, we must recognise that many industries occupy their present locations because that is where they started. This *inertia* means that the major industrial regions of the developed world today are little different from those of a century ago.

Large-scale, modern industries are relatively new to most LDCs, where for the majority of workers industry means small workshop activities and village crafts. Recently many LDCs have made great efforts to develop modern industries, in the belief that they would bring the prosperity enjoyed by DCs. Although some countries have succeeded, notably Japan and possibly Taiwan and South Korea, industrialisation on its own is unlikely to solve the problems of the Third World. More and more LDCs are now turning to small-scale industries and rural development programmes (as we shall see in Chapter 7) as the most likely way of improving the quality of life of the people.

Further exercises

1 a Figure 5.53 shows six possible locations (A–F) for an iron and steel works. Imagine that you are the minister responsible for industry in an LDC, and that one of the six locations has to be chosen as the site of a new steelworks. Assume that you will want to use your own coal and iron ore resources, and that all the steel is marketed at A. Transport is by rail, and the costs of transporting raw materials (per tonne kilometre) or *collection costs* (pages 105–6) are twice as high as the costs of transporting the steel to market or *distribution costs*. Select the location which should give the lowest transport costs, and briefly explain your choice. (For the location of Clabecq, see Figure 6.21)

b Select a steelworks from Table 5.13 which has a similar location to the one you chose in the last question. Describe the location of the steelworks.

Table 5.13

Sheffield (UK)	Jamshedpur (India)
Redcar-Lackenby (UK)	Yawata, Northern Kyushu (Japan)
Clabecq (Belgium)	
Warri (Nigeria)	Nagoya (Japan)
Bokaro (India)	

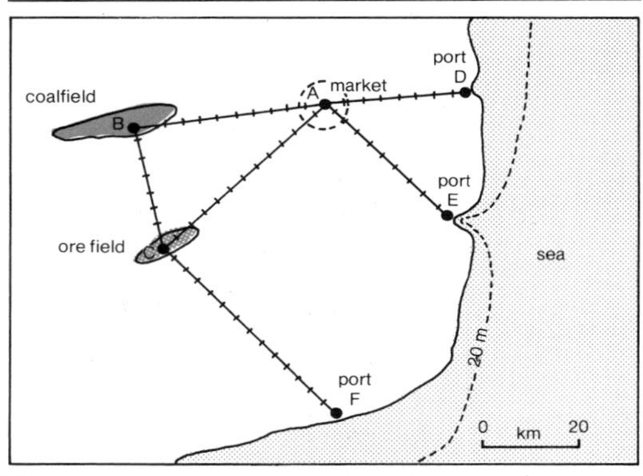

Figure 5.53 Locating an iron and steel works

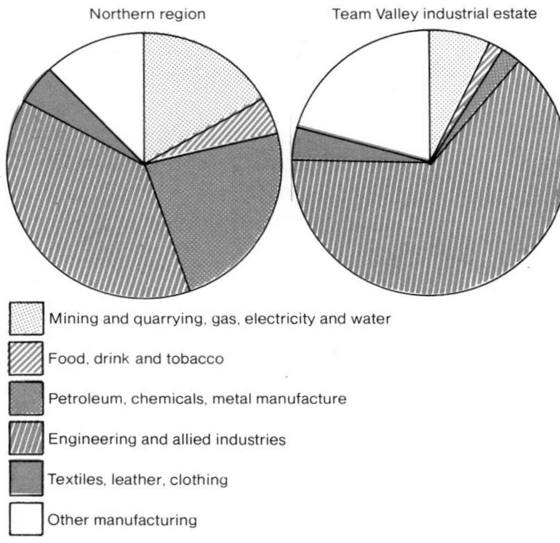

Figure 5.54 Manufacturing industry: the Northern Region and Team Valley industrial estate, Gateshead

2 Figure 5.22 shows the distribution of assisted areas in the UK. These areas are generally the poorest parts of the country and face problems such as high unemployment, and the decline of many of their basic industries. As a result they receive assistance from the government in the form of special grants, to help them attract new industry. Look at the distribution of assisted areas, and then read pages 132–3 on the distribution of industry in Nigeria. Is there any indication of a rich 'core' region and poorer outer region in the UK, like that in Nigeria? Give your answer in a short paragraph.

3 Explain the meaning of the following terms: location quotient; material index; footloose industry; assembly industry.
In each case use examples from the following industries to illustrate your explanation: motor vehicles, sugar refining, shipbuilding, electronics.

4 Explain the difference between light and heavy industries. Say how the material index might help you to distinguish between them.

5 Team Valley is a modern industrial estate in Gateshead, Tyne and Wear. Like Glenrothes new town, it is situated in an assisted area, has good road communications, and many modern, single-storey factories, designed to attract new industries. Study Figure 5.54 and say what type of industries are most important on the estate. Can you suggest ways in which the location of traditional industries like steel, chemicals and shipbuilding in the Northern Region, might differ from those at Team Valley. (Figure 6.20 might help you to answer.)

6 The planning of the Damodar Valley in India can be described as a 'multi-purpose' development project.

a Outline the three main purposes of the project.

b To what extent has it been possible to fulfil all three purposes satisfactorily?

Key ideas	Examples
The employment structure in a country can be divided into three sectors: primary, secondary, tertiary.	■ Manufacturing employs a much larger proportion of the working population in DCs than in LDCs. ■ The importance of the manufacturing sector as a source of employment is declining in DCs. In LDCs it is increasing, but only slowly. ■ LDCs are unlikely to follow the same changes in employment structure as DCs underwent as a result of industrialisation and urbanisation.
Various types of manufacturing industry can be defined using the following criteria:	
1 location	■ A simple division into material- and market-oriented industries.
2 heavy and light industries	■ Heavy industry eg iron and steel; light industry eg electronic engineering.
3 level of technology	■ High technology eg computers; low technology eg domestic textile industry.
4 use of labour / capital	■ Labour intensive eg pottery industry; capital intensive eg petrochemicals.
5 task performed.	■ Assembly industries eg motor vehicles; processing industries eg oil refining.
The purpose of manufacturing industry is to make a profit.	■ Profit is the difference between income and costs. A location is normally chosen where a satisfactory level of profit can be made.
Many factors may influence the location of industry:	
1 site	■ Many heavy industries eg steel, oil refining, require special sites. Sites may have to be flat, extensive, with access to deepwater, etc.
2 transport	■ This may be very important for industries with high transport costs eg steel, brick making. Transport costs are less important in DCs where communications are good. Processing industries whose materials undergo large weight loss may be material-oriented eg sugar beet. Industries whose products weigh more than materials may be market-oriented eg brewing. Perishability of a product eg bread, may also pull an industry to the market. Most light industries rely on road transport and require good access to fast roads. High tech industries may require access to international airports eg high tech industries in the Western Corridor. Many modern industries are not affected in their location choice by transport: they are said to be 'footloose'.
3 labour	■ The quality of labour is often important eg skills needed in electronics or mechanical engineering. Attitude of the workforce may be important eg Glenrothes' strike-free record.
4 linkages with other firms	■ An important factor which leads to the growth of large concentrations of industry eg Tokyo–Yokohama. The finished product of one firm may be the material for another eg component suppliers and assembly plants in the motor industry.
5 energy supplies	■ If large amounts of energy are needed an industry may be drawn to energy supplies eg aluminium smelting, electricity generation from coal or oil.

Key ideas	Examples
6 inertia	■ Industries remain where they first located because it is too costly to scrap existing plant and locate elsewhere eg steel at Ravenscraig.
7 government	■ In Japan the government has played a major part in the development of industry. In LDCs large projects may be planned by government eg Damodar Valley, Nigerian steel. Some industries may be owned by government eg British Steel. Governments may take location decisions on social rather than profit-making grounds eg the location of the motor vehicle industry on Merseyside in the 1960s.
8 attractive recreational areas.	■ Important for some footloose industries which need to attract highly qualified workers eg the 'Sunbelt' of the southern USA, the Thames Valley and Silicon Glen. The old, congested conurbations eg north east USA, London, are becoming less attractive to modern industry.
There are many difficulties for LDCs aiming to achieve development by industrialisation.	■ Among the many obstacles are: shortages of capital; shortages of skilled workers and technical 'knowhow'; small home markets; poor government; poorly developed transport networks; rapid population growth. When modern industries have been successfully established they are often based on low technology eg textiles, steel.
Raw materials and energy supplies are helpful, but not essential for industrialisation.	■ Japan has become a powerful industrial country in spite of having few mineral resources, and little coal, oil and natural gas.
Much manufacturing industry in LDCs is in the traditional sector.	■ Workshop and cottage industries may be as numerous as modern industries. They are labour intensive and therefore able to absorb large numbers of workers.
Many LDCs rely on a very narrow range of exports.	■ Often raw materials eg minerals, agricultural products, which have not been processed because of a lack of manufacturing industries. There is the potential for developing industries such as oil refining, petrochemicals and food processing based on these materials.
In most countries there is a division between the prosperous and less prosperous regions.	■ There is often a single prosperous (core) region with many successful industries eg Lagos, south east England. Outside this core the rest of the country (periphery) is less prosperous and may have few industries (eg in LDCs) or many declining industries (eg DCs). Most governments aim to even out the differences in wealth between regions.

Transport

Distance

Transport links places together and so enables the movement of people, goods and information. Thus it provides the means of overcoming the distance which separates places. Normally we think of distance as *physical distance*, measured in kilometres or miles. The greater the physical distance separating places the less movement or *interaction* there is between them. For instance, thousands of people travel from the home counties to work in central London each day, but few commute to London from the Midlands, and even fewer from northern England, because of the *time* and *costs* involved.

Physical distance is not always an accurate guide to movement: if a housewife undertakes a shopping trip, or parents are deciding which school their child should attend, they may be more concerned about the time involved in travelling, rather than the actual distances in kilometres. Journey times, however, unlike physical distances, are not unchanging: in the 1970s Concorde reduced the travelling time between London and New York to $3\frac{1}{2}$ hours (Figure 6.1), and in 1983 France's '*train à grand vitesse*' (TGV) brought Lyon to within 2 hours of the capital, Paris (Figure 6.2). These examples show that improvements in transport systems can bring places closer together in time, and that the physical distance separating places may often be irrelevant in the decision to travel.

Exercise

1 To show the link between physical distance and distance as time, complete the following.
   a Keep a record over one week of the time it takes you to travel to school or college each day. Calculate your average journey time for the week.
   b Measure the distance in kilometres of your route to school using your local 1:25 000 or 1:50 000 OS map.
   c Compile a table of journeys-to-school information for all members of your class, showing journey time, physical distance and the transport used (walk, cycle, bus, train, car) for each individual.
   d To show how interaction decreases with physical distance, use the information on the length of the journey to school (in kilometres) in your table, and count the number of students with journeys of less than 1 km, 2–2.9 km, 3–3.9 km and 4 or more kilometres. (Note that if your school draws its students from a wide area, you may have to use larger distance categories.)
   e Draw a histogram (like Figure 7.30A) to show the information in the previous question. Does your graph support the idea of decrease in movement with distance? If your graph does not show a continuous decrease of numbers with

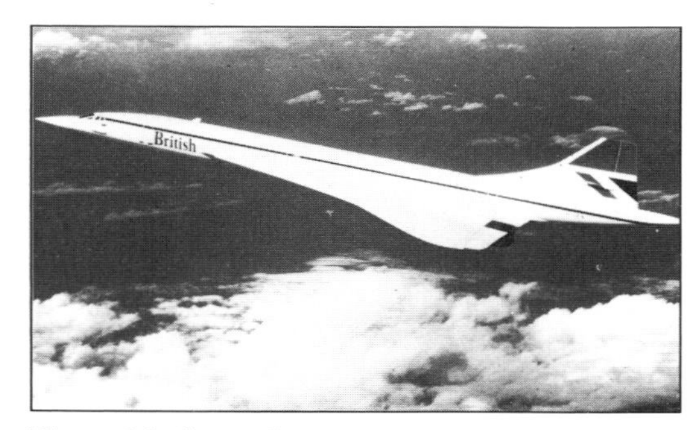

Figure 6.1 Concorde.

Figure 6.2 France's TGV (*train à grand vitesse*) was introduced in 1983, and covers the 426 km between Paris and Lyon (south east France) in two hours. With a maximium speed of 270 kmph it has halved the journey time between the two cities. A second TGV, linking Paris with Bordeaux (south west France) is already under development

distance, try to find out why eg differences in population density in the school's catchment area, school buses serving particular neighbourhoods and so on.

2 Using the information in your table from question 1, draw a scatter graph for each student, plotting physical distance on the horizontal axis, against journey time on the vertical axis. Colour the dots to distinguish the different means of transport used.

3 How closely related are the two measurements of distance on your scatter graph? Remember that the more closely they correspond to a straight line, the more strongly related they are. You will probably find that many points do not follow a straight line. Try to explain this by looking at the different means of transport used, the directness of some students' routes to school, problems of traffic congestion on certain routes and so on.

Exercise

1 With reference to Figure 6.3, complete the calculations of the cost of air travel per kilometre for the places in Table 6.1.

2 Which of the 10 cities in Table 6.1 has a) the cheapest b) the most expensive air travel from London measured as cost per kilometre?

3 Which continent has the cheapest air travel (again measured in cost per kilometre)?

4 How do you think that this pattern of transport costs is likely to affect a) air travel within Europe b) interaction between the UK and North America?

Table 6.1 Cost of air fares with distance from London

Destination	Distance (km) from London	Cost £	Cost per km (p)
Athens	2400	273	11.38
Copenhagen	950	147	15.47
Lisbon	1550	183	11.81
Los Angeles	10800	252	2.33
Miami	6500	189	2.91
New York	5500	?	?
Paris	350	?	?
Rio de Janeiro	7000	?	?
Rome	1420	?	?
Vancouver	10000	?	?

Distance may also be measured as cost. Figure 6.3 illustrates how the usual map of Europe and the Americas can be transformed when it is redrawn using the cost of air travel, rather than physical distance. In terms of cost, London is actually closer to New York, than to some European capitals such as Lisbon, Athens and Rome! This type of map tells us much more about the heavy volume of air traffic between Britain and the USA's east coast than any conventional map could.

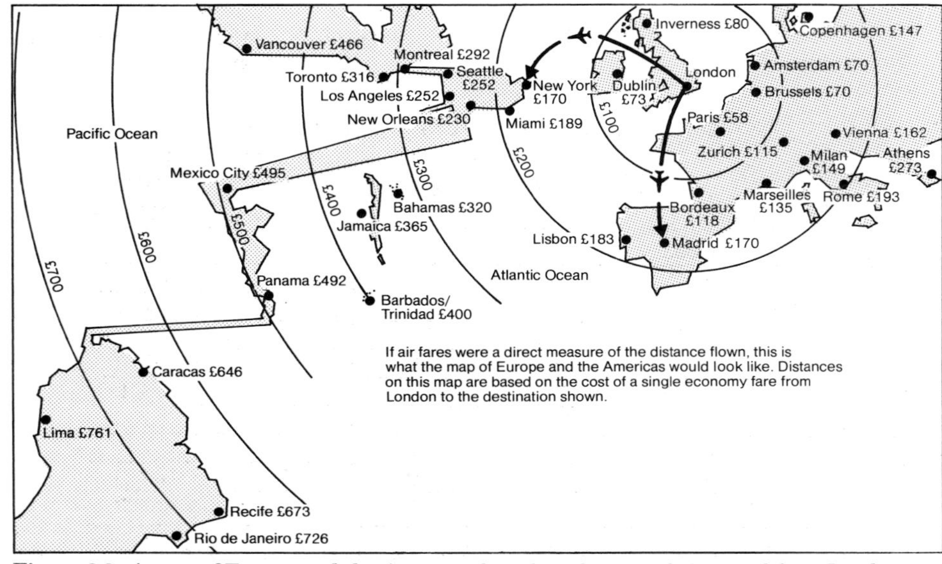

Figure 6.3 A map of Europe and the Americas based on the cost of air travel from London

Estimating flows of people and goods

Flows of people and goods occur when there is a *demand* in one place and a *supply* in another. Two factors have an important effect on the volume of flow between places: the distance which separates them, and the size of the places. Thus places which are close together, such as Manchester and Liverpool, should *interact* more than places which are far apart, like London and Edinburgh. Equally, we would expect larger centres such as London and Birmingham to generate more traffic between them than smaller centres like Ipswich and Norwich (Figure 6.4). It is possible to estimate the volume of movement between places using a simple formula:

$$\text{volume of movement} = \frac{\text{population of place A} \times \text{population of place B}}{\text{distance between A and B}}$$

Worked example

Using the figures for south east England and Wales in Table 6.2, we can estimate the number of people moving between the two regions by using the formula:

$$\text{volume of movement} = \frac{16.893 \times 2.777}{215\ (\text{km})} = 0.219$$

The value of 0.219 now has to be scaled-up to give an accurate estimate of population movement. In this example we use a constant value of 80.9. Thus our total population flow is given by:

$$0.219 \times 80.9 = 17.71\ (\text{thousands})$$

This compares quite well with an actual movement of 15000 people between the two regions.

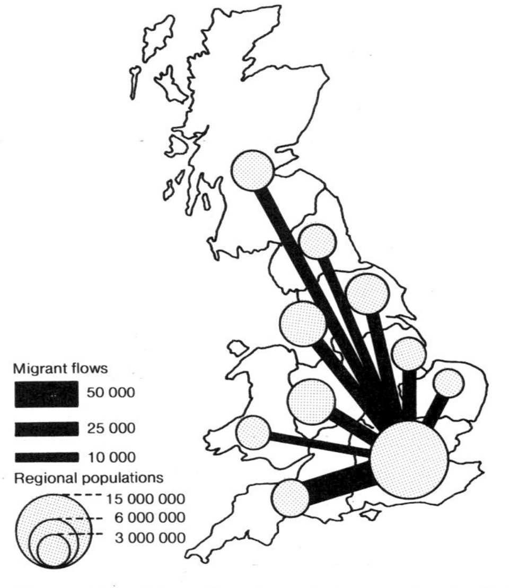

Figure 6.4 Migration flows between the South East and other regions in Britain

Table 6.2 Migration between the South East and other regions in Britain

	Population (millions)	Actual migration (000s)	Distance from London (km)	Estimate of migration using formula	Estimate × 80.9* (000s)
South East	16.893				
North	3.082	15	400	0.130	10.517
Yorks and Humber	4.884	22	275	0.300	24.270
East Midlands	3.779	24	175	0.365	?
East Anglia	1.881	24	115	?	?
South West	4.343	50	175	0.419	33.900
West Midlands	5.154	27	160	?	?
North West	6.450	30	260	?	?
Wales	2.777	15	215	0.219	17.710
Scotland	5.153	22	550	0.158	12.780

*This figure is obtained by dividing the total number of migrants (229) by the total estimated flows from the formula (2.83).

Exercise

1 Complete the calculations in Table 6.2.

2 Compare the actual and estimated numbers of migrants in Table 6.2. How similar are they? You may find it easier to comment by drawing a scatter graph and fitting a trend line.

3 How important would you say distance and population size are in explaining the movement of migrants between the South East and the other regions? Can you think of other factors which might explain the movement of migrants?

Figure 6.5 shows two maps of Britain. Figure 6.5A is a familiar map, with distance measured in kilometres. Figure 6.5B, however, is unusual because it has been drawn using fastest journey times by rail from London to 37 towns and cities in Britain. The average speed of train services to these places is 100 km per hour, which means that on average a place that is 60 minutes from the capital will be 100 km distant, one which is 120 minutes away will be 200 km distant and so on. However, only a small number of places – for example Ipswich and Norwich – have journey times close to the average speed. Most are either faster than average, making them 'nearer' to London than their actual distance indicates (Figure 6.5A), or slower than average, making them further away. Thus when distances are transformed into journey times, Leeds is seen to be closer to London than Sheffield, and Darlington as close to the capital as Hull! (Figure 6.5B)

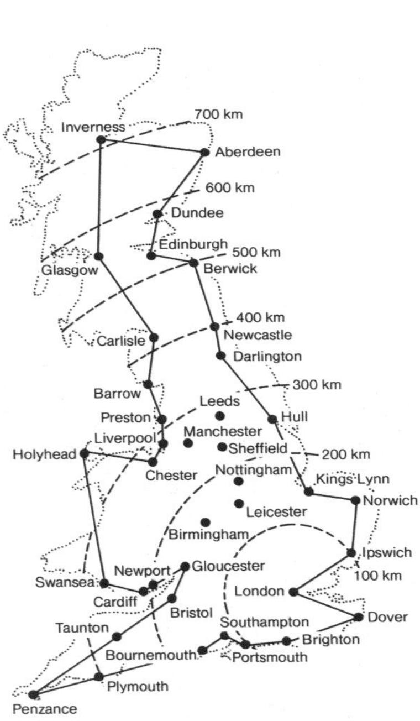

Figure 6.5A Actual distances

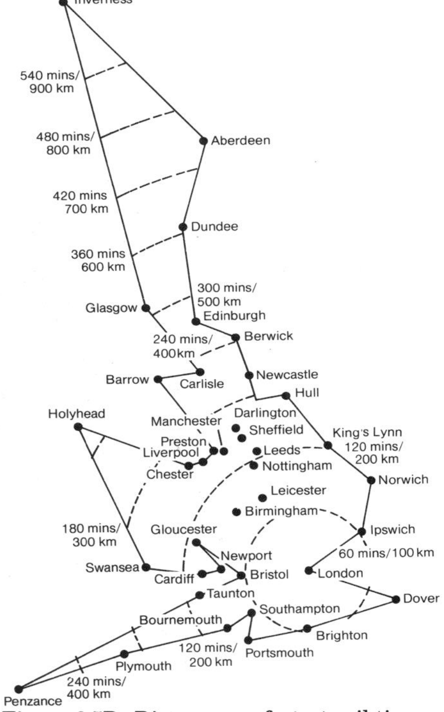

Figure 6.5B Distances as fastest rail times from London

Exercise

1 a Make a copy of the simplified outline in Figure 6.5A

b Make a tracing of Figure 6.5B and fix it as an overlay to Figure 6.5A. (You can line them up on the London–Ipswich route.)

c Shade in the areas of overlap. Distinguish those areas which are 'closer' to London in time compared with their actual distance, from those which are further away, by using two different colours.

d Write a brief paragraph on the location of the two types of area in the last question.

2 Study Figure 6.5 and arrange the following towns and cities into the three classes shown in Table 6.3:

Aberdeen	Hull	Leeds
Bournemouth	Gloucester	Norwich
Cardiff	Inverness	Preston
Dover	Ipswich	Southampton
Edinburgh	King's Lynn	Swansea
		Taunton

Table 6.3

Places closer to London in time than actual distance	Places further away from London in time than actual distance	Places as close to London in time as you would expect from their distance
Bristol	Portsmouth	Southampton

3 Hold a class discussion to consider the reasons for the patterns you observed in questions 1 and 2. Here are a few suggestions to help you:
— directness of the route
— speed of the route
— distance from London
— size and importance of various towns and cities.
Following your discussion write a summary of your reasons.

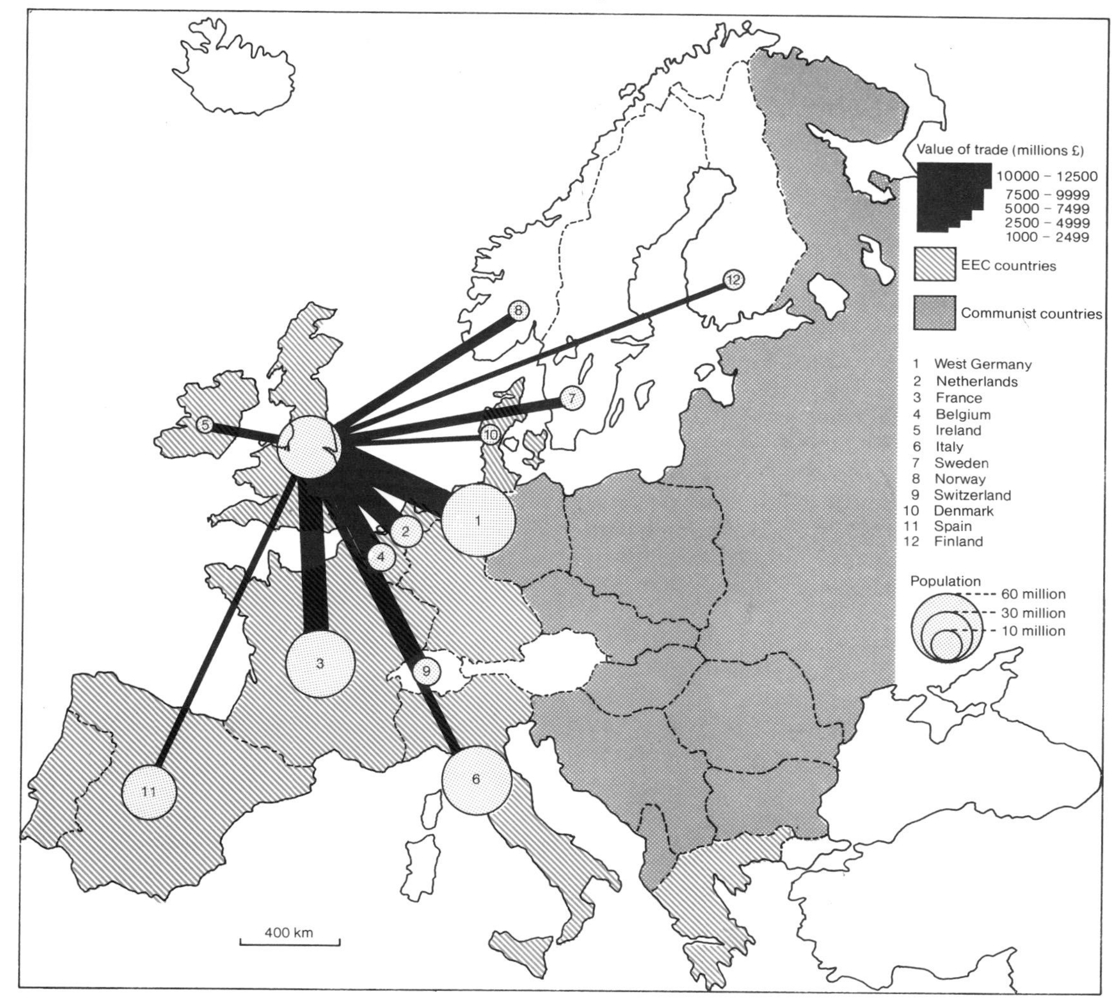

Figure 6.6 UK's main European trade partners

Exercise

Study Figure 6.6 which shows the volume of trade between the UK and its twelve most important European trade partners.

1 Name the UK's two most important trade partners.

2 Name two countries outside the communist bloc with which the UK has very little trade.

3 To what extent does a) population size b) distance have an effect on trade between the UK and its European neighbours? Write a paragraph, mentioning the countries which appear to be most influenced by these two factors.

4 Apart from population and distance, politics are an important influence on patterns of trade. With this in mind, how many of the UK's top 12 European trade partners are members of the EEC? How many are in the communist bloc of Eastern Europe?

The flow of goods or trade between countries is also affected by the resources and industries found in each. Some countries, like the Netherlands, have favourable conditions for farming; Finland has vast resources of timber for pulp and paper manufacture; the UK has rich resources of coal, oil and natural gas; and some countries have an advantage in certain manufacturing industries, such as motor vehicles in West Germany, and aerospace in France. It is often to the advantage of a country to specialise in producing items it can supply most cheaply, and import the other goods it needs from foreign countries. This means that trade often occurs between countries that have contrasting or *complementary* resources and industries.

Exercise

Look at the graphs in Figure 6.7.

1 Make a list of the main items which account for most of the trade between the UK and West Germany, Sweden, Denmark and Ireland. What are the main complementary areas of trade between the UK and these countries?

2 With which country would you say that the UK's trade was most complementary? Name the products of these two countries which most complement each other.

3 With which country is the UK's pattern of trade least complementary? Explain why this is so.

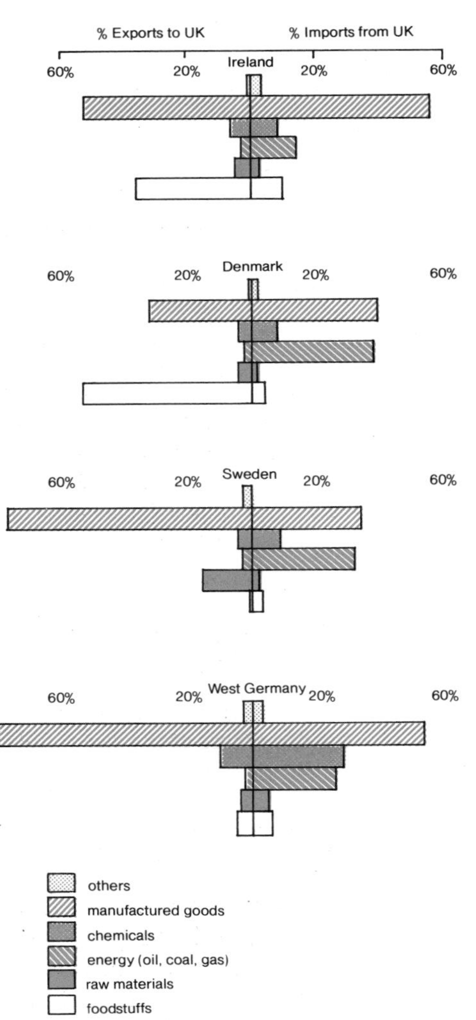

Figure 6.7 The pattern of trade between the UK and Ireland, Denmark, Sweden and West Germany.

Transport routes and Ordnance Survey maps

The physical geography of an area often has an important influence on the location of transport routes. The routes followed by roads, railways and canals have usually been chosen in order to limit the costs of building, and avoid natural obstacles such as steep slopes and land which is poorly drained or liable to flood. Rivers act as barriers to routeways, and as bridging is always expensive, routes may follow lengthy detours to places where rivers can be conveniently crossed. Natural features which offer gentle gradients are often followed to reduce costs; for instance roads may make use of cols or passes over high ground, and all types of route are attracted by valleys, and in areas of strong relief tend to follow the contours.

If it is impossible to maintain gentle gradients by following physical features, or if this can only be done at the expense of long detours, it will be necessary to modify some of the physical features. Very steep slopes may be overcome by switchbacks or hairpin bends, which while increasing road length, will reduce the steepness. Railways are more sensitive than roads to steep gradients, and make frequent use of cuttings, embankments, viaducts and tunnels. However, it should be noted that many modern roads, and especially motorways, also use cuttings, embankments and viaducts, so that traffic can maintain fast and uniform speeds. Canals are most finely adjusted to relief, and often follow highly indirect courses, keeping to a selected contour: locks are expensive to construct, and delay traffic.

Exercise

Study the 1:50 000 OS map extract (Figure 6.8 – see colour section) and answer the following questions.

1 Which is the more direct route between Gargrave and Hellifield: the A65 between the church-with-tower (856565) in Hellifield and road junction (932541) in Gargrave, or the railway between Hellifield station (852573) and Gargrave station (932536)? Calculate the *directness index* of the two routes to obtain a precise answer.

$$\text{directness index} = \frac{\text{actual distance by road or rail}}{\text{straight line distance}}$$

2 Try and explain why there is a difference in the directness of the two routes.

3 Draw cross sections of the two routes between
a) 911550 and 855566 along the A65
b) 911550 and 854570 along the railway.
Describe the differences in gradients along the two routes, and give a brief explanation.

4 Compare the directness of the A59 and the Leeds and Liverpool Canal between 964 518 and 909 508

5 Make a sketch map of the canal between Priest Holm Bridge (918537) and Williamson Bridge (911511) to show how the course of the canal has been influenced by relief. What is the advantage of the indirect route followed by the canal?

6 Describe the route of the railway between 970514 and Hellifield station (852573). What are the problems of relief and drainage along the route, and how have they been overcome?

Types of transport

The cost of transport varies with the length of the journey, the kind of goods carried, and the *type* of transport used (Figure 6.9). Transport costs are made up of two items: terminal costs and haulage costs. Terminal costs include the costs of loading and unloading, storage, and the dues which have to be paid when ships use a port or planes use an airport. These costs are fixed regardless of the length of the journey, and are highest for sea transport and lowest for road transport. Haulage costs are the actual expenses of the journey and cover the cost of fuel and wages; unlike terminal costs they increase with distance. Haulage costs tend to be cheaper the greater the amount of cargo carried: for instance, it is more expensive to transport a 35 tonne container over 100 km by juggernaut lorry, than it is by container ship. This is because whereas the lorry is limited to carrying a single container, a container ship might carry up to 500 of such units. Figure 6.9 shows how transport costs increase with distance for different types of transport. When terminal costs are high, short journeys are expensive; long journeys are cheapest when haulage costs are low.

Exercise

Study Figure 6.9 and answer the following questions.

1 Which type of transport has the lowest terminal costs, but one of the highest haulage costs?

2 Which type of transport has the highest terminal costs, but lowest haulage costs?

3 Which type of transport is best suited to a) short journeys b) intermediate journeys c) long journeys? Can you explain why?

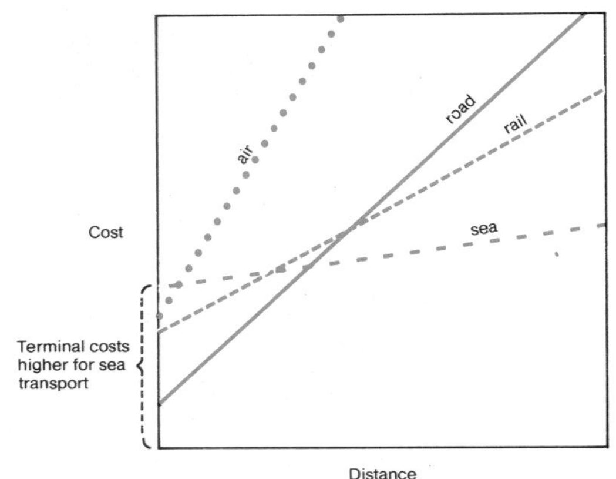

Figure 6.9 Types of transport and journey costs

Sea transport

There are two types of cargo transported by sea: general cargo and bulk cargo. General cargo is very varied, and includes items such as foodstuffs and manufactured products, which are usually packed in small lots. Bulk cargo is transported without packing, and consists mainly of fuel (eg crude oil) and mineral ores. Compared with general cargo, bulk cargo is shipped in larger consignments, has a lower value, and per tonne is cheaper to transport. Major changes have occurred in methods of shipping and handling of general and bulk cargoes in the last 25 years, which will be described later in this section. Figure 6.10 shows the principal ports in Britain.

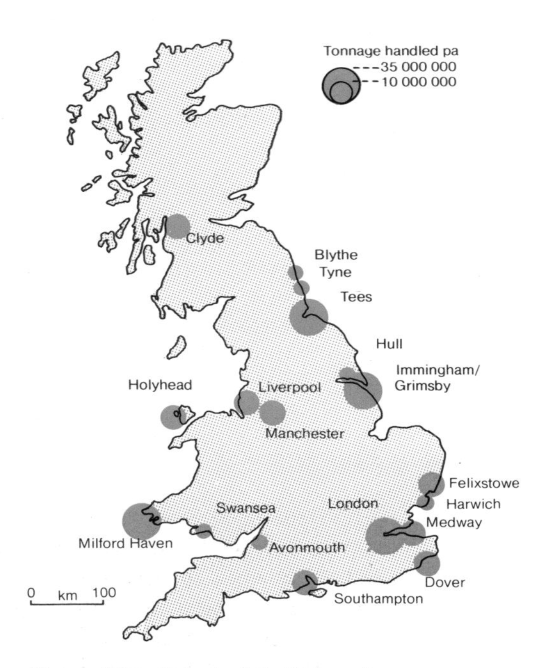

Figure 6.10 Principal British ports

Figure 6.11 Loading containers at the Dooley terminal, Felixstowe. Note the highly mechanised loading operation and the ease with which containers can be transferred from sea to road transport

Figure 6.12 The port of Felixstowe, located on the north bank of the Stour estuary in Suffolk, is the UK's largest container port. In the foreground is the Languard container terminal; in the middle distance is the original dock basin, built over 100 years ago; and in the far distance are the new Dooley and Walton container terminals

Felixstowe – a general cargo port

Felixstowe in Suffolk is one of the UK's largest general cargo ports (Figures 6.11 and 6.12). Most of this cargo is shipped through the port in standard-sized metal boxes, known as *containers*. The port has the capacity to handle 750 000 containers a year – more than any other UK port. Felixstowe's first container terminal was opened in 1967, and since the late 1960s containers have revolutionised the transport of general cargo in DCs. Today, nearly two-thirds of all general cargo handled at British ports is shipped by container. Clearly the advantages of containers must be considerable; some of them are listed in Table 6.4.

Table 6.4 Advantages of container transport

Advantage	Explanation
Cargo can be loaded and unloaded faster.	This means that ships spend less time in port, and more time at sea earning money. The average container ship only spends 12% of its time in port.
Cargoes can be transferred easily and cheaply to other forms of transport.	Containers are units of standard size. They can be loaded rapidly on to lorries and specially-built 'freightliner' rail wagons.
Fewer dock workers are needed.	Loading and unloading is highly mechanised. On average, each dock worker at a container terminal can handle twenty times the tonnage per day, compared with a worker at a conventional berth.
Cargo is more secure.	There is little loss of cargo owing to spillage/ breakage or pilfering.
Packaging costs are reduced.	Because goods are stored inside metal containers, less packaging is needed. Containers are also reusable.

In spite of these advantages, containerisation does have a number of drawbacks. The greatest is the enormous cost: at Felixstowe, two new container terminals, complete with gantry cranes, transit sheds and other storage areas, have recently been built at a cost of £32 million. Then there is the cost of building special container ships and thousands of aluminium containers.

Further disadvantages include the reduction in the number of dock workers, which may leave many men unemployed; and a decline in dockside industries, as cargoes transported in containers can easily be transferred from the port, by road or rail, to other locations.

Felixstowe has three container terminals: each is equipped with rail-mounted gantry cranes capable of lifting 35 tonnes and stacking containers up to three units high, and an extensive container park. Two freightliner terminals serve the container berths, and handle about 20% of the container traffic. There are daily freightliner services from Felixstowe to several major cities in the UK (Figure 6.13).

Figure 6.13 Felixstowe's European trade area

Roll-on/roll-off (ro-ro) is an even speedier method of cargo handling. Cargoes are transported on lorries and trailers which are driven directly on to (and off) specially designed ships, so there is no transfer of cargo from sea to overland transport. Ro-ro provides a fast, 'door-to-door' service between firms, and is particularly suited to short sea journeys. At Felixstowe, four berths handle the ro-ro traffic, the main links being with Zeebrugge, Dunkirk, Europoort and Göteborg (Figure 6.13).

Felixstowe has grown rapidly in the last 20 years (Figure 6.14). This is partly due to investment in modern cargo handling facilities, and partly to the port's favourable situation in the South East, facing the continent. Felixstowe trades with a large number of European ports, and in its immediate trade area or *foreland* in Europe is a market of 80 million people. Many sailings are to Rotterdam (the world's largest port) where containers are transferred to ships bound for North America, Africa, the Middle East and East Asia. Felixstowe's trading links are thus worldwide. The distribution of goods to the port's trade area in the UK (its *hinterland*) is helped by a network of modern dual carriageways which give good access to the M11 (for London), A1 (for the North) and the M1/M6 (for the Midlands and North West).

Exercise

The situation of Felixstowe, on the east coast of England facing Europe, explains much of its success as a port in the last 20 years.

1 Which towns and cities on the continent in Figure 6.13 are nearer to Felixstowe than Manchester?

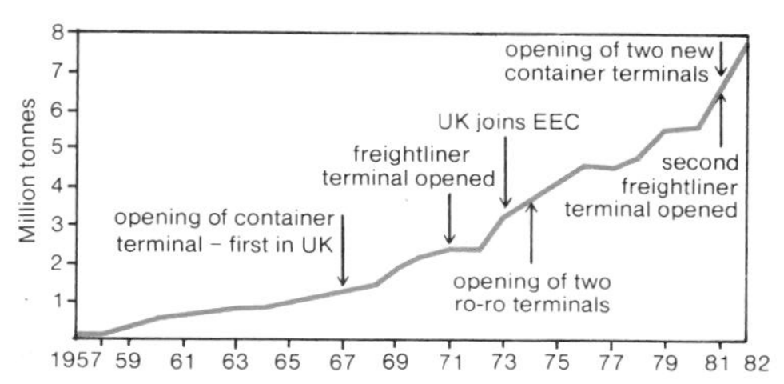

Figure 6.14 Felixstowe: growth of trade, 1957–82

2 The ten leading European ports (including the UK) in terms of tonnage handled are:
   1 Rotterdam
   2 Le Havre
   3 Marseille
   4 Antwerp
   5 Hamburg
   6 Genoa
   7 Bremen
   8 Dunkirk
   9 Bruges
   10 Calais.

   Find these ports in an atlas (some are shown in Figure 6.13) and find out which ones are within 150 km of Felixstowe.

3 14% of Felixstowe's trade (Figure 6.15) is with non-EEC European countries. Look at Figure 6.13 and say in which part of Europe most of these countries are situated.

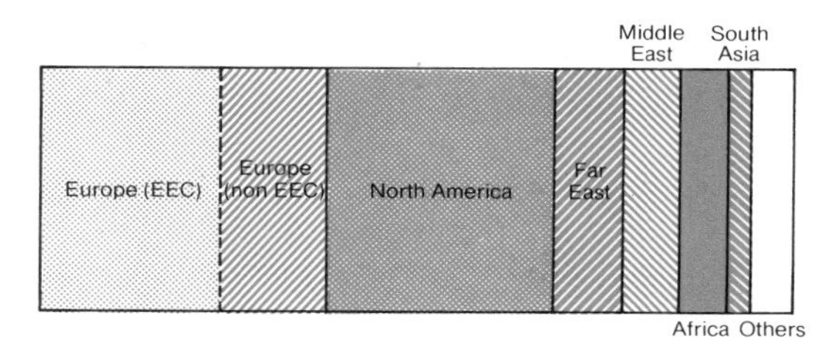

Figure 6.15 Felixstowe: pattern of overseas trade, 1982

4 Write a paragraph describing the area covered by Felixstowe's *foreland* in Europe. Do you think that the port is well situated to serve the major centres of population and industry in the UK?

5 Liverpool is one of the UK's leading general cargo ports but unlike Felixstowe, its trade has declined from 29.3 million tonnes in 1970, to just 11.9 million tonnes in 1981. Look at Figure 6.13 and say why the situation of Liverpool, in relation to a) Europe b) the main centre of population in the UK, is not as good as Felixstowe's.

6 Draw a plan of Felixstowe based on the air photograph of the port (Figure 6.12). On your plan label the following features: River Stour estuary; container park; warehouses/transit sheds; container quays; ro-ro terminals; oil jetty; oil storage tanks; original dock basin (completed 1886).

Teesport – a bulk cargo port

Teesport consists of Tees Dock and the various oil, gas, chemical and ore terminals which line the banks of the Tees downstream of Middlesbrough. In relation to tonnage handled, Teesport ranks as the third largest port in the UK, after Shetland and London.

Exercise

Figure 6.16 shows how Teesport has developed downstream from the old river port of Yarm over the last two centuries.

1 Using the information in Figure 6.16 draw a four-stage diagram to summarise the development of the port. The four stages are:
   1 simple quays and wharfs
   2 enclosed docks
   3 open docks
   4 specialised terminals.
   For each stage record a few simple details of port facilities, their location in relation to the river mouth, and approximate dates. The first stage is shown below.

2 Write a paragraph to explain why the port has expanded downstream over the last 200 years. Look at Figure 6.17 and give two reasons why so much port development has occurred at the mouth of the river since 1960.

3 Name two advantages of Tees Dock over the old Middlesbrough Dock.

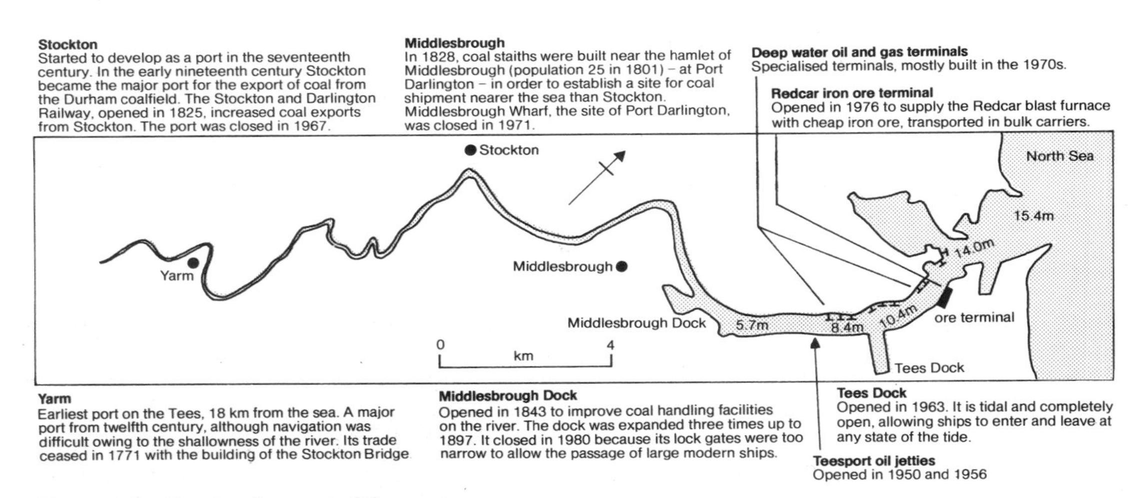

Figure 6.16 The development of Teesport

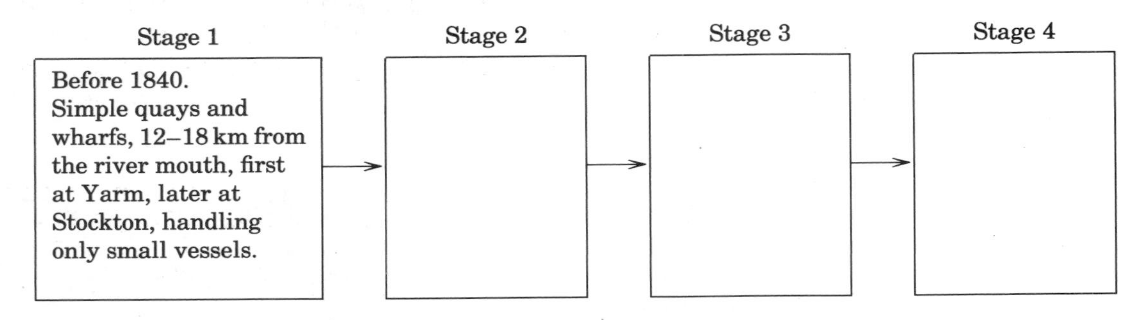

In contrast to Felixstowe, Teesport specialises in the handling of bulk cargoes (Figure 6.18), especially oil which accounts for 70% of its trade. The costs of transporting bulk cargoes such as oil, iron ore, chemicals and grain has fallen

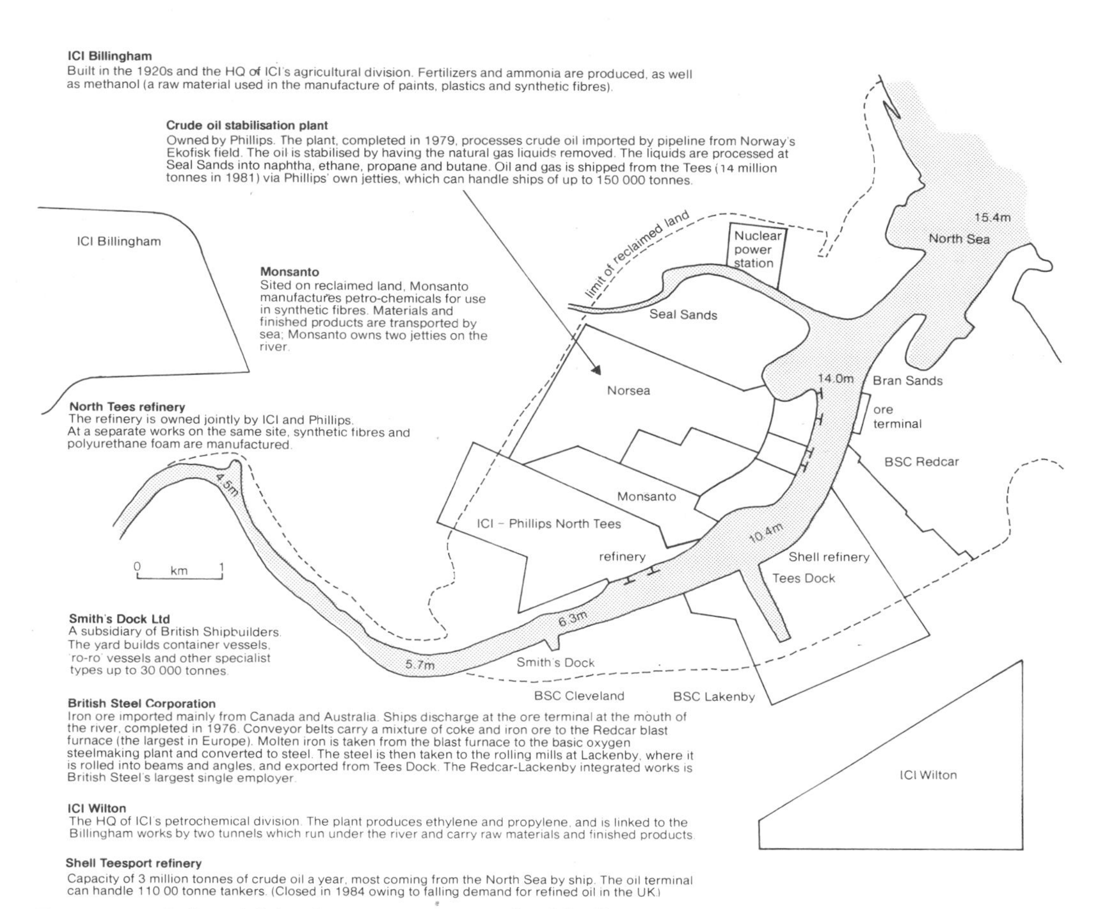

Figure 6.17 Industrial development at the mouth of the Tees

enormously in the last 20 years, with the development of huge bulk-carrying ships. These ships are cheaper to operate than smaller vessels because less money per tonne of cargo carried is spent on fuel, insurance, wages for the crew and so on. One result of cheaper sea transport has been the shipping of bulk cargoes from the most distant parts of the world. For instance, iron ore is imported into Teesport from as far away as Brazil and Australia. However, the huge vessels which transport bulk cargoes require special port facilities, which can only be provided by a handful of UK ports. The most obvious requirement is deep water; Teesport can offer over 14 m near the mouth of the river, which is sufficient for ships of 150 000 tonnes. The only ports on the mainland which offer deeper anchorages are Milford Haven in west Wales, and the Finnart oil terminal near Glasgow (Figure 5.8).

Exercise

Use an atlas and Figure 6.10 and make a list of the estuaries which offer the deepest anchorages for bulk cargo vessels. (You can assume that any port which handles more than 10 million tonnes of cargo per year relies heavily on bulk cargo.)

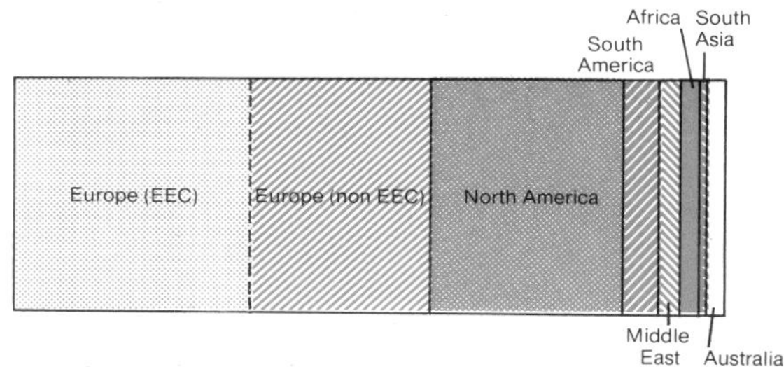

Figure 6.18 Teesport: pattern of overseas trade, 1982

A further requirement is special handling facilities to unload massive amounts of cargo rapidly. For example, at the Redcar ore terminal three mobile cranes are used to unload ships. The ore is then transferred on to conveyor belts which carry it to the steelworks.

The deep water channel near the mouth of the Tees has attracted several heavy industries, which rely on imported raw materials (Figure 6.17). Oil refining, petrochemicals and steel, associated with companies like Shell, ICI, Phillips and British Steel, are found at this *tidewater* location. Large areas of flat land have been reclaimed from the estuary for these industries; indeed reclamation is still taking place, as the recent drainage of Seal Sands shows.

The example of Teesport shows how ports can often be attractive locations for manufacturing industry. This is particularly so when there are expensive handling costs, as bulk cargo is transferred from sea to land, or from land to sea transport.

Exercise

1 Name two other industrial complexes at tidewater, which are similar to Teesside. (You may need to refer back to Chapter 5 to find examples.) State three location factors that all three complexes share.

2 Can you think of any reasons why Felixstowe has attracted few manufacturing industries compared with Teesport? (Clues – types of goods carried in containers, handling costs.) Write a paragraph of explanation.

The UK trade area or *hinterland* served by Teesport is not very large. This is because most imports are raw materials destined for the oil refining, chemical and steel industries of Teesside. Similarly, most exports originate from these tidewater industries. However, the principal export, accounting for 50% of the port's trade, is oil from the North Sea. Although some of this oil is brought in by tanker, most of it is transferred by pipeline, direct from the Norwegian Ekofisk oilfield.

Europe is Teesport's most important area of trade overseas: the port's east coast situation, and the UK's trading links with the EEC account for this. North America also figures prominently, the USA importing large amounts of crude oil from Teesport, and Canada being British Steel's major source of iron ore. There is also some trade in oil with the Middle East, and Datsun cars for the UK market are imported through Tees Dock at the rate of 65 000 a year (Figure 6.19B).

Exercise

1 Look at the composition of trade at Felixstowe and Teesport (Figures 6.19). Which port is the more specialised? Can you suggest how specialisation might be a weakness, and what might be done to strengthen the port's position?

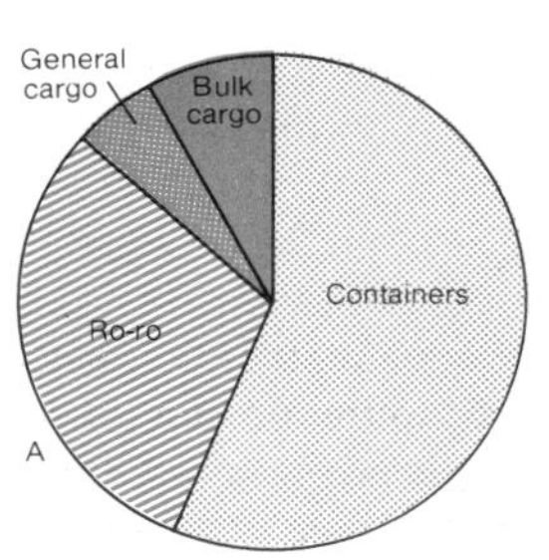

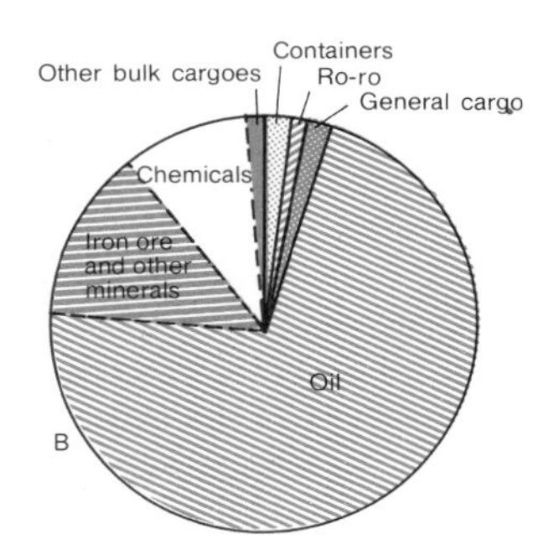

Figure 6.19 (*right*) A Felixstowe, B Teesport: nature of cargo handled, 1982

2 Figure 6.20 is an aerial view of the mouth of the Tees. Compare the photograph with Figure 6.17, and answer the following questions.
   a) From which bank of the river was the photograph taken?
   b) In which direction was the camera pointing?
   c) Identify each of the features indicated by the letters A to D.

Figure 6.20 The industrial complex on reclaimed land at the mouth of the Tees estuary in north east England

Inland waterways

Like sea transport, inland waterways (which consist of canals and navigable rivers) are most effective in moving bulk cargoes over long distances. However, their importance as a means of freight transport varies considerably from country to country: while 36% of all freight in the Netherlands, and 18% in Belgium is transported by inland waterways, the proportion in the UK is less than 1%.

Conditions in the UK are generally unfavourable for inland waterways. Many of the largest towns and cities are located on the coast, and in the UK coastal shipping performs the task of inland waterways in countries such as the Netherlands, Belgium and West Germany. Relief is also unfavourable compared with the UK's European neighbours, and many British rivers have short lowland courses, are small and steeply graded, and unsuitable for navigation. The canal network of the UK was largely built between 150 and 200 years ago, and for the most part has not been improved. The narrowness of the canals and locks makes them inadequate for commercial traffic; nowadays the main use of most canals is for leisure and recreational activities. One exception is the Manchester Ship Canal, completed in 1896 and linking the port of Manchester with the Mersey estuary. This canal, which is nearly 60 km long and has a minimum depth of 8.5 m, is the only one in the UK capable of accommodating ocean-going ships.

Exercise

1 a Look back at Figure 1.25 and list the major cities and conurbations located on or near the coast which are likely to be accessible to coastal shipping.
  b Compare West Germany with the UK by referring to Figure 3.21, which shows the 10 largest German cities; find out from an atlas how many are located on the coast. Of those cities not found on the coast, which ones are located on or near the River Rhine, or on one of its major (navigable) tributaries such as the Mosel, Neckar or Main?

2 a The Rhine, Elbe and Meuse are important navigable rivers in Western Europe. Use your atlas to estimate their approximate lengths. How do they compare with three of the UK's longest rivers: the Thames, Severn and Trent?
  b How do you think that the length of a river might affect its navigability? Apart from length, what other factors might determine whether a river is navigable or not?

3 Explain why areas of low relief are best suited to canal building (page 149). Compare the relief of Belgium with its pattern of inland waterways (Figure 6.21). Does relief appear to influence the network?

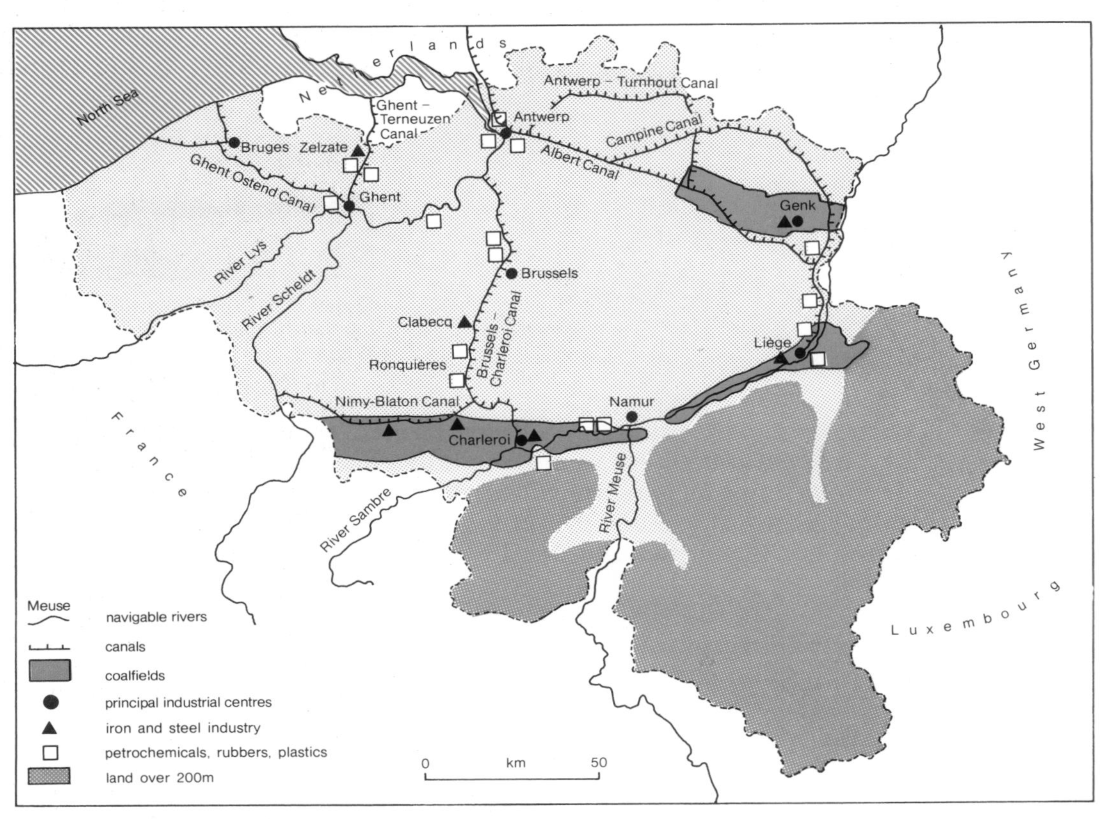

Figure 6.21 Heavy industries and inland waterways in Belgium

Belgium's inland waterways

The Belgian inland waterway network is based on the rivers Scheldt and Meuse, both of which have their sources in France and drain into the Rhine Delta. Other important navigable rivers are the Lys, a tributary of the Scheldt, and the Sambre, which joins the Meuse at Namur. To this natural system of waterways a comprehensive canal network has been added. The total length of the inland waterway network is almost 2000 km, with around 40% of it accessible to vessels of over 1000 tonnes (Figure 6.22).

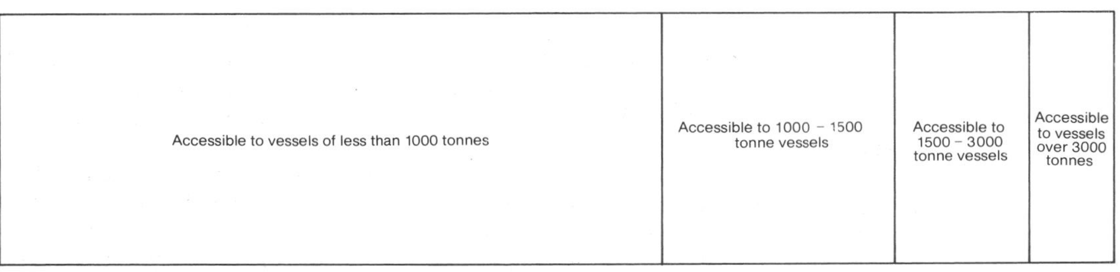

Figure 6.22 Belgian navigable waterways: 1944 km

The busiest waterway is the lower Scheldt valley (Figure 6.23) where the Brussels–Rupel canal and the River Rupel merge with the Scheldt. Of almost equal importance is the Albert Canal, which links the port of Antwerp with the Campine coalfield and the South Belgian industrial region. The canal, completed in 1940, is 130 km long and handles nearly 50 million tonnes of cargo a year (Figure 6.24). The Ghent–Terneuzen Canal, which links the port of Ghent with the North Sea, is accessible to 60 000 tonne vessels. Much of the cargo it handles is connected with the integrated steel plant located alongside the canal at Zelzate.

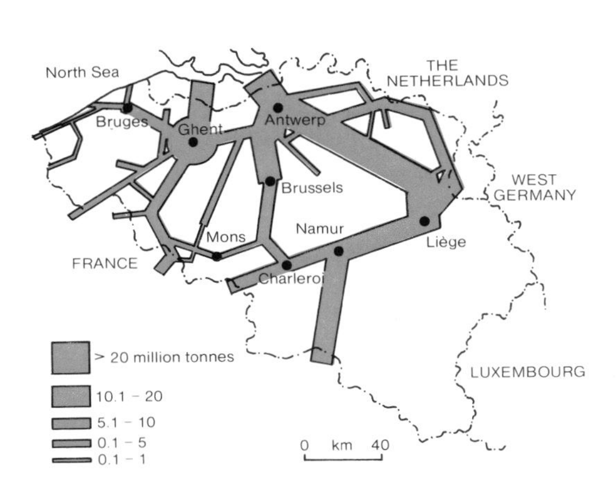

Figure 6.23 Freight traffic on Belgian inland waterways

Figure 6.24 A push barge in a lock on the Albert Canal near Liège, Belgium. Canal transport is particularly efficient in carrying heavy and bulky cargoes, like the crushed roadstone in the photograph

Since 1947 a programme of modernisation of the inland waterway network has been undertaken, with the aim of accommodating barges in the 1300–2000 tonne class. However, to some extent the need to widen and deepen canals and locks has been reduced by the introduction of the new technique of push-tugs. For example, individual tugs on the Albert Canal can push barges in convoys weighing up to 10 000 tonnes. Present policy is still to reduce the number of locks as far as possible, as they greatly slow down traffic. The most spectacular achievement has been the building of the inclined plane at Ronquières, on the Brussels–Charleroi Canal, which has replaced no fewer than 20 locks. The inclined plane is able to carry barges of up to 1350 tonnes from one level to another by giant lifts. The most recent improvement has been the completion of a new canal link between Antwerp and the River Rhine in the Netherlands.

Exercise

1 Say what evidence in Figure 6.21 supports the idea that canals are most important for the transport of high bulk, low value materials.

2 Assuming that the Belgian steel industry relies heavily on imported iron ore from overseas, which steel making location in Figure 6.21 is likely to be most favourable? Write a short paragraph of explanation, making some reference to the location of other steel making centres in Belgium.

3 Measured by tonnage handled, Antwerp is Europe's fourth largest port. Study Figures 6.21 and 6.23 and describe the advantages of Antwerp's situation in relation to the network of canals and navigable rivers.

Road transport

Motorways and trunk roads in Britain

In 1983 the UK had 2562 km of motorways with a further 672 km either under construction or planned, and nearly 12 000 km of major trunk roads (Figure 6.25). In Western Europe only West Germany, Italy and France have larger motorway networks.

The motorway network started in the UK with the completion of the Preston by-pass section of the M6 in 1958. The following year saw the opening of the Rugby to Watford section of the M1, and by 1970 there were just over 1000 km of motorway completed. The aim of motorway building is to provide safe, fast and efficient routes, and relieve congestion on the older trunk routes and within towns (Figure 6.26). Motorways have been primarily built to handle road freight traffic, which accounted for 82% of freight movements in the UK in 1981; for this reason the network links the major industrial areas in the country, while few routes have been built to ports or tourist areas. There is no doubt that the motorways have been highly successful: although they only form 1% of the UK's total surfaced road network, they carry 10% of all road traffic. Indeed, the motorway system is used by a far greater volume of traffic than was planned, and for this reason costly repairs are constantly required to maintain the roads in good condition.

Exercise

1 Motorways carry 10% of road traffic but account for only 6% of road accidents. Explain why motorways are safer than other roads.

2 Motorways were designed so that traffic can maintain average speeds of 80 km an hour. Describe the main differences between motorways and conventional roads which make these higher average speeds possible.

3 Which of the seven conurbations in Britain are not joined to the main motorway network? (If necessary refer to pages 15–17 to remind yourself where the conurbations are.) Look at Figure 6.25 and suggest how they could be most easily linked to the system.

4 Study Figure 6.25 and say which stretch of motorway in Britain is likely to be the busiest. Give your reasons. (Figure 1.25, Table 1.10 and page 16 contain useful information.)

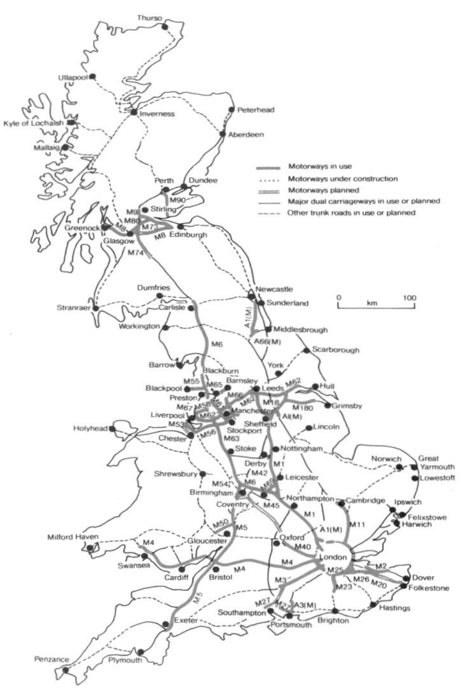

Figure 6.25 Britain's trunk road network

Transport networks are collections of routes (they may be roads, railways or pipelines) which link places together so that movements of freight and passengers can occur between them. The motorway system in Britain is such a network, though as yet, it is incomplete. You may think that the motorway network is rather sparse, and indeed there are several parts of the country, such as East Anglia and much of Wales and Scotland, which are not served by any motorways at all. However, when you consider the cost of building motorways this is not so surprising. For example, a 10 km stretch of the new M25 between Wisley and Chertsey in Surrey cost £30 million, while a 4 km section of the same motorway near Brentwood in Essex cost £17 million! Costs increase considerably when cuttings, embankments, viaducts or tunnels have to be built. As Table 6.5 indicates, a river tunnel such as the Tyne Tunnel near Newcastle can cost 50 times as much to build as an equivalent level section of road.

Table 6.5 Average building costs of various types of motorway based on the cost of a given length of ground level road

	Cost index
Ground level	100
Cutting	150
Embankment	200
Viaduct	750
River tunnel	5000

This means that the major factor which determines the features of transport networks is the need to keep building costs to a minimum. The limited extent of the UK's motorway network reflects the over-riding influence of cost, even though a partial or incomplete network increases the costs to the user (arising from longer journeys, more fuel used and higher labour costs).

The overall effectiveness of the British motorway network is reduced by the existence of several important gaps. There is, for example, only one trans-Pennine route (M62); there is no A1–M1 link, which would give the Midlands and the North West easier access to the east coast ports of Felixstowe and Harwich; and the absence of a motorway (or dual carriageway road) between the Midlands and the south coast, is another vital missing link. In addition, within the existing network there are some small, but important gaps, which urgently need filling. The M20 which links London with the Channel ports has a short section missing between Maidstone and Ashford; the M3 has still to be extended as far as Southampton; and the M42, which is intended to join the M5 and M6 south of Birmingham, has been at a standstill since 1978.

However, the most important motorway which has yet to be completed, is the M25 or orbital motorway, around London (Figure 6.27). The final section should be finished in 1986, by which time the project will have cost £630 million. Before the building of the M25, traffic had to pick its way slowly through London, or round it on congested roads. When complete, traffic will have a fast motorway route which entirely by-passes the capital. Already, traffic bound for the Channel ports from the North and Midlands can by-pass London on the north east section of the M25, cross the Thames through the Dartford Tunnel, and link up with either the M2 to Dover, or the M20 to Folkestone. The benefits of the new route are already being felt in north east areas of Greater London such as Enfield, Romford and Epping, where traffic congestion has been greatly relieved. Overall, the M25 should reduce journey times between the M2 and A1 by up to 60%. It will also give a motorway connection between Heathrow, Gatwick and Stansted airports.

Figure 6.26 The M1 near Sheffield; here it crosses the heavily industrialised Don Valley

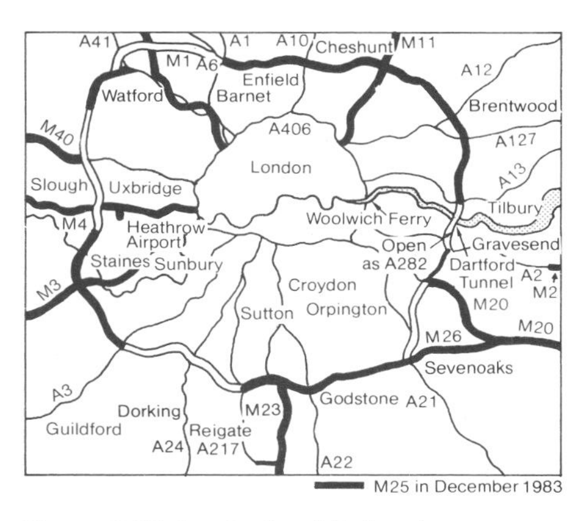

Figure 6.27 London's orbital motorway

Not all the effects of the M25 will be beneficial: while traffic within London should shrink, it will increase on the motorway radials (M1, M2, M3, M4) linked to the orbital road. The M1 for instance, which even now is used by 66 000 vehicles a day, could be taking 100 000 vehicles a day by the mid 1990s! Furthermore, many manufacturing and office activities might be attracted out of central London by the new motorway, and this would not only mean a loss of jobs in an area where they are badly needed, but would also cause planning problems, as the M25 for the most part runs through London's green belt.

Exercise

1 If you were planning a journey between the following pairs of cities, which motorways would you choose in order to travel by the most direct route? (See Figure 6.25.)
— Birmingham and Hull
— London and Bradford
— Leicester and Blackpool
— Swansea and Leeds

2 Following only those motorways in use in Figure 6.25, plan the shortest possible route starting from London, and visiting Bristol, Birmingham and Leeds (in any order) and finishing in London. Measure the distance of your route and compare it with alternative routes chosen by other members of your class.

3 Figure 6.28 is a simplified version of the motorway network of Britain. In it the actual network has been reduced to a series of straight lines or *links*, which connect places and junctions (*nodes*). When we look at transport networks in this way, it is possible to estimate the relative accessibility of places in the network. This is done by counting the number of links between a place, and all the other places in the network (Table 6.6). For example, in Figure 6.28 there are four links separating London from Bristol, and seven links between London and Leeds. If we add together all the links between London and the other 28 places in the motorway network, we get a total of 151 (Table 6.6). This figure tells us how well connected London is to the network: the lower the value for a place, the more accessible it is. However, you should note that this method takes no account of actual distances between places, and that in Table 6.6 London for instance, is just as close to Southampton as it is to Reading!
Complete the missing calculations in Table 6.6 and find the overall accessibility of Leeds, Hull, Coventry, Worcester, Cambridge, Bristol, Exeter and Swansea.
Which are the three most, and the three least accessible places in the motorway network?

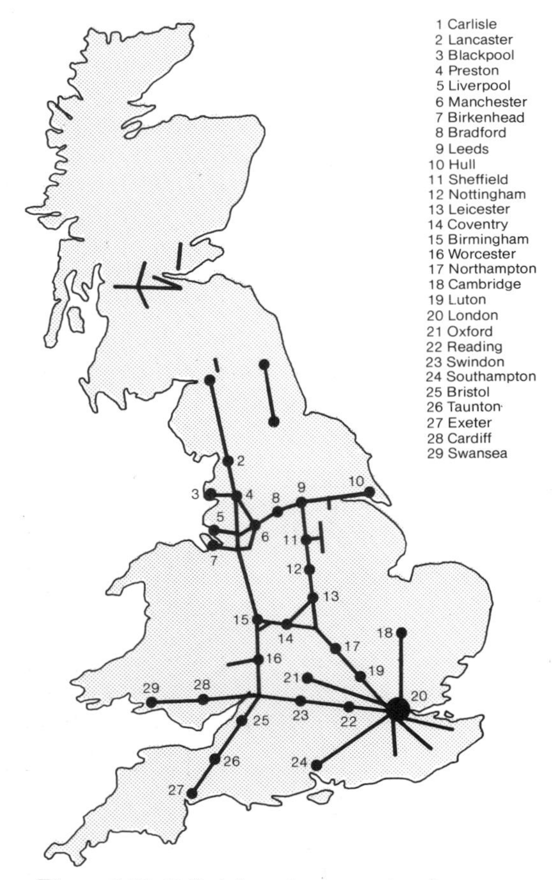

Figure 6.28 Britain's motorway network

4 On an outline map of England and Wales, plot the total scores for all of the places in Table 6.6. Draw in isolines to show relative accessibility at the following intervals: 130, 150, 170, 190. In order to help you, the 150 isoline has already been plotted in Figure 6.29.

5 Study the isoline map, and answer the following. Which region could reasonably claim to be at the centre of the motorway network of England and Wales? How does the accessibility of London compare with other places – is it more or less accessible than you expected?

6 If a manufacturing firm relied on fast, efficient road transport for the assembly of its materials and the distribution of its products to market, where (other things being equal) would be the best area in England and Wales to locate?

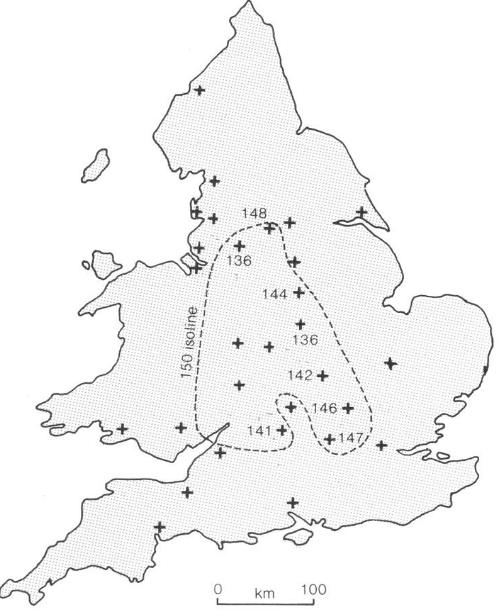

Figure 6.29 Motorway accessibility in England and Wales

Table 6.6

		1	2	3	4	5	6	7	8	9	10	11	12	13	14	15	16	17	18	19	20	21	22	23	24	25	26	27	28	29	TOTAL
1	CARLISLE	×	1	3	2	4	3	5	4	5	7	6	7	8	7	5	7	9	12	10	11	12	10	9	12	9	10	11	9	10	208
2	LANCASTER	1	×	2	1	3	2	4	3	4	6	5	6	7	6	4	6	8	11	9	10	11	9	8	11	8	9	10	8	9	181
3	BLACKPOOL	3	2	×	1	3	2	4	3	4	6	5	6	7	6	4	6	8	11	9	10	11	9	8	11	8	9	10	8	9	183
4	PRESTON	2	1	1	×	2	1	3	2	3	5	4	5	6	5	3	5	7	10	8	9	10	8	7	10	7	8	9	7	8	156
5	LIVERPOOL	4	3	3	2	×	2	3	3	4	6	5	6	6	5	3	5	7	10	8	9	10	8	7	10	7	8	9	7	8	168
6	MANCHESTER	3	2	2	1	2	×	2	1	2	4	3	4	5	4	2	4	6	9	7	8	9	7	6	9	6	7	8	6	7	136
7	BIRKENHEAD	5	4	4	3	3	2	×	3	4	6	5	6	5	4	2	4	6	9	7	8	9	7	6	9	6	7	8	6	7	155
8	BRADFORD	4	3	3	2	3	1	3	×	1	3	2	3	4	5	4	5	6	9	7	8	9	8	7	9	7	8	9	7	8	148
9	LEEDS									×																					
10	HULL										×																				
11	SHEFFIELD	6	5	5	4	5	3	5	2	1	3	×	1	2	3	5	6	4	7	5	6	7	7	8	7	8	9	10	8	9	151
12	NOTTINGHAM	7	6	6	5	6	4	6	3	2	4	1	×	1	2	4	5	3	6	4	5	6	6	7	6	7	8	9	7	8	144
13	LEICESTER	8	7	7	6	6	5	5	4	3	5	2	1	×	1	3	4	2	5	3	4	5	5	6	5	6	7	8	6	7	136
14	COVENTRY														×																
15	BIRMINGHAM	5	4	4	3	3	2	2	4	5	7	5	4	3	2	×	2	4	7	5	6	7	5	4	7	4	5	6	4	5	124
16	WORCESTER																×														
17	NORTHAMPTON	9	8	8	7	7	6	6	6	5	7	4	3	2	2	4	5	×	3	1	2	3	3	4	3	6	7	8	6	7	142
18	CAMBRIDGE																		×												
19	LUTON	10	9	9	8	8	7	7	7	6	8	5	4	3	3	5	5	1	2	×	1	2	2	3	2	5	6	7	5	6	146
20	LONDON	11	10	10	9	9	8	8	8	7	8	6	5	4	4	6	4	2	1	1	×	1	1	2	1	4	5	6	4	5	151
21	OXFORD	12	11	11	10	10	9	9	9	8	10	7	6	5	5	7	5	3	2	2	1	×	2	3	2	5	6	7	5	6	178
22	READING	10	9	9	8	8	7	7	8	8	10	7	6	5	5	5	3	3	2	2	1	2	×	1	2	3	4	5	3	4	147
23	SWINDON	9	8	8	7	7	6	6	7	8	10	8	7	6	5	4	2	4	3	3	2	3	1	×	8	2	3	4	2	3	141
24	SOUTHAMPTON	12	11	11	10	10	9	9	9	8	10	7	6	5	5	7	5	3	2	2	1	2	2	3	×	5	6	7	5	6	178
25	BRISTOL																									×					
26	TAUNTON	10	9	9	8	8	7	7	8	9	11	9	8	7	6	5	3	7	6	6	5	6	4	3	6	1	×	1	3	4	176
27	EXETER																											×			
28	CARDIFF	9	8	8	7	7	6	6	7	8	10	8	7	6	5	4	2	6	5	5	4	5	3	2	5	2	3	4	×	1	153
29	SWANSEA																													×	

As we saw earlier, motorways are costly, they take a long time to plan and build, and often their effectiveness is reduced by gaps in the network. An alternative to motorway building, which overcomes these problems, is *road improvement*. Here the aim is to upgrade *existing* trunk roads, often by building dual carriageways. The best example is the A1 between London and Newcastle-upon-Tyne, which consists of alternating sections of dual carriageway and motorway. Other important dual carriageway trunk routes, which permit speeds almost as fast as motorways, include the A38 between Birmingham and Derby, the A74 between Glasgow and Carlisle, and the A45 between Cambridge, Ipswich and Felixstowe.

Many smaller towns in the UK which are route centres, suffer badly from heavy traffic, which may cause severe congestion at peak times, pollute the central shopping areas with exhaust fumes, damage buildings and bridges by vibration, and, most seriously, cause road deaths and injuries (Figures 6.30 and 6.31). The effects of a by-pass (which diverts through traffic around the town) not only solves the immediate problems, but often improves the whole quality of life in the town. People are attracted to the town once the heavy traffic is removed, parking is easier, and many new businesses may open up.

Figure 6.31 The problem of traffic congestion and heavy lorries in small market towns is common in Britain. The solution – the building of by-passes – is a simple, but expensive one.

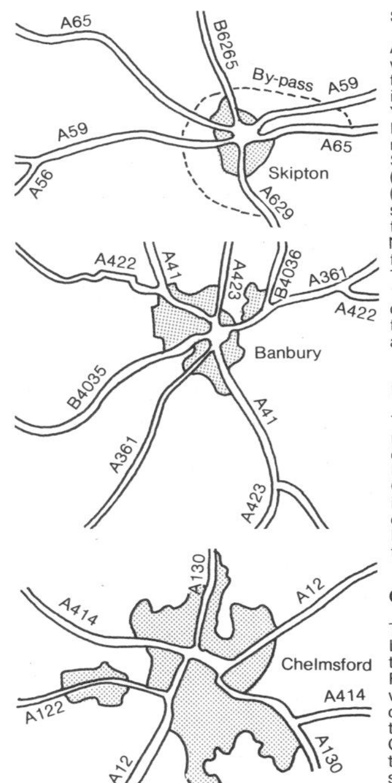

Skipton, North Yorkshire

An important route centre, with traffic converging on the town from the large industrial centres of West Yorkshire and East Lancashire. Also busy routes to Cumbria and Scotland (A65), Humberside (A59) and West Lancashire (A59). Congestion was most severe in summer, when tourist traffic to the Dales National Park was added to the normal freight traffic. The by-pass, completed in 1982, has relieved congestion and made the town an even more attractive shopping centre.

Banbury, Oxfordshire

The town needs a by-pass to relieve pressure from converging routes. With no M40 (West Midlands – Oxford) extension, the A41 is a major trunk road carrying traffic from Birmingham to Oxford and the south coast.

Chelmsford, Essex

The busy A12, which links London with Ipswich and the major ports of Felixstowe and Harwich as well as east coast resorts, is dual carriageway except for the section through Chelmsford (15 km). This, together with the town's situation as a route focus, leads to congestion. A by-pass is needed.

Figure 6.30 Important route centres and their traffic problems

Exercise

'Leydon' is a busy market town, where several important roads converge. Through traffic is heavy and is increasing; there is severe congestion in the town centre at certain times, where the noise, exhaust fumes and the movement of vehicles, makes the area unpleasant and dangerous for pedestrians.

Your task is to plan the route for a new by-pass round the town. The by-pass must:
a) link together the A659, A660 (west), A660 (east) and A6038 trunk roads b) keep costs of building as low as possible on behalf of the County Council.

Costs

Four factors affect the cost of building: slopes; flooding from the river; the possibility of having to demolish parts of the built-up area of Leydon; the possible need to bridge the river.

a Slopes increase the costs of building. The steepness of slopes is shown in Figure 6.32A by the difference in height (in metres) between the highest and lowest contour in each square. Building costs with slope are shown in Table 6.7.

b Land alongside the river is liable to flooding (Figure 6.32A), and the need to build embankments in this area increases costs. For any length of road *within a square* affected by flooding in addition to the building costs according to slope (Table 6.7) there is an extra £600 000 per ½ km (or square on the map).

c The County Council will accept plans which include some limited demolition on the outskirts of the town (see Figure 6.32B). However, building is costly in these areas because of the high price of land and the need to compensate owners whose property has to be demolished. For any length of road, *in a square*, affected by demolition, in addition to the building costs according to slope (Table 6.7) there is an extra £500 000 per ½ km (or square on the map).

d Your plan may involve a bridge across the river. In addition to building costs according to slope, each bridge costs £1 000 000 to build.

Table 6.7	Cost of building with slope
0–14 m	£100 000 per ½ km (ie per square on Figure 6.32A)
15–29 m	£150 000 ,, ,,
30–59 m	£300 000 ,, ,,
60–119 m	£600 000 ,, ,,

A

	10–11	11–12	12–13	13–14	14–15	15–16	16–17	17–18	18–19	19–20	20–21	21–22	22–23	23–24
06–07	76	31	30	31	46	61	61	76	91	107	107	91	61	0
05–06	61	76	107	92	92	107	107	107	107	107	76	31	31	31
04–05	0	0	0	0	15	15	15	15	15	0	0	0	0	0
03–04	0	0	0	0	0	0	0	0	0	0	0	0	0	0
02–03	15	0	0	0	0	0	0	0	0	0	0	0	0	0
01–02	15	15	15	15	30	15	31	15	31	31	15	15	30	30

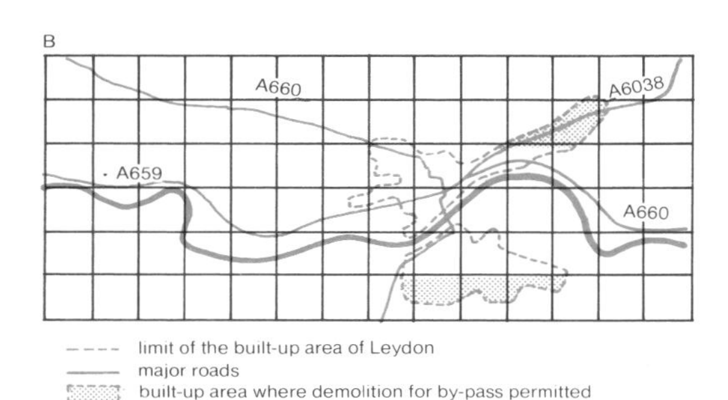

limit of the built-up area of Leydon
major roads
built-up area where demolition for by-pass permitted

Figure 6.32 Planning a by-pass for 'Leydon'
A Slopes and flooding B Base map

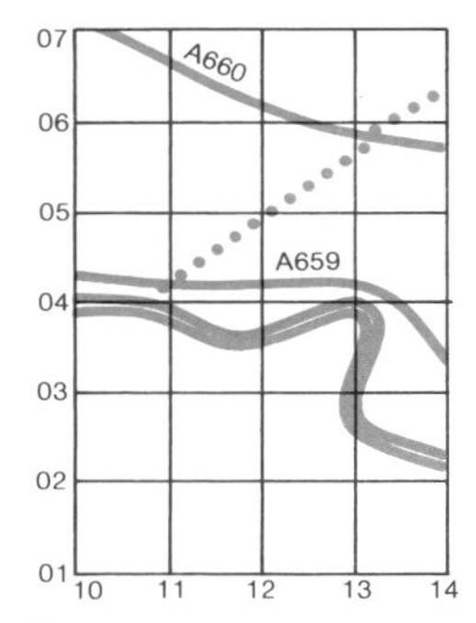

Figure 6.33

1 Taking into account all of the costs, draw your route for the by-pass on a traced copy of Figure 6.32B. Your route must consist of a series of straight lines, which can only change direction when they cross the boundaries between the grid squares (look at the example in Figure 6.33).

2 Estimate the cost of your route by entering the details of each section in a copy of Table 6.8. (The figures refer to the example in Figure 6.33.)

Table 6.8

Recording sheet for costs of building							
Grid square 4-figure reference	Slopes	Route length (mm)	Cost £	Extra costs £ Flooding	Demolition	Bridge	Total
1104	0	13	130000	130000	None	None	260000
1205	107	11	660000	None	None	None	660000
1305	92	5	300000	None	None	None	300000
1306	31	7	210000	None	None	None	210000
					Total cost		

3 How much did your by-pass cost? How does it compare with the cost of other routes chosen by members of your class?

4 In a paragraph or two, explain how you chose your route. Look at the routes chosen by others (especially those who devised the lowest cost routes) and suggest what alterations you might make to your original plan to make it even cheaper.

Road transport in the Third World

Poorly developed transport systems are a feature of most countries in the Third World. The example of Nigeria in the previous chapter (pages 130–4) showed how industrial progress can only be achieved through improvements in port, road and rail facilities. Equally, we shall see in Chapter 7 that agricultural development in Ecuador and Mauritania depends largely on road construction.

Madagascar

Madagascar, the large island off the coast of East Africa, is typical of many Third World countries in having an inadequate transport system (Figure 6.34) which has hindered development. There are only 850 km of railways, and an equally sparse road network. A problem of the road network is that only one-fifth of the 40 000 km have tarred, all-weather surfaces. During the rainy season dirt track roads become impassable, leaving many small towns cut-off. Great efforts are being made to improve the road system with money received as aid from DCs and the World Bank. Recent road construction projects include improvements to sections between Antananarivo, the largest city and capital, and Antseranana, and Toamasina (the main port), and Moramanga.

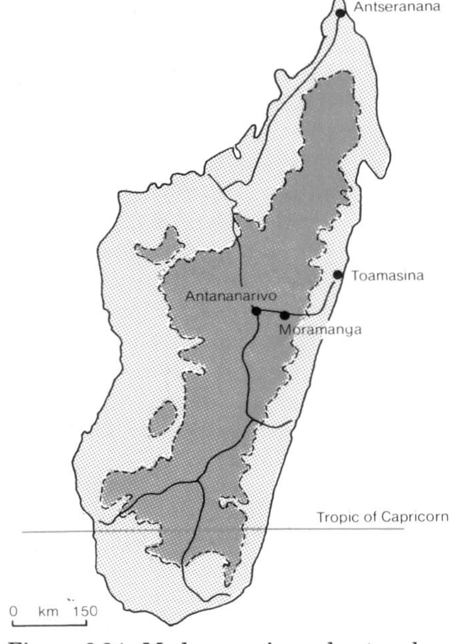

Figure 6.34 Madagascar's road network

Exercise

1 In addition to a lack of capital for road building, another factor hinders the development of roads in Madagascar. Have a look at Table 6.9 and say what it is.

2 Find the countries in Table 6.9 in your atlas. In which country would you say that relief is the biggest obstacle to road building?

3 Look at the figures in Table 6.9.
 a What happens to the density of the road network, as population density increases?
 b Try to suggest a reason for your answer.

Table 6.9

	Surfaced road network (km)	Population density per km^2	Length of road per km^2 (metres)
UK	340000	228	1380
Nigeria	43360	83	47
Madagascar	8364	15	14
Peru	4547	14	4

Brazil

The development of the state of Rondônia, deep in the Amazon jungle of Brazil (Figure 6.35) has until recently been hampered by the lack of roads. Getting in and out of the region was by way of a single 1450 km long dirt road from Cuiaba (Figure 6.35). In the rainy season this would turn into a quagmire, trapping trucks bringing in vital food and fuel supplies for days at a time. Conditions were so bad, that journeys between Rondônia and São Paulo states could take up to 30 days! The problem was solved in 1984 with the paving of the road between Cuiaba and Porto Velho, the capital of Rondônia. The World Bank financed the project, which has opened up the whole of the frontier land of north west Brazil to settlement. Between 1981 and 1984 the World Bank committed more than £600 million to the region, and nearly all of it has been spent on the main road, and 1000 km of feeder roads.

In the future this improved transport link will have a considerable effect on Rondônia and the whole of north west Brazil. It will certainly lead to even more rapid population growth as landless farmers from the south pour into the region. It will make commercial farming possible, growing crops like coffee, cocoa, bananas and rice for export and for the people living in the large cities such as São Paulo and Rio de Janeiro. And finally it will hasten the destruction of the rainforest, which is already disappearing rapidly throughout the Amazon basin (see Chapter 7, pages 232–40).

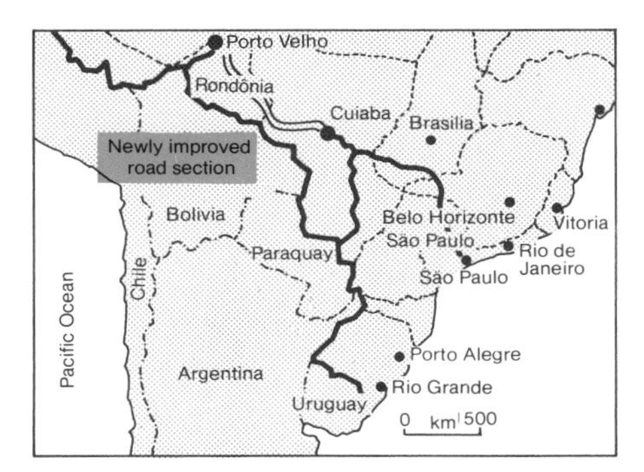

Figure 6.35 The Cuiaba–Porto Velho highway and the development of Rondonia, north west Brazil

Rail transport

Railways in the UK

Railways are important carriers of passengers and freight in the UK. However, compared with other forms of transport, the railways' share of passenger and freight traffic has been declining steadily for the last 40 years. For example, in 1982 the railways carried only two-thirds of the passengers, and half the freight which they transported in 1945. Today the railways carry only 7% of all passengers, and around 10% of the nation's freight. As traffic has declined, the railway network has been reduced in length: in 1950 there were 32 000 km of track, compared with 17 400 km in 1982. Although the network has altered little since the 1960s, it is possible that several underused and unprofitable lines will close during the 1980s (Figure 6.36).

Exercise

1 Compare the UK rail network (Figure 6.36A) with the distribution of population in the UK (Figure 1.25). Are the distributions similar? Say how, and write a brief explanation.

2 Figure 6.36B is a plan which reduces the rail network to around 2500 km. Such a network would only serve the major cities, but it would make the railways profitable (they needed government assistance of £900 million in 1982).

a Refer to Figure 6.36B and your atlas and list some of the cities in the UK which would no longer be served by rail if the network in Figure 6.36B were adopted.

b What do you think that Figure 6.36B tells you about the profitability of existing routes between London and the major cities, and between the major cities themselves?

c Can you suggest two additional routes to the network in Figure 6.36B which would substantially improve connections between the major cities?

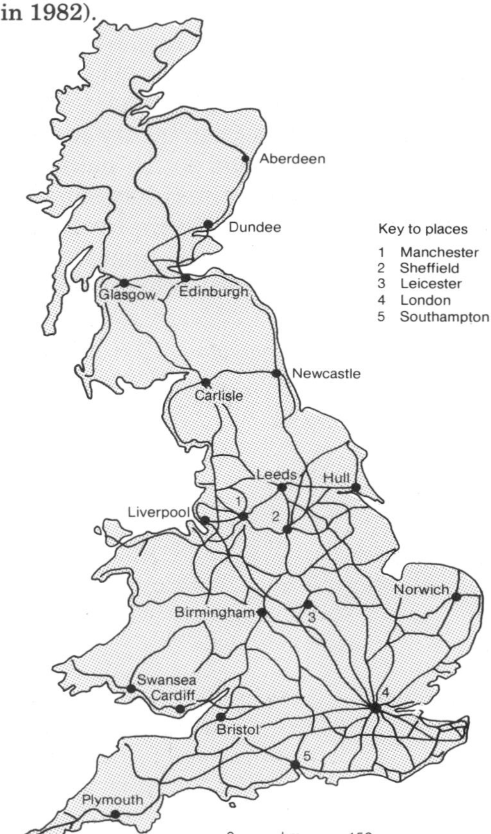

Figure 6.36A Britain's rail network, 1983

Figure 6.36B A proposed rail network for Britain

The decline of rail traffic is largely due to competition from road transport. Freight traffic has declined more than passengers, and today two-thirds of British Rail's income is from passenger traffic. The decline of freight traffic is the result of several factors. Few modern factories have a direct rail connection through their own sidings; road transport is usually quicker and can offer a door-to-door service; and there has been a massive decline in coal production (Figure 6.37) which has deprived the railways of hundreds of millions of tonnes of traffic over the last 25 years. In the 1970s the contraction of the steel industry also lost British Rail traffic (the movement of iron ore and finished steel), though to some extent this has been compensated for by a growth in oil and chemicals, and building and construction traffic (Table 6.10).

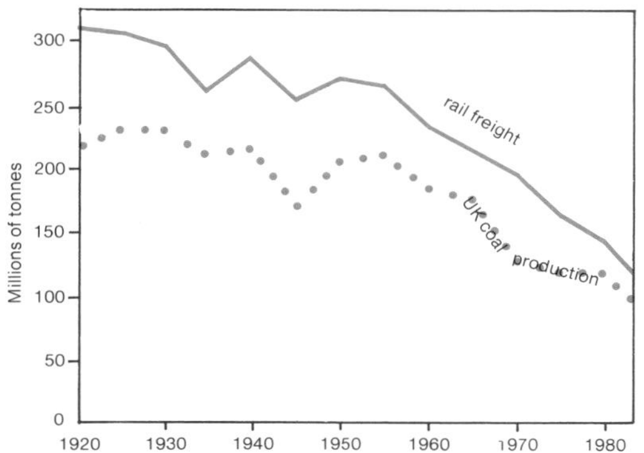

Figure 6.37 Rail freight traffic and coal production in the UK, 1920–82

Table 6.10
British Rail freight 1982: millions of tonnes carried

Coal	88.4
Iron and steel	14.3
Oil and chemicals	14.6
Building and construction	16.1
Freightliner	6.5
Others	2.0
Total	141.9

New developments

British Rail has made strenuous efforts to modernise its operations, and attract traffic back from road transport. Several routes – notably the west coast route from London to Glasgow – have been electrified; steam locomotives were phased out in the 1960s, and replaced by more efficient diesel and electric traction; passenger services between major cities have been greatly speeded up and made more frequent; and methods of handling freight have been streamlined and made more effective.

Railways are most competitive as carriers of freight when goods are moved regularly in large quantities over distances of 250 km or more. Traditionally the railways have relied on the transport of bulky, low value items, such as coal and iron ore. This kind of freight remains very important, even though the actual tonnages transported have declined considerably.

Exercise

1 Draw a pie chart to show the information in Table 6.10. Make the distinction between bulk and non-bulk freight on your chart clear.

2 What % of British Rail's freight traffic in 1982 was a) coal b) bulk commodities? (NB only 'Freightliner' and 'Others' are non-bulk items in Table 6.10.)

3 In 1950 the railways carried 286 million tonnes of freight, of which 170 million tonnes were coal. Has there been much change in the *relative* importance of coal traffic to British Rail since 1950?

4 Rail transport is most competitive over longer distances – at least 250 km for freight, and between 160 and 640 km for passengers. In which of the following countries is rail transport likely to be a) most important b) least important: UK, Netherlands, USA? Explain your answer.

British Rail has modernised its freight operations in a number of ways. *Unit* trains have been introduced for the movement of coal and iron ore. Permanently coupled trains carry coal from the Yorks, Notts and Derby coalfield to huge thermal power stations on the Rivers Trent and Aire. Loading and unloading is automatic and highly efficient, and as the trains move in a circuit, from mine to power station to mine, they are known as 'merry-go-round' trains (Figure 6.38). Similar unit trains transfer iron ore between Immingham and Scunthorpe on Humberside, Port Talbot and Llanwern in South Wales, and Hunterston and Ravenscraig on Clydeside. These unit trains show that rail can be competitive over short distances providing goods are moved regularly and in large quantities (up to 2000 tonnes at a time).

Figure 6.38 A merry-go-round train. Introduced in 1965 these trains now supply 60 million tonnes of coal a year to 11 power stations in Britain

Figure 6.39 A freightliner train. These trains cover long hauls between terminals – usually overnight – at high speed. Local delivery and collection is usually by road

While the railways have been fairly successful in attracting bulk cargoes, manufactured goods are mainly transported by road. 'Freightliner' is a service which aims to capture manufactured goods from road transport. It consists of container trains which travel at high speed on standard daily schedules, between major cities and container ports (Figure 6.39). The containers are assembled by road transport at specially equipped container terminals, where they are made into trains. Distribution of containers from the terminals is also by road. This service can compete with road hauled containers, but again only over longer distances. Altogether, British Rail now operates 40 freightliner terminals, and in 1982 handled over 750 000 containers. 'Speedlink' is a newer development, designed to provide a fast, direct freight service between all the major cities. It offers overnight, scheduled services for traffic in *wagonload* quantities, in contrast to the unit trains which usually carry a single load, for a single customer. Parcels, paper, lime, bottled drinks, fertilizers, cars, chemicals and bricks make up some of the varied freight carried by Speedlink. (See Figure 6.40 for a comparison of UK road and rail freight traffic.)

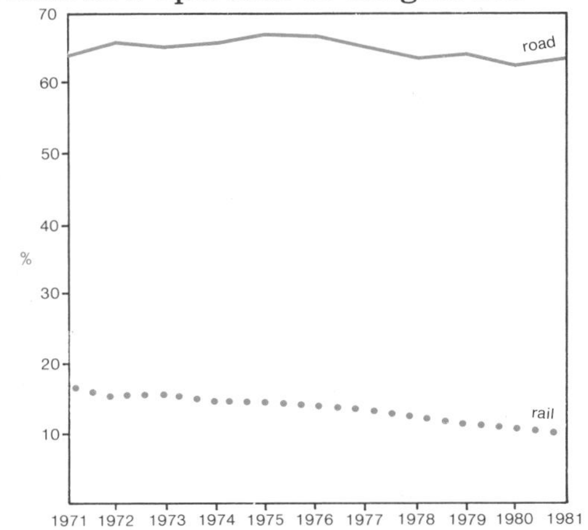

Figure 6.40. Percentage freight traffic by road and rail in the UK, 1971–81

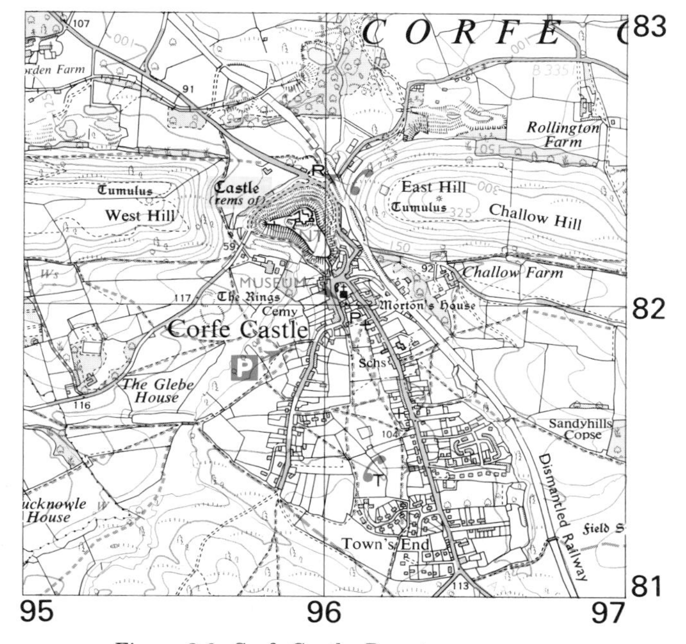

Figure 2.6 Corfe Castle, Dorset

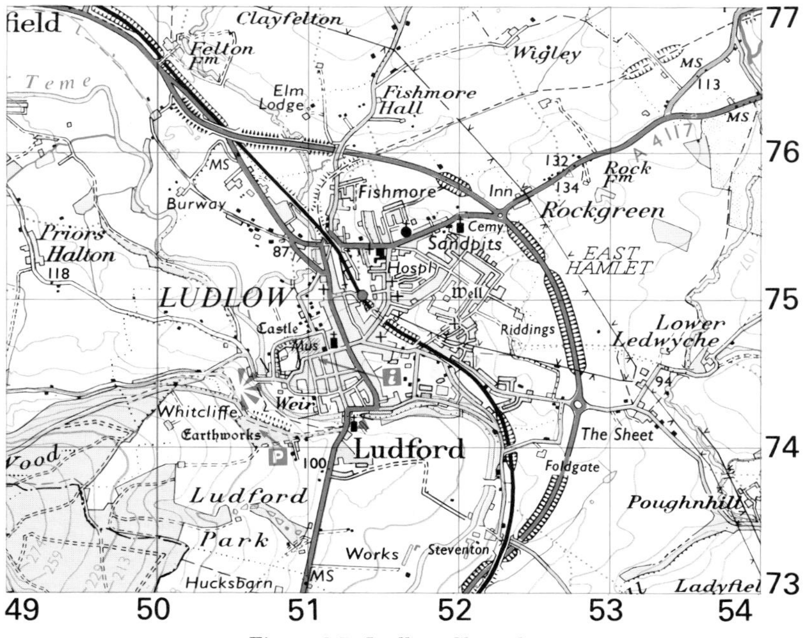

Figure 2.7 Ludlow, Shropshire

Figure 2.10 Preston, Lancashire

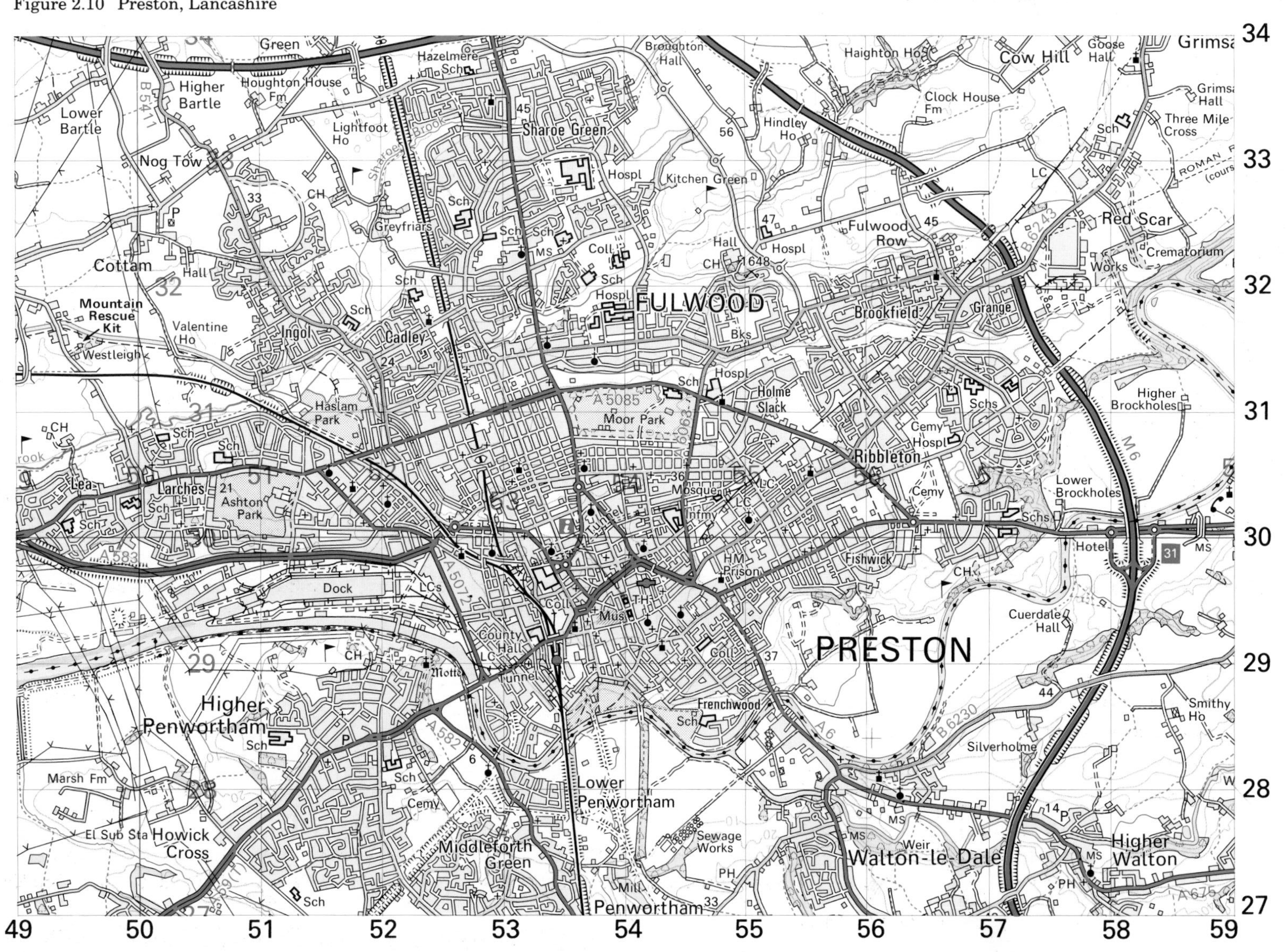

Figure 2.30 1:50 000 OS map extract of part of the Mendips and Somerset Levels

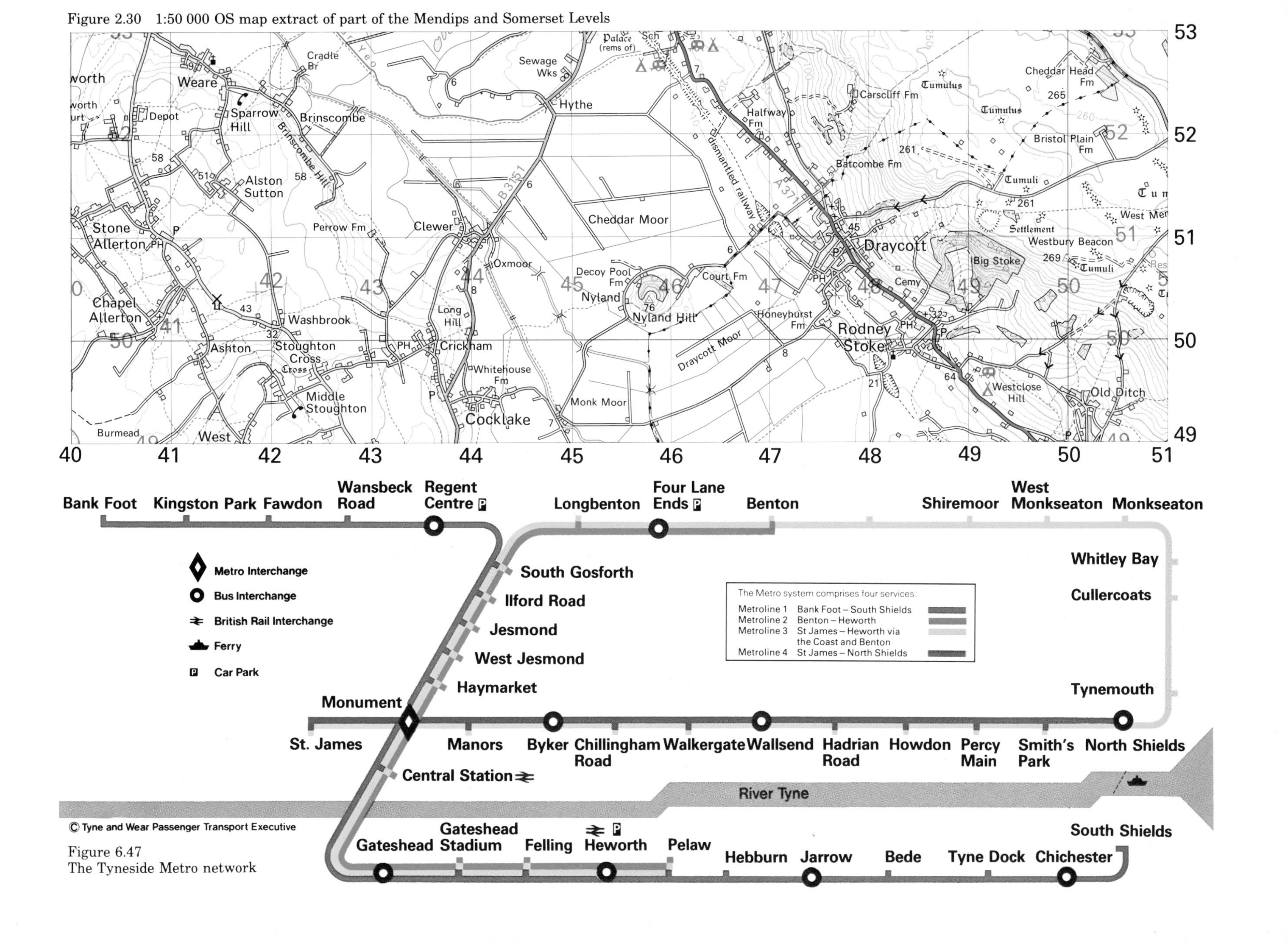

Figure 6.47
The Tyneside Metro network

Figure 6.8 1:50 000 OS map extract of the Gargrave area, North Yorkshire

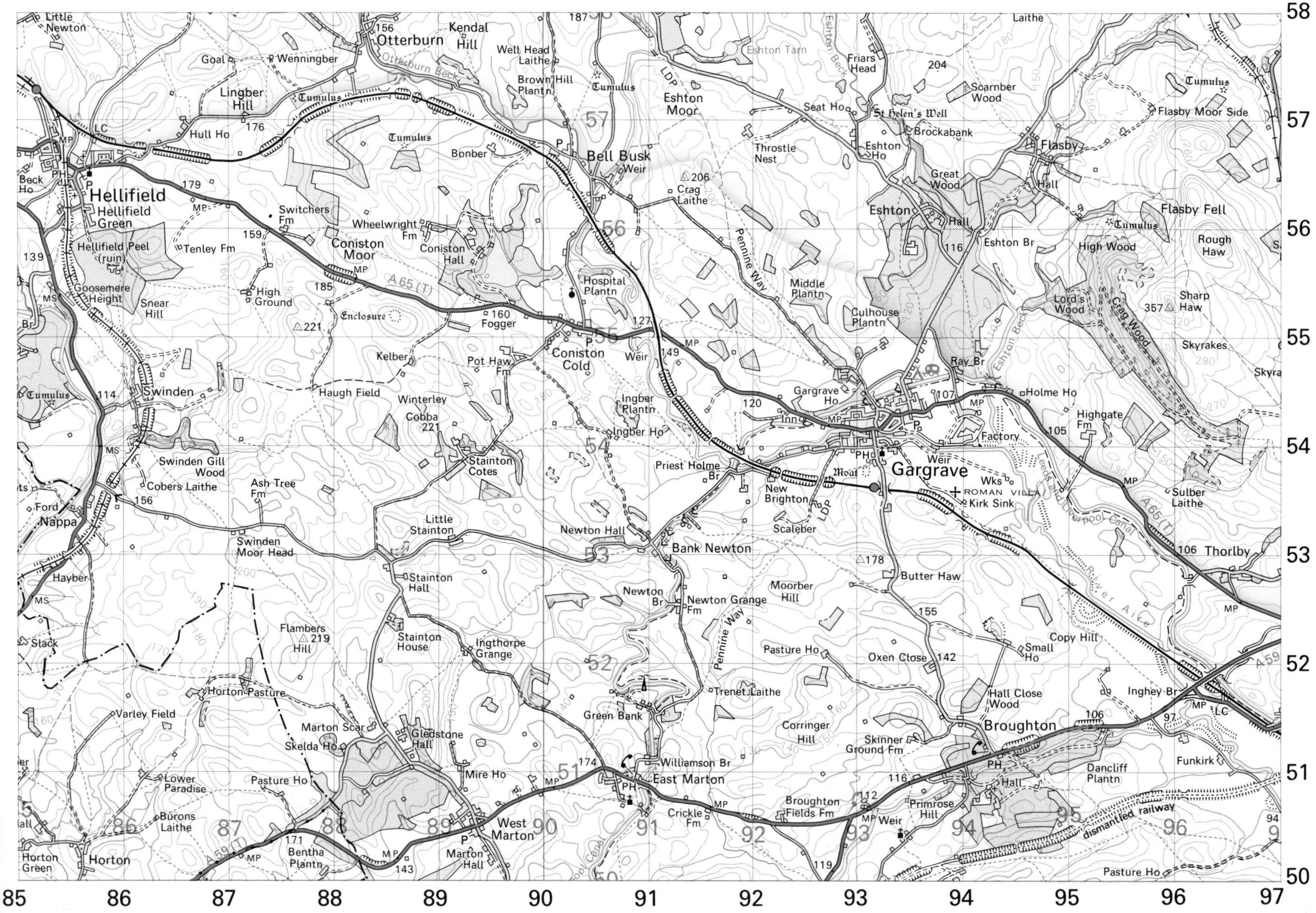

Exercise

1 Read through Table 6.11, and then make a similar table of your own which lists the disadvantages of rail transport compared to road transport.

2 In which of the factors in Table 6.11 would you say that the railways have the biggest advantage? Explain in a paragraph.

3 In 1982 Britain's railways received support from the government amounting to over £900 million. Do you think that this is too much to pay for a railway system? Figure 6.36B shows what the rail network would look like if British Rail were to receive no government support, and had to make a profit relying only on fares paid by passengers, and charges for freight to industry. Would you be in favour of such a network? Give your opinions either in a class discussion, or in a written form.

Table 6.11 Advantages of rail transport over road transport

Length of journey	Very efficient on longer journeys. Cost of moving a tonne of freight over 1 km at distances over 160 km is cheaper in terms of amount of fuel used and wages paid to drivers.		Railways take up less space. Compare a three lane motorway such as the M1 between Watford and Rugby, with the double-track west coast mainline between the same towns.
Type of fuel	Where electric traction is used, power can be obtained from coal, oil or natural gas.	Speed	Faster on major inter-city routes, such as London–Glasgow or London–Manchester.
Environment	Railways are highly efficient in transporting large numbers of commuters to city centres. They take traffic from overcrowded roads and help to reduce congestion. In the transfer of freight. A single merry-go-round or Freightliner train, could take 30 or 40 heavy lorries off the roads.	Flexibility	Developments such as Freightliner and Speedlink combine long rail hauls with short lorry trips to provide a service which competes with the door-to-door service of road transport.

Although the proportion of passengers carried by the railways has fallen from 9% in 1970 to around 7% today, the number of passengers using the railways has remained more or less the same. British Rail's inter-city services have been successful in competing against bus and air travel. Improvements in the speed and regularity of services have brought an increase in traffic (Figure 6.41).

Figure 6.41 British Rail's inter-city 125 passenger trains. Introduced in 1976 they are currently the world's fastest diesel train services. The prototype holds the world speed record for a diesel train of 229 kmph

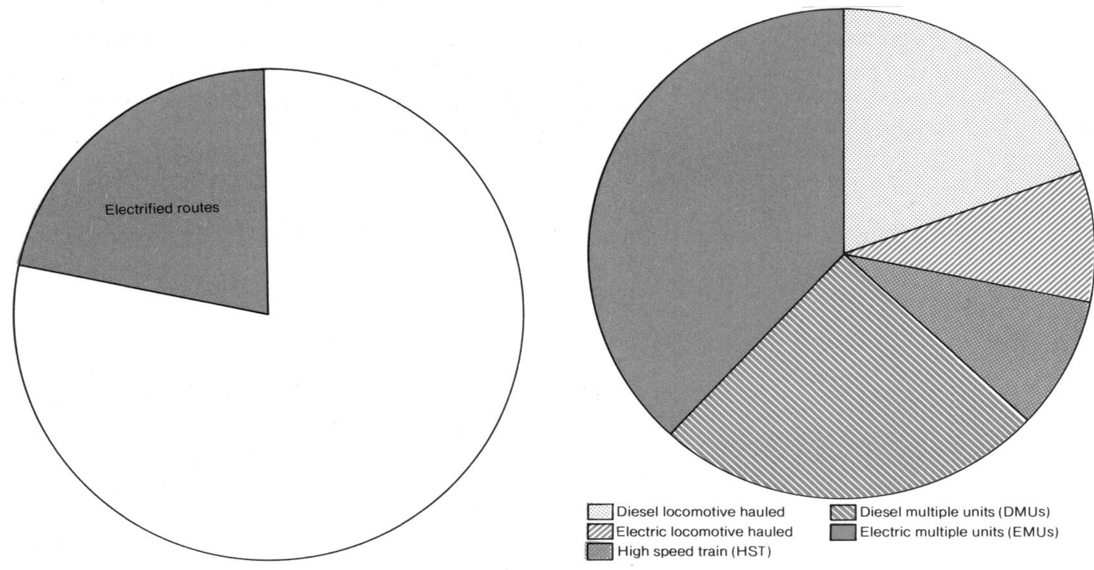

Figure 6.42 UK rail route network, 1982 (17431 km)

Figure 6.43 Loaded train kilometres

Electrification of the west coast mainline, linking London with the West Midlands, Greater Manchester, Merseyside and Clydeside conurbations, completed in the early 1970s, was an important development, and British Rail has plans to electrify the east coast mainline from London to Edinburgh, and other major routes out of London (Figure 6.42). Meanwhile, high speed diesel trains (HSTs) have been introduced on important non-electric routes, such as London–Leeds, London–Cardiff, London–Edinburgh and London–Plymouth. The HSTs are designed to operate at speeds of up to 200 kmph: today 45% of inter-city mileage is covered by these trains (Figure 6.43).

Suburban services are dominated by the South East, and the Southern Region. The importance of these services can be seen in Figure 6.43: most of BR's electric multiple units (EMUs) operate these commuter services, and they account for around one-third of all the mileage covered by the railways. As London has expanded outwards, rail commuting has grown, particularly as journeys-to-work from beyond the green belt become longer. One of the features of suburban services is that demand is very high at the peak morning and evening rush hours, but quite low for the rest of the day. Therefore although many trains have to be provided, they are underused for most of the day.

Railways in LDCs

Although the size of the UK's rail network has been cut drastically since 1960, it is still large compared with the networks of most LDCs. A feature of networks in LDCs is the small number of direct connections which exist between places. This is illustrated in the example of Tanzania (Figure 6.44D) where the network is sparse, and travelling to any place other than Dar-es-Salaam is difficult.

Many networks in the Third World consist of no more than a simple trunk route extending inland from the country's main port and capital city, with one or two branches linking the larger towns. Many networks of this type, such as those of Tanzania and Nigeria, were built during the period of colonial rule, and their purpose was to carry raw materials and agricultural products from the interior to the port, for shipment to the mother country. (Look back at Chapter 3, pages 55–6) for an explanation of how this led to the growth of primate, 'gateway' cities.) To a large extent many railways in Africa still have the same purpose: Nigeria's railways take groundnuts from the north to Lagos for export; Mauritania's only railway is used entirely for the transport of iron ore to the coast; and the prime concern of Zambia's rail network is to carry copper ore to the coast, through the neighbouring countries of Tanzania, Mozambique and Angola.

A Belgium

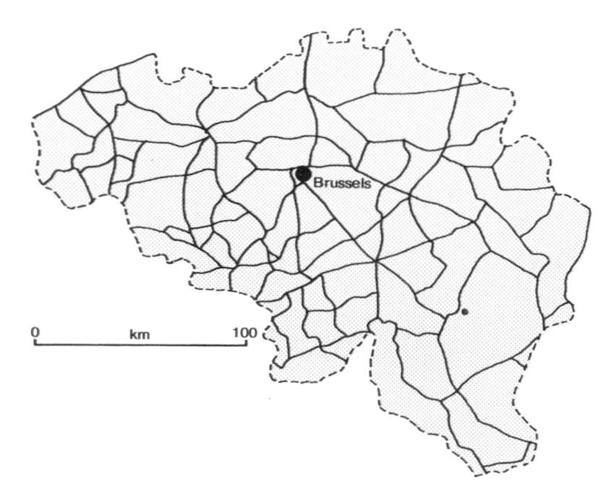

B Czechoslovakia

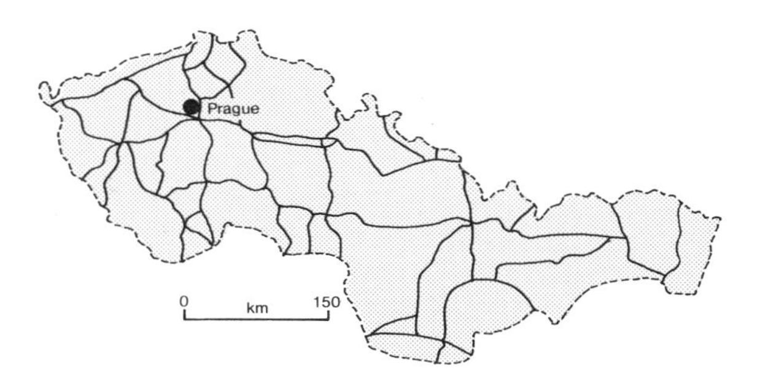

C Mexico

D Tanzania

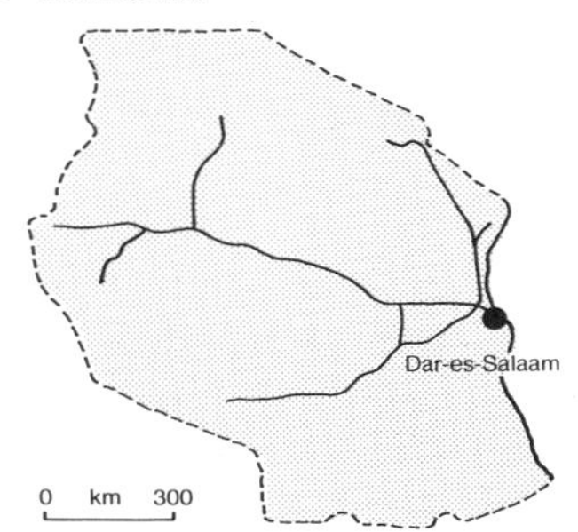

E Nigeria

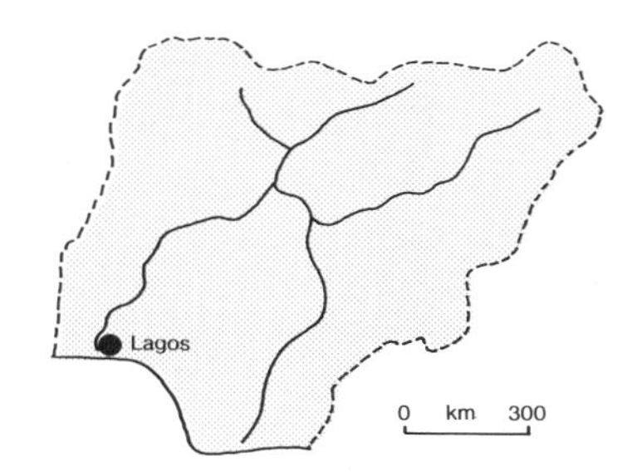

F Bolivia

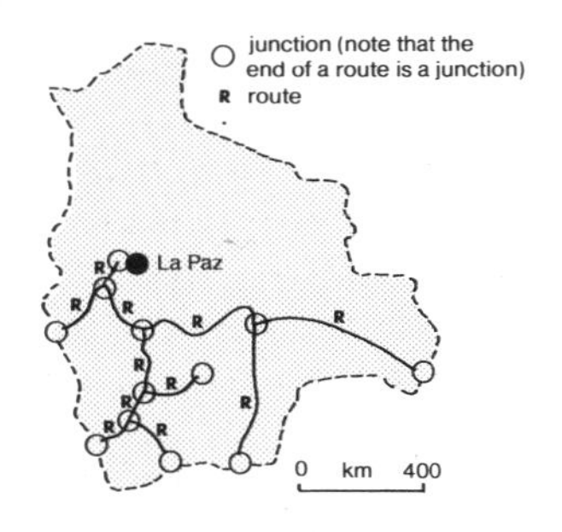

G Africa's expanding railways. Many African countries are today extending and improving their railways. However, lack of traffic, development funds and rundown economies, means that progress is slow

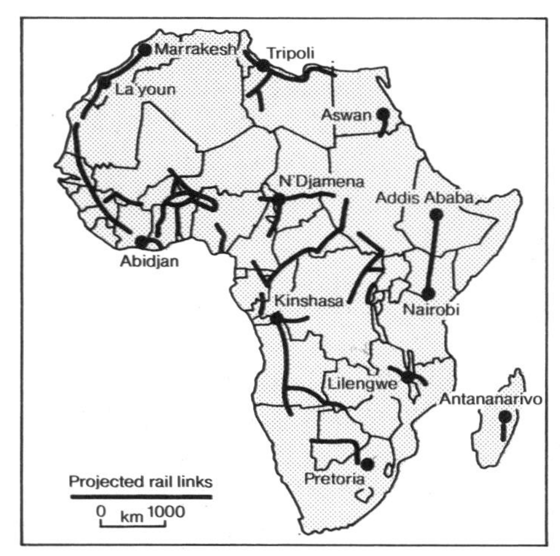

Figure 6.44 Railway networks

Exercise

1 Look at the rail networks in Figure 6.44. What are the main differences between the networks of Belgium and Czechoslovakia, and those of the other countries? Which network would you say is a) most connected b) least connected?

You probably had some difficulty in deciding which country had the most poorly connected network. This can be overcome by measuring some of the features of the networks, and obtaining an index which will tell us how well connected they are. A simple index which will do this expresses the number of routes as a ratio of the number of junctions (Figure 6.44F). We call this ratio the Beta Index. In the example of Bolivia, the network contains 11 routes and 12 junctions, giving a Beta Index of 11/12 or 0.92. This is a relatively low value, indicating that the network is poorly connected. Beta values normally range from around 0.5 to 1.5, and the higher the value the more complex and better connected the network is.

2 Complete the calculations of the Beta indices in Table 6.12, for the networks shown in Figure 6.44.

3 From your calculations of the Beta indices, which is the a) most b) least connected network? How does this result compare with your original estimate in question 1? Because we now have a measure of the complexity of the rail networks of the countries in Figure 6.44 we can test the idea that the more developed a country is, the more complex is its rail (or road) network. A simple measure of development, which we used in Chapter 1, is gross domestic product per person. (See Chapter 1, page 2 for a definition.) For each of our six countries this value is:

Belgium	£7507
Bolivia	616
Czechoslovakia	1629
Mexico	1166
Nigeria	478
Tanzania	254

4 Compare the Beta indices and the gross domestic product per person values by placing each set of values in rank order from 1 (highest) to 6 (lowest). Plot a graph like the one in Figure 4.36.

5 Would you say that there is a strong/moderate/weak relationship between level of development and the complexity of transport networks in a country? Write a few sentences explaining your results.

Table 6.12
Calculating the Beta Index

	Number of routes (r)	Number of junctions (j)	Beta Index (r/j)
Belgium	151	119	1.27
Bolivia	11	12	0.92
Czechoslovakia	78	64	1.22
Mexico	?	?	?
Nigeria	?	?	?
Tanzania	?	?	?

Although the level of development of a country explains much about the nature of its transport networks, other factors also have an influence. In many LDCs rail networks are still in the process of being built: whereas the UK's network was largely completed in the nineteenth century, in Nigeria the first railway was not opened until 1901, and as we saw in the last chapter, work is in progress to extend the system. Finally, in large parts of the Third World, population densities are low (eg the Amazon and Zaire Basins, and the Sahara) and there is simply no demand to build either railways or roads. However, we must not forget that communications are often the key to development, and that once a railway or road is built in an area, it opens up the prospect of industrial (Chapter 5) and agricultural (Chapter 7) progress.

Urban railways: the Tyneside Metro

The Tyneside Metro is a rapid transit railway, designed to link up with bus services, and gives Tyneside Britain's first *integrated transport system*. By the early 1970s the Tyneside conurbation, and in particular the central area of Newcastle-upon-Tyne, was suffering badly from traffic congestion. Buses and railways were run as completely separate systems, and as more people began to use private cars for journeys-to-work and shopping trips, congestion became acute. While the roads were congested, the existing railway network, with its slow, uncomfortable and infrequent trains was underused.

The planners decided to tackle these problems by introducing a light rail or metro system, which would be linked to a new and more extensive bus service, and which would provide fast, direct access to Newcastle's CBD from most of the conurbation. In order to keep the costs as low as possible, the idea was to use the existing rail network: thus while the total length of the Metro network is 54 km, only 13 km is new track. The hub of the Metro is 6.4 km of underground route in central Newcastle, which is the main employment and shopping area in the region. In addition to the tunnelling in central Newcastle, other major building projects have included a new bridge across the Tyne (Figure 6.45) between Newcastle and Gateshead, and the Byker viaduct across the Ouseburn valley.

The Metro trains consist of two units (Figure 6.46) with a seating capacity of 84 passengers. They can be operated singly or in pairs, and are powered by overhead electric wires. There are 43 stations on the network (Figure 6.47; See colour section) which are fully automated and therefore unmanned.

Figure 6.45 Metro train crossing the new Queen Elizabeth II bridge over the River Tyne

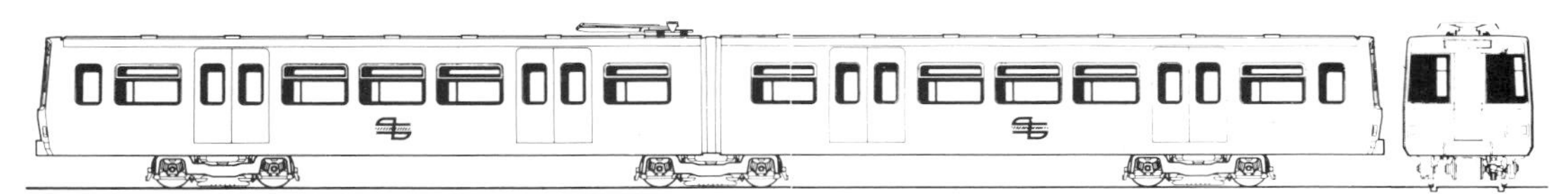

Figure 6.46 Rapid transit car for Tyneside Metro

The Metro is not just a railway, but part of wider integrated transport system which serves the entire conurbation. New bus routes serve the Metro stations, and where stations are located on major radial roads, interchanges (ie bus stations alongside the Metro stations) have been built. Thus passengers can interchange freely from rail to bus, often with just one ticket. Many bus services which used to terminate in the city centre have been diverted to the Metro interchanges, in order to discourage traffic from central Newcastle and to avoid competition between buses and the Metro. 900 car parking spaces have been provided at stations around the system to encourage private motorists to complete their journeys by Metro, and more are planned.

In its first few years of operation the Metro has proved highly successful. The high frequency of service (trains every 3–5 minutes) and the comfortable and quiet ride it provides, attracted 90 million passengers between 1980 and 1983. 7% of these passengers would previously have travelled by car, and 66% of all journeys have combined rail and bus transport. The Metro has actually encouraged Tynesiders to travel more often, and this growth of traffic has occurred at a time of very high unemployment and severe economic recession in the region.

Exercise

Study Figure 6.47 (colour section) and answer the following questions.

1 Which station gives access to all four services operated by the Metro?

2 Measure the accessibility of this station using the method you followed in the exercise on page 174. Compare its accessibility with that of South Shields and Cullercoats.

3 What physical feature on the map reduces the overall accessibility of the network? Suggest one additional link which would greatly improve accessibility.

4 Near its mouth the River Tyne is a busy shipping river, and flows in a deep, steep-sided valley. What would be the problems of building a bridge or a tunnel in this area?

5 If you were to travel from South Shields to North Shields, following the most direct route, where would you need to change trains?

6 Imagine that you want to travel from Bank Foot, and visit every station on the Metro network following the shortest route.
  a Describe the route you would choose.
  b Say where you would change trains.
  c Count the number of stations you will pass through (some of course you will pass through twice), and compare your number with others in the class.

Air transport

Heathrow Airport

Heathrow was chosen as the location of London's first airport in 1943. It occupies a flat terrace of the River Thames, and the site is well drained and underlain by gravels. Heathrow is conveniently situated 25 km west of London (Figure 6.48) and is linked to the capital by the underground rail system: the journey time from central London is around 40 minutes.

Heathrow is easily the UK's largest airport: in 1982–3 it handled 26.6 million passengers, which represent nearly 45% of all passengers using British airports (Figure 6.49). It retains its position as top of the league of *international* airports, because though a number of USA airports handle more passengers (Table 6.15), Heathrow handles the largest number of international passengers (Figure 6.50) as well as serving more international destinations by direct flight than any other airport in the world. However, compared with passenger traffic, the amount of freight transported through Heathrow (and other major airports) is small, averaging around 500 000 tonnes a year. The high cost of air transport compared with surface forms, makes it too expensive to air freight bulky, low value goods. Nonetheless, there are some industries which use Heathrow as an export outlet, principally the high tech electronics business, which is concentrated along the M4, close to the airport. More importantly, a location

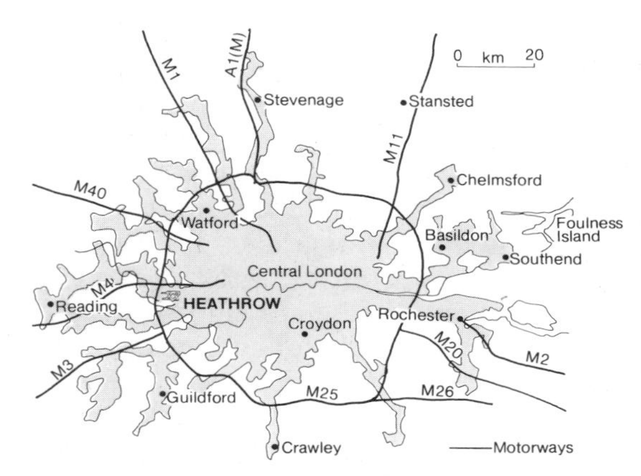

Figure 6.48 The situation of Heathrow airport

Figure 6.49 Heathrow airport: looking north east along terminal 1's international pier

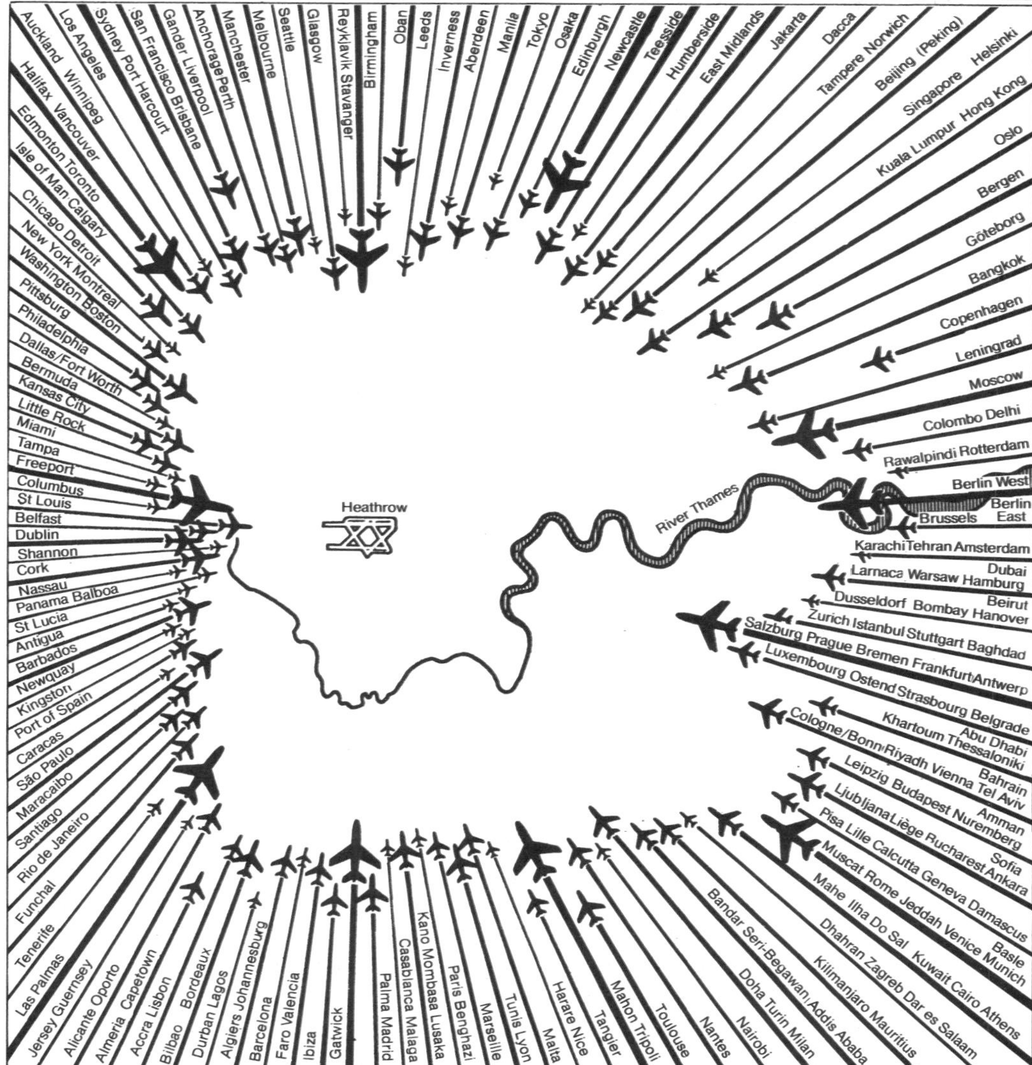

Figure 6.50 Heathrow airport: origins and destinations of flights

close to Heathrow gives businessmen unrivalled access to Europe and North America – 2193 flights a week, to 204 different destinations (Figure 6.51)!

Exercise

Figure 6.52 shows the destination of all European flights from Heathrow.

1 List some of the factors which might influence the distribution of places in Figure 6.52. In order to help you, you might consider why there are direct flights from Heathrow to places such as Norwich, Paris and Palma (Mallorca).

2 One factor you should have listed in question 1 was distance. We saw in pages 143–5 that the further apart two places are, the less movement or traffic there is between them.

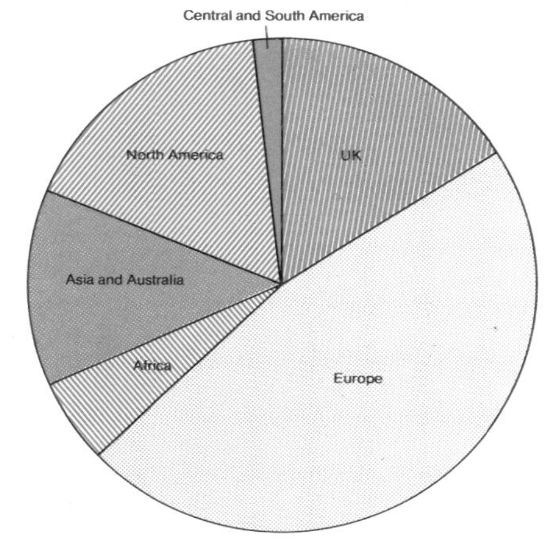

Figure 6.51 Origin and destination of passenger traffic at Heathrow (proportion of passengers carried)

You can test this idea using Figure 6.52.

a Count the number of places in each of the five concentric rings, centred on Heathrow. Enter them in Table 6.13 and calculate the number of places per million km^2 in each ring.

b Plot the number of places per million km^2 against distance, as a bar graph (histogram).

c Does traffic decline with distance? Describe the change of traffic with distance. (Eg Is it a straight line, a gentle curve, a steep curve, or a combination of all three?)

d Do you think that the graph might look any different if Europe were not divided into Western and Eastern political blocs?

Table 6.13 Decline of air traffic with distance from Heathrow

Ring	Number of places	Area of ring million km^2	Places per million km^2
0– 500 km	26	0.786	33.1
501–1000 km		2.357	
1001–1500 km		3.928	
1501–2000 km		5.499	
2001–2500 km		7.070	

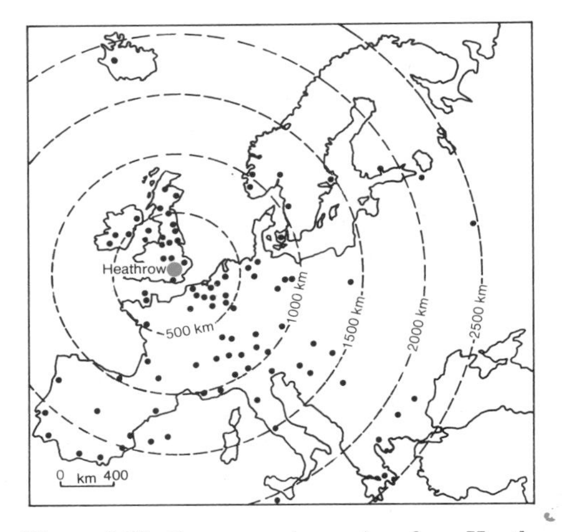

Figure 6.52 European air services from Heathrow

Table 6.14 Location requirements for London's third airport

1	large area of flat, well drained land
2	the site should be well away from existing built-up areas to reduce noise problems to a minimum
3	good access to London (less than one hour travelling time)
4	a site with good visibility and which is little affected by fog

As well as an airport, Heathrow is a large centre of employment, with nearly 44 000 people working on the site. The rapid growth of air transport, and of Heathrow in particular, has on several occasions in the last few years prompted a search for a site for a third London airport (after Gatwick) (Table 6.14). New York, Paris and Moscow have each built new international airports to accommodate the increases in air traffic, but until 1985 no firm decision had been made on London's third airport. In the past, sites have been chosen at

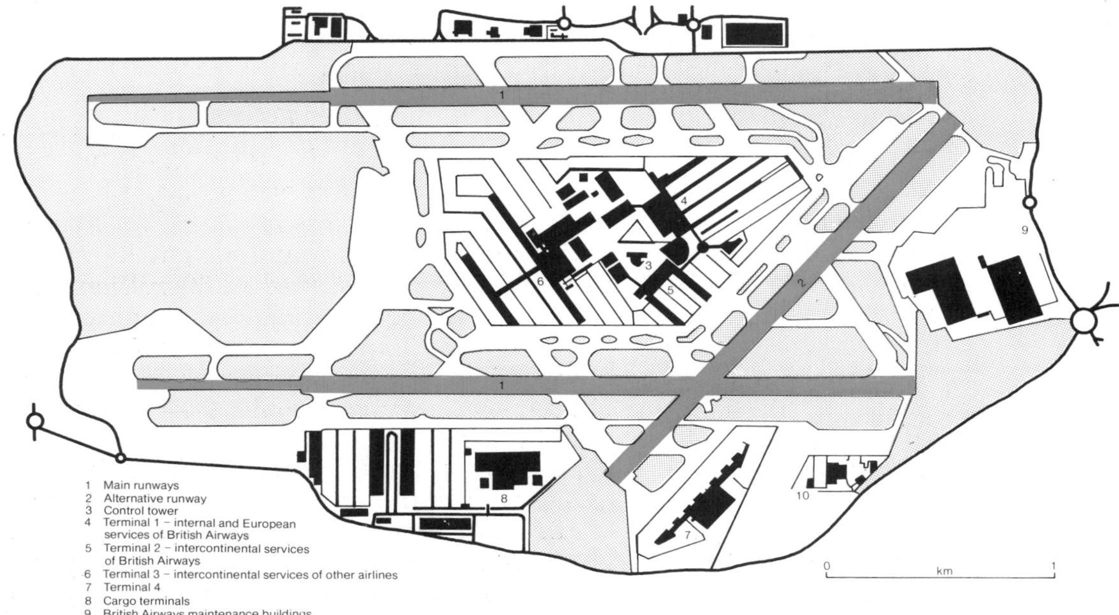

Figure 6.53 Heathrow airport: layout

Exercise

1 Figure 6.53 shows the layout of Heathrow. Estimate the area of the airport in km^2.

2 Large areas of flat, well-drained land are likely to be in demand for other uses besides airports. Can you say what these might be and how they might cause opposition to the location of a new airport?

3 Look at the location of Heathrow in Figure 6.48. How well located is it in relation to aircraft noise pollution in surrounding urban areas? You should note the alignment of the main runways – east–west – and consider the flight paths of aircraft as they approach, and take-off from Heathrow.

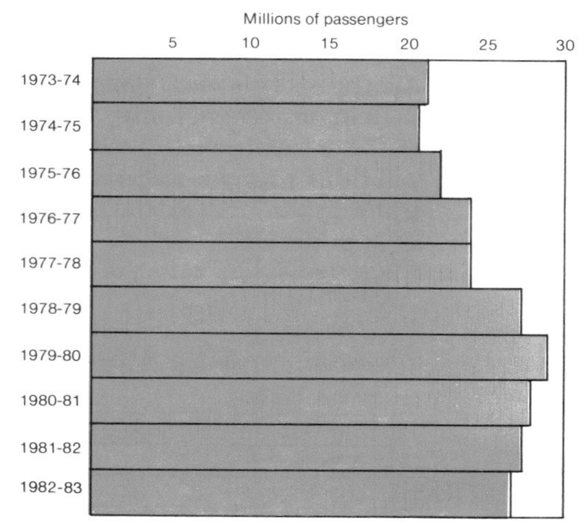

Figure 6.54 Heathrow: passenger traffic, 1973–83

Stansted (Essex), Cublington (Buckinghamshire), Thurleigh (Bedfordshire) and Foulness Island (Essex): each has met with strong opposition, and has eventually been abandoned. In a small, densely populated country like the UK, siting a new airport is always going to be difficult and cause controversy, and this is especially so in the overcrowded South East.

Foulness Island, in the Thames estuary (Figure 6.48) was the site most favoured for London's third airport in the early 1970s. The site had many advantages: it is fairly close to London; it is on the coast and in an area which was largely unpopulated, hence aircraft noise would not be a problem; extensive areas of flat land are available, and because the airport was to be sited on Maplin Sands – an area which would be reclaimed from the sea – there would be no loss of farm land.

In spite of these considerable advantages the whole project was abandoned in 1974. The site would certainly have been very expensive to develop (about £700 million at 1974 prices), and there had been strong opposition from naturalists and conservation groups because of the adverse effects the airport would have had on wildlife (particularly birds) in the area. However, the main reason the project was abandoned was lower estimates of passenger growth up to the mid 1980s following the massive increase in oil prices in 1974. For example, in 1971 it was estimated that by 1985 British airports would have to handle 85 million passengers, but by 1983 the total had only just reached 60 million. Indeed, since 1979–80 there has been no increase in the volume of passenger traffic using Heathrow (Figure 6.54). Another factor behind the cancellation of the Foulness project was the introduction of wide-bodied air liners such as the Boeing 747 and the DC10; this meant that more passengers could use Heathrow without any increase in the number of flights.

In the long term, however, traffic will grow, and airport facilities in south east England will have to be expanded. With this in mind, a fourth terminal opened at Heathrow in 1985, which caters for an extra 8 million passengers a year. Planning further ahead, the British Airports Authority is hoping to build a new terminal at its small Stansted airport. The government has already given the go-ahead for this project which, by 1990, will make Stansted London's third airport.

Exercise

1 With the help of an atlas, find out in which countries each of the top 20 airports is located (Table 6.15).

2 Air transport is more important in the USA than in any other country. Most of the air traffic is between cities within the USA. Can you think of any reasons why domestic air traffic in the USA should be more important than in the UK?

3 In the USA the growth of air traffic has been greatest in the south and west, and smallest in the north. This is partly explained by faster rates of population, manufacturing and service industry growth in these two regions (Figure 3.19) in the last 15 years; and by the wider spacing of major cities, which encourages air transport. Look at the information in Table 6.16. Does it suggest that air transport is becoming relatively less important in the north? Write out your conclusions in a paragraph.

Table 6.15 World top 20 airports in order of passenger traffic

1	Chicago
2.	Atlanta
3	Los Angeles
4	HEATHROW
5	New York (JF Kennedy)
6	Dallas/Fort Worth
7	Denver
8	Tokyo (Hareda)
9	San Francisco
10	Miami
11	New York (La Guardia)
12	Frankfurt
13	Paris (Orly)
14	Osaka
15	Boston
16	Honolulu
17	Toronto
18	Washington (National)
19	Paris (Charles de Gaulle)
20	Houston

Table 6.16 Top 10 largest cities, and top 10 airports in the USA

10 largest cities		10 largest airports	
1	New York	1	New York (JFK and La Guardia)
2	Los Angeles	2	Chicago
3	Chicago	3	Atlanta
4	Philadelphia	4	Los Angeles
5	Detroit	5	Dallas
6	San Francisco	6	Denver
7	Washington	7	San Francisco
8	Dallas	8	Miami
9	Houston	9	Boston
10	Boston	10	Honolulu

Summary

Transport is the means of overcoming the obstacle to movement presented by distance. Distance is usually thought of as kilometres or miles, but often movement can be better understood when we think of distance as cost, or time.

Transport systems have three essential features: networks, flows and different means of transport. Overland transport systems, such as roads and railways, form networks of routes which join places together. A feature of these networks is that they are usually sparse and incomplete because of the enormous costs involved in their building. Networks are particularly sparse in LDCs and in areas of low population density.

Transport networks provide channels for flows of goods and people between places. These flows, which vary in volume, direction and the type of items being moved, are carried by several different transport methods, which themselves vary in the cost and speed with which they can carry payloads over distance. However, developments in technology in the last 30 years have shown that the effectiveness of any form of transport can change quite rapidly, and can have important influences on the location of industry and service activities.

Further exercises

1 a On a piece of tracing paper used as an overlay to Figure 6.55 design a road network which links together towns A, B, C, D and E. You should aim to keep the building costs to a minimum.
  b Describe the main features of your network, saying what landforms and other physical features have been followed or avoided, and what measures have been taken to overcome natural obstacles.
  c Choose two locations on your network where in your view the advantages of situation would favour the growth of new towns. Explain your choices.
  d If you were to design a rail network to link the five towns, in what ways if any, would it differ from your road network?

2 Figure 6.56 shows five possible sites for a new airport in an area. Describe the advantages and disadvantages of each site, and explain which you think would be the most suitable location.

3 Look at the distribution of container ports and deepwater terminals in Britain (Figure 6.57) and answer the following questions.
  a Which part of Britain (NE, SE, SW, NW) has the largest concentration of container ports? Give two advantages for the location of such ports in the region you have selected.
  b How does the cargo handled by deepwater terminals differ from that handled by container ports? Which of the following methods of overland transport are likely to be most important for deepwater terminals and for container ports: road, rail or pipeline? Briefly explain your answer.
  c Name two manufacturing industries which need to be located near to deepwater terminals.
  d For one of the ports shown on the map, write an account of its importance under the following headings:
  — site
  — hinterland
  — communications and trade.

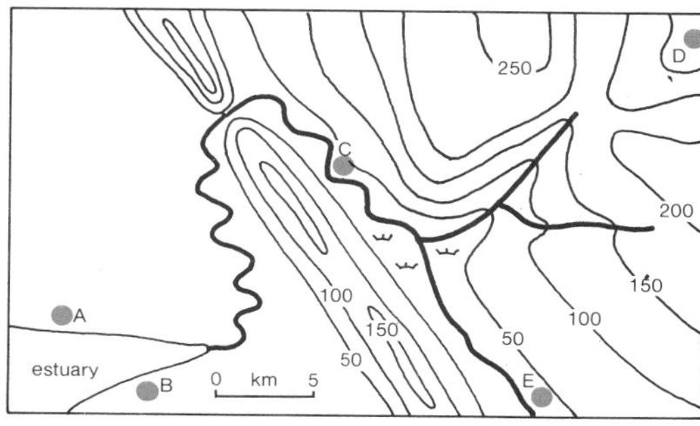

Figure 6.55 Locating a transport network

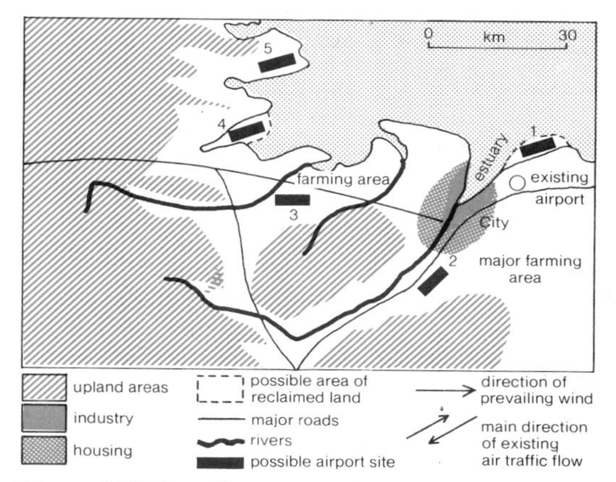

Figure 6.56 Locating a new airport

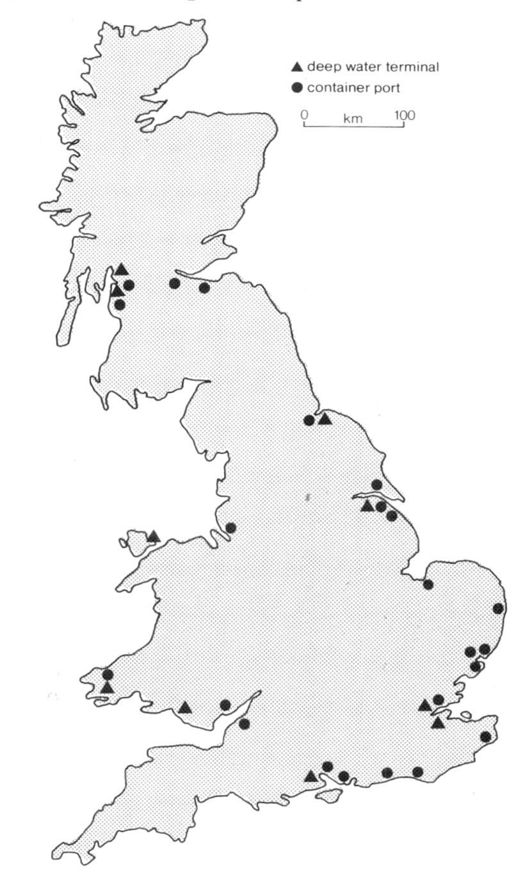

Figure 6.57 (*right*) Container and deepwater terminals in Britain

Key ideas	Examples
Distance can be defined in several different ways.	■ Physical distance – the number of kilometres separating places. This is often the least useful measure. ■ Distance as cost – may be a more accurate indication of movement eg North Atlantic air fares. ■ Distance as time – faster transport services eg Concorde, electrified rail routes, may encourage greater movement of people and goods.
Distance influences the volume of traffic of people, goods and information between places.	■ As distances increase, interaction declines eg volume of commuting to London, volume of migration between UK regions and the South East, the amount of trade between countries.
Patterns of movement are influenced by other factors, apart from distance.	■ The attractiveness of places eg the prospect of employment in large cities, the number and range of shops in a shopping centre. ■ Political factors may hinder or help movement. Differences between western and eastern Europe limit trade and the movement of people. The EEC makes movement between member countries easier. ■ Physical factors may reduce movement eg high mountain ranges, deserts, large rivers, islands, etc. ■ Movement often occurs when a demand in one place, is met by a supply in another eg the movement of iron ore from Australia to Japan, or of people from areas of high unemployment eg north east USA, to areas of full employment eg southern USA.
Methods of transport vary in their advantages in terms of types of goods carried, and length of journey.	■ Transport costs consist of haulage and terminal costs. ■ Where terminal costs (loading and unloading) are high eg sea transport and inland waterways, long journeys are most economic. Where terminal costs are low, but haulage costs (fuel and labour) are high eg road transport, shorter journeys are more economic. ■ Heavy or bulky, low value goods are most effectively carried by sea, inland waterways or railways. ■ Where speed and door-to-door service are important, road transport is most efficient.
Roads, railways, inland waterways and pipelines form networks of routes, which link places together.	■ Transport networks are usually sparse, with few direct connections between places. This reflects the need to keep the costs of building as low as possible. ■ Networks are particularly sparse in LDCs (lack of capital and demand) and in areas of low population density. ■ The access to places in a network varies; generally, the larger and more important a place, the better the accessibility eg Paris in the French rail network.

Key ideas	Examples
The location of routes is influenced by physical and human factors.	■ The location of routes can be examined on OS maps. ■ Physical factors include relief, flooding and drainage. Some features may attract routeways eg valleys, other may repel them eg steep slopes. ■ Routes may deviate in order to gain extra traffic, though major routes, linking large towns, are usually fairly direct. ■ Physical obstacles may be overcome by the use of tunnels, indirect routes which follow contours, cuttings, embankments, bridges, etc.
Changes in technology lead to the expansion of some forms of transport and the decline of others.	■ The growth of road transport in all DCs, and the decline of railways.
Changes in methods of cargo handling can influence the location of industry.	■ Containerisation has greatly reduced the costs of handling cargo. It has made ports less attractive as locations for industry. ■ Bulk cargo handling costs have declined as cargoes such as iron ore and crude oil are carried in larger ships. This trend has emphasised tidewater locations for heavy industries dependent on imported materials eg steel in Japan, petrochemicals on Southampton Water.
Traffic in towns and cities can often cause congestion.	■ Problems are caused by peak hour traffic in large cities. Solutions include the rapid transit system eg Tyneside, and the integration of bus and rail services. ■ There are problems of congestion in smaller towns which serve as route centres eg Banbury, Chelmsford. The construction of by-passes is a solution.

Agriculture

Part 1: The pattern of world agriculture

Agriculture is the production of food and materials by the growing of crops and the management of livestock.

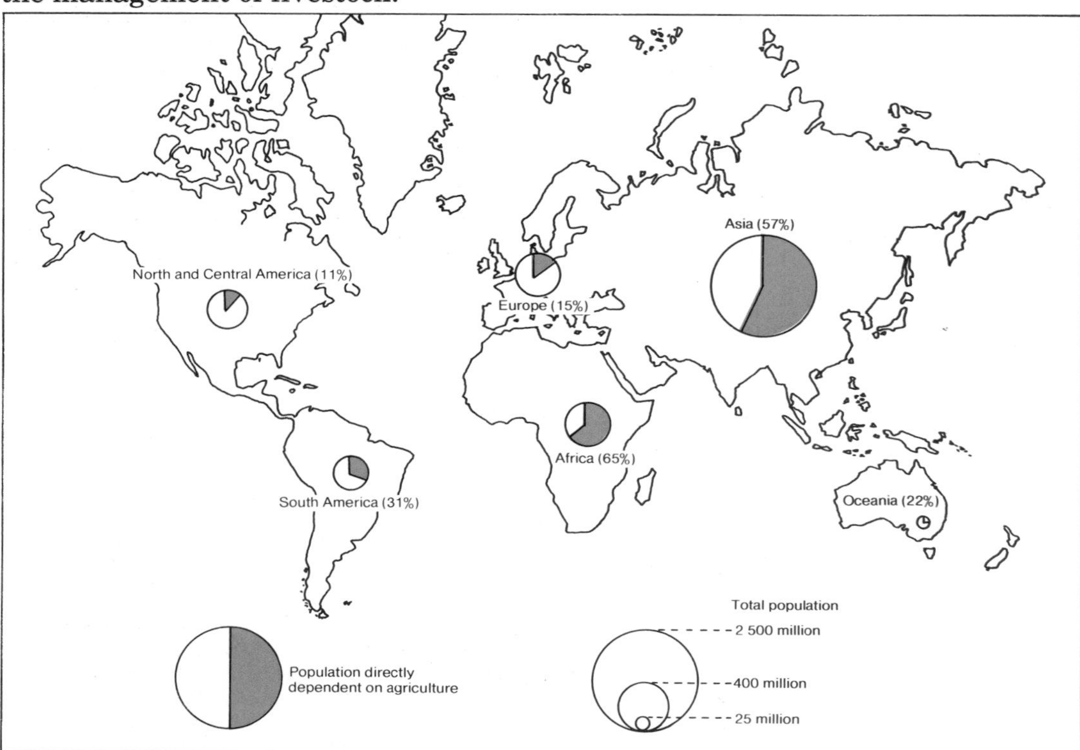

Figure 7.1 The world's agricultural population

In the early 1980s 45% of the world's working population was engaged in agriculture, and over 2 billion people depended directly on agriculture for their livelihood (Figure 7.1). However, the distribution of the world's agricultural population is very uneven, with 9 in every 10 agricultural workers living in the Third World (Figure 7.2). The vast majority of these people practice *subsistence* farming, growing crops and keeping livestock for their own consumption. This situation contrasts with farming in DCs, where crops are grown for cash, and to feed the 88% of the population who do not work on the land.

Figure 7.2A Percentage of world's population by continent

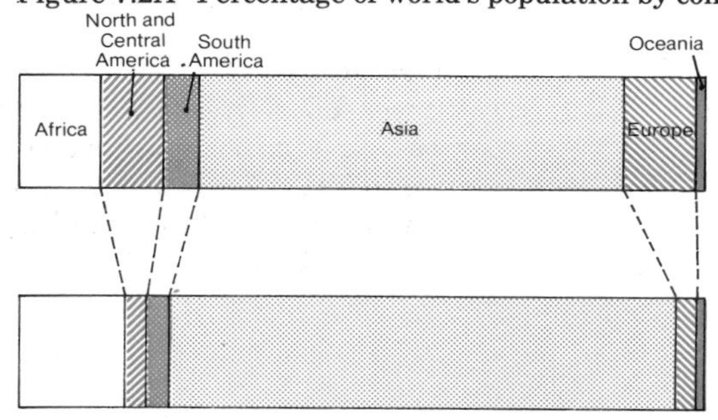

Figure 7.2B Percentage of world's agricultural population by continent

Table 7.1 shows that although DCs have only a small fraction of the world's agricultural workforce, their production of major food crops such as cereals and roots is equal to that of LDCs. This is because over the last 150 years, farm workers in DCs have been steadily replaced by machinery, making modern farming *capital intensive*. In contrast, we describe farming in the Third World, with its huge labour force, as being *labour intensive* (Figure 7.3).

Table 7.1 Agricultural area, employment and production in DCs and LDCs

	Arable area (1000 ha)	Population working in agriculture (1000s)	Arable land per worker (ha)	Output of major food crops (1000 tonnes)	Output per worker (tonnes)
Developed countries	648828	65942	?	1061520	16
Less developed countries	709603	763036	0.93	1163875	?

Exercise

1 Complete the calculations in Table 7.1. How much more labour intensive is farming in LDCs compared with DCs?

2 How do you think that DCs are able to produce virtually the same output of major crops as LDCs, with only a fraction of the agricultural workforce?

3 Using the figures in Table 7.1 try to calculate how many tonnes of major crops are produced on average per hectare of arable land in DCs and LDCs. State your conclusion in a sentence.

4 Given that in 1981 the population of DCs was 1178 million, and that of LDCs was 3335 million, how much food is produced per head of the population in each of the two areas?

5 Food shortages are a common problem in Third World countries. Two factors which contribute to this problem are inefficient farming and too many mouths to feed. (Look back at Chapter 1, pages 4–9 to remind yourself of the rate of population growth in the Third World today.) Using the figures in Table 7.1, which of the two factors would you say is mainly responsible for food shortages? Explain your answer in a sentence or two.

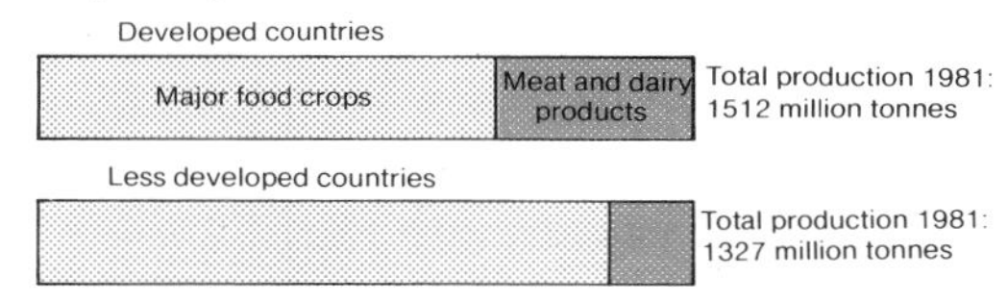

Figure 7.4 Agricultural production in DCs and LDCs

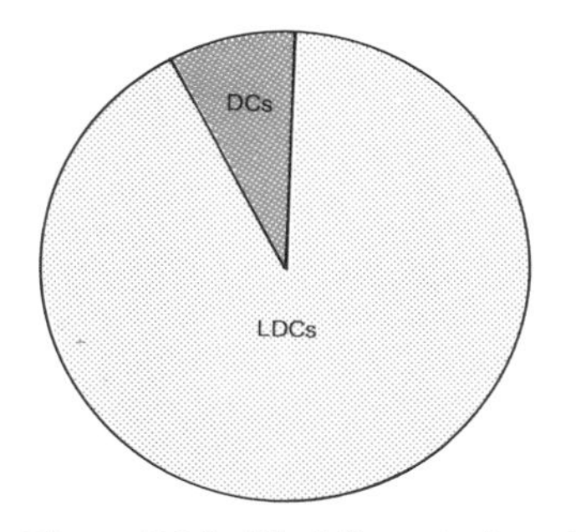

Figure 7.3A World's agricultural workforce

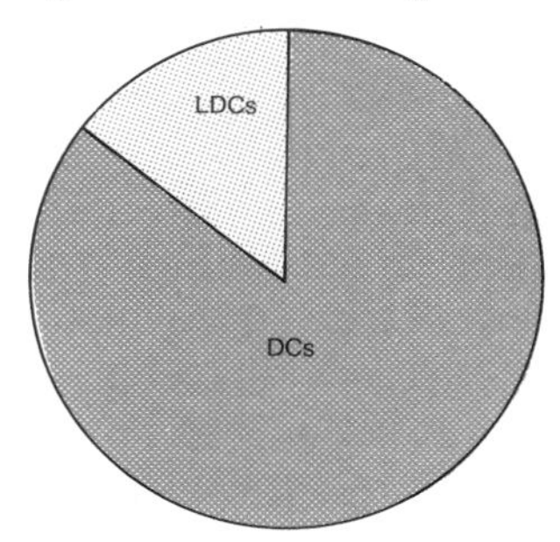

Figure 7.3B Tractors used in agriculture

6 Figure 7.4 shows a further contrast in farming between DCs and LDCs. Write two sentences to state what this difference is.

7 On average it requires 10 tonnes of grain or root crops fed to livestock to produce 1 tonne of meat. On the basis of this fact and the figures in Table 7.1, can you suggest why meat and dairy production in LDCs is so much lower than in DCs?

The nature of agriculture

The nature of agriculture or farming in any part of the world can be considered by asking four simple, but important questions (Figure 7.5). The answers to these questions will tell us what a farmer grows, where he grows it, how he grows it, and who will eventually consume it. However, we are also interested in *explaining* the nature of farming, and understanding why types of farming vary from place to place. Figure 7.5 shows that many factors influence farming, and that most of them put some sort of limit on what a farmer can do. In the next section we shall see how some of these limits or *constraints* influence the pattern of agriculture in the developed world.

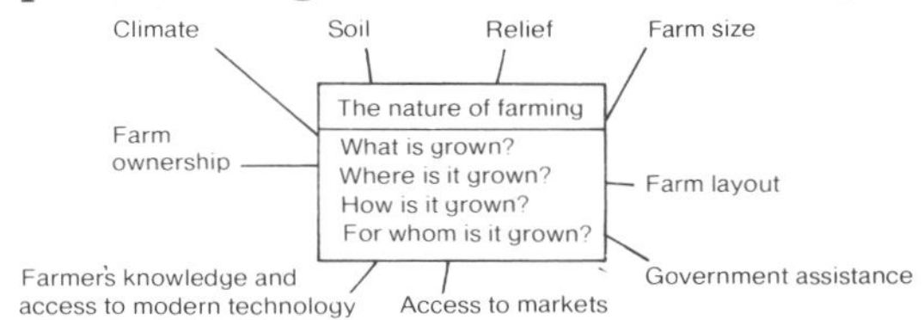

Figure 7.5 Factors affecting the nature of farming

Part 2: Agriculture in the developed world

Agriculture in the UK

Physical factors

Agriculture, more than any other activity that we have looked at in previous chapters, is strongly influenced by physical geography, especially climate, relief and soils. These factors not only control which crops can be grown successfully in an area, but more importantly the size of yields and the profit which the farmer can make.

Climate

In the UK cereals like wheat and barley grow best in areas which have fairly warm summers (16°C+ July mean), and moderate rainfall in the range 600–800 mm a year. Where these conditions are found the cultivation of cereals and root crops like sugar beet, which we call *arable farming*, gives higher profits than livestock farming, and tends to dominate land use (Figure 7.6). Areas of high rainfall (above 900 mm) make arable farming difficult; however, in these areas grass growth is improved by plentiful rainfall, and grassland for livestock farming is most profitable. Summer temperatures and mean annual rainfall are not the only climatic factors which influence agriculture. The length of the growing season (Figure 7.7) which is defined as the number of days a year when the temperature of the soil is 6°C and above, varies from 7–9 months in lowland Britain, to less than 4 months in northern uplands. This means that in some parts of the country some arable crops would have too short a growing season to ripen. Also important, particularly to the farming of fruit and vegetables, is the date of the last frost. This occurs later with increasing altitude and latitude; in the lowland parts of England it ranges from early April in west Cornwall, to late May in north Northumberland.

Figure 7.6 Wheat drilling on a large arable farm in Norfolk

Exercise

1 Imagine a lowland area where soils are equally fertile everywhere and the mean July temperature is 16°C, but where rainfall varies from 600 mm a year in the east, to more than 1000 mm in the west. We can assume that all farmers in this area want to make a profit. Study Figure 7.8, which shows this situation, and answer the following questions.

a At what point (ie mean annual rainfall) will dairy farming become more profitable than arable?

b Make a copy of Figure 7.8 and put in the following labels where appropriate:
(1) mainly arable, with some dairying
(2) mainly dairying, with some arable
(3) dairy farming only.
The first label has already been put on the diagram to help you.

c Where is the best location for dairy farming, and why is dairying unlikely to be important there?

2 Now look at Figures 7.10 and 7.11 which show the varying importance of arable and grassland, and mean annual rainfall in England and Wales. Try to explain the pattern of arable and grassland in England and Wales using the ideas in the previous question.

3 The actual pattern of land use in England and Wales (Figure 7.11) is of course more complicated than that in Figure 7.8. Apart from rainfall, can you suggest why a) Wales contains so much improved pastureland, and b) Merseyside has so much arable land? (Figures 7.9 and 7.15 suggest the answers.)

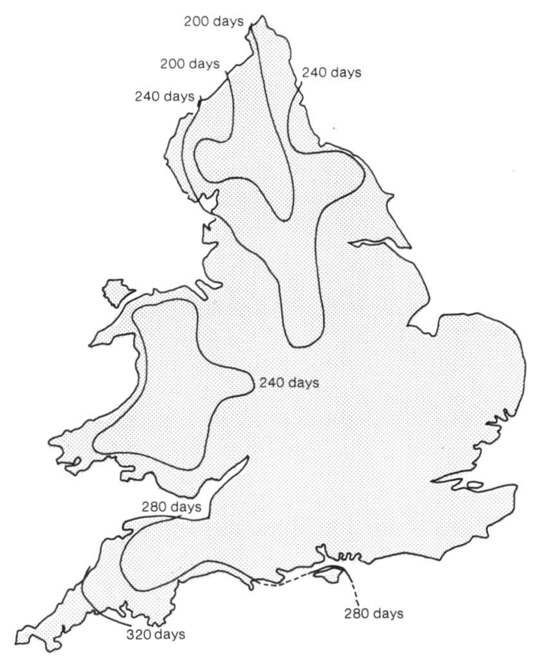

Figure 7.7 Length of growing season in England and Wales

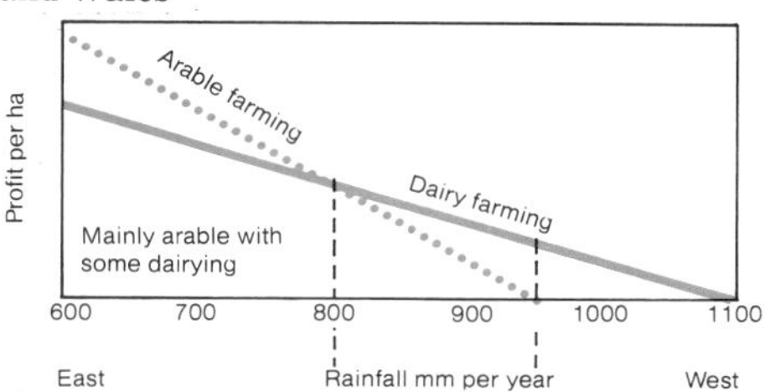

Figure 7.8 The influence of rainfall on arable and dairy farming

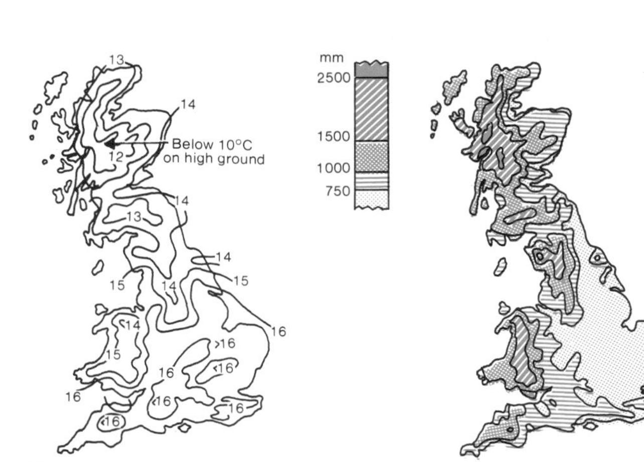

Figure 7.9 Actual isotherms for July: generalised

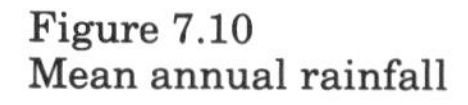
Figure 7.10 Mean annual rainfall

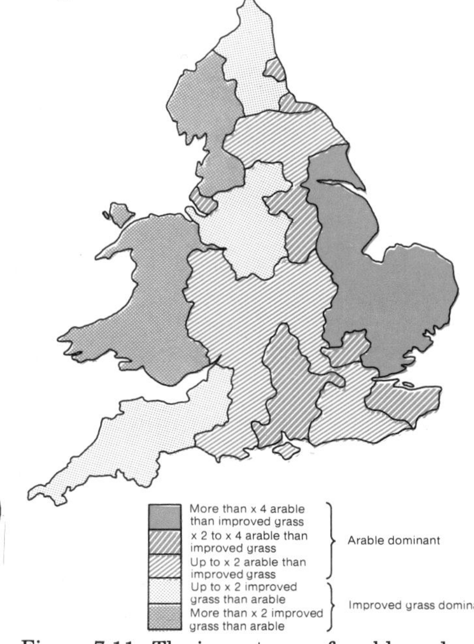

Figure 7.11 The importance of arable and improved grass in England and Wales

Exercise

Look at Figures 7.12A and 7.12D which show the distribution of wheat growing and rough grazing (ie hill sheep farming) in Britain. Now compare these distributions with rainfall (Figure 7.10) and average July temperatures (Figure 7.9):

1 Trace the outline of Britain in Figure 7.12A and plot the areas which have a) less than 750 mm of rainfall a year (Figure 7.10) b) average July temperatures of 16°C and above (Figure 7.9). Shade the areas which have *both* features on your tracing, and place it as an overlay on Figure 7.12A showing the distribution of wheat growing. Would you say that climate has a weak/moderate/strong influence on wheat growing in Britain?

2 Follow the same method as in the previous question, only this time plot areas with 1000 mm or more rainfall, and those with average July temperatures of 14°C or less on your tracing paper. Compare the distribution of areas with both climatic features with the distribution of rough grazing land, largely used for hill sheep (Figure 7.12D). Comment as in question 1 above.

Figure 7.12A Distribution of wheat

Figure 7.12B
Distribution of barley

Figure 7.12C
Distribution of improved grassland

Figure 7.12D
Distribution of rough grazing

Table 7.2 Climate and farming in three counties

Average July Temp.	Mean annual rainfall	Agricultural land use % arable	improved grass	rough grazing
16.9°C	577 mm	13.7	34.1	52.2
15.9	865	82.4	12.6	5.0
13.7	1829	30.9	60.0	9.1

Exercise

The figures in Table 7.2 refer to climate and land use in the counties of Essex, Somerset and Gwynedd.

1 Locate each county in your atlas.

2 Using the information in Table 7.2, and comparing it with Figures 7.9–7.12 identify each of the three counties according to the climate and the land use pattern which you think fits each one best.

3 Explain your choice and the main differences in land use between the counties.

Exercise

Look at Figure 7.7 showing the length of the growing season in England and Wales and answer the following questions.

1 Which part of the country has the longest growing season?

2 Dairy farming is important in this region. However, a major cost to any dairy farmer is the forage required by cattle in winter. Explain what advantage this region has for dairy farming in this respect.

3 Figure 7.10 suggests another reason why dairy farming is important in the region. Describe briefly what it is.

4 The region also specialises in producing 'early' vegetables and flowers, which command a high price in January and February. What advantage does the region have to enable it to do this?

Relief

Throughout the uplands of the UK, relief, in the form of steep slopes and high altitude, severely limits the scope of farming. Tractors can only plough slopes of up to 15°, while combine harvesters are restricted to slopes of less than 5°. Quite apart from the shortness of the growing season and high rainfall, arable farming is greatly limited by the problems of using machinery in the uplands. The disadvantages imposed by relief mean that in the uplands the farmer has little choice of crops and livestock; on better land he may cultivate improved pasture for hay, but in the more rugged areas such as central Wales, the Pennines, the Lake District and the Scottish mountains, he will rely almost entirely on rough grazing for his sheep, on the hills and moorlands (Figure 7.13).

Exercise

1 Draw a scatter graph using the figures in Table 7.3, with altitude plotted on the horizontal (x) axis, and growing season on the vertical (y) axis.

Figure 7.13 (*right*) A typical hill farm in central Wales, with pastures at an altitude of nearly 600 m. Can you see any evidence on the photograph which suggests that soils are thin and poorly drained?

2 Draw a best-fit trend line through your scatter of points, trying to ensure that the same number of points occur above and below the line.

3 From your graph, estimate how much the growing season decreases for every 10 m of altitude.

4 Use your graph to find the average length of the growing season in northern England at: sea-level, 150 m and 300 m.

5 What other factors are likely to influence the length of the growing season at the places you have plotted on your graph?

Table 7.3 Length of growing season and altitude: northern England

Growing season (days)	Altitude (metres)
237	67
238	66
200	214
237	109
189	315
248	97
190	341
230	172
238	116
258	28
209	287
232	138
245	39
247	54

Soils

Soil is the third of the physical factors which have an important influence on farming. However, although farmers can do little to modify relief and climate, soils can be, and have been, greatly improved through drainage and the use of fertilizers. Figure 7.14 illustrates the influence that soil quality can have on agricultural land use in Lincolnshire and Leicestershire in lowland England. In both counties, climate and relief are similar, and therefore cannot explain the large differences in land use. The main difference is in soil quality: Lincolnshire has one of the largest areas of first class arable land in Britain in the Fens around the Wash (Figures 7.15 and 7.16). The soils are derived from fen peat and silt and give high yields of vegetables, fruit, potatoes, sugar beet and cereals. Leicestershire, in comparison, has soils of moderate quality: most are clayey and poorly drained, and favour grass rather than arable land. The poorest soils in Britain are found in the uplands, which adds a further disadvantage to farming in these areas. Most of the essential minerals needed by crops have been washed out or *leached* from upland soils by heavy rainfall, and waterlogging is common. Thus, even when climate and relief permit cultivation, infertile, wet soils are likely to support only improved grassland at best.

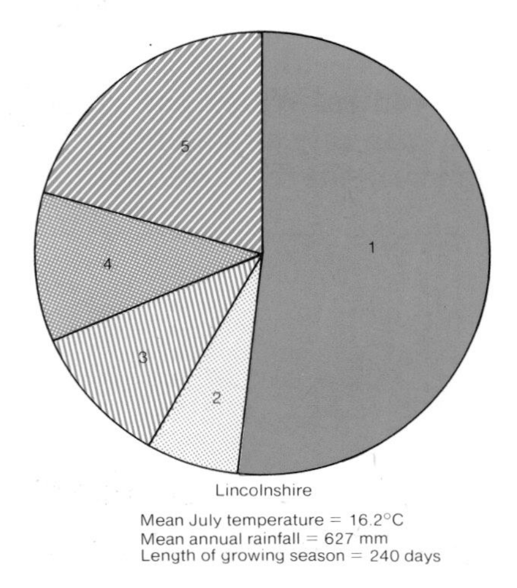

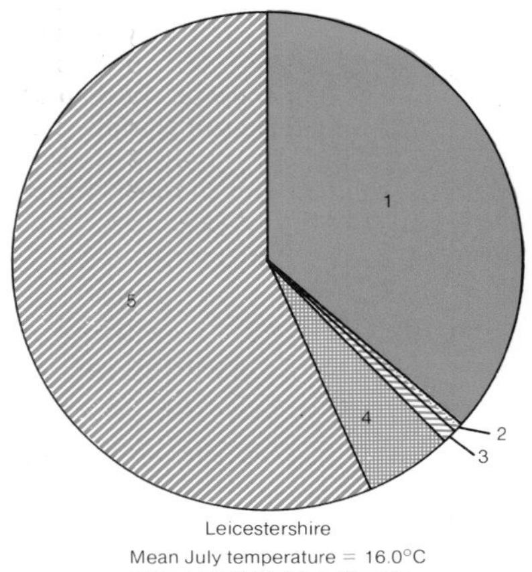

Key
1 cereals
2 sugar beet
3 fruit and vegetables
4 other arable
5 grassland

Figure 7.14 Agricultural land use A Lincolnshire B Leicestershire

Exercise

1 Look at Figure 7.17 and by referring to an atlas write down the names of the most important areas for fruit and vegetable growing (horticulture) in England and Wales.

2 How close are the main fruit and vegetable growing districts to the areas of first class arable land (Figure 7.15)?

3 Bearing in mind your answer to question 2, how profitable do you think fruit and vegetable growing is on the best quality land with very fertile soils? Answer this question by making a copy of Figure 7.18 which shows how the profitability of different types of farming varies with soil fertility. On your graph draw in the likely gradient of profit for fruit and vegetables.

4 Which group of farmers (ie those farming good, moderate or poor soils) has a) the greatest b) the least choice of crops and livestock?

Figure 7.16 The landscape of the Fens in eastern England. The Fens are the largest area of first class arable land in Britain. The fertile silt and peat soils are intensively farmed, with cereals, vegetables, fruit and sugar beet especially important. The photograph shows part of the Fens near Downham Market in Norfolk: note the typical rectangular fields, straight roads, isolated farms and traces of old stream channels which crossed the area before drainage and reclamation in the 17th century

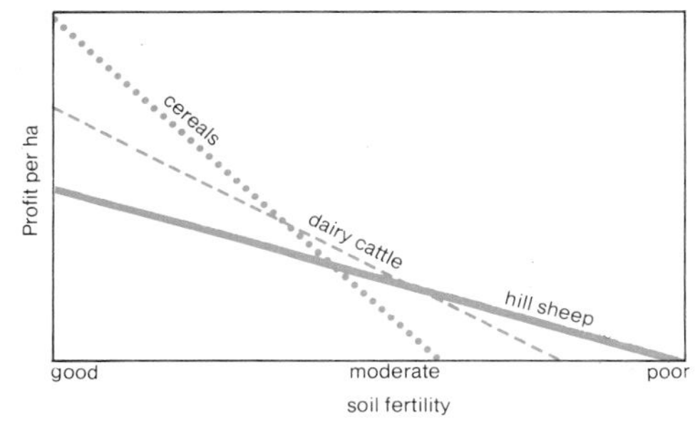

Figure 7.18 The influence of soil fertility on types of farming

Figure 7.15 Distribution of best quality soils in Britain

Figure 7.17 Distribution of soft fruit and vegetables in England and Wales

Government

We have already seen that climate suits the growth of grass in western Britain, and that arable farming is not very profitable in this area. However, the distribution of dairy farming is also affected by government policy which is designed to protect farmers, especially in the remoter areas, and ensure an ample supply of fresh milk to meet the demands of people in towns. This is done through the Milk Marketing Boards (MMBs), which were established by the government in 1933. Scotland has four MMBs but England and Wales are covered by one MMB which is split into eleven regions (Figure 7.20). All milk leaving farms is sold to the MMB at a guaranteed price, which is fixed each year by the government. The price per litre is the same *within* each region, but varies slightly *between* regions. This is because it is more expensive to collect milk and transport it to dairies in regions like north Wales and Cornwall, where farms may be more remote and smaller than in eastern England or the North West. Its transport to market is paid for by the Board (Figure 7.21).

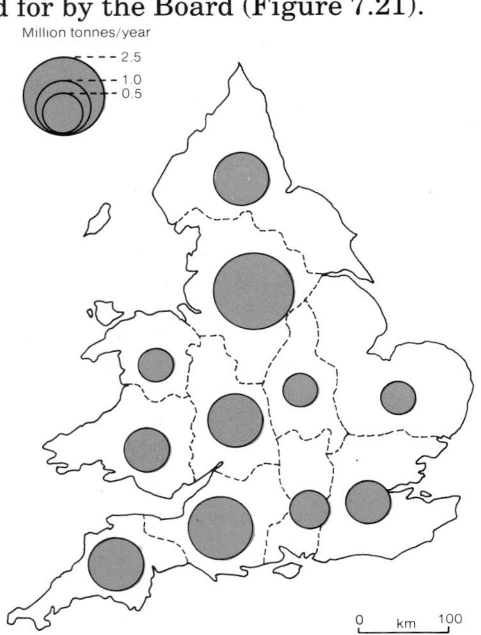

Figure 7.20 Milk production in England and Wales

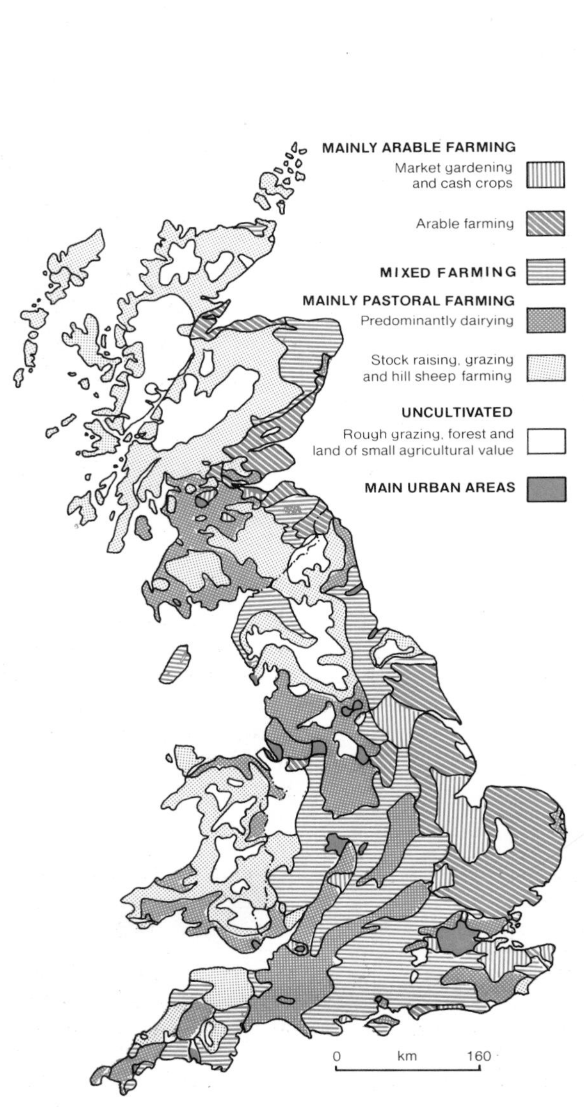

Figure 7.19 Farming types in Great Britain (from *Agriculture in Britain*, HMSO)

Figure 7.21 All milk leaving British farms is sold to the Milk Marketing Board. Milk is collected from farms by tanker lorries and transported to nearby dairies and creameries.

This policy clearly favours the more isolated, distant dairy farmers in areas such as north and west Wales, Cumbria, Devon and Cornwall: it makes little difference to the profits of the farmer, if he is situated near to, or at a considerable distance from the market. Similarly, within any MMB region, distance from any of the 700 dairies or collection centres does not affect a farmer's profits. Without the government's policy towards milk producers, many dairy farms in remote western areas of England and Wales would be uneconomic, and these farms would be forced to concentrate on other types of farming, such as sheep or cattle rearing. Do you think that this government policy is fair?

Exercise

1 Milk is heavy, bulky and expensive to transport. If farmers were required to pay the full cost of transport, where would you expect to find the dairy industry concentrated? (To remind yourself of the effect of transport on location, look back to Chapter 5, pages 105–6.)

2 Now look at the distribution of milk production in England and Wales (Figure 7.20) and compare it with the location of the main markets for milk (Figure 7.22). How does the distribution of milk production differ from that you expected in your answer to the last question?

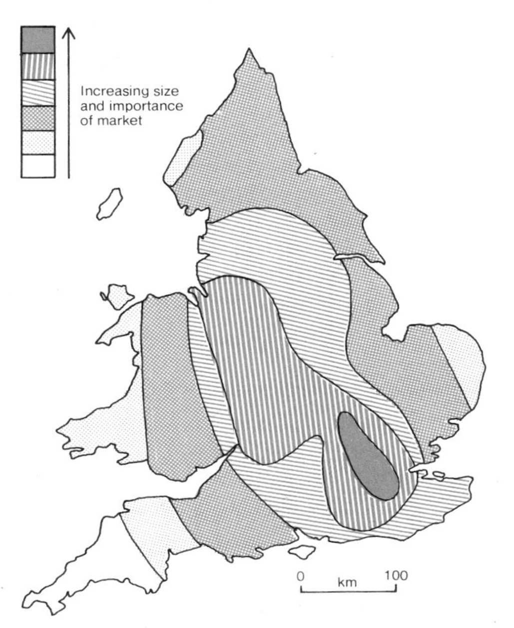

Figure 7.22 Areas of greatest demand for milk in England and Wales

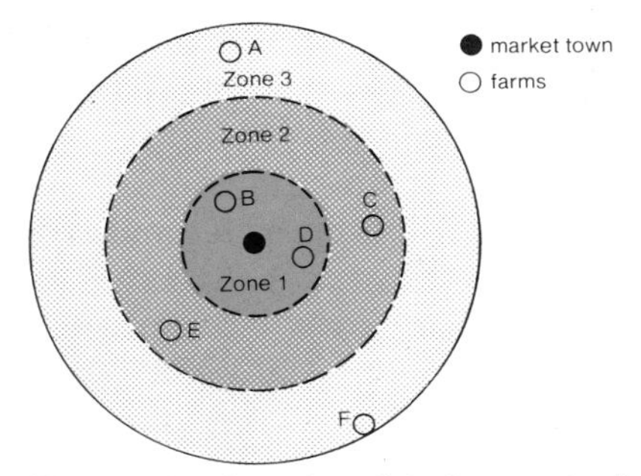

Figure 7.23 Location of six farms round a market town

Exercise

Figure 7.23 shows the location of six farms in an area which surrounds a market town. The town has a dairy operated by the MMB, and a livestock market for cattle and sheep. All milk produced on the farms is sent to the dairy, and all livestock are sold in the market town.

Table 7.4 Profits from dairy and sheep farming where farmers pay full transport costs

	Dairy farming			Sheep farming		
	Income per ha per year	Transport cost per ha per year	Profit per ha per year	Income per ha per year	Transport cost per ha per year	Profit per ha per year
ZONE 1	£1000	£100	£900	£800	£20	£780
ZONE 2	£1000	£200	?	£800	£40	?
ZONE 3	£1000	£300	?	£800	£60	?

1 Study Table 7.4 which shows the income and transport costs of dairy farmers and sheep farmers. In this example it is assumed that milk producers pay transport charges for the collection of their milk, which are in proportion to the distance from the dairy.
   a Draw a bar chart based on Figure 7.24 which shows how the profitability of dairy and sheep farming varies in the three zones.
   b Which farms will specialise in milk production, and which in sheep farming?
   c Why do you think that dairy farmers are likely to pay higher transport charges than sheep farmers?

2 Now assume a situation where the government subsidises the dairy farmers, by charging a standard transport rate of £100 a year for each hectare's production.
   a Draw a second bar chart to illustrate this new situation.
   b Which farms will now specialise in milk production?

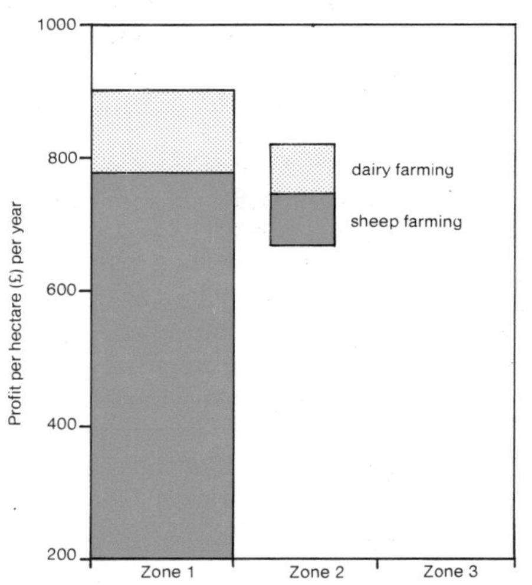

Figure 7.24 Profitability of dairy and sheep farming in zones round a market town

Farm size

The size of a farm can have important influences on the types of crops which are grown, the yields per hectare, and the methods of cultivation used. If a farmer depends wholly on his farm for his living, and his farm is small (for example less than 20 ha), he will need to grow crops and use methods of cultivation which will give him a large return from each hectare. This may only be possible through heavy expenditure on machinery, buildings, labour, fertilizers, pesticides and other *inputs*. Farming which relies on high inputs, to produce high *outputs* (yields), is described as *intensive* (Figure 7.25).

Some of the most intensive farming systems, such as glasshouse cultivation of salad crops, pig breeding and poultry, may give the farmer a good living on as little as one hectare of land! However, although these farms have a small area they are large in the sense that the amount of money invested in them is probably many times greater than that of a hill farm of 2000 ha.

Exercise

1 *Extensive* farming is a system where low inputs produce low outputs per hectare. Extensive farms are thus always large where farming is the full-time occupation of the farmer. Draw a diagram similar to Figure 7.25 to illustrate an extensive farming system.

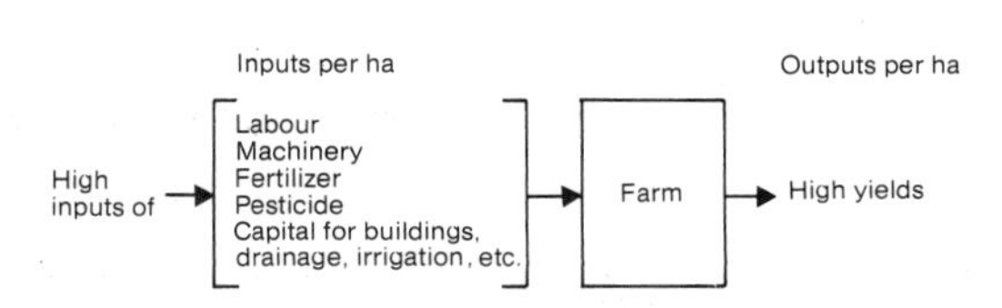

Figure 7.25 An intensive farming system

2 Study Table 7.5 which shows farm sizes for three different types of farming in England and Wales, and answer the following questions.
  a Which type of farming is most characteristic of the larger farms (over 60 ha)?
  b Which type of farming is most common on the smaller farms (under 60 ha)?
  c Which type of farming do you think is a) the most intensive b) the least intensive? Explain your answers.

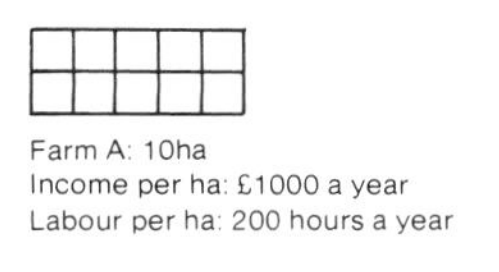

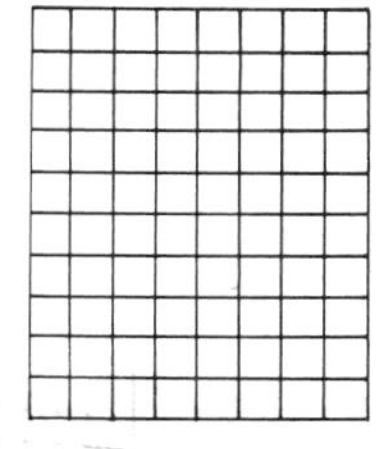

Figure 7.26

Table 7.5 Farm sizes and types of farming in England and Wales

Farm sizes	% total farm area	% total wheat area	% total dairying area	% total orchard area
under 20 ha	7.5	1.6	8.3	18.9
20–40 ha	12.5	3.8	21.4	15.0
41–60 ha	12.1	4.6	18.5	11.1
over 60 ha	67.9	90.0	51.8	55.0

Methods of cultivation, and in particular the use of machinery in farming, may be strongly influenced by farm size. On very small farms of just a few hectares there would be little justification for expensive machinery, when much of the work could be done by hand. Smallholdings, concentrating on fruit and vegetables (horticulture), compared to other types of farming, are often for this reason *labour intensive*. In contrast, very large farms growing cereal and root crops justify the purchase of large amounts of machinery, including tractors, combine harvesters, spraying machines, crop driers and many others. Without the use of machinery, cultivation of very large farms would be impossible.

Exercise

Figure 7.26 shows two farms, A and B, of 10 and 80 hectares. For the farms to be successful, they each need to provide an income of £10 000 a year. Conditions on the two farms, in terms of climate, soil, relief and all other factors are the same, and farmers have the choice of growing either potatoes or wheat (Table 7.6).

1 Assuming that each farmer works for 2000 hours a year, which crop would each farm specialise in, and what would be the income of the two farms?

2 Which farm is more intensively cultivated? Can you say why?

3 Would farm B achieve a higher income if it grew a combination of potatoes and wheat?

4 Which farm has a) the higher yield in money per hectare b) the higher yield in money for every hour worked?

Table 7.6 Profitability of potatoes and wheat

	Yield per ha (tonnes)	Value per tonne	Yield per ha (£)	Hours of work per ha per year
Potatoes	30	£33.33	£1000	200
Wheat	5	£50.00	£250	25

Agriculture in the Netherlands

Nearly 70% of the land area of the Netherlands is used for farming. However, the Netherlands is a small country and the total cultivated area is only 2 500 000 hectares. Given the Netherlands' relatively large population of 14 million, the density of population per square kilometre of farmland is one of the highest in Europe (Table 7.7). In spite of this, Dutch agriculture produces a large surplus for export; indeed one quarter of all Dutch exports consists of agricultural products.

Crops and livestock

There are many different types of farming in the Netherlands (Figure 7.27). This results from a combination of physical and human factors, especially soil and drainage conditions, population density and nearness to markets.

Climate sets the broad limits on which crops can be grown. Average rainfall for the whole country is 750 mm a year, and as all districts are within a short distance of the sea, maritime influences have a strong effect on temperature.

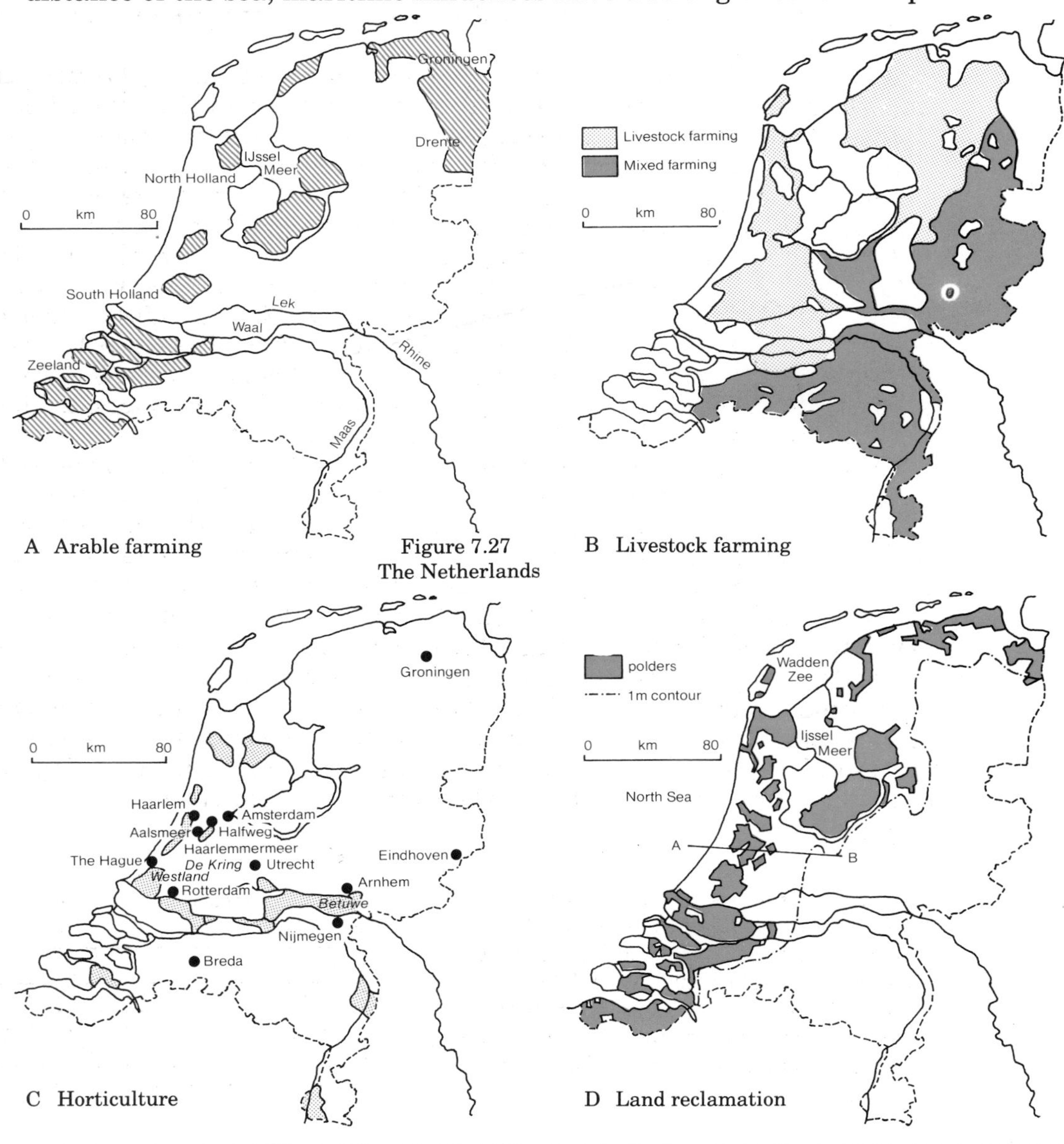

A Arable farming

B Livestock farming

C Horticulture

D Land reclamation

Figure 7.27 The Netherlands

The mean January temperature is a relatively mild 1.7°C, and the mean July temperature a moderate 17°C. In western areas there are no more than 60 days a year when frost occurs.

While climate in this small country, with little variation in relief, is much the same everywhere, soils show a much greater variety. Sandy soils are found close to the dune coastline, and on the glacial deposits which cover much of the eastern 'high' Netherlands. In the west, in the provinces of North and South Holland, there are large areas of marine clay and peat on land which was formerly lake and sea bed. These artificially drained areas protected from flooding by dykes, are known as *polders*, and are the best farmlands in the country (Figure 7.27D).

An important feature of Dutch agriculture is its high intensity. This stems from the Netherlands' high population density, and is reflected in the small size of the average farm (15.6 ha). The home market for farm products is dominated by Randstad, and intensive fruit, vegetable and dairy farming are found in several areas close to the conurbation (Figure 7.27C). The foreign market is also important, particularly West Germany: the largest concentration of population in Europe, the Rhine–Ruhr in north west Germany, is barely 175 km from the Randstad.

Two-thirds of farmland is under grass (Figure 7.28). Dairy farming produces important butter and cheese exports, and fresh milk for the six million people living in Randstad. Dairying occupies the less well-drained clay and peat soils of the polders, which are too wet for arable farming. Mixed farming dominates the sandy soils of the south and east, but in recent years there has been increasing *specialisation*, particularly in pig and poultry farming.

Arable farming, which is largely geared to producing cereals for animal feed, is found on the fertile, well-drained, clay soils of the west. Many of these areas in the 'low' Netherlands are polders, the largest being the IJssel Meer polders where over 90% of the farmland is arable. Apart from cereals, potatoes and sugar beet are major crops; sugar beet being best suited to areas of heavy clay soils, such as those in Zeeland. Arable farming is also important on the peat soils of Groningen and East Drente (Figure 7.27A).

Horticulture or market gardening is the most famous farming activity in the Netherlands. It is concentrated almost exclusively in North and South Holland, where there are several important specialisms. Behind the dunes of the North Sea coast, on the lime-rich sandy soils of the Haarlemmermeer polder, are the famous bulb fields, growing tulips, daffodils, crocuses and hyacinths. Not only are the bulbs a valuable export, but the bulb fields in spring are a major tourist attraction. The Westland, situated between The Hague, Hook of Holland and Rotterdam, is primarily an area of glasshouse cultivation. Crops are grown here on minute holdings in heated glasshouses: salad crops, especially cucumbers, lettuce and tomatoes, are most popular. Other local specialisms include flowers in the Aalsmeer district, ornamental trees and garden shrubs at Boskoop, and orchards in the Betuwe, between the Rhine and Waal rivers.

Exercise

1 Draw 10 squares measuring 2 × 2 cm to represent the 10 countries in Table 7.7. Using a scale of 1 dot for every 10 persons per km^2, place the appropriate number of dots for each country in the squares. Belgium for instance, will have a square containing 66 dots. Make sure that you place the dots uniformly in each square.

Table 7.7 Population density per km^2 of cultivated land in the EEC

Country	Density	Country	Density
Belgium	657	Italy	319
Denmark	182	Luxembourg	364
France	169	Netherlands	569
Greece	104	UK	302
Ireland	59	West Germany	501

2 One reason why the Dutch have gone to such expense to reclaim land and create polders, is that the dykes which are built strengthen the country's sea defences. Look at Figure 7.27D and say where most of the polders are found. Why are they found in this part of the Netherlands? (Figure 7.27D gives you a clue.)

3 Table 7.7 suggests a second reason why land reclamation has taken place on a large scale. What is it?

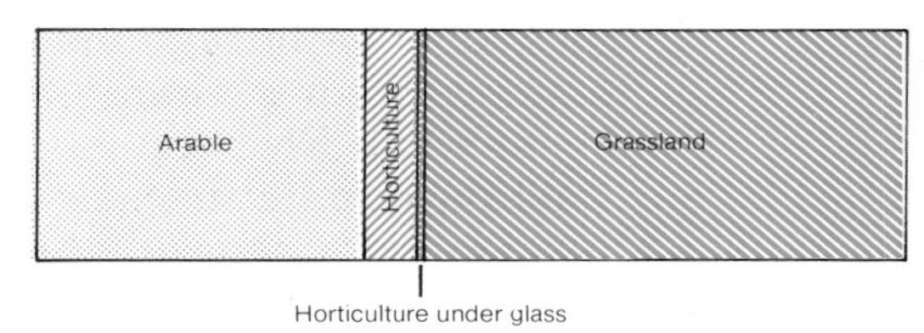

Figure 7.28 Agricultural land use in the Netherlands

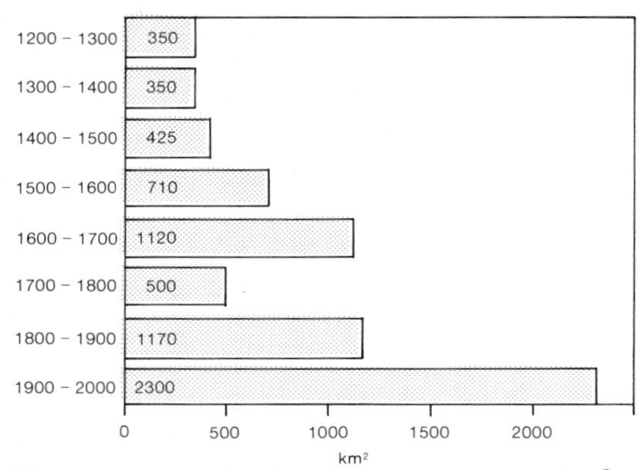

Figure 7.29 Land reclamation per century in km^2

Organisation of farming

Land reclamation has added 17% to the Netherlands' total area since AD 1200, and in the 'low' Netherlands half the farmed area is polderland. Figure 7.29 shows that by far the largest reclamation has occurred in the twentieth century; indeed the reclamation of the Zuider Zee and the draining of the four IJssel polders alone, added 6% to the country's land area. Many of the polders lie below sea level, and this creates special problems for farming: farm land has to be artificially drained by pumping water into the surrounding dykes. The cost of drainage has to be paid for by the farmers, as well as the expense of maintaining the dykes and pumps. A further problem in the low-lying areas is that salt water continually seeps under the dykes and, unless controlled, affects the quality of crops in some polders (Figure 7.31).

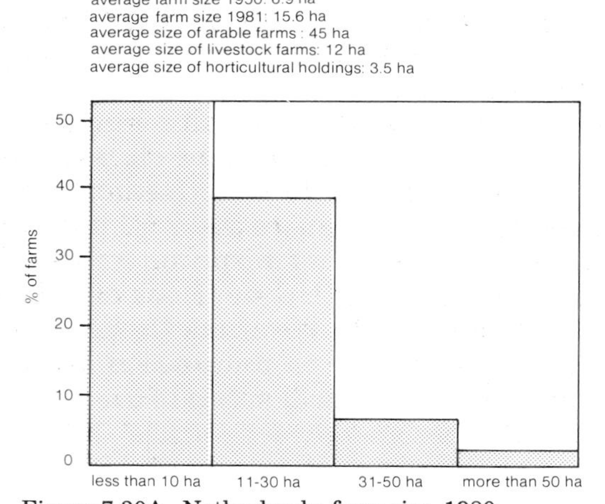

Figure 7.30A Netherlands: farm size, 1980

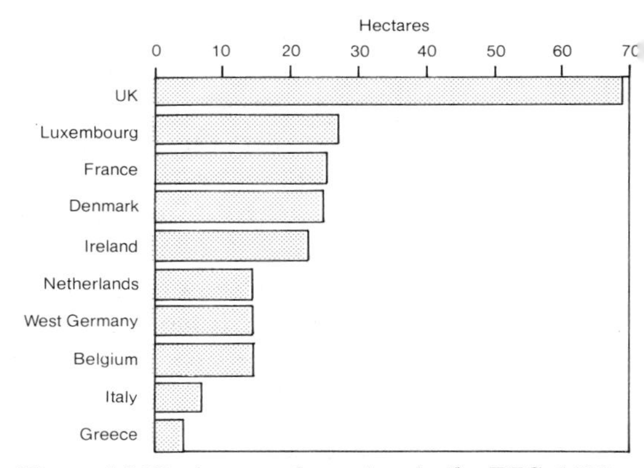

Figure 7.30B Average farm sizes in the EEC, 1980

The average Dutch farm is only 15.6 hectares in size, and this fact partly explains the highly intensive nature of Dutch farming. Over half of farms are less than 10 hectares (Figure 7.30) and many horticultural holdings are less than 1 hectare. Arable farms are largest, averaging 45 hectares, followed by livestock farms (12 hectares) and horticultural smallholdings (3.5 hectares). However, since 1950, when the average farm was only 6.9 hectares, there has been a steady increase in farm size, and the total number of holdings has fallen correspondingly. The EEC, concerned to improve the efficiency of farming, gives grants to encourage the joining of scattered plots of land into single blocks: since 1950 over 1 million hectares have been *consolidated* in this way.

As in all EEC countries farming in the Netherlands has become more mechanised, farmers better trained, and supporting services concerned with research and advising farmers have become more extensive in the last 40 years. It is not therefore surprising that yields have increased sharply during this period – wheat by 53%, potatoes by 36%, milk by 26% and sugar beet by 16%. Another aspect of improved efficiency has been a large decline in the agricultural workforce: whereas in 1947 agriculture employed 1 in 5 of the workforce, in 1981 the proportion was little more than 1 in 25.

The pattern of farming in the Netherlands is strongly influenced by the EEC, which is the main market. Three-quarters of Dutch farm exports go to other EEC countries, and membership of the EEC has encouraged farmers to specialise in products such as fresh fruit, flowers, vegetables, veal and pig meat almost exclusively for the Common Market. Clearly the Netherlands' geographical situation, which gives it easy access to the huge urban populations of northern Germany, Belgium and the Paris region, has assisted this trend.

Agricultural policy in the EEC

Within the EEC agriculture is the only industry for which the member states have a common policy. The Common Agricultural Policy (CAP) is based on two main principles.

1 It provides member countries with a single market of 270 million people. Within this market there is free movement of farm products, so countries do not have to pay duties on the goods they export.
2 It protects EEC farmers from cheap imports by imposing tariffs and by giving them subsidies to produce certain crops. For instance, many essential products like grain, meat and milk have a guaranteed minimum price: if prices fall to this level then the EEC buys them from the farmers and either stores them, until the market improves, or sells them off to non-EEC countries.

The aims of the CAP are to give farmers a reasonable income, assure the EEC's essential food supplies, and keep prices for the people as steady as possible. There is no doubt that for a country like the Netherlands, with a large and efficient farming sector, membership of the EEC has proved very successful. One effect of the CAP has been that with free competition farmers have been encouraged to specialise in those crops and livestock which they can produce most cheaply. In the Netherlands the trend towards specialisation in the production of fruit and vegetables and dairy products has been strongly influenced by membership of the EEC.

Exercise

Figure 7.31 is a cross-section through the western Netherlands (see Figure 7.27D), and shows three contrasting landscapes, each with distinctive soil, drainage and farming conditions. Make a copy of the cross-section and the table. Look carefully at the maps of farming in the Netherlands (Figure 7.27) and complete the table using the appropriate descriptions below it.

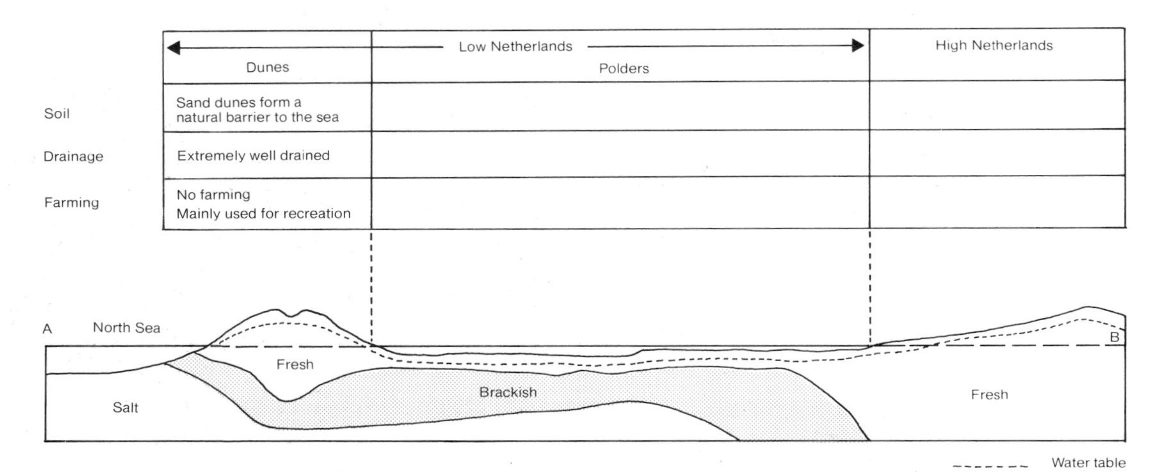

Figure 7.31 Cross section through a polder

'Marine clay soils and peaty soils which are very fertile.'

'Sandy soils formed from glacial outwash material which are not naturally very fertile.'

'Coarse sandy soils which are very well drained. The water table is a long way below the surface. Shortage of water can be a problem.'

'Artificial drainage is necessary as the whole area lies below sea level. In some areas the water table is almost at the surface and soils are too wet for cultivation. Salt water seepage can be a problem.'

'Intensive cultivation: bulb growing on sandy areas behind the dunes; dairy farming on damper soils for Randstad conurbation.'

'Less intensive farming, combining livestock production and the growing of cereals, roots and grass for fodder.'

Case studies of Netherlands' farming

Arable farming in Eastern Flevoland

Between 1930 and 1968 four polders were drained in the former Zuider Zee – known since its sealing off as Lake IJssel (Figure 7.32). In the south west of the Lake IJssel polder of Eastern Flevoland, Mr de Boer farms an arable holding of 60 hectares (Figures 7.33 and 7.34). Eastern Flevoland, the third in the series of polders, covers 54 000 hectares and fell dry in 1957. The first harvests were taken from it between 1960 and 1970 when it was farmed by the government-controlled Polders Development Authority. In 1970 Mr de Boer obtained his farm, having previously made three unsuccessful applications for a farm in the polders. (The number of applicants is many times the number of farms available.) He gave his farm the name of 'Ex Undis', which appropriately enough means 'from the waves'.

Mr de Boer's farm is divided into four large fields. He devotes one field to each of the following crops: winter wheat, potatoes, sugar beet, and either beans, peas or oats (Figure 7.35). He follows a system of rotation so that each field is never planted with the same crop for more than one or two years. The choice of the first three crops – wheat, potatoes and sugar beet – is explained by the very fertile soil, which gives a good profit from this crop combination. His choice of the fourth crop depends largely on market prices in any one year.

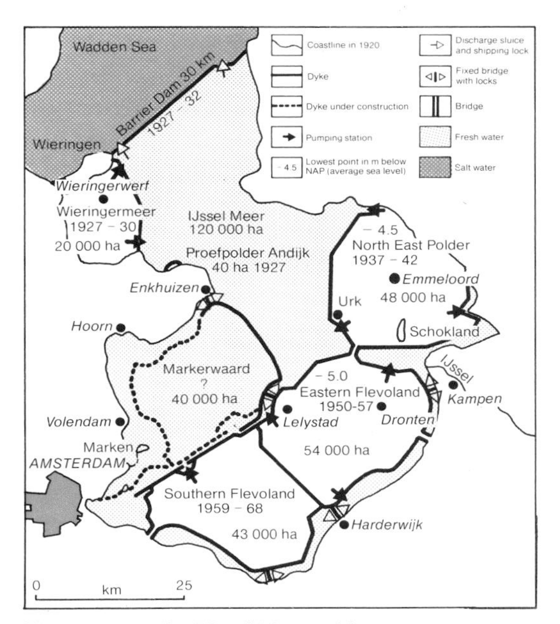

Figure 7.32 The IJssel Meer polders

Figure 7.33 The location of Mr de Boer's farm

Mr de Boer pays great attention to the soil, which is already of high quality. Samples of soil are taken regularly by the Agricultural Soil and Crop Research Laboratory, which then tells him which fertilizers to use. The soil is so fertile because it was part of the sea bed until a few years ago. The remains of shell fish and fish give the soil a high lime and potassium content, though there is a shortage of vegetable material, bacteria and worms. In the growing season pesticides are used, and are generally sprayed by the farmer himself, though sometimes he employs a specialist firm to spray his crops from an aircraft. 'Ex Undis' is highly mechanised, with a wide range of equipment for sowing, planting and harvesting, including four tractors, a spreader for artificial fertilizer, a spraying machine (for pesticides) and separate machines for planting and harvesting sugar beet, cereals and potatoes. As the farm is so highly mechanised, Mr de Boer does not employ any outside labour.

Figure 7.34 Mr de Boer's farm in Eastern Flevoland, looking NNW. 'Ex Undis' is marked with an X.

Figure 7.35 'Ex Undis' cropping plan

The sugar beet is sent to a factory in Halfweg, between Amsterdam and Haarlem. The seed potatoes are sold to a trading company, which exports them to Brazil and other countries. The wheat, which is grown only for seed, goes to a trading company in Groningen, and the peas and beans are grown under contract for a canning factory.

Mr de Boer's income can vary greatly from year to year: in a good year he can earn up to four times as much as in a bad one. The main reason for this is not so much differences in the size of the harvest caused by climate or disease, but variations in market prices. Even so, 'Ex Undis' is one of the most profitable farms in the country – an indication of the almost ideal conditions for arable farming on the IJssel Meer polders.

Exercise

1 Look at the figures of crop yields in Table 7.8 and explain why it is that in the IJssel polders the number of applicants for farms has been many times the number of farms available.

2 Write a short account to describe and explain the ideal conditions for farming on Mr de Boer's farm, and in the IJssel Meer polders generally. Use the following headings as a guide:
— soil quality
— farm size compared with national average (page 198)
— relief (look at Figure 7.34)
— farm layout (access to land, shape of fields, etc. – see Figure 7.34).

Table 7.8 Crop yields: 'Ex Undis' and Netherlands' average

	'Ex Undis'	Netherlands
Wheat	6.5 tonnes/ha	5.2 tonnes/ha
Potatoes	50.0	34.0
Sugar beet	60.0	46.5

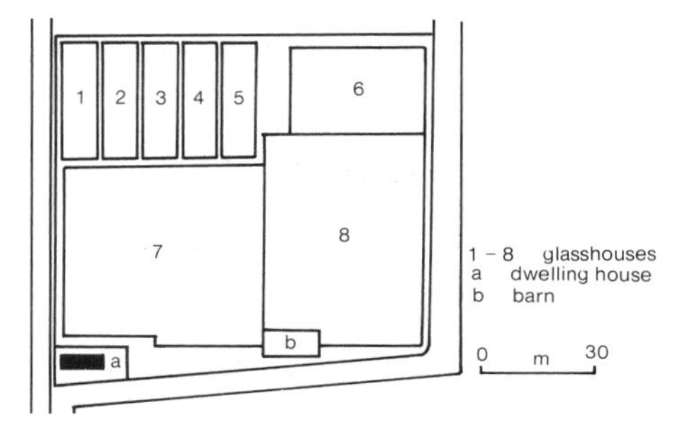

Figure 7.36 Plan of Mr P Steekelenburg's holding

Horticulture in the Westland

The most intensive form of horticulture is the growing of fruit, vegetables, ornamental plants and flowers in heated glasshouses. The largest and best known area of glasshouse cultivation in the Netherlands is the Westland, situated between The Hague–Delft–Rotterdam to the north and east, the New Waterway to the south and the North Sea to the west (Figure 4.32). Farming methods are extremely intensive, and the average size of holding is only one hectare. Owing to the high costs of labour, mechanisation and automation have been taken to remarkable lengths on many holdings.

The locational advantages of the Westland include the nearness of the Randstad region, with its huge market, and the region's mild, maritime climate (the Westland lies immediately behind the dunes). However, the climate is only important to the extent that heating costs are somewhat lower than areas further inland. In other respects, the Westland is not an ideal location. Partly because of its location in the Randstad, land prices are extremely high (an average of £70 000 per hectare). Also, because of its location on the polluted lower reaches of the Rhine, the quality of surface and ground water is poor. Finally, in view of the importance of the West German market for horticultural products, its situation is somewhat isolated.

Mr Steekelenburg's smallholding (Figures 7.36 and 7.37) is situated on the northern side of the Westland, close to the outskirts of The Hague. His holding is only one hectare, and adjoins his father's holding which is the same size. This allows labour (provided by the family), machinery and transport to be shared.

In the large, continuous glasshouses Mr Steekelenburg grows such vegetables as spinach and endive in the spring, cucumbers in summer, and lettuce in autumn and winter. He also grows grapes in smaller, detached glasshouses. His choice of crops is influenced by market prices and competition from other EEC producers. Competition from French and Italian grapes for example, has caused a decline in grape growing in the Westland.

All crops are grown under glass, and are heated by gas heaters, suspended from the roofs of the glasshouses. The gas heating is thermostatically controlled, and an alarm system sends a warning to Mr Steekelenburg's house if the heating fails. A 'rain machine' enables the time and duration of watering of crops to be set in advance. There is also a semi-automatic ventilation system, by which windows in the roofs of the glasshouses can be opened and closed. This is not the last word in automation: there are holdings with a fully automatically controlled climate, where heating, watering, ventilation and carbon dioxide content of the air are all regulated by computer!

The soils in the glasshouses are mainly fed with artificial fertilizer, and crop rotation is practised to combat disease. The average labour supply is two to three persons, though during harvesting periods more labour is needed, which is usually provided by the family or sometimes school children. All produce is sold through the Westland-Noord co-operative, situated only 6 km from the holding.

The Canadian Prairies

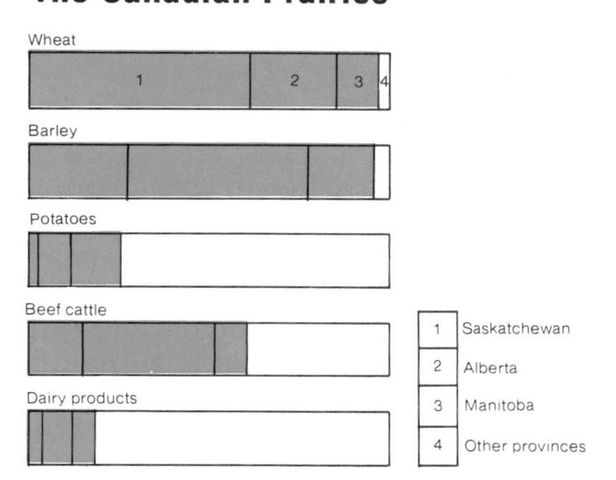

Figure 7.38 The importance of farming in the Prairies: selected agricultural products by value, 1982

7.37 The Westland glasshouse district, looking ESE, with the outskirts of The Hague in the background. Mr Steekelenburg's holding is marked with an X.

The Prairies of western Canada are one of the most important farming areas in the developed world. They form the most northerly part of the Great Plains, which extend as far as Texas in the southern USA. The whole region is highly productive: each farmer produces sufficient grain and meat to feed an average of 55 people for a year! Little wonder that the Great Plains have been described as the 'breadbasket' of the western world.

The Canadian Prairies consist of the three provinces of Alberta, Manitoba and Saskatchewan. Between them they account for 79% of Canada's farmland, produce 98% of the country's wheat, 94% of the country's barley, the entire oilseed crop, and nearly 60% of Canada's beef (Figure 7.38). They form an eastward sloping plain, between the Rocky Mountains in the west, and the barren Laurentian Shield to the north and east. They are covered with glacial and lake deposits, which have formed fertile brown and black soils, ideal for cultivation.

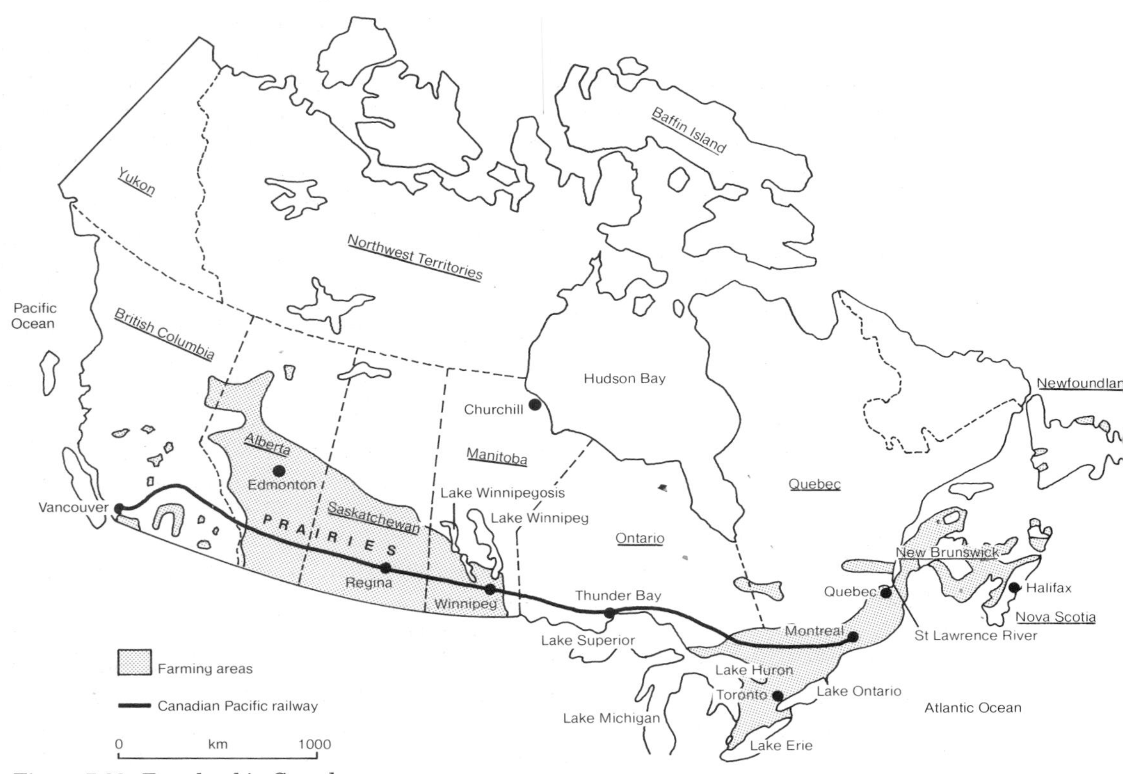

Figure 7.39 Farmland in Canada

Unlike the farming areas we have described earlier in this chapter, farming in many parts of the Prairies has been established for little more than a century. Settlement first began in 1812 in the Red River Valley, near the present day city of Winnipeg, but for much of the nineteenth century settlement occurred very slowly. The main obstacle was the isolation of the Prairies in the centre of the continent, with little prospect of commercial farming until the building of the railways after 1850. The real breakthrough came with the completion of the Canadian Pacific railway in 1885, which linked British Columbia with the eastern provinces (Figure 7.39). Both the government and the railway companies granted land to settlers, normally in standard homesteads of 160 acres (64 ha). Settlement followed the railways, and was initially confined to a zone of 15 km on either side of the track. Thus, as well as providing the essential transport for farm products, the railways were vital in the settlement of the Prairies and the development of farming there.

Exercise

1 Canada is the largest country in the western hemisphere and the second largest in the world. Consult your atlas and find out which country has a larger area than Canada.

2 Refer to Figure 7.39 and measure the approximate distance between a) the northernmost part of Baffin Island in the north, and Lake Erie in the south b) the Atlantic and the Pacific.

3 To give you some idea of the remoteness of the Prairies before the building of the railways, measure the straight line distances between Regina in Saskatchewan, and the ports of Thunder Bay (Ontario), Vancouver (British Columbia) and Churchill (Manitoba). (For comparison, the straight line distance between London and Glasgow is approximately 550 km.)

4 Study the air photograph showing part of the Canadian Prairies (Figure 7.40).
  a Describe the landscape of the Prairies by considering the following features: the shape of farms (roads and tracks form most farm boundaries); the shape of fields; the pattern of roads; and settlement (nucleated or dispersed?).
  b The lower part of the photograph is crossed by a railway. Explain briefly the importance of the railway in the development of farming in the Prairies.
  c Suggest a possible advantage to farming of the regular farm and field shapes found in the Prairies.
  d Suggest a reason for the location of the larger, nucleated settlement in the bottom left of the photograph. What are the most likely functions of this settlement?

Figure 7.40 An aerial view of the farming landscape of the Canadian Prairies

Farming in Manitoba

Manitoba is the most easterly of the three Prairie provinces. The farmed area of the province is entirely concentrated in a triangular shaped block in the south (Figure 7.41). On one side of the triangle runs the USA–Manitoba border, the second along the Saskatchewan–Manitoba boundary, while the third cuts diagonally across the province from the south east corner, to a point west of Lake Winnipegosis. It is easy to underestimate the size of the province: in fact its total area is three times greater than the UK, and the farmed area is twice as large as Denmark's!

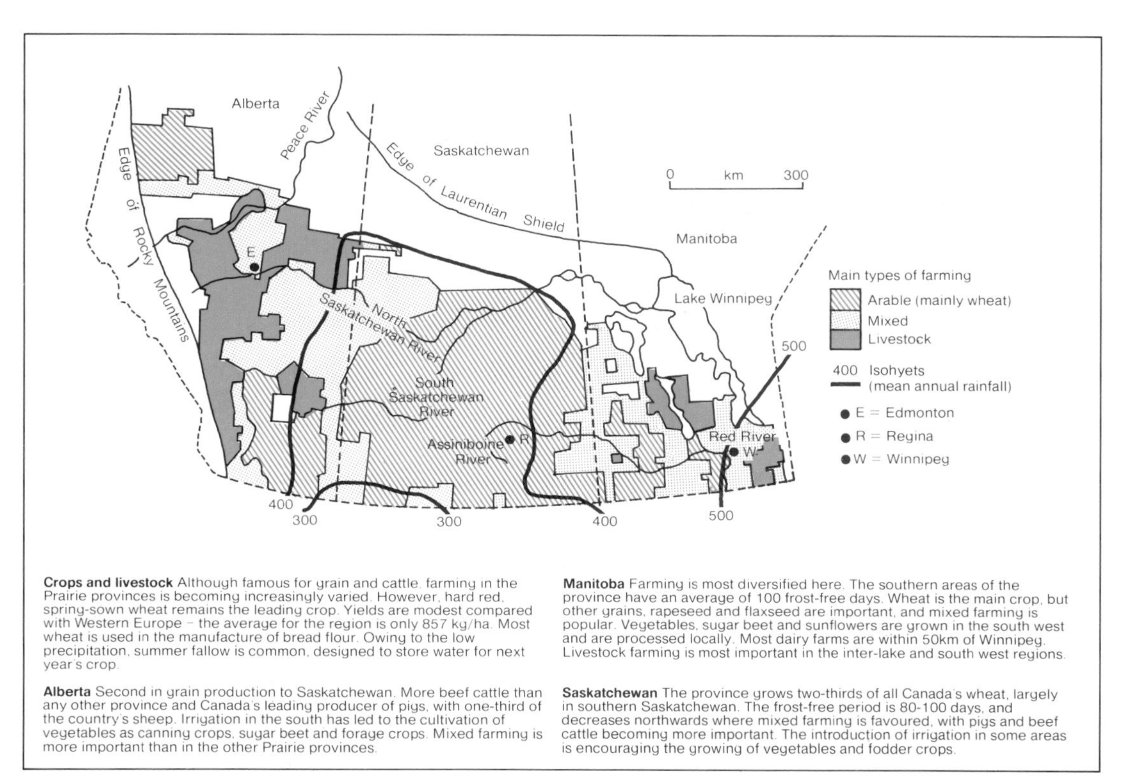

Figure 7.41 Farming in the Prairies

Climate

The distribution of farmland is largely determined by climate, though farming would extend further north were it not for the rugged, infertile Laurentian Shield. Throughout the Prairies, the length of the frost-free period is critical for farming. In southern Manitoba it varies between 100 and 120 days a year (Figure 7.47A), which is just sufficient for crops like wheat, barley, oats, oilseeds and suger beet to ripen. However, although summers are short, they are warm (Winnipeg's average July temperature is 19.7°C) and there are long hours of daylight. Nonetheless, wheat growing in the Prairies would not have been possible without the breeding of special wheat varieties such as spring red and amber durum, which mature quickly and can resist drought. Winters are long, cold and dark, and with only a light snow cover, the frost is very penetrating. For this reason most crops must be spring-sown.

Precipitation in the Prairies is light, ranging from 350 mm in southern Saskatchewan, to around 550 mm in south east Manitoba. Drought is a major hazard and indeed in the last century large parts of the southern Prairies were considered to be too dry for successful cultivation. Although the amounts of precipitation are only just sufficient for rain-fed farming, it is the unreliability of precipitation which is a more serious problem: wide variations around the average precipitation are a feature of the climate (Figure 7.42).

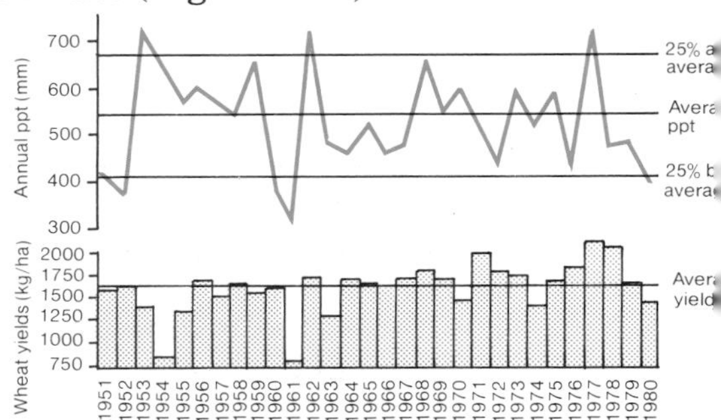

Figure 7.42 Annual precipitation and wheat yields in Manitoba

Exercise

Figure 7.43 is a climate graph for Winnipeg, which is fairly typical of the Prairie provinces of Canada. Study the graph and answer the following questions.

1. Which season has the most precipitation? Is this distribution of precipitation likely to help the farmer?
2. How many months have average temperatures below freezing?
3. What is the mean annual temperature range?

Look at Figure 7.42 which compares annual wheat yields in Manitoba with annual precipitation.

4. Between 1951 and 1980 how many years had a) above average b) below average precipitation? How many years recorded a) 25% above average b) 25% below average?
5. What happened to the wheat harvest in years when precipitation was 25% from normal?
6. Comparing the two graphs in Figure 7.42 would you say that the amount of precipitation had a large/moderate/small influence on wheat yields? What other features of climate influence yields? (Read the previous and next sections.)

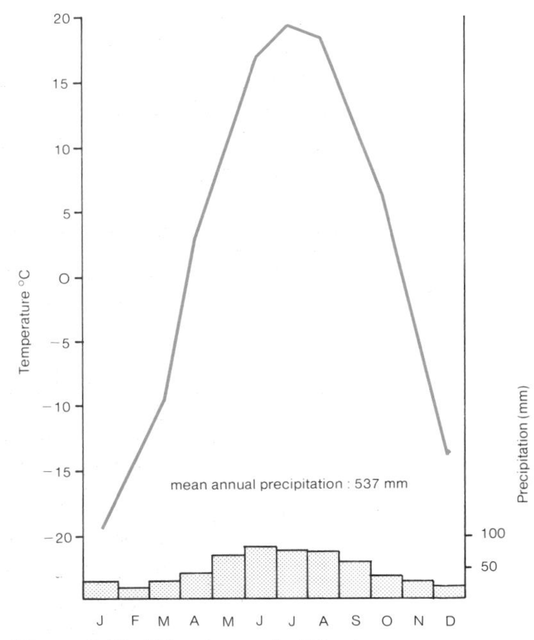

Figure 7.43 Climate graph: Winnipeg

Exercise

Figure 7.44 shows the dates of seeding and harvesting of wheat in Manitoba between 1970 and 1980. Look carefully at the diagram and answer the following:

1 What was the date of a) the earliest b) the latest seeding?

2 What was the date of a) the earliest b) the latest harvesting?

3 What was the length of a) the shortest b) the longest, growing period?

4 Does the average temperature for May (Table 7.8A) determine the date of seeding? Find this out by drawing a scatter graph of May temperature (x) against dates of seeding (y). Comment briefly on your result.

Table 7.8A Average May temperatures at Winnipeg 1970–1980 (May average: 10.6°C)

1970	9.3°C	1974	8.6°C	1978	14.5°C
1971	10.1°C	1975	12.2°C	1979	7.3°C
1972	14.6°C	1976	11.8°C	1980	15.7°C
1973	10.6°C	1977	17.8°C		

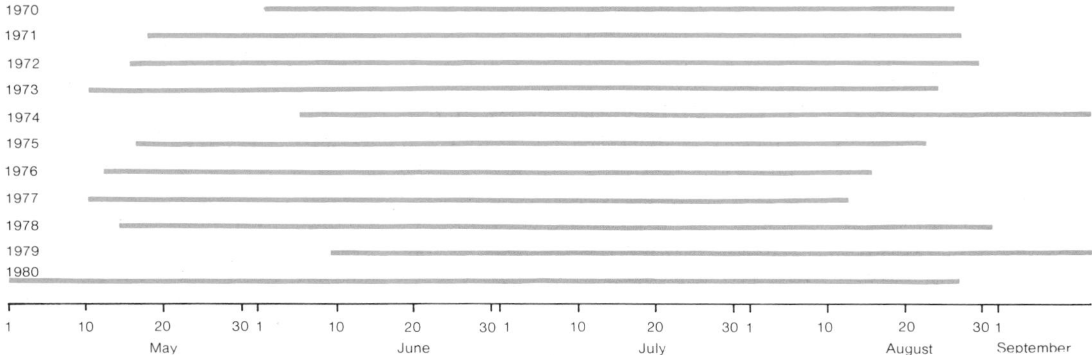

Figure 7.44 Dates of wheat seeding and harvesting in Manitoba, 1970–80

Hail storms are a third climatic hazard (Figure 7.47D). Unlike drought and frost, their effect is usually confined to quite small areas, although locally the damage to crops can be devastating. The wind also presents a potential hazard, causing erosion of the soil, especially in spring when the soil has dried out but is not protected by crops. The lighter soils are most easily eroded by the wind, which is particularly strong in the level, treeless landscape of the Prairies (Figure 7.45). Poor drainage is a major hazard to farming in southern Manitoba. This is a problem confined to spring, particularly if there has been a heavy winter snow cover. As the snow thaws it leaves the soil waterlogged and cold, which may seriously delay the planting of crops – in some years until as late as June.

Table 7.9 A farmer's diary 1980–1: southern Manitoba

Spring	Light snow cover; melting snow did not result in waterlogging, and seeding began early. Temperatures in March and April well above average. Heavy spring frost resulted in losses of vegetables, especially onions, cauliflowers and cabbages.
Summer	Dry conditions in July prevented good seed development of cereals. Yields of barley were reduced. Warm, dry conditions promoted many insects and diseases which affected vegetables. Hail caused considerable damage to crops south of Winnipeg.
Autumn	Heavy rainfall delayed harvesting of field crops in some areas. Freezing temperatures and snow during October meant that large acreages of potatoes and root crops were left in the ground to freeze.
Winter	A light snow covering did not provide good protection against frosts for many autumn-sown crops.

Figure 7.45 A farm on the Canadian Prairies. Note the large barn where livestock are kept and fodder is stored during the long and severe winter, and the shelter belt of trees around the farm, which provides some protection from the wind, in a flat, largely treeless landscape (see Figure 7.40)

Figure 7.46 Combine harvesting of barley in the Prairies. By European standards Prairie farms are huge, averaging over 300 hectares in Saskatchewan, and over 250 hectares in Alberta and Manitoba. Arable farms of this size can only be cultivated with the large scale use of machinery

Farming methods

Although crop yields are generally increasing (Figure 7.42), farming in the Prairies remains *extensive* compared with Europe. Inputs of labour, fertilizer, machinery and pesticide are fairly low for each hectare farmed, and yields of principal crops are barely half those of Dutch or British farmers. However, low yields are unimportant when land is plentiful and farms are large: in Manitoba

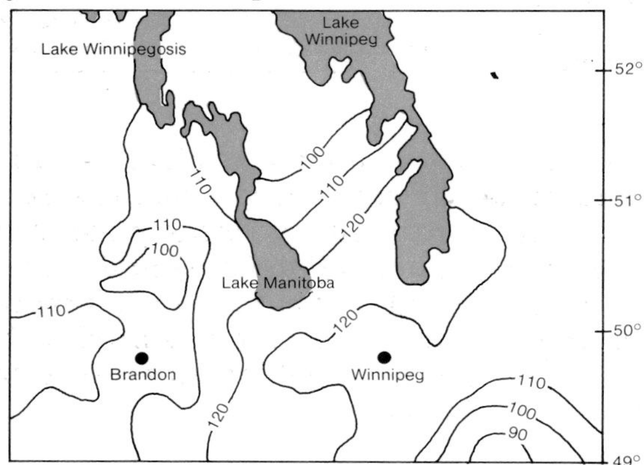

Figure 7.47A Length of frost-free period in southern Manitoba (days p.a.)

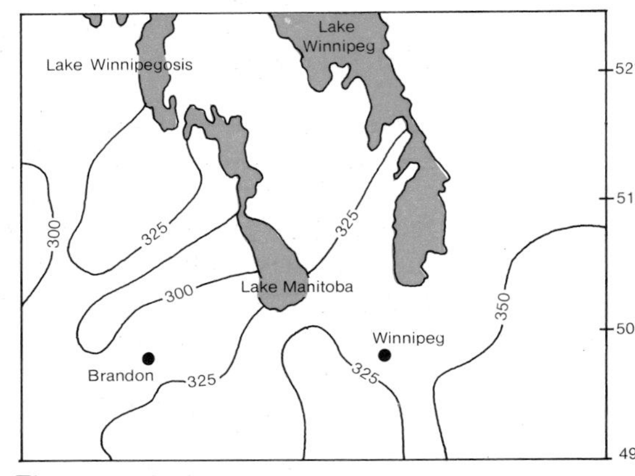

Figure 7.47B Average precipitation in southern Manitoba from 1 May to 30 September (mm p.a.)

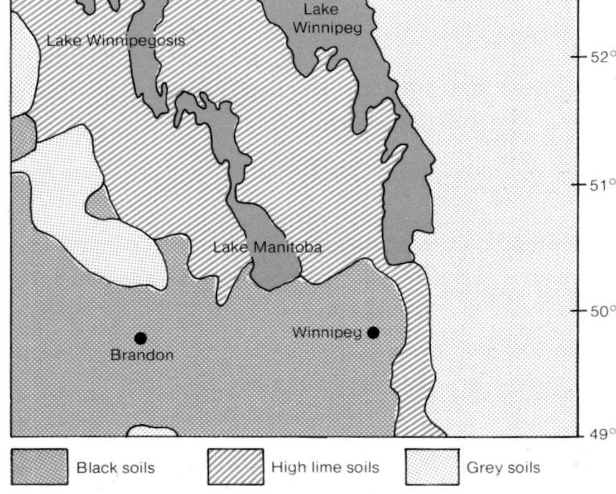

Figure 7.47C Soil types in southern Manitoba

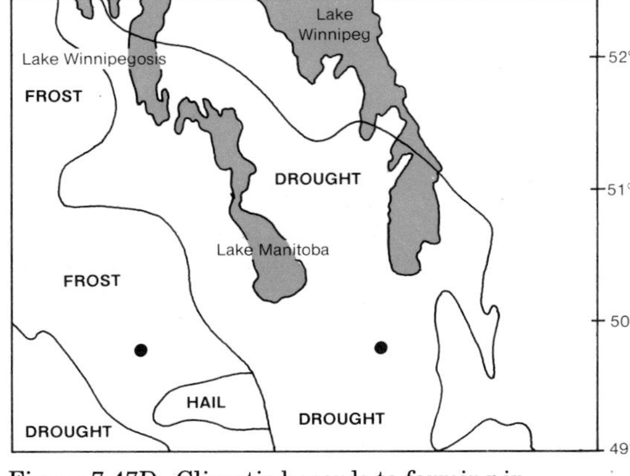

Figure 7.47D Climatic hazards to farming in southern Manitoba (waterlogging of the soil in spring is a widespread problem)

the average farm is 259 hectares, and clearly, even with only a small profit from each hectare, a farmer can make a living.

It would be impossible to cultivate farms of this size without the large-scale use of machinery, and indeed Prairie farming is probably the most highly mechanised in the world. The purchase of machines for ploughing, seeding, spraying, harvesting, drying and transporting involves a huge investment by farmers. Individual farmers may own several combine harvesters, and the use of machines rather than farm labour is such that self-propelled combines are a common sight in the Prairies at harvest time! (See Figure 7.46.)

Exercise

1 Use the information in Table 7.10 to draw two diagrams (similar to Figure 7.25) to show farming in Manitoba and Denmark as simple systems. Show inputs per hectare (labour, machinery, fertilizer) and output (income per ha) as arrows, proportional in width to their values. The box in the diagram should be a square, proportional in area to the average farm size.

2 If a farmer needs an income of £30 000 a year to make a living, how large a farm would he require in a) Manitoba b) Denmark? Write a brief paragraph explaining the difference.

Table 7.10 Farming in Manitoba and Denmark, 1981

	Manitoba	Denmark
Population working in agriculture	43 000	120 000
Farmed area	5 504 000 ha	2 897 000 ha
Average farm size	259 ha	26 ha
Number of tractors	67 342	181 000
Number of combines	22 631	39 000
Number of farms	29 442	110 812
Chemical fertilizer	90 kg/ha	243 kg/ha
Average crop yields:		
wheat	2110 kg/ha	5560 ka/ha
barley	2450 kg/ha	3920 kg/ha
oats	1905 kg/ha	4220 kg/ha
Average farm income	£165 per ha	£925 per ha

Crops and livestock

In southern Manitoba, differences in climate, relief and soil are small (Figure 7.47). While climate broadly determines what can be grown, the acreage devoted to various crops is most strongly affected by market prices and government policies. Wheat is the main crop in all districts and is found on 70% of farms (Figure 7.48A). The area sown to wheat has remained largely unchanged in the last 20 years, and the overall acreage is controlled by the Canadian Wheat Board. Most of the crop is exported; its great advantage is its hardness and suitability for milling for bread flour.

Figure 7.48 Trends in Manitoba's agriculture

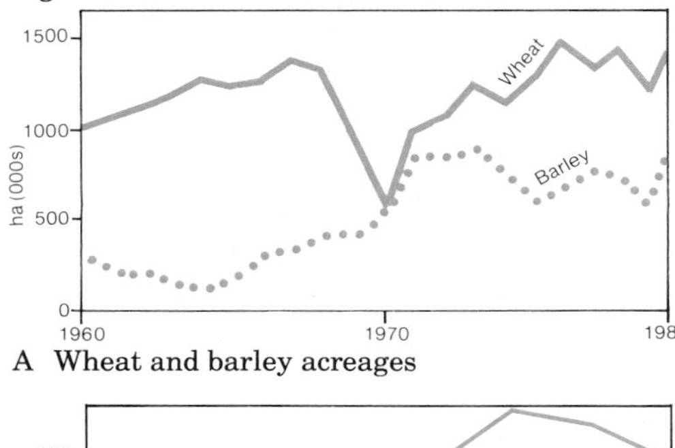

A Wheat and barley acreages

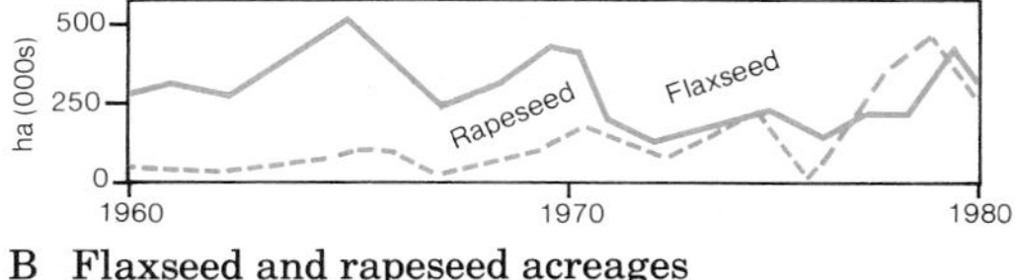

B Flaxseed and rapeseed acreages

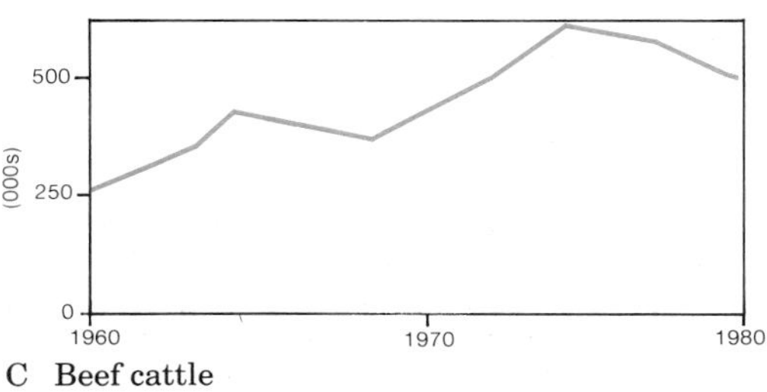

C Beef cattle

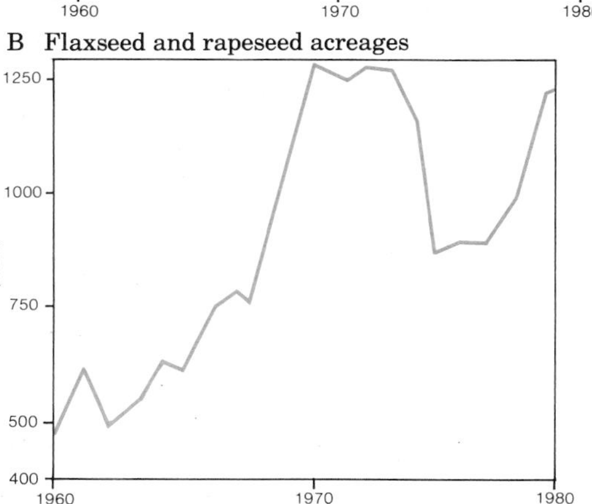

D Pigs

In the Brandon–Winnipeg area, oilseeds almost achieve the same level of importance as wheat (Figure 7.48B). The main oilseed crops are flax and rape, though sunflowers occupy a small, but growing, acreage. The crop is processed to produce vegetable oils for human consumption or industrial use, and high quality fodder for livestock. Barley is also grown widely as livestock feed, while special crops, such as sugar beet, buckwheat and peas are found in the most southerly areas, where the frost-free period is longest. Vegetables are a speciality in the Red River district near Winnipeg, and around Brandon. Half of Manitoba's one million population lives in Winnipeg, which is an important market for fresh vegetables, as well as being the centre of the food processing industry.

In 1981, 11% of cropland in Manitoba was left fallow. This is a very high proportion by European standards, though quite typical of the Prairies. The purpose of the fallow is to store moisture in the soil, prior to cultivation the next year. Although weeds are cut from time to time, the soil is disturbed as little as possible. Another system, which has the same purpose, is called *zero tillage*. This involves the planting of a crop into unploughed stubble land – with little soil disturbance, losses of moisture are kept to a minimum.

Livestock play an important part in Manitoba's farming industry, and contribute nearly 40% of the value of agricultural production. Cattle are widespread throughout the province, and are found on a majority of farms. Beef cattle are most numerous, and their importance has increased rapidly in recent years (Figure 7.48C). European breeds have been introduced and are now dominant. Beef farming is not as intensive as in Europe, and the cattle are mainly grazed on the unimproved, Prairie grassland. About half the cattle bred in the province are sold for fattening elsewhere. Dairy farming has declined in the last 10 years, but retains its importance around Winnipeg, where it concentrates on the production of fresh milk. Cheese is produced in large quantities and is manufactured in eight factories in the province.

Exercise

1 Look at the graphs in Figures 7.48 and 7.49 and summarise briefly the main trends in farming in Manitoba since the 1960s. Can you suggest a possible link between the trends in the beef cattle and pig numbers and the acreages devoted to barley and rapeseed?

2 Using Figures 7.38 and 7.50 compare farming in Manitoba with that in Alberta and Saskatchewan under the following headings: overall size of production; the importance of crops compared with livestock; dependence on wheat; the importance of beef cattle; diversity of production.

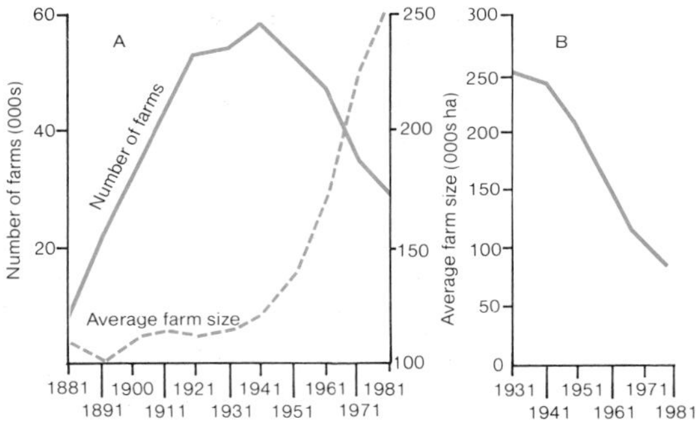

Figure 7.49A Number of farms and farm sizes in Manitoba; 7.49B Farm population in Manitoba

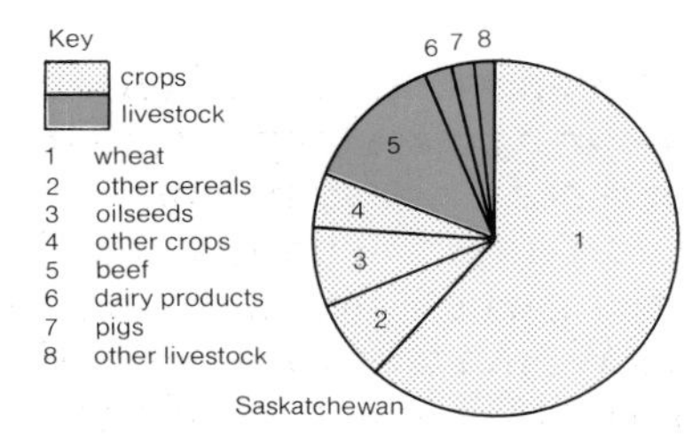

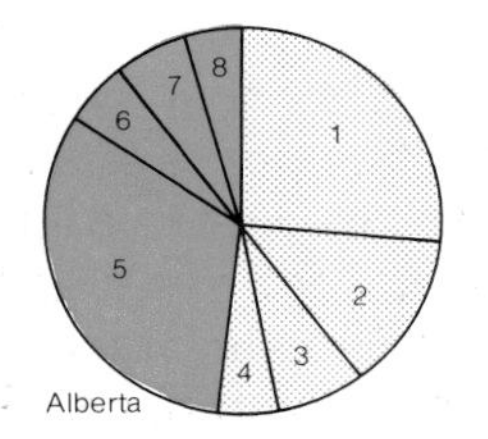

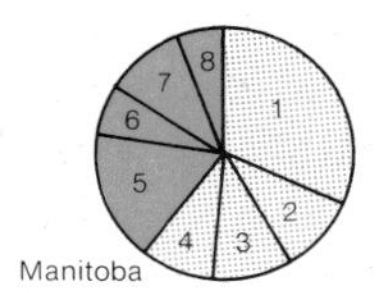

Figure 7.50 Value of farm products in the Prairie Provinces, 1982

Organisation of farming

In common with the other Prairie provinces, the number of farms has fallen rapidly in Manitoba in the last 40 years, and with this the farm population (Figure 7.49). Small farms have become increasingly difficult to manage profitably: modern farming requires a great deal of expensive equipment which is often beyond the means of the small farmer. The result is that the smaller farmers go out of business and move to the towns, and farms get fewer, but bigger. Farming in Canada is a highly organised and thoroughly efficient industry and, as in the examples of Britain and the Netherlands, farmers are supported by a large number of organisations, which include marketing boards, advisory services, research stations, credit corporations and co-operatives.

Figure 7.51 Country grain elevators in Saskatchewan. Elevators are designed for the bulk storage and handling of grain, and are operated by farmers' co-operatives and elevator companies. All are situated along railway lines or near roads where it is convenient for farmers to deliver their grain. Grain is taken from the small country elevators, to the large terminal elevators where it is stored, cleaned and graded before shipment overseas.

Figure 7.52 Grain being loaded in Vancouver harbour, a major outlet for grain exports from the Canadian Prairies. What is a) the main advantage b) disadvantage of Vancouver as an export outlet compared with the Great Lakes' ports or Churchill on Hudson Bay?

Transport

Commercial farming depends on good transport facilities. Farm products are shipped by road, rail and water. With good roads in most areas, farmers play a large part in transportation by carrying their own grain to elevators (Figure 7.51), and their other products to markets and processing plants. Practically all livestock are now moved from farms to stockyards and packing plants by road, and much of the former rail traffic in farm products has been diverted to road. However, rail is still the standard means of transporting millions of tonnes of grain a year over long distances from country elevators to ports and mills. It is also used for long hauls of livestock and meat going from the stockyards in the Prairies to British Columbia.

The Great Lakes have long been used for transporting grain from the port elevators at Thunder Bay to eastern Canada during the shipping season from May to November. The opening of the St Lawrence Seaway has made this route even more attractive, as ocean-going vessels can now reach the Great Lakes. Another seasonal route for grain is through the port of Churchill on Hudson Bay. Churchill offers the shortest sea route to Western Europe, but suffers from being ice-bound from November to June. Vancouver, on the Pacific coast, is more distant, but it does offer an ice-free port all year round (Figure 7.52).

Summary

Only a small fraction of the world's farmers are found in DCs, and yet the annual production of food in the developed world equals that of the less developed world. This is made possible by a farming industry in DCs which is highly organised, highly mechanised and highly efficient.

Farming in DCs is undertaken almost exclusively on a commercial basis, with crops and livestock produced for cash. Farmers are in business to make a profit and will generally choose the type of farming which, given the restrictions set by physical and human factors, will give the best return. Of the physical controls, climate is the most important as it sets broads limits on what can be grown. However, in small countries like Denmark and the Netherlands, soil quality may be more significant in influencing the pattern of farming. Overall, in DCs the influence of physical factors is weakening: irrigation is widely used in the summer to offset drought; new varieties of crops are produced which can thrive in the short growing period in high latitudes; soils are transformed by drainage and fertilizers; and over small areas a completely artificial environment may be created in glasshouses.

Human factors assume considerable importance in farming in DCs. The location of the market and the prices for farm products have a clear effect on profit. So too do government policies which provide the farmer with subsidies, guaranteed prices and quotas. In addition, farmers benefit from a wealth of supporting services, including co-operatives, credit agencies, research into crop and livestock breeding, and many others.

Despite the success of farming, changes are taking place throughout the developed world. Yields continue to increase and farmers are tending to specialise more and more. Meanwhile, smaller farmers find it more difficult to compete and go out of business. The result is fewer, but larger farms, and everywhere a steady fall in the farm population.

Further exercises

1 Figure 7.53 shows an imaginary city, surrounded by a series of farming zones. The city is the only market for farm products and within the area the following types of farming are practised: sheep farming, dairying, market gardening and cereal farming.

a If the cost of transport to market depends on the weight of production per hectare and distance from the city, and is the only factor influencing the choice of crops and livestock, which zone would each farming type be found in? Show your answer by making a copy of Figure 7.53 and shading each zone according to farm type.

b Describe what happens to the intensity of farming with distance from the city on your diagram.

c Name two factors, other than transport, which might influence the choice of location of farming types in the four zones.

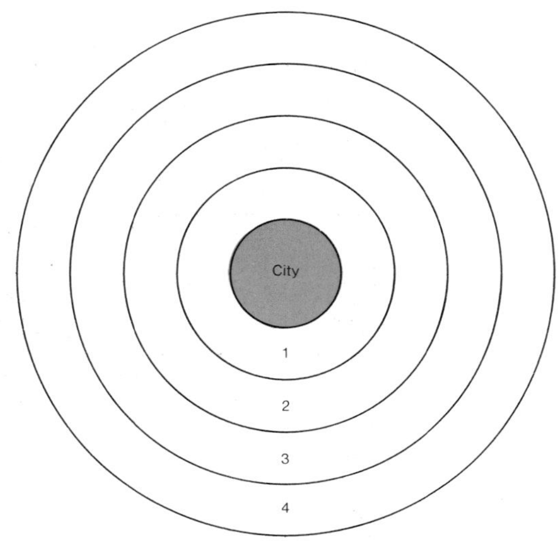

Figure 7.53 An imaginary city

2 a Describe what has happened to the following aspects of farming in DCs in the last 30 years:
— sizes of farms
— number of farms
— size of the farm population.
b Refer to actual examples, and explain the trends in farming you have described in a.

3 Look at Figure 7.54 which shows five farming regions (A–E) in England and Wales, and answer the following questions.
a In which of the regions is rough grazing land more important than either arable or improved grassland?
Explain your choice.
What type of farming would you expect to find in this region?
b Which of the regions has the following climatic characteristics:
mean January temperature – 7°C
mean July temperature – 17°C
mean annual precipitation –1000 mm?
Why do you think that the production of early vegetables and spring flowers is important in this region?
c Which of the following types of farming has a distribution like that in region E: dairying, cereals, fruit, sheep, beef cattle, market gardening? Explain your answer.
d Which region best fits the following description?
'The region has between 800 and 900 mm of precipitation a year, which suits the growth of grass and favours dairy farming; winter temperatures are relatively mild which lengthens the grass growing season. The large urban populations nearby give rise to a strong demand for fresh milk, which further encourages dairying.'
e Which region contains 'the largest area of first class arable land in Britain, between 550 and 600 mm of precipitation a year, is flat, and is entirely devoted to cereals, roots, fruit and vegetable crops'?

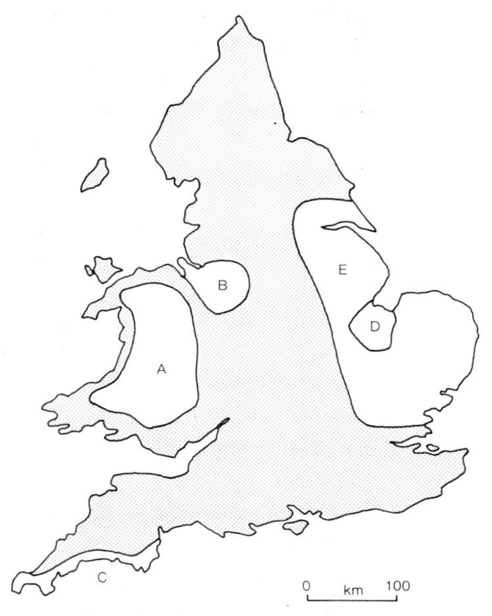

Figure 7.54 Five farming regions in England and Wales

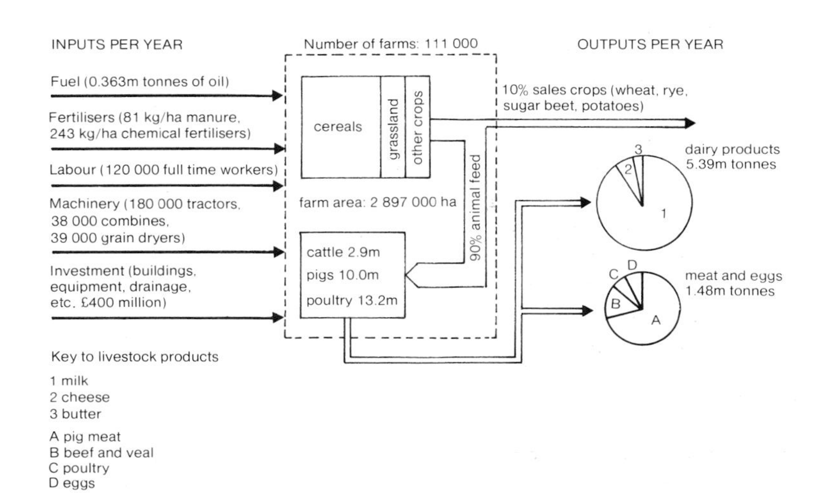

Figure 7.55 Danish farming – a highly intensive system

4 Figure 7.55 shows Danish farming as a system, with inputs and outputs.
   a What happens to most of the crops grown in Denmark?
   b How is this different to crops grown in LDCs? Can you explain the difference? (Refer back to the exercise on page 185 earlier in this chapter.)
   c With reference to Figure 7.55 write a paragraph to explain why Danish farming can be described as 'highly intensive'.

5 Crop yields in the Prairies are influenced by farming methods, climate and soil fertility. There are three main groups of soils: brown, dark brown and black. Their distribution in Saskatchewan is shown in Figure 7.56.
   a Describe the distribution of soil types in Saskatchewan.
   b Look at Figure 7.41 and suggest one factor which might explain the pattern of soils in the province.
   c Using the figures on wheat yields in Table 7.11 plot three graphs (one for each soil type) similar to those in Figure 1.3. On each graph show the median wheat yield. In this instance the median will be the sixth value, when yields are ranked in order of size from 1st to 11th. (To remind yourself of how to calculate the median refer back to Chapter 1, pages 2–3.)
   d Match the three soil types to the following three descriptions:
      'Highest yielding soils which are found in the wettest areas.'
      'Lowest yielding soils, confined to the driest parts of Saskatchewan.'
      'Moderate-high yielding soils found in areas with between 300 and 400 mm of rainfall a year.'

Table 7.11 A sample of wheat yields by crop district according to soil type (kg/ha): Saskatchewan 1973–82

Brown soils	Dark brown soils	Black soils
574	661	697
689	640	762
680	672	743
609	631	781
702	748	727
640	770	746
713	724	716
667	686	754
798	667	768
615	686	762
531	708	702

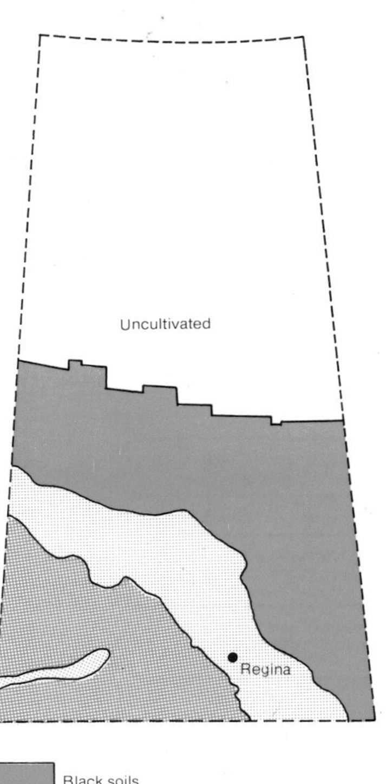

Figure 7.56 Soils in Saskatchewan

Part 3: Agriculture in the less developed world

India

We saw on pages 184–185 that people in the Third World depend on agriculture to a much greater extent than people in DCs. India is no exception: 62% of its workforce is engaged in agriculture, and altogether more than 400 million people depend directly on agriculture for their living. The scale of Indian agriculture dwarfs that of any single European country, and even a group of countries such as the EEC. For instance, India has nearly twice as much farm land as the whole of the EEC, and more than twenty times the number of farm workers!

In DCs farmers grow crops to sell either directly for cash, or to feed to animals which are later sold. Such a system is known as *commercial* agriculture. In India, commercial agriculture is found in some areas, and cotton, rubber, tea and tobacco are important *cash crops*, especially in the south. However, most farmers grow crops for food or *subsistence*, for themselves and their families, and compared with countries such as Canada and the Netherlands there is a strong emphasis on basic food crops, particularly rice, wheat and millet. We shall explore these and several other differences between farming in India and in DCs, in the next few pages.

Crops

In most of India, temperatures are ideal for farming all year round: only in the hills of the far north do winter temperatures drop below 10°C and prevent cultivation. The main influence on farming is rainfall, rather than temperature. With the exception of the dry north west (Figure 7.57) there is enough rain everywhere to support at least one crop a year, and where crops can be watered artificially through *irrigation*, two, and maybe three crops a year, can be grown. The problem with rainfall in India is not the amount, but the fact that most of it (between 75–90%) comes in a short burst, from June to September (Figure 7.59), leaving the rest of the year dry. Only in the far north and south of India is it possible to grow rain-fed crops in the dry, winter period of the year.

Figure 7.57 India: mean annual rainfall (mm)

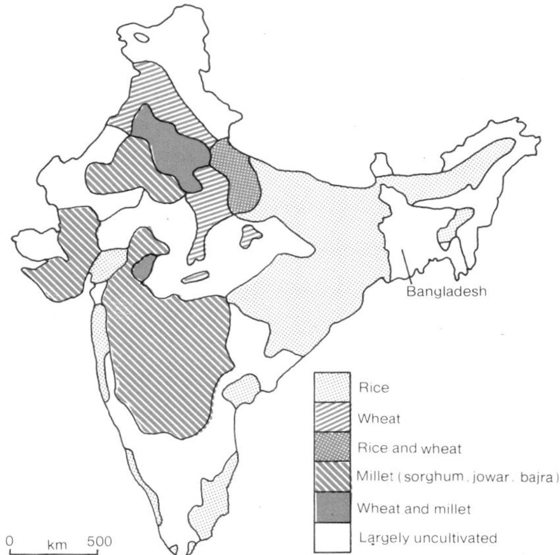

Figure 7.58 India: distribution of principal food crops

Exercise

Look carefully at the climate graph of Calcutta (Figure 7.59) and answer the following questions.

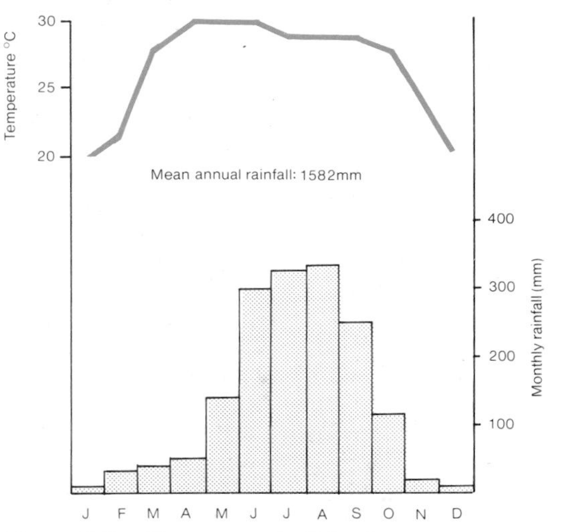

Figure 7.59 Climate graph: Calcutta

1 India's climate is normally divided into three distinct seasons: a) cool and mainly dry b) hot and dry c) hot and wet. Name the months for each of these seasons at Calcutta, and calculate the percentage of total rainfall which comes in each season.

2 What is the mean annual temperature range at Calcutta (ie the difference in temperature between the warmest and coldest months)? Is frost likely in any month? Do you think that temperatures might hinder the growth of crops in any month? (Look back at page 186 to find the temperature above which plants and crops start to grow.)

3 Calcutta receives only small amounts of rain between November and April. However, what little falls is less effective for farming than it would be in the UK or Netherlands. Look at the temperatures during this period and suggest why this is so.

4 If a farmer wanted to grow crops between November and April how could this be done?

The 1000 mm isohyet (Figure 7.57) in India is an important one. It divides India into two areas: above 1000 mm where rain-fed, rice cultivation is possible; and below 1000 mm where rain-fed wheat and millets are dominant. Rice is India's principal food crop and is grown on one quarter of all cultivated land. It is the highest yielding cereal crop, but it is the one which uses most water and can only be grown in areas with less than 1000 mm of rain a year with irrigation. Rice is thus a wet season or *kharif* crop throughout India. Wheat is second in popularity to rice, occupying nearly 14% of the farmed area. Everywere it is grown as a winter or *rabi* crop relying on moisture left in the soil from the monsoon rains. Millets cover three distinct plants – bajra, jowar or sorghum, and ragi – and together they account for around 20% of the cultivated area. Sorghum is the most popular, but where conditions permit, rice and wheat (which are both higher yielding) are preferred.

Exercise

Study carefully the maps of rainfall and cropping patterns in India (Figures 7.57 and 7.58), and then match the following three descriptions with the cereals: rice, wheat and millet. With the appropriate crop type as a heading, copy each description.

crop A: 'Often found in the drier, poorer areas such as Maharashtra, north Karnataka, east Rajasthan and western Anhdra Pradesh, unsuited to other cereals. The crop is mainly rain-fed and comparatively drought-resistant.'

crop B: 'Although it is mainly grown as a rabi crop without irrigation, irrigation is necessary to produce good yields. Its importance has increased considerably in recent years, and it is the leading crop in Punjab, Haryana, western and central Uttar Pradesh, and northern Madhya Pradesh.'

crop C: 'Its area of dominance is in the wetter parts of India, principally from the eastern parts of Uttar Pradesh and Madhya Pradesh to include the whole of east India, and along the west coast from southern Gujarat to Kerala. Without irrigation it needs three consecutive months with more than 300 mm of rainfall.'

Figure 7.60 Traditional rice farming in South Asia. Note the flooded and embanked padi fields, the lack of machinery and the simple techniques used

The problems of Indian farming

According to the Food and Agricultural Organisation (FAO), in 1980 56% of India's population, the vast majority of whom are peasant farmers and their families, lived in poverty. Poverty is at the centre of most of the problems which face India's farmers today (Figure 7.60). Rural poverty also spills over into the towns and cities, as millions of farmers, unable to make a living on the land, leave the countryside and, as we saw in Chapter 4, create major urban problems. Poverty, however, is caused by many different problems, which in the Indian countryside include an acute shortage of farmland, inefficient farming methods, fragmented farms, unfair rents, a shortage of capital, and too many children (Figure 7.61).

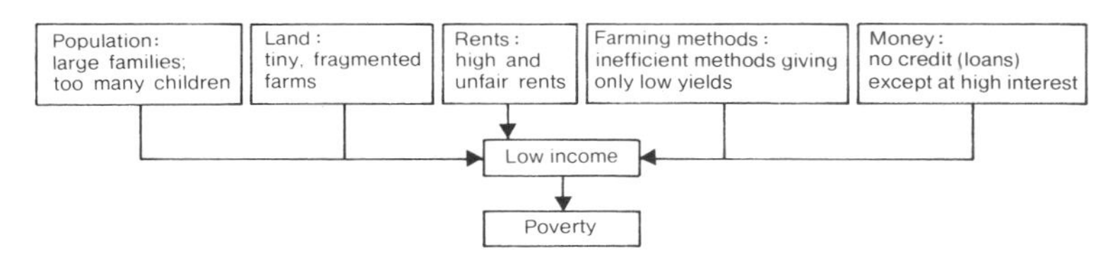

Figure 7.61 The causes of rural poverty

Small farms

Farms in India are tiny: 55% of holdings are less than 1 hectare in size, and of these 30% are less than 2000 m^2! (Figure 7.62). Yet in a sense, those that have farms are the lucky ones, for two in every five farmers are landless, and this group is the poorest of all. The reasons for these tiny units is the continual subdivision of farms resulting from the laws of inheritance among the Hindus and Muslims, where property is divided equally among all the heirs. Hence successive generations inherit smaller and smaller shares of land. No matter how efficiently he farms, if a farmer has insufficient land, the result is always a low income and poverty.

Exercise

1 What happens to food consumption as farm size increases in LDCs like India? (Table 7.12) What does this suggest to you about the amount of food consumed on small farms?

2 Which shows the larger % increase with farm size: total food or protein consumption?

3 Can you suggest a reason why the amount of protein (meat) eaten by peasants on small farms is so small? (Refer back to pages 184–5) for some ideas.) What do you think that the main diet of small farmers and their families is likely to be?

Table 7.12 Food consumption per person per day in relation to farm size in India

Farm size	Total food (grams)	Protein (meat) (grams)
landless	694	53.9
0.01–0.49 ha	697	54.6
0.5 –0.99 ha	745	57.7
1.0 –2.99 ha	785	62.5
over 3 ha	843	67.6

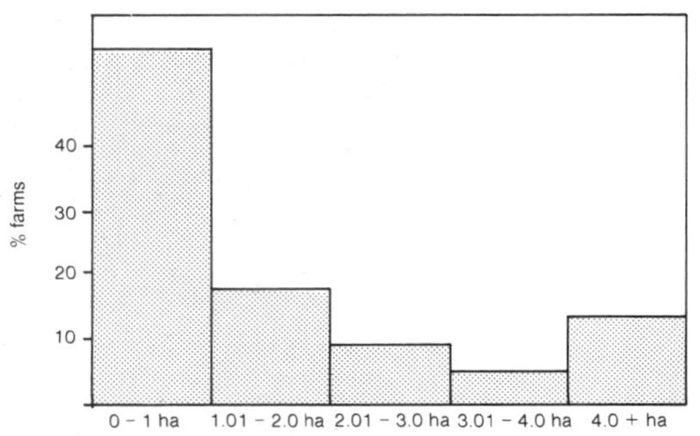

Figure 7.62 Farm sizes in India

Fragmented farms

Another problem, closely related to farm size, is *fragmentation* of land. Fragmented land is owned by one individual, but is scattered in small plots, separated by land owned by other farmers (Figure 7.63). A similar situation existed in Denmark before the nineteenth century, and fragmentation is common today in several parts of Mediterranean Europe. Again, the problem in India is related to the inheritance laws, which state that all heirs should be given an equal share of good and bad land. Clearly it would be impossible to divide up land fairly if it had to be maintained in large, separate blocks. If small farms are inefficient, small, fragmented farms are doubly so. Think of the time wasted in moving men, cattle, seed and irrigation water from one plot to another; the loss of land in field boundaries; the disputes that can arise when access is needed during the growing season; and the impossibility of planning effective drainage and irrigation schemes for the land.

Unfair rents

A third problem connected with land is the level of rent, which in a country where land is scarce, tends to be high. *Sharecropping* is a frequent arrangement where a farmer, in return for the cultivation of the land, gives to the landlord a proportion or share of the crop as rent. Often the share that is left to the farmer may be so small that he is doomed to a life of poverty. Furthermore it is common in India to find that many tenants (ie farmers who rent their land) have little or no security, and can be evicted at any time. Such a system does not instill confidence, and farmers are naturally reluctant to make improvements to the land where there is no guarantee that they will benefit from them.

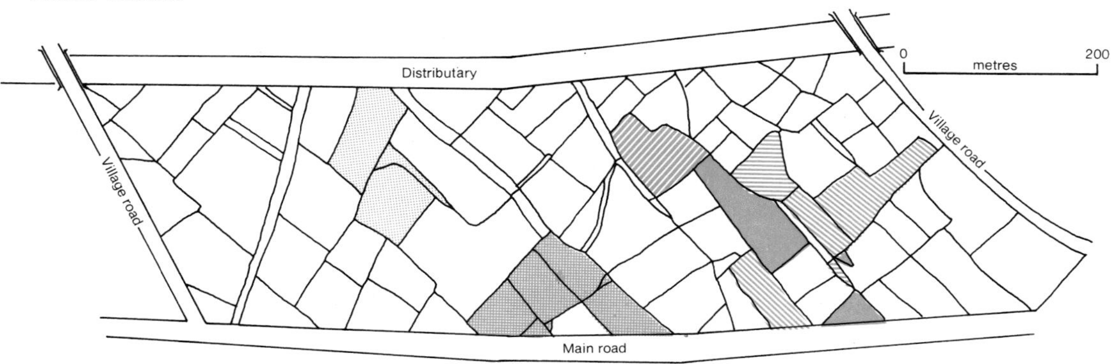

Figure 7.63 Land reform in an Indian village: Before

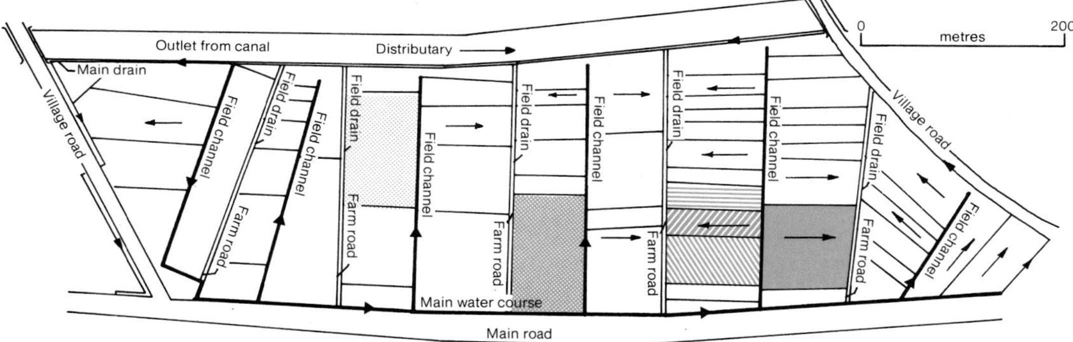

Figure 7.64 Land reform in an Indian village: After

Land reform

Many of the problems associated with land can be solved by re-organising the size and layout of farms (Figure 7.64), and abolishing unfair arrangements between landlords and tenants. This process, which has been successfully carried out in several LDCs, is known as *land reform*. India has already made a start, though progress is slow and there are still large areas where landlords exploit the peasant farmers. The severe shortage of land and the lack of employment outside agriculture helps to maintain this situation. However, most states have introduced laws which place an upper limit on the size of farms, and fix rates of compensation for those who have been forced to sell land. In the northern states of Punjab and Haryana *consolidation* of fragmented plots is now almost complete. There is no doubt that the prominence given to land consolidation has been an important factor in the recent agricultural development of Punjab and Haryana (see the next section).

Exercise

1 With reference to Table 7.13, why do you think that farmers are allowed to own more non-irrigated than irrigated land in Punjab?

Table 7.13 Maximum size of holding in Punjab (for a family of 5)

Irrigated land capable of two crops a year	7 ha
Irrigated land producing one crop a year	11 ha
Non-irrigated arable land	20.5 ha
Other land	21.8 ha

2 Figures 7.63 and 7.64 show a small area in India where land reform has recently been carried out. Write a brief account on the effect of land reform in this area, using the following themes as a guide:
 a shape and size of plots and their likely influence on farming efficiency before land reform
 b the consolidation of plots and the improvements this will bring
 c the introduction of irrigation (why has this been possible?) and its likely benefits.

Improved farming methods

Improved farming methods, particularly irrigation and the growing of high yielding varieties (HYVs) of rice and wheat, can increase the amount of food produced, and provide extra employment in agriculture (Figure 7.65). As long as the population does not grow too rapidly, these developments could improve the standard of living of many peasant farmers, and help to stem the flow of migrants from the countryside to the towns.

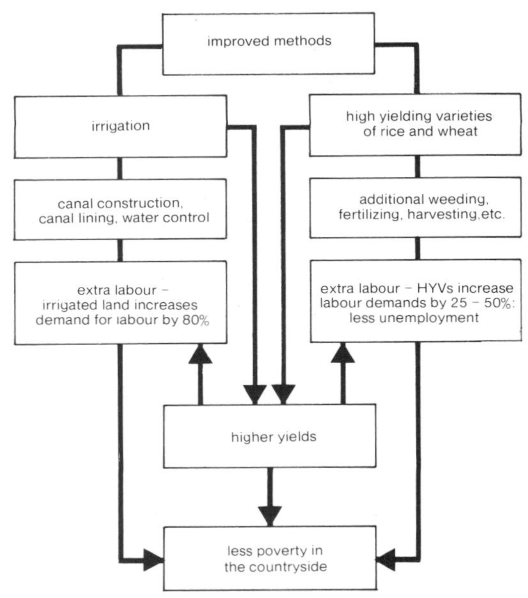

Figure 7.65 The beneficial effects of improved farming methods

Irrigation

At the moment only 13% of India's farmland is irrigated, though as Figure 7.66 suggests, there are huge resources of water which are not used. If some of this water could be used for agriculture, the benefits in terms of food production would be enormous. The region with the greatest potential is the eastern Gangetic Plain: with the proper use of its water supplies and the introduction of land reform, it has been estimated that this one region could produce half the world's total grain production!

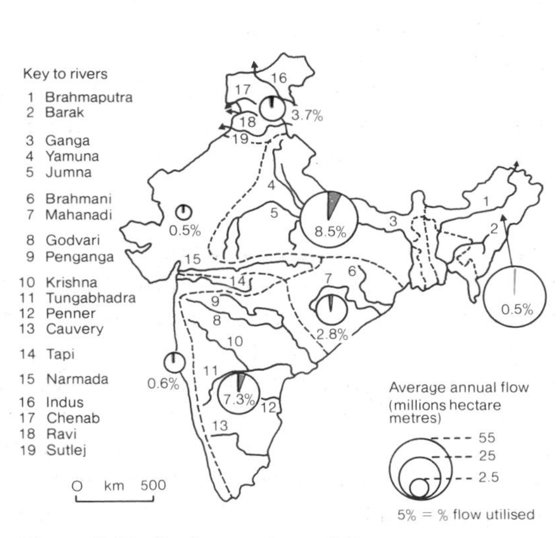

Figure 7.66 Surface water and its use

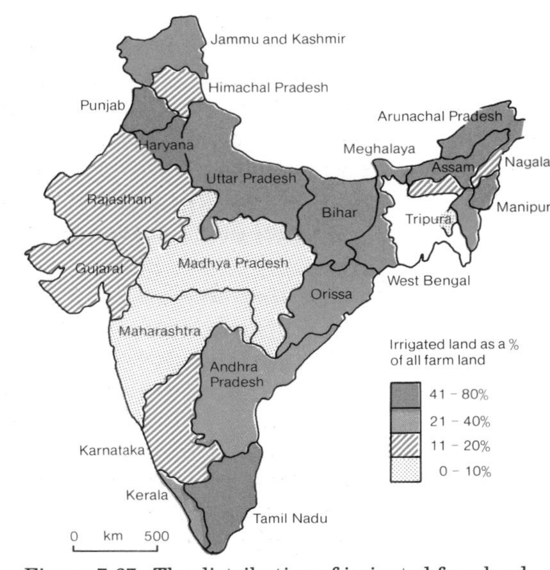

Figure 7.67 The distribution of irrigated farmland

One reason why only a fraction of the total rainfall is used is that most of it comes during the three or four months of the monsoon season. At this time rivers are in flood, and as there is far more water than can be used, most of it drains wastefully into the sea. If some of this water could be stored, it could be used for irrigation during the rest of the year, permitting a second or third crop to be grown. Moreover, a controlled supply of water throughout the year would raise yields and eliminate the prospects of poor harvests when the monsoon rains failed.

Exercise

1 Compare the pattern of river flow (Figure 7.66) with the distribution of rainfall (Figure 7.57) in India. Can you think of other factors which might influence the volume of flow of the major rivers?

2 Which parts of India have the greatest potential for further irrigation?

3 How can the problem of uneven seasonal rainfall be overcome? Re-read Chapter 5, pages 136–9 and describe what was done in the Damodar Valley of north east India to extend irrigation.

Figure 7.68 High yielding rice in Maharashtra state, India

India is making steady progress in increasing the area of irrigated land: in the 1970s the irrigated area grew by one-third, and now stands at 4 million hectares (Figure 7.67). This has been a major factor in helping to make India self-sufficient in cereal production since the late 1960s. At the same time irrigation has created many new jobs, partly through the building and lining of irrigation canals, and partly because double and triple cropping has meant more planting, weeding and harvesting needs to be done. On average, one hectare of unirrigated farmland will provide work for one man for 64 days a year, while a similar area of irrigated land will provide 115 days of work a year.

Water for irrigation is not only taken from streams and rivers, but also from wells, which tap *groundwater* supplies. Large numbers of tube wells have been sunk throughout India in recent years, the number actually doubling between 1960 and 1975. Unfortunately, many of these wells rely on mechanical pumps, and shortages of electricity (the majority of villages have no electricity) and diesel fuel often cause problems.

Feeding India's hungry millions – the Green Revolution

The Green Revolution is the term used to describe the introduction of new high yielding varieties (HYVs) of cereals, especially dwarf rice and wheat (Figure 7.68), in the Third World. Growing these HYVs requires new farming methods, including the use of irrigation, chemical fertilizers and pesticides. In India the HYVs were first introduced in the late 1960s, and quickly boosted cereal production by nearly one third (Figure 7.69). This increase has been such that in spite of severe droughts in 1979 and 1980 India did not have to import any extra grain – something which had proved impossible during the droughts of the early 1960s.

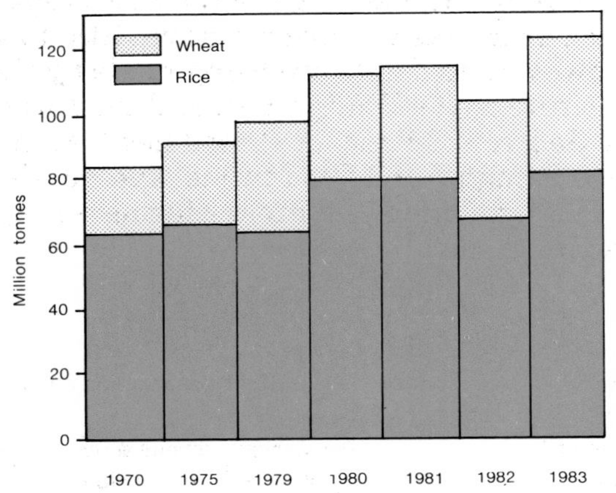

Figure 7.69 India: rice and wheat production, 1970–83

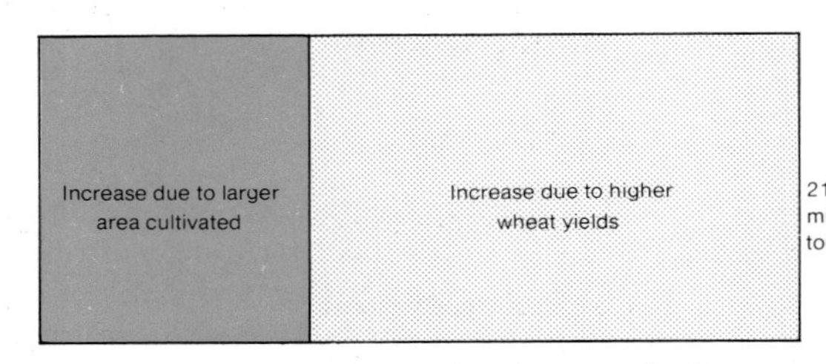

Figure 7.70 India: increase in wheat production, 1970–83

Wheat has been the more successful HYV: while the wheat area increased by one third between 1970 and 1983, wheat production in this period more than doubled (Figure 7.70). However, the benefits of the new wheat varieties have only been felt in one or two regions, notably the Indo-Gangetic Plains of north India (Figure 1.23), from the Punjab and Haryana, to western Uttar Pradesh. Here conditions are exceptionally favourable for HYVs, and include established irrigation systems and fertile alluvial soils. Elsewhere, the impact of HYVs of wheat has been small, largely because irrigation is poorly developed in most regions (Figure 7.67) and there is insufficient rain to grow wheat as a winter crop. Figure 7.71 compares the wheat yields of various countries.

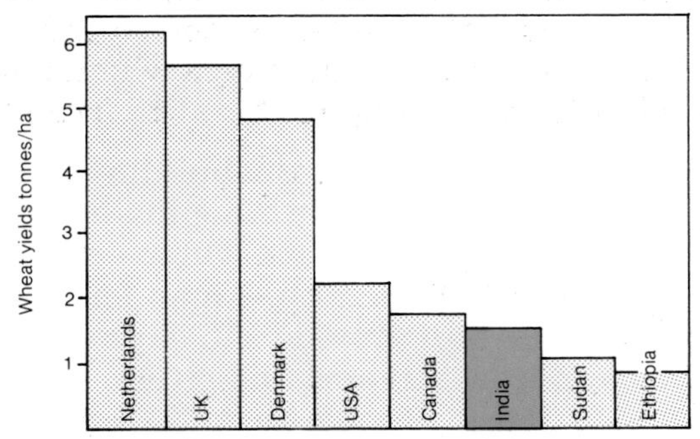

Figure 7.71 Wheat yields in selected countries in the developed and less developed world

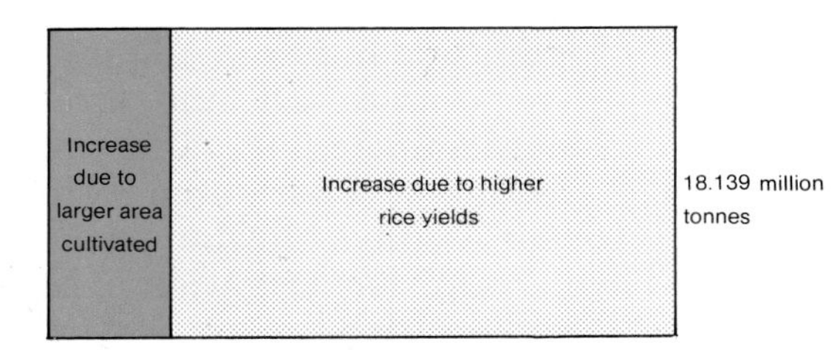

Figure 7.72 India: increase in rice production, 1970–83

HYVs of rice also depend on irrigation, yet two-thirds of India's rice acreage is unirrigated, and in these areas the so-called 'miracle' rice cannot be grown. Equally, the new rice has not been successful in delta and flood plain areas, where flooding and waterlogging are common, because unlike traditional varieties (TVs) they cannot tolerate being submerged for long. Finally, HYVs are less resistant to insect pests and diseases than most traditional varieties. Considering these problems it is not surprising that the overall increase in India's rice production in the last 14 years has been modest (Figure 7.72). Once again, however, it has been north India which has been most successful.

If the benefits of the Green Revolution have been somewhat uneven across the states of India, it is also true that the gains made by different groups of farmers have been unequal. Those who have prospered most are farmers who are already well-off. They have been able to afford the essential fertilizers, pesticides, tube wells and power pumps, needed to grow the new crops. Needless to say, the vast majority of India's poor peasant farmers have little to show for the Green Revolution. Today, however, attempts are being made by the International Rice Research Institute in the Philippines, and the International Maize and Wheat Improvement Centre in Mexico, to breed new varieties of cereals which are better suited to drought- and flood-prone, and non-irrigated areas. If they succeed, then for the first time the ordinary farmers may well be able to share the benefits of the Green Revolution.

Exercise

1 Complete the calculations in Table 7.14.

2 Has production of wheat and rice exceeded/kept pace with/fallen behind population growth?

3 Do you think that the figures in Table 7.14 mean that the mass of the people of India will necessarily be better fed? Re-read the previous section before writing a paragraph to answer this question.

Table 7.14 Cereal production and population growth: India 1970–81

	Population (millions)	Wheat & rice production (million tonnes)	Kg of wheat and rice per person/year
1970	552.469	83.720	151.2
1975	618.831	90.261	?
1981	697.974	116.675	?

Agricultural development – the example of Punjab

In India agriculture has shown most progress in the northern states, especially Punjab (Figure 7.73). Because of the development of its water resources, the Green Revolution has been highly successful in Punjab, and today this is India's richest state. Although Punjab has more winter rainfall than most other parts of the country, 80–90% of rain comes in the monsoon season, and without irrigation the prospects for farming during the winter season would be poor. However, Punjab is fortunate in having several large rivers which cross the state and provide plentiful and reliable water supplies for such irrigation (Figure 7.73).

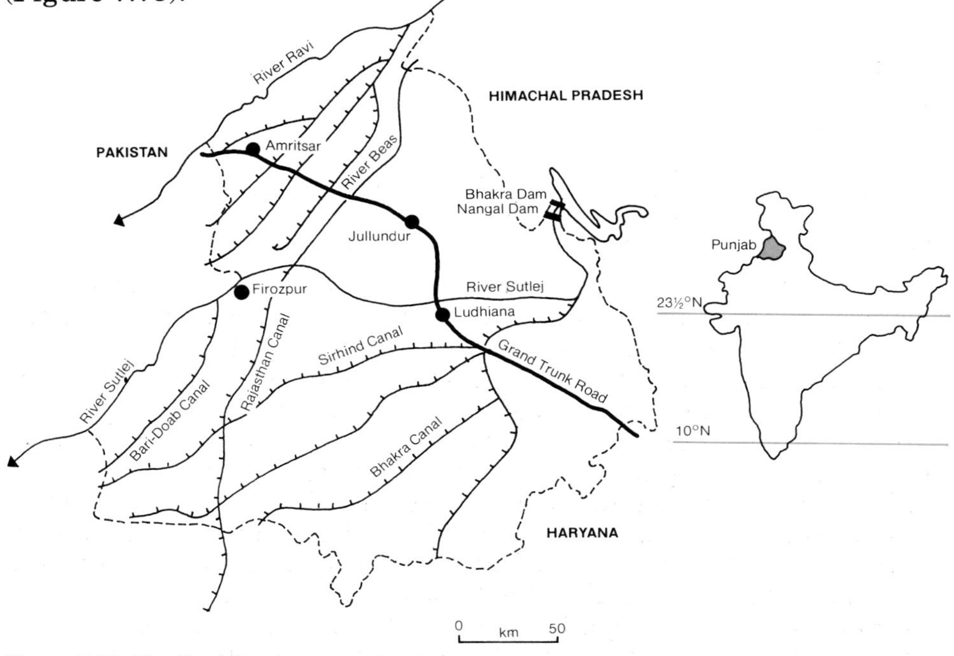

Figure 7.73 The Punjab

Figure 7.74A Villagers who will benefit from a new irrigation scheme in Bihar, North East India

Figure 7.74B Newly constructed irrigation channels. Note that the channels have been lined to prevent water loss through seepage

In addition to surface water, there are large supplies of groundwater at shallow depths beneath the alluvial plains of Punjab. These are tapped by tube wells and are a further source of water for farming.

Water from the rivers is transferred to the farmed areas by a network of canals, some of which were built by the British in the last century. More recently the Bhakra and Nangal dams have been constructed on the Sutlej River, and provide water for 15 million hectares in Punjab, Haryana and Rajasthan. This project also produces hydro-electric power, essential for the pumping of water from hundreds of tube wells in Punjab, and for the growth of new manufacturing industries.

The Green Revolution has been successful in Punjab because conditions are almost ideal for HYVs of cereals, especially wheat. Most importantly, over three-quarters of the farm land is irrigated (Figure 7.75), giving high yields (Punjab's wheat yields are higher than those in the USA and Canada), and allowing two crops a year to be grown in many areas. While most parts of rural India have a surplus of farmers and farm labourers, Punjab has recently had a shortage, and farmers have been forced to pay higher wages to attract workers from neighbouring states!

Exercise

1 Name the three major rivers which flow through Punjab.

2 Refer to an atlas and find the source of the rivers. Into which major river do these rivers flow?

3 Re-read pages 221–4 and study Figure 7.65 and try to explain why the Green Revolution creates extra work for farmers and farm labourers.

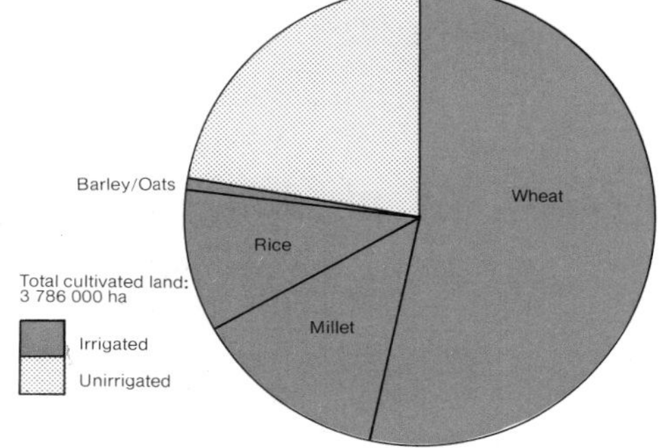

Figure 7.75 Punjab: irrigated land

In one other respect farming in Punjab is not typical of that in the rest of India: whereas most Indian farmers grow crops for food for themselves and their families, in Punjab crops are mainly grown for cash, and are sold at the market. On average in India, out of every 10 tonnes of cereals grown, only 3 tonnes are sold for cash. Nearly all of this surplus, which is needed to feed India's urban population, comes from Punjab, and neighbouring Haryana and western Uttar Pradesh, which might be described as the 'granary' of India. *Commercial* agriculture in north India has been encouraged by the building of metalled roads and increasing the number of market centres where farmers can sell their grain. The government has also helped by giving farmers fixed prices for their grain, and guarantees to buy all their production. Such policies may be commonplace in DCs, but they are unusual in the Third World, particularly in countries as poor as India.

As farming has prospered, manufacturing industries have grown up in Punjab in order to process farm products, and supply farmers with essential items like fertilizers, ploughs, electric pumps and so on. Altogether 50000 jobs in manufacturing are now linked directly to agriculture.

Unfortunately the success of farming has also created a number of problems. Most serious is waterlogging and the release of mineral salts into the soil, as a result of excessive irrigation of crops (Figure 7.76). In north India as a whole, over 3 million hectares of good farm land have been ruined in this way. The situation is even worse across the border, in the Indus Valley of Pakistan, where nearly one-third of all irrigated land has been made unfit for cultivation. Meanwhile, in Punjab, as everywhere in India, the population continues to grow rapidly and threatens to hold back further progress.

In spite of these difficulties, Punjab shows what can be achieved by encouraging agricultural development, without any specific attempt at industrialisation: the success of commercial agriculture has automatically led to the growth of related manufacturing industries.

Exercise

1. The majority of Indian farmers rely on rainfall to water their crops. Make a list of the disadvantages of rain-fed agriculture compared with irrigation.
2. Why has the Green Revolution been so successful in Punjab and north India?
3. How could the sort of developments which have occurred in Punjab help to solve some of the serious problems which face cities in LDCs today? (Look back at Chapter 4 which outlines the urban problems.)

Figure 7.76 Over-watering of crops and the lack of proper drainage has led to the failure of many irrigation schemes in the Third World. The photograph shows a failed scheme in Sudan: the soil, which has become saline and waterlogged, is no longer fit for cultivation

Mauritania – land of drought

Mauritania, one of Africa's poorest and least densely populated countries, is part of a wider region known as the Sahel (Figure 7.77). The Sahel stretches across Africa, from the Atlantic coast in the west, to the Sudan in the east and is sandwiched between the Sahara Desert to the north, and the tropical grasslands and woodlands to the south. In an average year the Sahel receives between 100 and 500 mm of rain. However, since 1970 the rains have been unreliable, and the whole region has suffered a series of disastrous droughts and famines (Figure 7.78). At their height in the period 1970–3, no fewer than 250000 people died of starvation in the Sahel region.

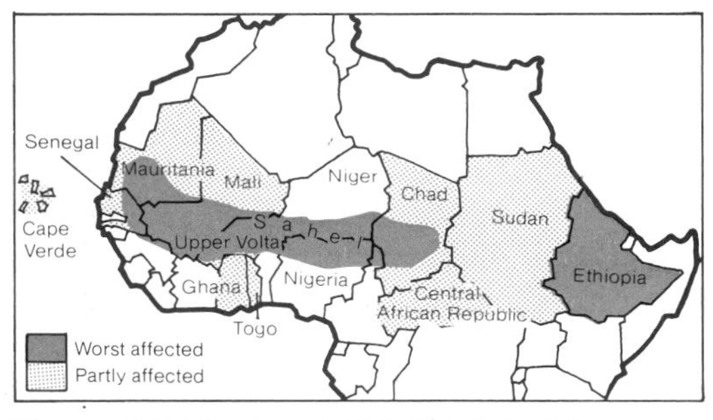

Figure 7.77 The drought-hit Sahel of Africa

The southern half of Mauritania lies within the Sahel belt. The rest of the country is desert and, except for scattered oases, uninhabited. The lack of rainfall and shortage of water means that a mere 0.2% of the country's total area is arable land. Grazing land, most of it of very poor quality, covers 38% of the land area, but by far the largest part of Mauritania is too dry to support any kind of agriculture.

Exercise

Look carefully at Figures 7.79 and 7.80A and then insert the missing words in the paragraph on Mauritania's climate.

Rainfall is sparse throughout Mauritania, but except for the desert areas of the east, the rains follow a seasonal pattern. The winter is a period of ________, although northern areas have occasional rain at this time from storms, heading eastwards through the Mediterranean. Most rain falls in ________, between July and October, with a peak in ________. The rains advance from the south, and gradually peter out as they move northwards. The extreme ________ of the country is the best watered, and the only area which can support rain-fed agriculture. As most of Mauritania is situated within the ________, temperatures are high throughout the year and do not hinder crop growth.

summer, August, tropics, south, drought.

With another three months to go before the rains are due, most of Mauritania and northern Mali and Senegal is utterly desolate. Wells are dry, the water tables are so low that trees are dying, crops have failed, animals are few and thin. In every village the granaries are empty. Food aid from outside is insufficient and, with dignified understatement, the people say they are "tired, very tired."

No one here eats more than once a day. Some only eat every three days, others exist by painstakingly picking out the seeds of the dry little "cram cram" berry to boil into gruel. And hundreds of thousands of people are on the move, the old traditions and structures of their complex societies broken by the drought.

Mauritania, home of the dead camel, has suffered the drought for most of the past 13 years. Perhaps as much as three quarters of the country's population of nearly 2 million has been driven into the towns by the drought. Virtually the entire remaining nomadic population has trekked over the borders, into Mali and Senegal, in search of water and pasture.

The herd itself was already 90 miles to the south — the last water-hole in the area. Here the men had begun to dig down an extra five or six metres. The water nearer the surface was drying up. Great herds of long-horned cattle browsed across a circle of sparse grass tufts round the water hole. Thousands of camels filled the horizon.

Normally in this dry season these herds cross from Mauritania into Mali. They return after a few months with Mali's own cattle herds, to secure a few additional months grazing in Mauritania. But this year no one will go back. Mauritania's only river, the Senegal, which runs along the country's southern border, is at its lowest level for 80 years. Last year's rain was only 30 per cent that of a normal year. "Even the birds have left us," said a Mauritanian official in the southern capital of Kaedi, pointing to empty nests swinging from thorn bushes.

Mauritania is a poignant victim of the dramatic increase in the growth of the world's deserts. Every day the road carries news to the government of death from starvation of vitamin deficiency so serious that people are losing teeth or sight, and of chronic malnutrition. "We are in a catastrophic situation," said Mr Ba Aliou Ilora, secretary to Mauritania's ruling Military Committee.

Figure 7.78 An extract from *The Guardian* 5 May 1984 – Continuing drought in the Sahel: the problem in the mid-1980s

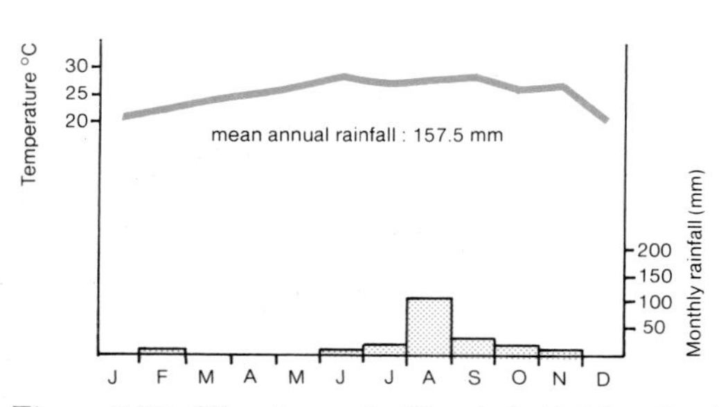

Figure 7.79 Climate graph: Nouakchott, Mauritania

Pattern of farming

In Mauritania farming is severely limited by the low rainfall and the existence of very few permanent streams and rivers which might supply irrigation water. Settled farming therefore occupies only a very small area, confined to the valley of the Senegal River and some of its tributaries, and districts with at least 450 mm of rain a year (Figure 7.80A). In the alluvial lands of the Senegal Valley the Soninke people practise rain-fed cultivation during the wet season. After the rains have finished, and the floods receded, they are able to grow a second crop on the damp alluvial soils. Their main crops are sorghum, millet, groundnuts and maize.

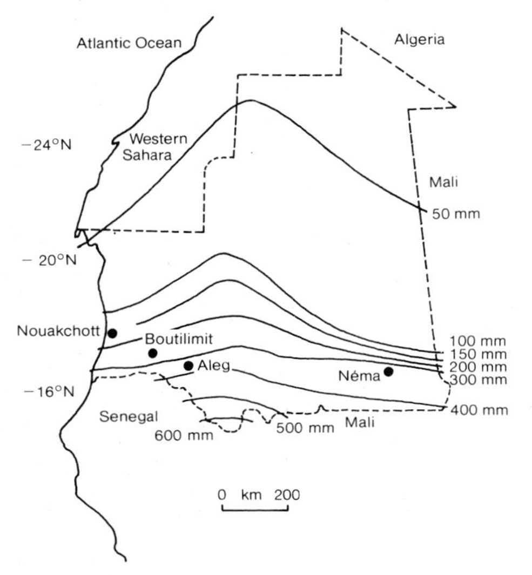

Figure 7.80A Mauritania: average annual rainfall

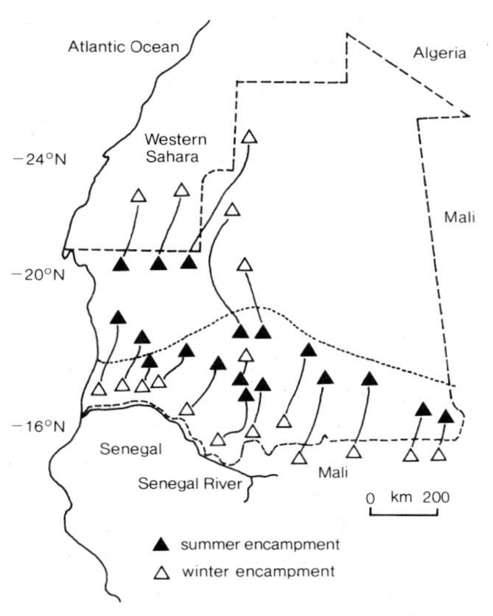

Figure 7.80B Mauritania: seasonal movements of nomads

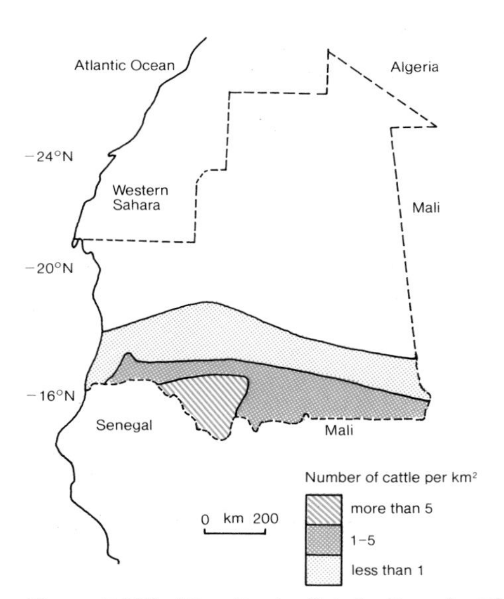

Figure 7.80C Mauritania: distribution of cattle

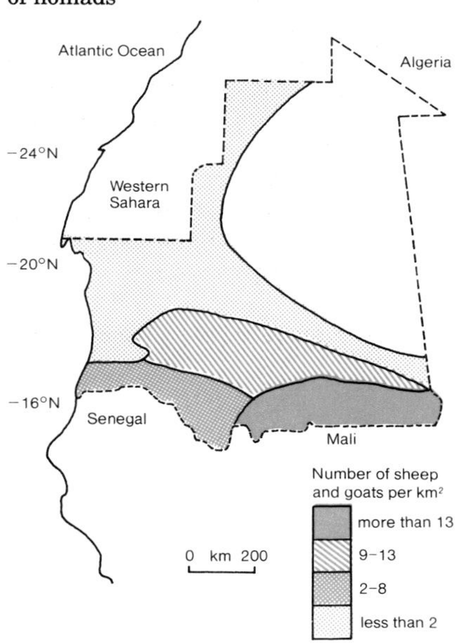

Figure 7.80D Mauritania: distribution of sheep and goats

In view of the difficulties of farming in Mauritania, it is surprising that so many people – over 80% – depend on farming for their living. The vast majority of those in agriculture are not settled cultivators, but *nomadic herders*, keeping cattle, camels, sheep and goats (Figure 7.81). These people do not live in permanent settlements, but are constantly on the move with their flocks and herds, in search of water and pasture. They follow traditional routes, visiting the same wells and pastures at the same times each year. A route involving a round trip of 800 km in a year is not unusual, and this would include longer stays at the summer, and particularly the winter encampments (Figure 7.80B). Nomads like the Moors of central and northern Mauritania, who concentrate on camels, goats and a few sheep, move their entire encampment as they follow their routes. In contrast, the Fulani cattle herders of the south do not move the entire tribe with the herds. Most of the tribes people remain on the northern margins of the Senegal River while Fulani herdsmen drive the cattle north in summer, following the rains. After the rains the herds return south to their winter encampment where there is water and pasture.

Figure 7.81A Owing to the recent drought, many nomadic groups in the western Sahel have been forced to abandon their nomadic way of life; many have settled around the larger towns and cities

Figure 7.81B Nomadic tribespeople of the Sahel. Note the sporadic vegetation cover, the dryness of the soil, and the tents which form their temporary encampments

Exercise

Look at Figure 7.82 and answer the following questions.

1 Which domestic animal's numbers have declined continuously in the period 1970–81?

2 Which domestic animal has had the least change in numbers between 1970 and 1981?

3 Which animals have shown the greatest change in numbers during the same period?

4 Can you suggest why cattle formed a smaller proportion of total livestock in 1981, compared with 1970?

5 Two factors account for changes in the number of camels, cattle, sheep and goats per person between 1970 and 1981 in Table 7.15. Can you say what they are? (Clue – have a look at Figures 7.83 and 7.86.)

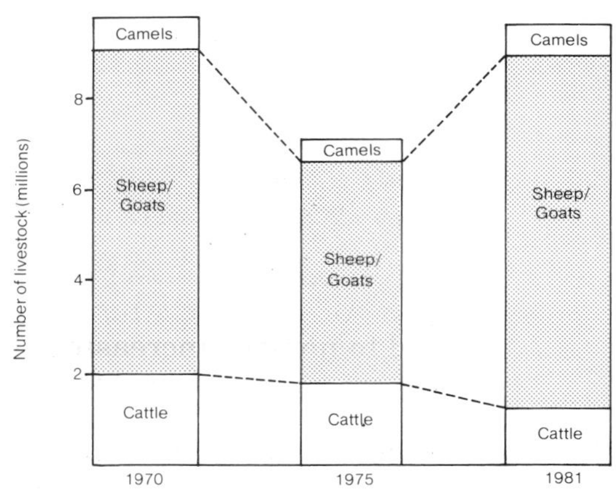

Figure 7.82 Numbers of livestock: Mauritania, 1970–81

Table 7.15

	Number of livestock per person
1970	7.9
1975	5.1
1981	5.8

The meagre supplies of pasture and water in the Sahel mean that nomadic herders require very large areas to feed each animal. For every square kilometre of grazing land, production of meat, wool, milk and other items is extremely small; we describe such a farming system as *extensive*. However, there is no doubt that nomadic herding is well suited to areas of low rainfall, which cannot sustain permanent grazing all year round. In spite of its success, nomadic herding in the Sahel is facing a crisis, and as we shall see in the next section, is under threat as a way of life.

Problems of nomadic herding

In 1965, three-quarters of Mauritania's population were nomadic herders: today, following the terrible droughts of the 1970s, the proportion has fallen to less than 30%. Prolonged drought caused huge reductions in the numbers of cattle, sheep and goats (Figure 7.82), especially in the period 1970–4, when conditions were at their worst. Thousands of nomads were forced to give up their traditional way of life and either migrate to the towns (Nouakchott's population rose from 20 000 in 1969 to nearly 200 000 in 1980!) or settle in the better watered south and become agriculturalists.

Figure 7.84A (*right*) Mauritania is one of the Sahel countries worst affected by drought. Rapid population growth and increasing numbers of livestock have combined with drought to destroy the vegetation cover over huge areas
Figure 7.84B (*lower right*) Overgrazing in the Sahel. Cattle, sheep, goats and camels have eaten or trampled all vegetation around this water source

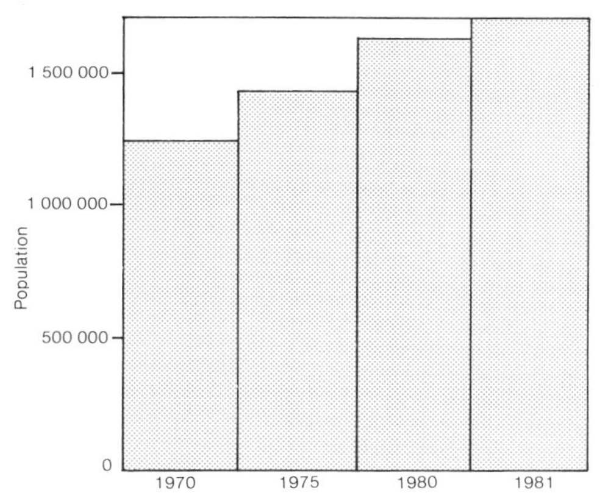

Figure 7.83 Population growth in Mauritania

Drought is not the only reason for the decline of nomadism. Rapid population growth in Mauritania (Figure 7.83), in common with other African countries, led to nomads increasing the size of their flocks and herds. With too many livestock, the already sparse pastures were soon *overgrazed*: the grasses and herbs preferred by the livestock were replaced by less attractive plants, and in extreme cases the vegetation was completely destroyed. In some areas, when animal feed became scarce, the nomads resorted to felling the trees and shrubs to allow their livestock to browse on the leaves and branches. The combination of drought and larger flocks and herds not only destroyed much of the vegetation cover, but exposed the soil to erosion by wind and water (Figure 7.84). This *desertification* of the land is now widespread in the Sahel, and each year, as the drought continues, the Sahara Desert advances further south (Figure 7.85). Indeed, in the last two decades Mauritania has lost 80% of its pasture to the sand.

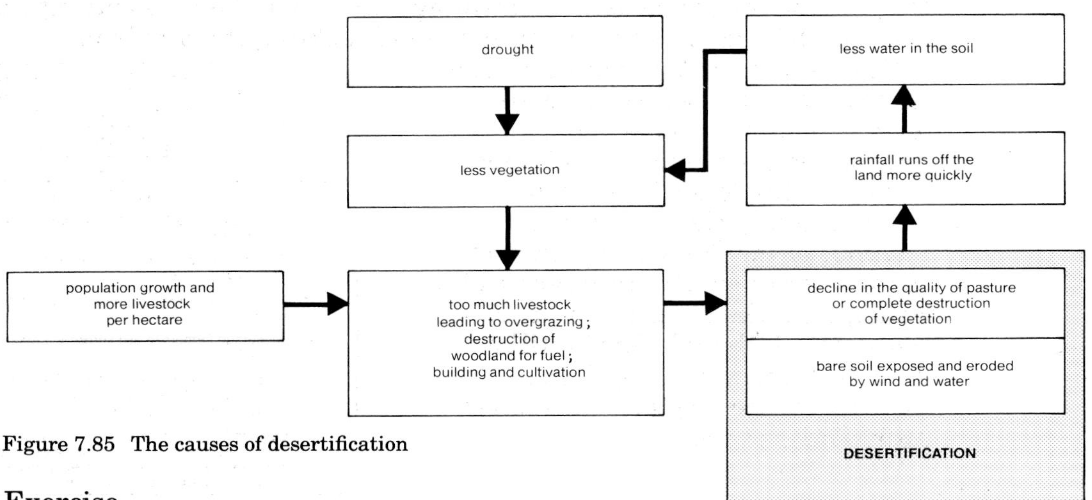

Figure 7.85 The causes of desertification

Exercise

1 Study Figures 7.80A, C, D and answer the following questions.
   a Which domestic animal is most/least affected by drought?
   b Where in Mauritania do you think that (i) camel herders (ii) cattle herders, are most likely to be found?

2 Using Figure 7.80B as your source of information, answer the following questions.
   a In which direction do most nomads move in summer? Try to explain this movement.
   b Can you say why some nomads in central and northern Mauritania move north in winter?

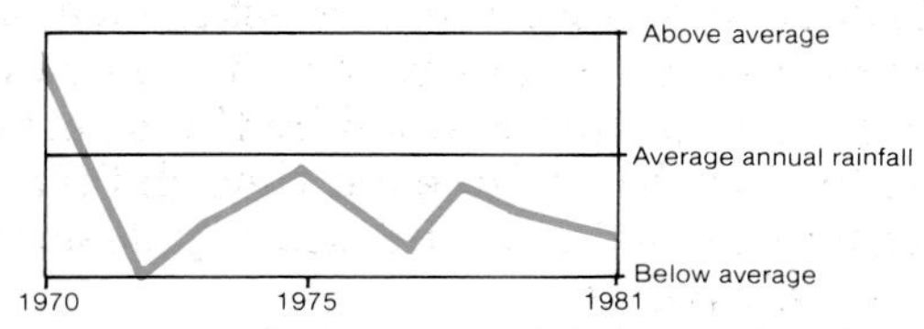

Figure 7.86 Rainfall in the Sahel, 1970–81

Exercise

Study Figures 7.86 and 7.87 and answer the following questions.

1 How many years between 1970 and 1981 had below average rainfall in the Sahel? Which was the year of greatest drought?

2 What happened to food production in Mauritania, Niger and Mali between 1970 and 1973? How would you explain this trend?

3 How long did it take for food production in Mauritania to recover to the levels of 1970?

4 What happened to population growth between 1970 and 1981 (Figure 7.83)? Compare the graph of population growth with food production in Mauritania in this period, and suggest any problems which might have arisen.

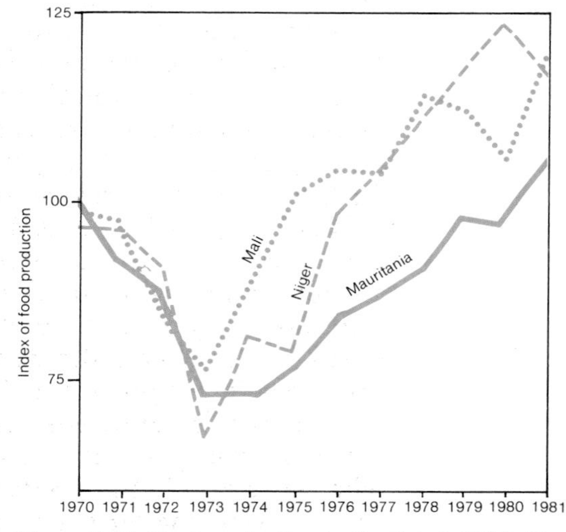

Figure 7.87 Food production in the Sahel, 1970–81

Solving the problem of desertification

Every year in the Sahel 200 000 km^2 of land are desertified to the point where they can no longer be used for farming, and the problem is getting worse. Figure 7.88 suggests a number of ways of tackling the problem.

One solution is tree planting on a large scale. This is already under way in several countries, but progress is slow, and has not kept pace with the loss of trees. One scheme to stop the southward advance of the Sahara Desert is to plant a 'green belt' of trees across the Sahel, from the Atlantic to the Red Sea coast. Although this is still a possibility, it would require the planting of the staggering number of 16 000 million trees!

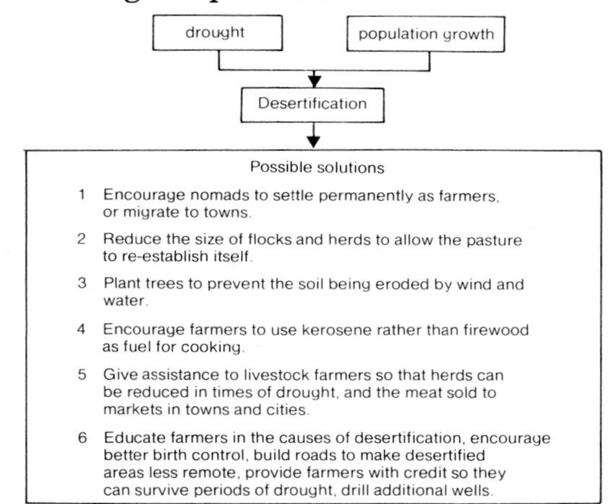

Figure 7.88 Solving the problem of desertification

If farmers could be persuaded to reduce the size of their flocks and herds, desertification might be halted. However, the countries of the Sahel are among the poorest in the world, so it is not easy to convince the people that it is in their interest to have fewer livestock. Another obstacle is the fact that the grazing lands are not the property of individual farmers, but are owned by everyone. Thus the reduction of livestock numbers would only be successful if it was accepted by everyone, and this would not be easy to achieve. Finally, ownership of cattle among people such as the Fulani of West Africa, and the Masai of East Africa, is often central to their whole way of life. For instance, the standing of a person in the tribe may be determined by the number of cattle he owns, and the more the better. In this situation, even though farmers may realise that overgrazing is damaging the pastures and causing desertification, they are often unwilling to reduce their herds.

Because drought is a feature of the Sahel climate, any plan aimed at development must take account of it. When drought begins, farmers need to be able to reduce their herds quickly, if they are to prevent damage to the pastures and soil. Their surplus animals could be sold for meat, providing roads are built to the markets in the main towns and cities. With money from foreign aid the Mauritanian government is currently building a road in the south of the country, between Nouakchott and Néma (Figure 7.80A). Collection points could be established along the road and, in times of drought, animals could be moved quickly to market. The government could pay the farmers a guaranteed price for their animals, and the money would help them through the drought.

However, the best solution is a full-scale programme of rural development. Farmers should be educated in sound livestock methods; they should be encouraged to have smaller families; credit should be made available to improve the pastures and drill new wells; and roads should connect rural areas to the markets and allow some degree of commercial farming. Unfortunately, there are few signs of this happening: the governments of the Sahel countries have shown little interest in improving traditional agriculture, preferring instead large, prestige projects such as the irrigation schemes of central Sudan, where the aim is the production of export crops like cotton and groundnuts, rather than food for the people.

Shifting cultivation – traditional farming in the tropical rainforest

The tropical rainforest covers large areas of lowland, close to the equator, in South America, Africa and South East Asia (Figure 7.89). The climate of these areas is ideal for plant growth, with constant high temperatures and rain all year round. The result is the richest and most varied forest in the world dominated by huge, evergreen trees (Figure 7.90). From looking at Figure 7.90 you might think that the rainforest grows on highly fertile soils, and that if the trees were cleared, farmers would be sure to obtain good crops. Nothing could be further from the truth. The rainforest soils are in fact extremely poor, and are incapable of sustaining permanent cultivation. The reason for this is clear in Figure 7.91 which shows that most of the essential minerals that plants need for their growth, are stored in the forest trees, and not in the soil.

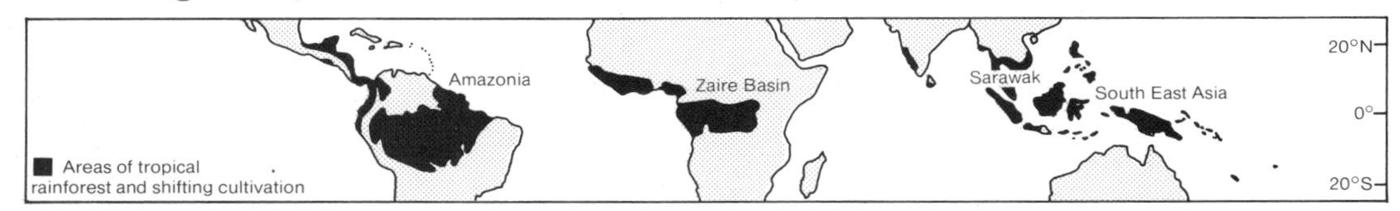

Figure 7.89 Areas of tropical rainforest and shifting cultivation

Figure 7.90 The tropical rainforest of Amazonia

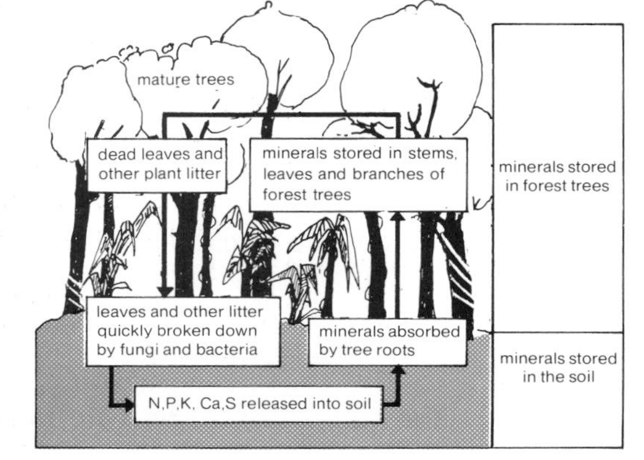

Figure 7.91 The cycling of minerals in the rainforest

Shifting cultivation, the traditional method of farming in the rainforest, successfully overcomes the problem of low soil fertility. Shifting cultivators, like the Iban tribe of Sarawak on the island of Borneo in South East Asia (Figure 7.92), have learned that the soils are too poor for permanent cultivation, and must be rested for long periods. They make small clearings in the forest (about 2 ha for a family of six), felling the trees with axes a metre or so above the ground, but rarely bothering to dig out the roots (Figure 7.93). The plots are cleared in June and July, and in the relatively dry month of August the branches and leaves are burned. The ash from the burn provides sufficient fertilizer for the soil to allow cultivation for up to two years. Crops are grown entirely for subsistence, the principal one being hill rice, which does not require irrigation. The seeds are sown directly into the ashes, in holes made with a simple tool known as a dibbling stick. Initially, yields of rice are good, with the Iban averaging nearly three-quarters of a tonne per hectare for the first crop. However, as the crops and heavy rains remove the vital minerals from the soil, yields quickly decline. In addition, weeds become an increasing problem, and take more and more of the Iban's time to clear. After nearly two years, cultivation is no longer worthwhile, and the plot is abandoned and a fresh clearing made.

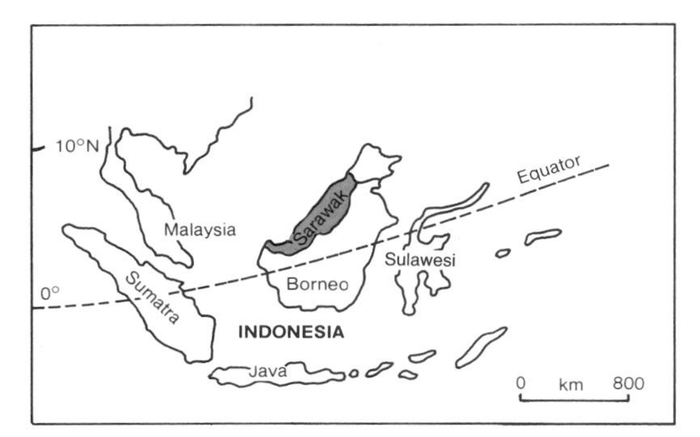

Figure 7.92 Location of Sarawak, Malaysia

Figure 7.93 Clearing and burning of the rainforest in Amazonia for cultivation by newly arrived colonists

Exercise

1 Draw a diagram like Figure 7.94 to illustrate the cycle of cultivation followed by the Iban tribe. Use the information below to complete the diagram by writing in the segments the main tasks done in each month.

DATE

1.6	Clearing the jungle begins.
1.8	Clearing is completed.
14.8	Trees are burned.
18.9	Dibbling and sowing of rice begins.
27.10	Sowing is completed.
12.2	Quick ripening rice is harvested.
26.3	Threshing of quick ripening rice.
22.4	Harvesting of later ripening rice.
2.5	Storing of rice.
	Weeding takes place from the completion of burning, to the final harvesting of rice.

2 Present the figures in Table 7.16 as two pie charts.

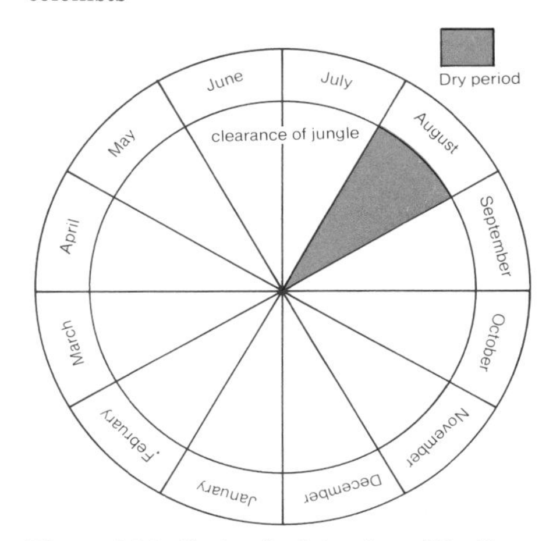

Figure 7.94 Cycle of cultivation of the Iban

Table 7.16 Time spent by the Iban in man-hours per hectare

	Jungle not previously cultivated	Jungle on plots previously cultivated
Clearing	367	221
Dibbling	57	57
Sowing	65	65
Weeding	228	285
Harvesting	277	277

3 What are the main differences in the effort required to cultivate areas of new jungle, and areas which have been cultivated in the past? Try to explain them.

It takes at least 15 years for the forest to re-establish itself on the abandoned plots, and for the soil to regain its fertility. Provided the land is rested for this period, shifting cultivation can continue indefinitely. What threatens shifting cultivation is an increase in the population of shifting cultivators, which forces the forest to be re-cultivated too soon. The Iban are already facing this problem, as their population density begins to exceed 20 per km^2, which is thought to be the most which shifting cultivation can support in Sarawak (Figure 7.95).

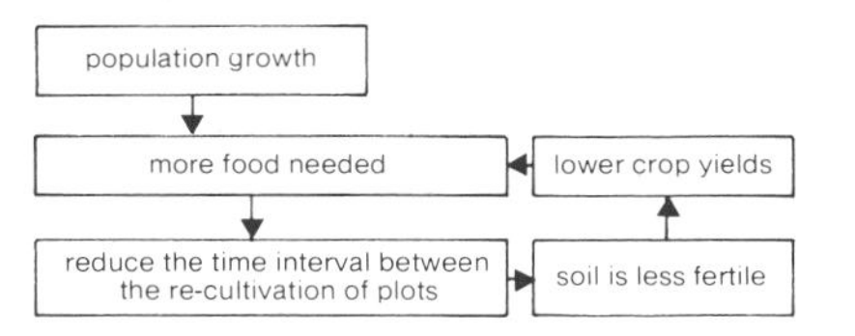

Figure 7.95 The spiral of decline of shifting cultivation

Exercise

Imagine that a small group of shifting cultivators farm an area of 1 km^2 (100 ha) in the rainforest, and that each person requires the food produced by $\frac{1}{4}$ hectare of land each year. What happens when the population begins to grow? Find out by completing the following questions.

1 Complete the calculations in Table 7.17.

Table 7.17 Population growth and the length of the fallow period

Population	Area of land needed per year (ha)	Length of fallow period given total area of 1 km^2
8	2	50 years
12	3	33.3
16	4	
20	5	
24	6	
28	7	
32	8	
36	9	
40	10	

2 Plot the values in Table 7.17 as a graph (Figure 7.96).

3 What happens to the length of the fallow period as population increases?

4 From your graph estimate the critical population level (ie density) when soil fertility and crop production begin to decline.

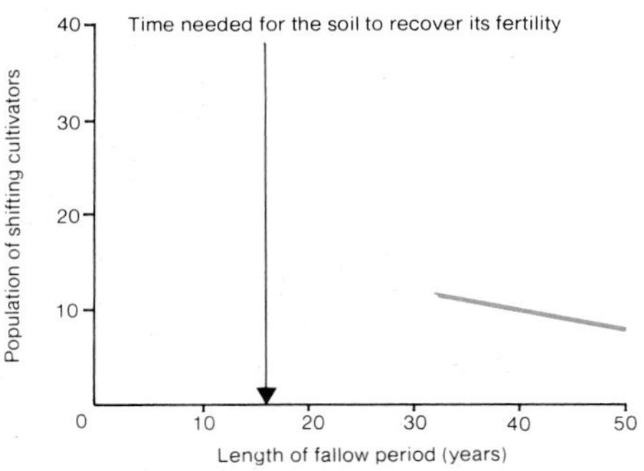

Figure 7.96 Shifting cultivation and population growth

The development of agriculture in Amazonia: example of north east Ecuador

The lowlands of the Amazon Basin (Figure 7.97) cover a vast, sparsely populated region in South America. However, Amazonia is currently being

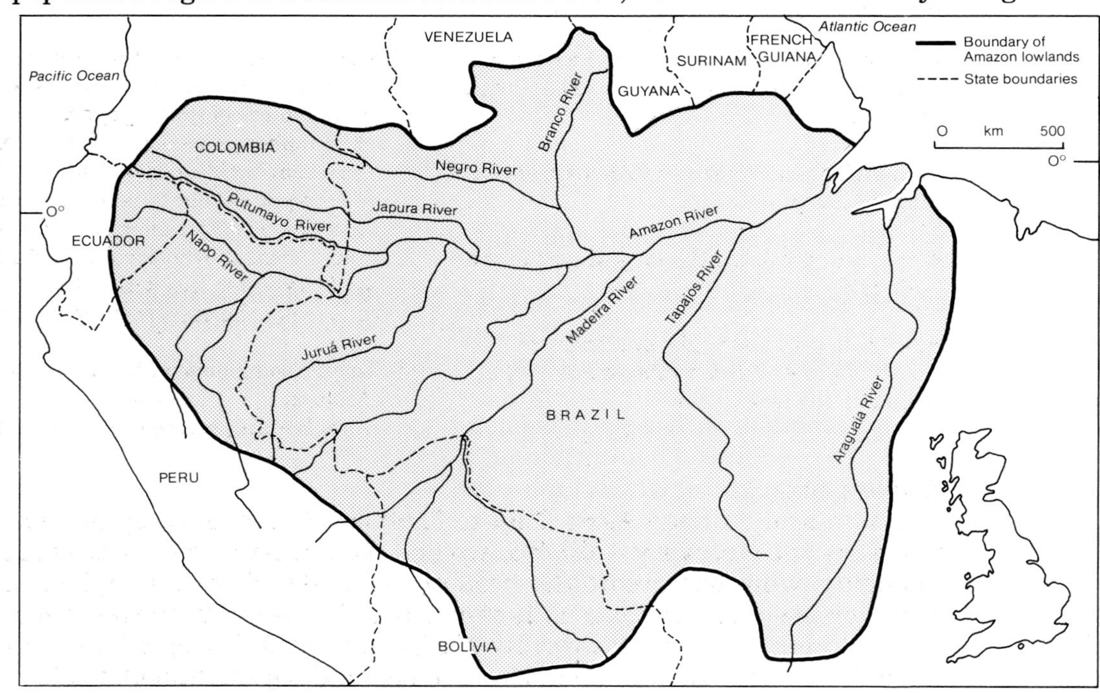

Figure 7.97 The Amazon lowlands

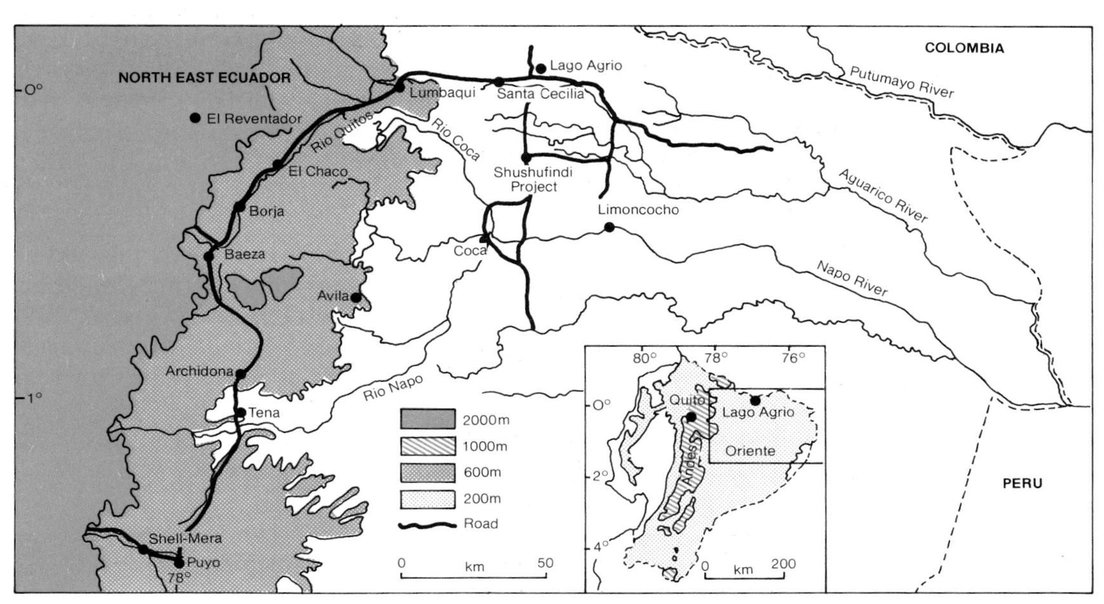

Figure 7.98 Principal areas of colonisation in Ecuador

settled and developed very rapidly: by the end of the century it has been predicted that the rainforest, which covers most of the region, will have been largely cleared for agriculture. So far, the colonisation of Amazonia has been unplanned, and has created a number of very serious problems. One small area which illustrates what is happening is north east Ecuador, an alluvial plain drained by the Upper Amazon, which has attracted large numbers of colonists since 1970 (Figure 7.98).

Exercise

With reference to Figure 7.97 which shows the Amazon lowlands, complete the following exercises.

1 Name the countries which form part of the Amazon lowlands.

2 Which country forms the largest part of the lowlands?

3 How far is it in a straight line from the mouth of the Amazon, to the source of the Napo in Ecuador?

4 Estimate the area of the Amazon lowlands. To do this trace their outline from Figure 7.97 on to a piece of graph paper, and then count the number of 1 × 1 cm squares (each representing 90 000 km^2) within the lowlands. Where you encounter squares which are crossed by the boundary of the lowlands, count them as whole squares if more than half their area lies within the lowlands. If this is not the case, then ignore them.

5 To give some idea of the vastness of Amazonia, estimate how much larger it is than Britain, whose total area is 230 000 km^2.

Settlement

The area around Lago Agrio (Figure 7.98) was first opened up in 1969, when following the discovery of oil, Texaco and Gulf constructed an all-weather road. Suddenly, what had previously been an isolated and remote region, became easily accessible, and thousands of colonists flooded in from the overpopulated, Andean highlands to the west. By 1980 nearly 40 000 people had settled in the Lago Agrio area. Little attempt was made by the government to plan the settlement in a sensible fashion. The first settlements were on the Lago Agrio–

El Chaco highway, spaced at intervals of 250 m, so that each farm would have a narrow frontage on the road. Farms were laid out geometrically in standard 50 ha blocks, measuring 250 by 2000 m. No regard was given to water supply, drainage, relief or soil fertility. Once all the sites on the highway were occupied, new farms were located on trails cut through the forest at intervals of 2 km, running parallel to the highway (Figure 7.99). In some areas, up to three parallel trails have been established, leaving some farms more than 6 km from the road.

The reason why the settlement pattern in Figure 7.99 developed is because it makes maximum use of the few roads in the region. Farmers need access to markets, and this consideration has over-ridden everything else. Nonetheless, now the majority of farms have no direct access to roads and unless small feeder roads to the main highway are built soon, most of these farms will not survive.

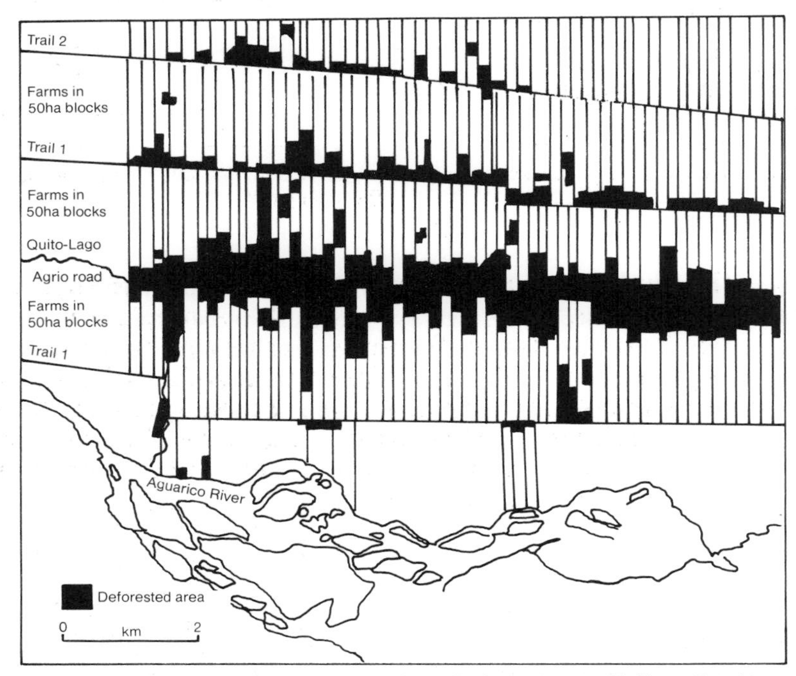

Figure 7.99 Spontaneous settlement along the Lago Agrio–El Chaco Road in north east Ecuador

Exercise

1 The shape of farm plots means that the distribution of good soils and water supplies is often highly uneven. Farmers unlucky enough to have only poor soils and no reliable water supply on their plot, have little chance of success.

 a In Figure 7.100 how many farms have both good soils and access to a stream for water?

 b How many have either some good soils or a water supply?

 c How many have neither good soils nor a supply of water?

 d Would you say that the distribution of good soils and water was fair/reasonably fair/unfair? State your reasons.

2 Figure 7.101 shows an alternative shape for the farms. Make a tracing of this farm layout, place it over Figure 7.100, and comment on the fairness of the distribution of good soils and water.

3 Can you suggest another disadvantage to farmers of the long, narrow plots in Figure 7.100?

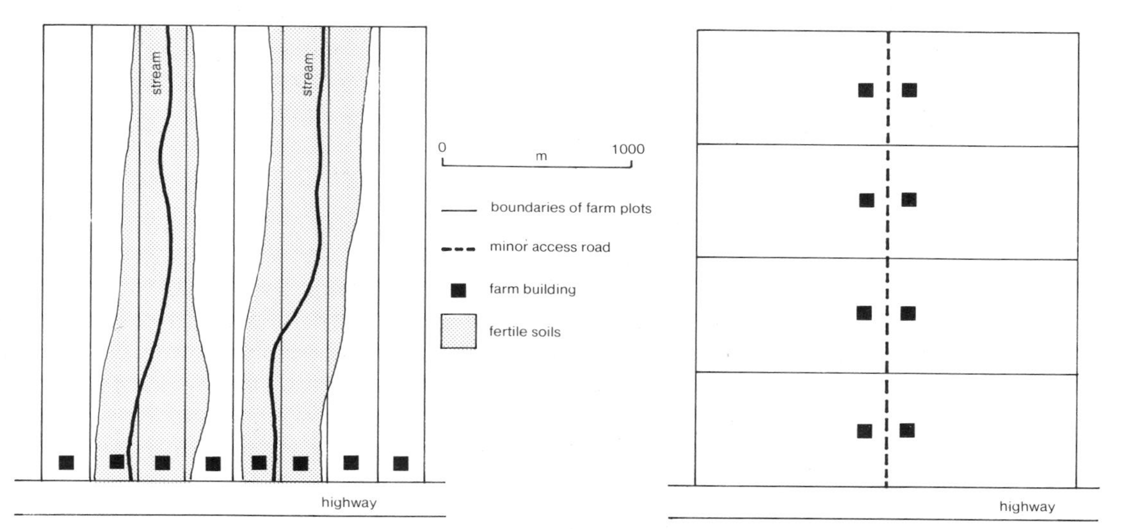

Figure 7.100 Farm plots along the Lago Agrio–El Chaco Road

Figure 7.101 Possible alternative layout for farm plots

In addition to the unplanned settlement of the colonists, there are a few government sponsored settlements in the region. One example is at Shushufindi (Figure 7.98), located on the main highway 35 km south of Lago Agrio. Here a village has been built for 80 families, together with a school, recreational facilities and other services. Around the village is a zone of private plots, with each family allocated 10 hectares; a large zone of pasture, owned by the village, surrounds the private plots; and this is encircled by an outer zone of forest, again owned by the village community.

Exercise

1 Can you suggest why the pattern of land use around Shushufindi – food and cash crops – cattle – forestry – in order of distance from the village, has been chosen (Figure 7.102)?

2 When land is owned by everyone in the village, rather than individuals, there needs to be a lot of co-operation between farmers. Can you think of an example where co-operation would be necessary in the use of the pasture zone in Shushufindi, and explain why?

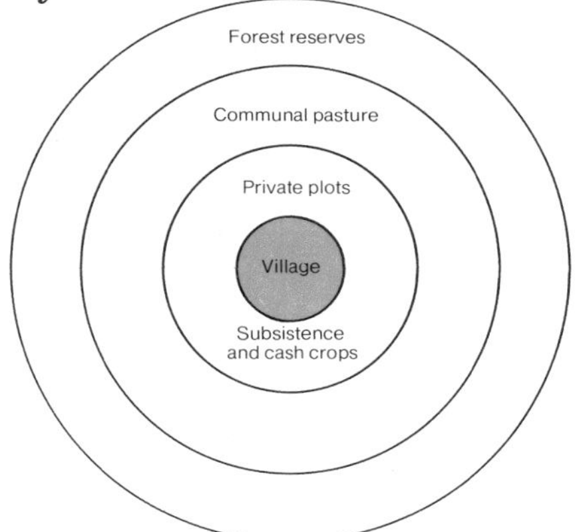

Figure 7.102 Planned government settlements in the Oriente of Ecuador

Planned settlements like Shushufindi have so far proved both expensive and unpopular with colonists. The new housing provided in the village is costly, and farmers are forced to practise ranching, even though many have never had experience of livestock farming. Farmers are expected to spend half their working day in the pasture zone, which leaves them little time to tend their own private plots. So far the scheme has made little money out of ranching, and many people have had to leave the village temporarily to find wage employment elsewhere. Others have left for good, disillusioned with the scheme.

Types of farming

Slash and mulch polyculture

This is the most common type of farming in the eastern lowlands, and is practised by almost all new settlers. In many respects it is similar to shifting cultivation, with the land farmed for only a limited period, before it is abandoned and a new plot cleared. However, unlike most shifting cultivation, the felled trees and undergrowth are not burned, but simply allowed to rot. Burning is not possible in the eastern lowlands where there is no dry season, and so crops are sown directly on the rotting cover of vegetation or 'mulch', which provides the essential minerals they need for growth.

Slash and mulch *polyculture* gets its name from the wide variety of food and cash crops grown by each farmer. Typical crops grown for subsistence include maize, rice and sweet potatoes, while crops such as coffee, cocoa and citrus are grown for cash (Figure 7.103). Growing a variety of crops has several advantages.

1. There is less chance of insect pests and plant diseases destroying the entire crop, which would be a high risk if only a single crop were grown.
2. Farmers are protected from sudden falls in price for cash crops, when several different kinds are grown.
3. Farmers and their families have a more balanced diet.
4. Crops ripen at different times, and tree crops give permanent cover to the soil; thus soil erosion is reduced.
5. The mixture of crops helps the soil to keep its fertility longer.

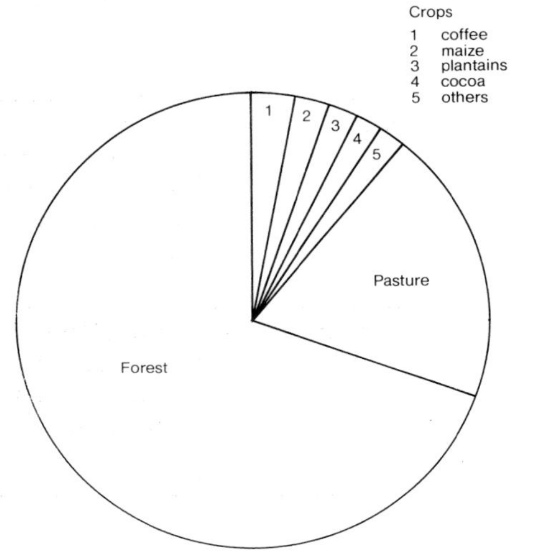

Figure 7.103 Land use on colonists' 50 hectare plots in Lago Agrio, Ecuador

Slash and mulch polyculture can continue on the same plot for up to 15 years before the soil loses most of its fertility, and a new clearing has to be made. This means that the rate of forest destruction is slowed, and that the land can support higher population densities.

Exercise

Slash and mulch polyculture in north east Ecuador is a relatively successful method of farming in the rainforest, compared to methods used by colonists elsewhere in Amazonia (Figure 7.104). Table 7.18 compares slash and mulch with these other methods. Make a copy of the table and insert the missing words.

Figure 7.104 (*right*) Cultivation of the rainforest is expanding rapidly, but is confined to areas opened up by the building of new highways. Note that in this area some plots still await forest clearance.

Table 7.18 Methods of crop cultivation in Amazonia

	Slash and mulch polyculture in north east Ecuador	Cultivation by colonists elsewhere in Amazonia	
Crops	A ________ variety of crops, including annual food crops and ________ cash crops.	A ________ range of crops, with a strong emphasis on annual food crops.	(narrow, wide, perennial)
Period of cultivation of plots	Usually between ________ years, before clearing a fresh plot becomes necessary.	There is a rapid decline in fertility with farmers often forced to abandon plots after ________ years.	(2 – 3, 10–15)
Pests and diseases	Owing to the variety of crops grown or ________, the effects of pests and diseases on harvests are ________.	The effects of pests and diseases are ________ especially when ________ or the growing of just one or two crops is practised	(considerable, small, monoculture, polyculture
Soils	Soil fertility is ________ for several years, and soil is also to some extent protected by a crop cover, which ________ erosion.	Soil fertility is soon ________. When crops are harvested the soil may be exposed to ________ by the heavy rains.	(erosion, maintained, exhausted, limits)
Effect on the forest	Rates of forest clearance ________. The land ________ support a higher population density.	Rates of forest clearance are ________. Only ________ population densities can be supported.	(low, slow, can, rapid)

Cattle ranching

Cattle ranching is the most important farming activity in Amazonia today. In north east Ecuador farmers regard slash and mulch polyculture as simply a means of clearing the forest and saving enough money before buying cattle. The climate in the region is ideal for grass, with constant high temperatures (around 24°C) and abundant rainfall (3000 mm a year) evenly spread throughout the year. Beef cattle are fattened in the eastern lowlands and later sold to the main markets in the highlands. Beef has several advantages over cash crops like coffee and cocoa: beef prices do not vary so much; poor transport is not a great problem, as cattle can be driven through the forest to a collection point on the highway; and the demand for meat in South America is increasing.

Unfortunately the drawbacks to cattle ranching are considerable. The variety of crops under polyculture is replaced by a single crop – grass – which is easily attacked by insect pests and diseases. As with shifting cultivation, the first few crops of grass are quite good, but as the soil's fertility is used up, weeds begin to infest the pastures, together with shrubs and small trees, until eventually the land is abandoned. Finally cattle damage the soil by trampling, and remove the vegetation by overgrazing. In both cases, the result is soil erosion, rivers become silt-laden and there is an increased risk of flooding.

While the 50 ha plots are large enough for polyculture, they are too small for ranching. Many colonists have insufficient land to make a living from ranching and are often forced to sell their farms to rich businessmen living in the capital Quito. Already, large farms of over 2000 hectares are beginning to appear along the Lago Agrio–El Chaco road, and this trend seems set to continue. If this happens, then one of the main purposes of colonisation in the eastern lowlands – to provide land for the poor peasant farmers of the more densely populated highlands – will have failed.

Exercise

1 What is polyculture? How does it differ from monoculture?

2 Write a short account comparing the advantages of polyculture with cattle ranching in North East Ecuador. Use the following headings to help you:
— size of population each can support
— number of farms and farm sizes
— effect on soil and vegetation.

Summary

Farming is the leading activity in the Third World, and in most LDCs employs more than half of the working population. The character of farming is very different from that of the developed world: production is largely for subsistence; it is based on simple methods which are often inefficient; it relies mainly on human labour; and produces yields which are so low that farmers are condemned to lives of poverty. These difficulties are increased by other problems: poor farmers in the Third World are hit hardest by natural hazards such as drought, flooding and disease, and where cash crops are grown, low world prices may work against them. On top of this there is the problem of continuing population growth. With more mouths to feed, farmers in desperation allow pastures to be overgrazed, overwater crops and attempt to cultivate land unsuited to farming. All too often the result is the destruction of soil and vegetation, and the loss of the vital resources on which farming depends.

What is needed to combat these problems, is the carefully planned development of rural areas, aimed at raising farm production, and thereby improving people's standard of living. Farmers need to be educated in the use of higher yielding crops, irrigation and the management of pasture. Money must be made available so that wells can be drilled, fertilizers can be bought, and roads built, and governments must be prepared to tackle problems of land ownership and inefficient farm layout where they exist. Although the task is a huge one, there is a growing realisation that the development of agriculture offers the best chance of improving the quality of life of the mass of the people in the LDCs.

Further exercises

1 a Explain the differences between the following pairs of terms:
— intensive and extensive farming
— monoculture and polyculture
— arable and mixed farming
— commercial and subsistence farming.
b Give an example of each of the above terms from regions or countries you have studied.

2 a What is soil erosion?
b Describe examples of farming practices in LDCs which have caused soil erosion.
c Suggest ways in which the problem could be solved.

3 a What is the Green Revolution?
b What changes to farming occur in a successful Green Revolution?

c With reference to India, state three reasons why the Green Revolution has had only limited success.

4 a Explain why shifting cultivation gets its name.
b With reference to an example, describe how under traditional shifting cultivation the land is cleared and farmed.
c Why is land abandoned after a few years?
d What happens to shifting cultivation if there is a rapid increase in population?

5 a What is nomadic herding?
b Give an example of a group of nomadic herders.
c Explain how climate influences the seasonal migrations of nomadic herders.

Test your skill as a farmer

In this game you play the role of a farmer, deciding the combination of crops and livestock on your farm, which will give you the highest profit after 10 years. The farm is shown in Figure 7.105 and is subdivided into 25 squares or fields; each square has to be allocated one of the following uses – sheep, cattle, cereals or market gardening. Thus you must decide not only *what* you produce, but also *where* on the farm you produce it. In making your decisions you have to weigh up several factors, including the profits you can reasonably expect from each type of land use, the value or capability of the land, and potential weather and market hazards.

Procedure

1. Using Tables 1 to 4 assess the value of each square for farming on the basis of relief, altitude and drainage. Table 5 gives an example of how the scores for the three factors are converted into grades.
2. Draw a square of 10 × 10 cm, subdivided into 25 2 × 2 cm squares (as in Figure 7.105). Choose a colour for each grade of land, and shade in the squares to show the pattern of land capability on the farm.
3. Study Tables 6, 7 and 8 carefully, and compare them with your map. You must now decide what you *think* is the best land use for each square. Draw up a balance sheet like Table 9 and enter the land use for each square in column D. Also complete columns C, E and F.
4. Select 10 consecutive numbers between 1 and 8 from the random number tables in Table 3.10 and enter them in the top row of your balance sheet as in the example (Table 9). These numbers refer to Table 8 and tell you the hazard for each year.
5. You can now calculate the profit for each of the 10 years. After 10 years add up your total profit, and to give a more realistic figure multiply it by 10. The winner of the game is the farmer who achieved the highest profit.

Follow-up work

1. Compare your profits with those of other members of your class. Would you say that your profits were high, about average, or low?
2. Explain your level of profit. Was it good/bad luck or good/bad decision-making which accounted for your result?
3. If you were to play the farm game again, what decisions would you alter in order to achieve higher profits?

Table 1 Relief	
Number of different contours per square	Score
0–1	5
2	3
3 or more	1

Table 2 Altitude	
Most of square:	Score
below 75 m	5
76–175 m	3
above 175 m	1

Table 3 Drainage	
Number of different contours per square	Score
0–1	1
2	2
3 or more	3

Table 4 Land capability	
Total score per square	Low grade
11 or more	1
7–10	2
less than 7	3

Table 5 Calculating land capability: example

Squares	Relief	Altitude	Drainage	Total	Land grade
A1	5	1	1	7	2
B3	1	3	3	7	2
D5	5	5	1	11	1

Table 6 Profits per square per year (£)

	Grades of land		
	1	2	3
Cereals	80	60	5
Market gardening	100	30	0
Cattle	60	50	10
Sheep	40	30	20

Table 7 Extra costs of cultivation with distance from the farm (£ per square per year)

	Distance from farm (metres)		
	0–200	201–400	over 400
Cereals	10	20	30
Market gardening	20	40	80
Cattle	10	20	40
Sheep	5	10	15

Figure 7.105 Farming game

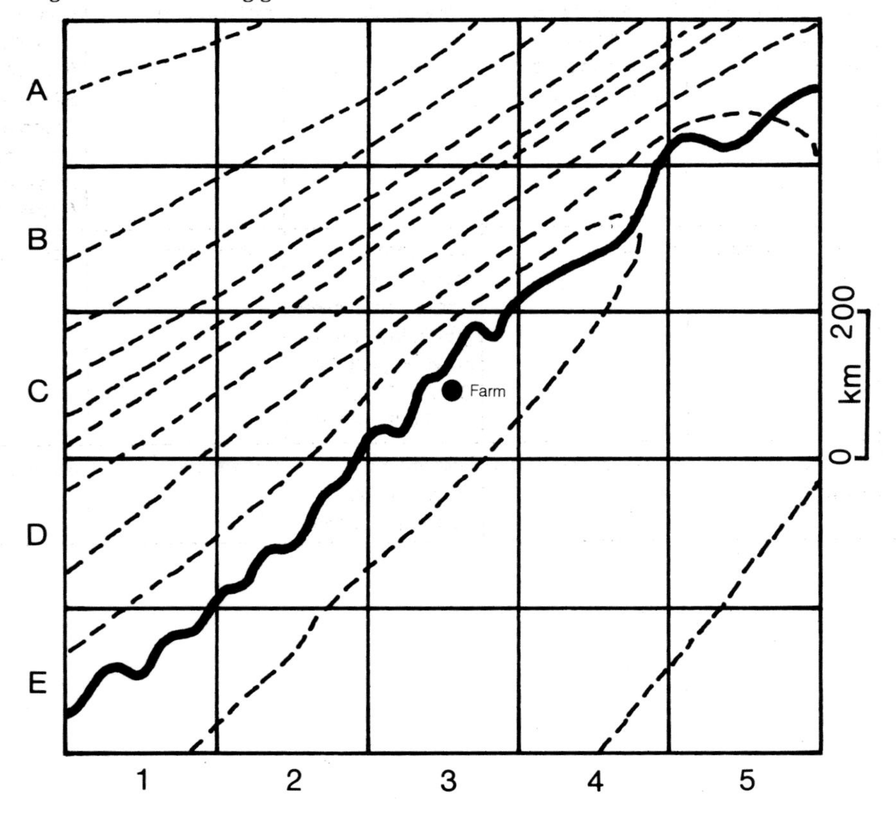

Table 8 Hazards to farmers and their effects on farming types

Random number	Hazard	Cereals	Market gardening	Cattle	Sheep
1	Severe summer drought.	Poor harvest even though prices are up. *Profits cut by half.*	*Not affected* owing to use of sprinkler irrigation.	Grass growth is poor and milk yields are down. *Profits down by half.*	Plenty of water in poorly drained uplands. Sheep *not affected.*
2	Valley land below 50 m flooded. Squares E1, D2 and C3 affected.	All cereal crops in these three squares destroyed.	All market gardening crops in these three squares destroyed.	*Not affected.*	*Not affected.*
3	Sudden increase in energy costs.	Use of oil for machinery *cuts profits by one quarter.*	Large-scale use of energy for heated glasshouses. *Profits cut by one third.*	*Not affected.*	*Not affected.*
4	Changes in government farm policy.	*Not affected.*	*Not affected.*	Subsidy to dairy farmers reduced. *Profits down by 10%.*	Subsidy to sheep farmers increased. *Profits up by 10%.*
5	Good weather conditions: record levels of production.	Glut on the market. Prices fall. *Profits down by one quarter.*	*Profits down by one quarter.*	Guaranteed prices mean profits *not affected.*	*Not affected.*
6	Harsh winter, with snow cover for six weeks.	Frosts help to kill many fungal and insect pests. *Profits up by one quarter.*	*Not affected.*	*Not affected.*	Heavy snow on land above 175 m (A1, A2, A3, B1, B2) and many sheep and lambs lost. *No profit from these squares if farmed for sheep.*
7	Late frost in May.	*Not affected.*	Severe frost in valley bottom. Profits from market gardening *halved* in B4, B5, C3, C4, C5, D2, D3, D4, D5, E1, E2, E3, E4.	*Not affected.*	*Not affected.*
8	Hail storms in August.	*Profits down* by one quarter.	Damage to orchards. *Profits down by one third.*	*Not affected.*	*Not affected.*

				(random numbers)		4		5		6		3		7		2		3		1		7		8	
A	B	C	D	E	F	Year 1		Year 2		Year 3		Year 4		Year 5		Year 6		Year 7		Year 8		Year 9		Year 10	
Squares	Distance from the farm in metres	Grade of land	Choice of land use	Normal profit (Table 6) before the effect of distance and hazards	Normal profit (E) minus distance costs (Table 7)	Gains /losses due to hazards	Final profit for the year	Gains/losses due to hazards	Final profit for the year	Gains/losses due to hazards	Final profit for the year	Gains/losses due to hazards	Final profit for the year	Gains/losses due to hazards	Final profit for the year	Gains/losses due to hazards	Final profit for the year	Gains/losses due to hazards	Final profit for the year	Gains/losses due to hazards	Final profit for the year	Gains/losses due to hazards	Final profit for the year	Gains/losses due to hazards	Final profit for the year
A1	560	2	SHEEP	30	15	+1.5	16.5	NONE	15	−15	0	NONE	15	NONE	15	NONE	15	NONE	15	NONE	15	NONE	15	NONE	15
A2	450																								
A3	400																								
A4	450																								
A5	560																								
B1	440																								
B2	290																								
B3	200																								
B4	290	2	CEREALS	60	40	NONE	40	−10	30	+10	50	−10	30	NONE	40	NONE	40	−10	30	−20	20	NONE	40	−10	30
B5	440																								
C1	400																								
C2	200																								
C3	0																								
C4	200	1	MARKET GARD.	80	70	NONE	70	−17.5	52.5	NONE	70	−23.3	46.7	−35	35	NONE	70	−23.3	46.7	NONE	70	−35	35	−23.3	46.7
C5	400																								
D1	440																								
D2	290																								
D3	200																								
D4	290																								
D5	440																								
E1	560																								
E2	450																								
E3	400																								
E4	450																								
E5	560																								
Total Profit for Year (£)																									

Table 9 Balance sheet for farm game

FINAL PROFIT AFTER 10 YEARS − (× 10)

Key ideas	Examples
Several *types* of farming are defined, based on: 1 crops and livestock	■ Arable, mixed, pastoralism, market gardening. Farmers may concentrate on a single product (monoculture) eg wheat in Prairies, or several (polyculture) eg slash and mulch cultivation in Ecuador.
2 what happens to crops and livestock	■ Subsistence farming eg Iban of Sarawak; commercial farming for cash eg farming in DCs.
3 methods of cultivation	■ The extent to which machinery, fertilizers, pesticides, etc. are used; the distinction between rain-fed and irrigation agriculture; intensive and extensive methods.
A farm can be seen as a *system*.	■ The farm has a number of features: size, ownership, layout, soils, relief and drainage of the land. Inputs include rainfall, sunshine, fertilizers, machinery, labour and pesticides; outputs comprise crops, livestock and waste products.
The *distribution* of farming types and systems is influenced by physical and human factors.	■ *Physical* a Climate sets the broad limits on which crops can be grown eg east–west contrast in the UK. b Soils vary in their fertility and their value for different crops eg fertile peat and silt soils of the Dutch polders, the infertile sandy soils of Jutland. c Land which is steeply sloping cannot be cultivated with machinery, and may be unsuitable to plough. ■ *Human* a The purpose of commercial farming is to make a profit – farmers will select the combination of crops and livestock which will give the best profits in the long term. b Access to market may affect the crops grown eg dairying and horticulture around Winnipeg, and whether farming is for cash or subsistence. c Farm size may influence the use of machinery eg Prairies, or dependence on labour eg India. Small farms are usually cultivated more intensively than large farms eg glasshouse cultivation in the Netherlands. d Governments often support farmers with subsidies, guaranteed prices, etc, or impose quotas on production eg MMB in the UK, the CAP in the EEC. Governments may invest in large-scale projects to develop farming eg irrigation in Punjab, land reclamation in the Zuider Zee.

Farming types and systems undergo change over time.	■ The declining farm populations in DCs, and the migration of people from the countryside to the towns in LDCs. ■ The decrease in the number of farms, and the corresponding increase in the sizes of farms in most DCs. ■ The trend towards greater specialisation in farming in DCs eg decline of mixed farming in Denmark and emphasis on special cereal or pig farms. ■ Introduction of new techniques eg the Green Revolution and irrigation in South Asia.
Farmers are faced with a range of problems and hazards.	■ *Physical* a Climatic changes eg long-term drought in the Sahel. b Weather hazards eg short-term drought, frost, hail. c Soil erosion, either by wind eg Prairies, or water eg the Sahel. In semi-arid areas of LDCs the destruction of soil and vegetation has led to desertification. ■ *Human* a Rapid population growth in LDCs and misuse of soil, water and vegetation resources eg desertification in the Sahel, soil salinity in Punjab and Pakistan, colonisation of Amazonia. b Small farms, not large enough to support a farmer and his family eg northern India. c) Fragmented farms, making farming inefficient and improvement difficult eg India. d High rents and sharecropping, which discourage farmers from making improvements in LDCs. e Isolation and remoteness from markets eg pastoral farming in Mauritania, cash crops in Amazonia.

Subject Index

Place Index